Critique, Norm, and Utopia
A Study of the Foundations of Critical Theory

CRITIQUE, NORM, AND UTOPIA

A Study of the Foundations of Critical Theory

SEYLA BENHABIB

New York   Columbia University Press

Library of Congress Cataloging-in-Publication Data
Benhabib, Seyla.
Critique, norm, and utopia.
Bibliography: p.
Includes index.
1. Criticism (Philosophy)   2. Ethics.   I. Title.
B809.3.B46   1986   142   85-13323
ISBN 0-231-06164-1
ISBN 0-231-06165-X   (pa.)

This publication has been supported by the National Endowment for the Humanities, a federal agency which supports the study of such fields as history, philosophy, literature, and languages.

Columbia University Press
New York   Guildford, Surrey
Copyright © 1986 Columbia University Press
All rights reserved

Printed in the United States of America

c 10 9 8 7 6 5 4 3 2

For Nesim Benhabib

CONTENTS

PREFACE AND ACKNOWLEDGMENTS

This book began with a question and a suspicion. As the "linguistic turn" of critical social theory became increasingly clear in the last decade, I asked myself whether Jürgen Habermas' efforts to base the normative foundations of critical theory upon a "communicative ethics" could succeed. The kinds of questions I was asking had an historical precedent, and my suspicion was that by going back to Hegel's critique of Kant and of modern natural right theories, one could develop an alternative normative foundation for critical theory. While this suspicion has proved untenable, the question of what one might learn from Hegel's critique of Kantian ethics in the context of a critical social theory continues to be valid. This book documents my conclusion.

My analysis begins in Part 1 with an examination of the concept of critique in Hegel's works and the transformation of this Hegelian legacy by Marx. Whereas for Hegel the purpose of critique is to further the integration of the autonomous individual into an ethical community, Marx views critique as crisis theory, the main function of which is to point to the contradictions of the present and to encourage the emergence of needs, patterns of interaction, and struggle which point the way toward a new society.

In Part 2, "The Transformation of Critique," I show how the dimensions of critique discovered by Hegel and Marx are radically altered in the work of the Frankfurt School, particularly in that of Horkheimer and Adorno. I conclude with a discussion of Habermas' program for a critique of functionalist reason in late-capitalist societies.

Despite the historical mode of presentation it follows, the intentions of this work are not historical but systematic. My purpose in tracing the origins and the transformation of critique is not to write a history of critical theory from Hegel to Habermas. Not only is it doubtful whether such a study can be successfully carried out in a single work, it is not even necessary. At present, the tradition of critical theory has been well presented to English-speaking audiences by a number of authors, most notably by Martin Jay, Thomas McCarthy, and David Held. Building on their comprehensive accounts of the Frankfurt School and of Habermas, in this book I follow an approach which can be characterized as the reconstruction of the history of theories from a systematic point of view.

In general, to understand a philosophical argument and to evaluate its cogency, it is necessary to know the questions and puzzles which such an argument proposes to answer. To understand these questions and puzzles, in turn, it is necessary to reconstruct those social, historical, and conceptual contexts which form the horizon of inquiry of different theories. This general rule of historical reconstruction has to be qualified in one respect. As Gadamer has shown, a reconstruction of past arguments and theories always involves a "fusion of horizons." Understanding always involves understanding from *within* a framework which makes sense for us. In this sense, *learning* the questions of the past involves *posing* questions to the past in light of our conceptual preoccupations in the present. The reconstruction of the history of theories proceeds like a dialogue in which one asks a question, seeks to comprehend whether this question is meaningful to the other, listens and reformulates the answer of the other, and in light of this answer rearticulates one's original position. It is in this spirit that I have approached the problem of the normative foundations of critical theory.

From a systematic point of view, this work pursues the question: how fruitful is Hegel's critique of early natural right theories and of Kantian ethics for reformulating the normative foundations of critical social theory? I answer this question by investigating the models of *human agency* and *autonomy* presupposed by various theories. Behind Hegel's critique of Kantian ethics is the model of a subject of history constituting the historical process through its "work." This model, which I name the "philosophy of the subject," provides Marx as well with a vision of emancipation, and continues as an implicit normative standard in Horkheimer's work as late as 1937. The philosophy of the subject privileges one mode of activity as history-shaping, namely, the "work model of activity." Since Hegel's *Phenomenology of Spirit*, it is also maintained that the goal of critique is to further the autonomy of the subject. Whereas Hegel and Marx— on this point I see no difference in their approaches—view autonomy as a process of *self-actualization* in history to be attained by the creative and transformative moment of work, Horkheimer and Adorno conceive of autonomy as a non-dominating relation to nature, as *mimetic reconciliation* with the other within and outside us. Both views presuppose the validity of the philosophy of the subject, and accept the historical and epistemological primacy of the work model of activity.

Against this background, Jürgen Habermas' contribution is to have initiated the shift in critical theory from the work model of activity to communicative action. In his view, autonomy means the communicative competence in examining and justifying the grounds of our actions from a universalist standpoint and the ability to act on such a basis. What distinguishes this communicative model of autonomy from the previous two is Habermas' assumption that social action is not to be defined in the light of the subject-object relation, named variously "objectification," "externalization," or "appropriation." Constitutive for social action is the subject-subject relation, which we can understand as a form of linguistically mediated communication.

The communicative model of action and autonomy initiates a justifiable shift in critical theory away from the primacy of work. Hence the question with which this book began is reformulated in the last chapter: how can Hegel's critique of natural right and of Kant be made fruitful for further developing the program of communicative ethics and autonomy?

The research leading to this work was supported by a most generous fellowship from the Alexander von Humboldt Foundation. I would like to thank this foundation for its rigorous stan-

dards and old-world commitment and generosity toward the
study of the humanities. I also thank Boston University, College
of Liberal Arts, for a Seed Research Faculty Travel Grant,
awarded in the summer of 1981, and for the consecutive leaves of
absence granted me to enable the completion of my Humboldt
fellowship. From June 1979 to December 1981, I was an Alexander von Humboldt Fellow at the Max-Planck Institut zur
Erforschung der Lebensbedingungen der wissenschaftlich-
technischen Welt, under the directorships of Professors Jürgen
Habermas and C. F. von Weizsäcker. Subsequent to the formation of the new Max-Planck Institut für Sozialwissenschaften
under the directorship of Professor Jürgen Habermas, I spent
the period from June to December 1981 again as an Alexander
von Humboldt Fellow at this institute. I would like to express
my deepest thanks to Professor Jürgen Habermas for his hospi-
tality during this entire period, as well as for his continuing
support and encouragement. My thanks also to the former Research Fellows of the Max-Planck Institut, especially to Wolfgang Bonss, Rainer Döbert, Helmut Dubiel, Klaus Eder, and
Günter Frankenberg, for their personal and intellectual companionship, and to Inge Pethran for her invaluable administrative and secretarial help during this period.

A number of people have read portions of this manuscript at
various stages of its readiness. I owe a special debt of gratitude
to Thomas McCarthy for reading the entire manuscript and for
his invaluable comments on the second half of this work in particular. His support and solidarity have been unfailing throughout. I have greatly benefited from comments and criticisms
made on earlier drafts of various chapters by Richard Bernstein,
Marx Wartofsky, György Markus, Paul Stern, Andrew Buchwalter, and Lorenzo Simpson. Needless to say, for the final content I
am alone responsible.

I have the good fortune of having philosophical friends on
both sides of the Atlantic, conversations with whom have shaped
my ideas over the years. Albrecht Wellmer was always willing to
share his thoughts with me; his clarity and precision in writing
about the tradition of critical theory have set an example I was
happy to follow. Exchanges with Moishe Postone, Axel Honneth,
Georg Lohmann, and Alfons Söllner on the history of the Frank-

furt School have been rewarding. On this side of the ocean, Dick Howard, Jean Cohen, Andrew Arato, Paul Breines, and Joel Whitebook will recognize the influence of their work and our conversations upon my thinking. To Wolf Schäfer, a special word of gratitude is due for his support, affection, and companionship. He has discussed many phases, stages, and permutations of this work patiently with me, and has led me to appreciate the utopian dimension in critical theory. Finally, I would like to acknowledge the diligent, conscientious, and painstaking efforts of Mark Colby in typing and copyediting this manuscript, and Maureen MacGrogan of Columbia University Press, for her interest in this work at its very early stages and for unfailing editorial competence in seeing it through.

This book is dedicated to the memory of my father, who passed away during its completion.

ABBREVIATIONS USED IN TEXT
AND NOTES

(Complete publication information will be found in the Bibliography)

DA   Adorno and Horkheimer, *Dialektik der Aufklärung*

KiV   Horkheimer, *Kritik der instrumentellen Vernunft*

LC   Habermas, *Legitimation Crisis*

M   Marx, *Texte zur Methode und Praxis, II, Pariser Manuskripte, 1844*

MEW   Marx and Engels, *Werke*

MukH   Habermas, *Moralbewusstsein und kommunikatives Handeln*

NR   Hegel, "Über die wissenschaftlichen Behandlungsarten des Naturrechts." The first number gives page references for the German edition/ the second for the English.

PhG   Hegel, *Phänomenologie des Geistes*. The first number gives page references for the German edition/ the second for the English.

PhR   Hegel, *Hegel's Philosophy of Right*

ThCA   Habermas, *The Theory of Communicative Action: Reason and the Rationalization of Society*, vol. I.

ThdkH   Habermas, *Theorie des kommunikativen Handelns: Zur Kritik der funktionalistischen Vernunft*, vol. II.

TuG   Marcuse, *Triebstruktur und Gesellschaft* (see under *Eros and Civilization*)

Wth   Habermas, "Wahrheitstheorien"

ZfS   *Zeitschrift für Sozialforschung*

Critique, Norm, and Utopia
A Study of the Foundations of Critical Theory

If I am not for myself, who will be for me?
If I am for myself alone, what am I?
If not now, when?

(Rabbi Hillel, *Sayings of the Fathers*)

Introduction

THE CRITICAL THEORY OF SOCIETY: BETWEEN PRACTICAL PHILOSOPHY AND SOCIAL SCIENCE

The traditional teaching of ethics and politics, designated as practical philosophy, came to an end in the latter half of the nineteenth century.[1] Since its inception with the Greeks, this tradition had maintained that questions of the good life for the individual, and of the best social and political order for the collectivity, could be answered rationally. Under the triple attacks of positivism, historicism, and "value-free" social science, practical philosophy lost its claims to reason. It was seen at best as belonging to the prehistory of the scientific study of society. Emile Durkheim's doctoral dissertation on Montesquieu's *Spirit of the Laws* is exemplary for the way in which the new science of society distinguished itself from the tradition of practical philosophy.

The traditional teaching of ethics and politics, from Aristotle to Montesquieu, claimed Durkheim, sought to answer the question: what is by nature the best form of social and political existence?[2] This tradition examined various social and political orders, always under the aspect of their appropriateness to realize the best for humans by nature. "Nature" was thereby understood equivocally as *fact*, as the totality of what is given, and as *norm*, as what ought to be, but is not. When Montesquieu claimed laws "to spring from the nature of things," he could have meant two things: either that laws follow from societies as an effect follows from the cause that produces it, or that laws are simply instruments that the nature of society requires to fulfill itself and to attain its ends.[3] Society could be understood as the efficient or as the final cause of laws. "Montesquieu," complained Durkheim, "does not even seem to suspect the possibility of the first of these meanings,"[4] and views laws as those sets of relations most appropriate to the nature of a given society, facilitating the objectives toward which it should strive. The task of the new science of society, by contrast, is to investigate social facts, "like all other things in nature,"[5] as having characteristics that can be described and explained scientifically.

Durkheim introduces two more criteria to *demarcate* the new science of society from the tradition of practical philosophy. First, practical philosophy prescribes to social agents the right, just, and prudential course of action and instructs them in its attainment. But a teaching oriented to action and to its future realization cannot be scientific. For action concerns the particular, that which must be realized here and now, whereas science has to comprehend the universal, the unchanging and the necessary, that which is at all times and places.[6] Second, because of its goal to instruct and to enlighten, the traditional teaching of ethics and politics has to confine itself to the visible and the apparent in social life. To instruct and to guide human action, the theorist has to proceed from that sphere of appearance and opinion shared by all and in which human action unfolds.[7] But science moves from the visible to the invisible, from *doxa* to *episteme*, from the daily activities, beliefs, and opinions of humans to the causes generating them.

Critical social theory, as formulated by members and associates of the Institut für Sozialforschung in the 1930s,[8] from the beginning rejected the demarcation between ethics and politics and the new science of society as drawn by the young Durkheim. Insofar as critical social theory analyzed society from the standpoint of its emancipatory transformation in the future into a "world which satisfies the needs and powers of men" (ZfS 1937:625/246), it shared the intentions of the traditional teaching of ethics and politics to unite the claim of reason with the happiness and freedom of individuals and the justice of the collectivity. Insofar as a critical social theory conceived of society as the totality of conditions under which social individuals produced and reproduced their existence, it shared Durkheim's intentions to analyze this totality and to comprehend it scientifically. The project of a critical social theory was situated between practical philosophy and social science, sharing and radically reformulating the intentions of both.

According to Horkheimer's by now classic statement,

> The critical theory of society . . . has for its object men as producers of their own historical way of life in its totality. The existing relations which are the starting point of science are not regarded simply as givens to be verified and to be predicted according to the laws of probability. Every given depends not on nature alone but also on the power man has over it. Objects, the kind of perception, the questions asked and the meaning of the answers all bear witness to human activity and the degree of man's power. . . . [Critical theory] is not just a research hypothesis which shows its value in the ongoing business of men; it is an essential element in the historical effort and powers of men. . . . Its goal is man's emancipation from relationships that enslave him. (ZfS 1937:625–26/244–46)

Whereas Durkheim juxtaposes the concept of nature as fact to the old teleological world view, Horkheimer, in a manner reminiscent of the young Marx, stresses that "every given depends not on nature alone but also on the power man has over it." The modern, mechanistic conception of nature which Durkheim takes for granted is criticized by Horkheimer for concealing the *social constitution* of nature through material praxis (ZfS 1937: 255/200). For Horkheimer the decisive question is not the choice between a teleological and a mechanistic conception of nature, but the fact that the modern concept of nature, which the new science of society accepts as its own, obscures "the question of the mediation of the factual through societal praxis as a whole" (ZfS 1937: 256/201).

Critical theory also rejects the second Durkheimian distinction between theoretical understanding of *nomological social necessity* and *practical instruction* in the specifics of moral and political action. If natural as well as social facticity is the consequence of social praxis—more specifically, if facticity is constituted in the material process through which individuals reproduce their existence by transforming externality—then the critical theory of society which recognizes this process cannot be "just a research hypothesis." For a theory which accepts as its basic premise the constitution of facticity through social praxis cannot view the conditions under which it is applied and put to use as being external to itself. Rather, since they view theoretical activity as a moment in the general life of society, for critical theorists, how, under which conditions, and to what ends theory enters social praxis is a question that they pose themselves. Critical theory comprehends itself "as an essential element in the historical effort to create a world which satisfies the needs and powers of men." A theory which intends to show that social necessity itself is a product of the praxis of individuals aims at enlightening these same individuals about the specifics of their actions and their future transformation. The relation of theory to practice or, in Durkheim's terms, of science to art, is not external, but internal to the self-understanding of critical theory.

Finally, the Durkheimian distinction between the *visible opinions* of social agents and the *invisible structures* grasped by the social scientist is given a new formulation by Horkheimer. He argues that critical theory does not dismiss the reality of the social world as it *appears* to individuals. The mode in which social life appears is an indication of the extent to which individuals are alienated from their own social praxis. Critical theory is also a critique of ideologies, for the manner in which individuals experience and interpret their collective existence is an essential aspect of their social effort. If individuals view their social life as dominated by impersonal, natural, or supernatural forces, this is due to the structure of the material praxis through which they appropriate nature.

The critique of ideologies does not merely disclose the dependence of thought upon social being, of consciousness upon material praxis. It also criticizes this dependence from the standpoint of the struggle for the future. Even when the idea of a reasonable organization of society appears hopeless and far away, precisely to members of that class whose existential situation should predispose them to an interest in emancipation, critical theory must exercise obstinacy and remain committed to the idea of a better future (ZfS 1937: 271/217). For critical theory, consciousness is both immanent and transcendent: as an aspect of human material existence, consciousness is immanent and dependent upon the present stage of society. Since it possesses a utopian truth-content which projects beyond the limits of the present, consciousness is transcendent. In insisting upon this utopian dimension, and in remaining faithful to the utopian content of the philosophical tradition, critical theory "resembles Greek philosophy, not so much in the Hellenistic age of resignation as in the golden age of Plato and Aristotle. . . . The new dialectical philosophy, however, has held onto the realization that the free development of individuals depends on the rational constitution of society. In radically analyzing present conditions it became a critique of the economy" (ZfS 1937: 626/246).

What distinguishes critical social theory from positivistic sociology then is its emphatic *normative* dimension. The scientific analysis of the social world is not an end in itself, but a necessary step of enlightenment in the process of transforming this world into one "which satisfies the needs and powers of men." Through this emphatic normative dimension, critical theory preserves the intentions of practical philosophy to rationally articulate a more adequate form of human existence and to enlighten them in its attainment. However, preserving the intentions of practical philosophy means neither accepting its validity as a form of inquiry to be carried on independently from the social sciences, nor that the normative dimension of critical theory is based upon a new form of practical philosophy. Even while retaining the intentions of the old practical philosophy, Horkheimer views its replacement by a scientific study of society as irrevocable. His reference to the "golden age of Plato and Aristotle" is also misleading, for the normative standards of critical theory are not based upon an ontology of nature which Plato and Aristotle share. Rather, critical theory stands in the tradition of the Kantian teaching of autonomy, and the Hegelian-Marxist transformation of practical philosophy into a philosophy of historical praxis. Let me clarify this context by a brief historical account of those developments which are decisive for Horkheimer but which are not explicated further by him.

Aristotelian practical philosophy was a unified teaching of ethics and politics that investigated the specificity and the conditions of human praxis. By "praxis" Aristotle meant the most human activity, the realization of which was only possible in the *polis*, in the human community where speech and action were not only acquired, but most significant, could be best actualized.[9] Aristotle analyzed and defined praxis within the broader context of a philosophical anthropology, or doctrine of the soul, which in turn was an aspect of the theory of life embedded in his philosophy of nature. At the other end of the spectrum, Aristotelian practical philosophy included a study of the kinds of human community which formed the necessary conditions of the good life. This study, to which the *Politics* is devoted, includes not only an examination of the political realm, in which the rule by law of equals over equals is exercised, but of the *oikos*, of the household in which the *despotes* rules over his wife, children, and slaves through personal insight and non-reciprocal fatherly prerogative.

The unity and architectonic of the Aristotelian teaching was first challenged by Hobbes and modern natural rights theorists.[10] Modern theories formulated the foundations of politics as a consensual contract among autonomous, right-bearing individuals and distinguished sharply between the sphere of morality and that of legality. From Hobbes to Kant, politics was emancipated from morals and seen as a sphere of strategic action, within which self-interested individuals mutually chose to subordinate their wills to a public authority for the sake of pursuing their privately defined interests.

Whereas the natural rights tradition initiated and legitimized the separation of ethics from politics, Mandeville and Adam Smith formulated the separation of economic activity from both ethics and politics. Economic reason and its moral foundations could no longer be dealt with within the confines of Aristotelian practical philosophy. As the pursuit of material interests was emancipated from moral passions,[11] and became in fact the ruling passion, a non-Aristotelian theory of "moral sentiments" had to be formulated to justify this development. A new political and moral theory was needed to justify processes through which "private vices" could become "public virtues" in the modern marketplace. Even prior to the challenge posed by Durkheim to the traditional teaching of ethics and politics, practical philosophy had disintegrated by the mid-nineteenth century into the study of politics, (political) economy, and morals.

In this context, Horkheimer's claim that the critical theory of society resembles Greek philosophy in the golden age of Plato and Aristotle is seriously misleading. For the fundamental problem of practical philosophy in this tradition is the actualization of a natural function and purpose, which for humans is only possible within the community. Why men should choose to live by that which is their function or should strive to realize that which is highest for them is an *ontological* question: it is in the nature of all that is to tend to its perfection. Man must make this *telos* toward actualizing himself an immanent goal by adopting it as a conscious aim. With the rise of the modern, non-teleological natural science, with the differentiation of the public realm into autonomous political and economic domains, with the privatization of morals and the emergence of an intimate familial sphere, the cognitive as well as social bases of the ancient tradition were destroyed. A critical theory of society which sought to remain true to the utopian intention of Greek philosophy could hardly do so on the basis of a no longer tenable ontology of nature.

Indeed, Horkheimer appeals to a second philosophical tradition to justify the normative-utopian dimension of critical theory. In the phraseology of German idealism, he writes: "Reason's intuition of itself, regarded by philosophy in former times as the highest degree of happiness, is transformed in modern philosophy into the materialist concept of a free, self-determining society" (ZfS 1937: 626/246). This appeal to "reason's intuition of itself" can hardly be reconciled with the ideal of contemplative happiness that both Plato and Aristotle share and the basis of which is the participation of human *nous* in an order of divine and eternal intelligence. Horkheimer, by contrast, appeals to the ideal of autonomy formulated by German idealism, according to which reason's intuition of itself is an act of freedom through which the will determines itself in accordance with rational principles. The materialist conception of a free, self-determining society is indebted not to the Greek tradition of practical philosophy, but to the Kantian teaching of autonomy.

Yet for Horkheimer the materialist idea of a "free, self-determining society" is not a mere "ought," a postulate of practical reason, but a possibility—albeit a historical, not a natural one. This ideal is an immanent, historical potential embedded in the development of the forces of production and the human mastery over nature. Unlike that of Aristotle, Horkheimer's nat-

uralism is not an ontological but a historicist one; it presupposes the Hegelian-Marxist transformation of practical philosophy into a philosophy of praxis. In this context "praxis" no
longer means the specifically human capacity to engage in "just
and noble actions," but the material activity of constituting the
objective conditions of existence. The decisive question is
whether Horkheimer's attempt to base the normative dimension
of critical social theory upon a historicized reason can avoid the
naturalistic fallacy of deducing the "ought" from the "is" any
more than the ancient ontological tradition of natural law
could. As Jürgen Habermas has observed,

> From the beginning there was a lack of clarity concerning the
> normative foundation of Marxian social theory. This theory was
> not meant to renew the ontological claims of classical natural law,
> nor to vindicate the descriptive claims of nomological sciences; it
> was supposed to be a "critical" social theory but only to the extent
> that it could avoid the naturalistic fallacies of implicitly evaluative
> theories. Marx believed he had solved this problem with a *coup de
> main*, namely, with a declaredly materialist appropriation of
> Hegelian logic. Of course, he did not have to occupy himself espe-
> cially with this task; for his practical research purposes he could
> be content to take at its word, and to criticize immanently, the
> ruling bourgeois theories of modern natural law and political
> economy—a content that was, moreover, incorporated into the rev-
> olutionary bourgeois constitutions of the time.[12]

To analyze this "lack of clarity" concerning the normative
foundations of critical theory is a major purpose of this book.
This unclarity is not due to a lack of conceptual acuity or to
analytical confusion. It is endemic to the mode of inquiry known
as "critique" that, despite its emphatic normative dimension, it
considers itself to have transcended the normative naïveté of
evaluative theories prescribing an ideal ethics and an ideal
politics.

The rejection of prescriptivism and of traditional practical
philosophy are the Hegelian legacy within the Marxist critique
of political economy upon which Horkheimer bases his program
of a critical social theory. The Hegelian-Marxist transformation
of practical philosophy into a philosophy of praxis has two aspects to which Horkheimer is indebted: first, Hegel rejects not

only the natural law ontology of the ancients but the prescriptivism of Kantian moral philosophy as well. In order to avoid the naïveté of openly evaluative and prescriptive inquiries, Hegel develops the method of immanent exposition and critique. Second, the purpose of such critique is to demystify the apparent objectivity of social processes by showing them to be constituted by the praxis of knowing and acting subjects. Let me call the first moment of the critical enterprise *immanent critique*, while naming the second aspect *defetishizing critique*. My thesis is that the lack of clarity concerning the normative foundations of critical social theory must begin with an analysis of this Hegelian legacy.

Hegel develops the method of immanent critique in order to avoid the pitfalls of criteriological and foundationalist inquiries both in epistemology and in moral, political philosophy. Even prior to the *Phenomenology of Spirit*, where an alternative epistemological inquiry named the phenomenological method of "watching on" is articulated,[13] in his 1802–3 essay on *Natural Law*,[14] Hegel uses a similar argument to criticize empiricist and formalist theories of modern natural right. I begin my discussion of the origins of the method of immanent critique in chapter 1 with this essay. The method of non-criteriological inquiry, which allows its practitioners to criticize the opponents' arguments by showing their internal inconsistencies and contradictoriness, is used in this essay to reject modern natural right theories. The Marxian critique of political economy is indebted to Hegel's method of immanent critique, and, following Hegel, Marx also rejects modern natural right theories of the Lockean and the Kantian sort for being dogmatic and prescriptive. Marx's famous attack on the Robinsonades of modern political economy was foreshadowed by Hegel's critique of state-of-nature methodologies in 1802–3.

Although this methodological critique of modern natural right theories contains much that is valid, it leads both Hegel and Marx to underestimate the normative content of these theories. Modern political philosophy, from Hobbes to Kant, maintains that rational consent is the basis of legitimate political authority. In dismissing this claim as the ideology of bourgeois civil society, Hegel, as well as Marx, reveals a profound ambivalence toward modernity and its characteristic differentiation of social life into the public, private, and intimate realms. This early critique of modern natural right presupposes the normative ideal of a unified ethical community (*Sittlichkeit*).

Chapter 2 shows that Hegel's discovery of labor and of the emancipatory moments intrinsic to it leads him to a "retreat from Eleusis" and sets him upon the path of reconciliation with modernity. By focusing on the *Phenomenology of Spirit*, I analyze the claim that history is the "work" of a collective subject and that the individual can find reconciliation with objective reality insofar as he becomes aware of the identity of constituting and constituted subjectivity. The presuppositions that the social-historical world is the "work" of a collective singular subject and that constituting and constituted subjectivity are identical are named "the philosophy of the subject." My goal in the second half of chapter 2 is to show that the philosophy of the subject is not rejected but entailed by Marx's materialist critique of Hegel in the *1844 Manuscripts*.

This preliminary analysis of the normative presuppositions of immanent and defetishizing critique sets the stage for the more properly systematic goals of this work. In approaching the problem of the normative foundations of critical theory, my purpose is to illuminate a dominant model of action, named the "work model of activity." This model is first articulated through Hegel's analysis of *Entäusserung* (externalization), is then materialistically translated into "production" by Marx in the *1844 Manuscripts*, and continues as an implicit normative standard in Horkheimer's 1937 essay on "Traditional and Critical Theory." The work model of action is the cornerstone of the vision described as the "philosophy of the subject." From Marx to Horkheimer, the vision of a demiurge-like mankind, producing externality, unfolding its capacities in this process, and destined to emancipation by appropriating its own alienated forces, dominates. The philosophy of the subject and the work model of action privilege collective singularity over plurality. In Hegel's critique of Kantian moral philosophy, in Marx's emphasis on concrete, sensuous finitude and individuals in social relations, and in Adorno's critique of identity philosophies, one can discover traces of a more intersubjectively oriented and pluralistic conception of self, society, and politics. To develop the full implications of these scattered elements and insights, however, the shortcomings of the work model of action and of the philosophy of the subject must be seen more clearly.

My argument against the work model of action and the philosophy of the subject focuses on two dimensions. First is the philosophical clarification of the concepts of action, interpretation, and autonomy entailed by this model. I criticize the prelinguistic and mentalistic language which Hegel and Marx use to characterize intentionality, as well as rejecting Hegel's attempt to exclude interpretive indeterminacy from the sphere of human interaction. This analysis is presented in chapter 4, section 4.

In the *Dialectic of Enlightenment*, Adorno and Horkheimer repudiate the assumption that the history of the humanization of nature through labor contains an emancipatory dynamic. They undermine the very model of mankind as a demiurge, shaping nature after its own image, upon which nineteenth-century Marxism rested. Yet the vacuum left by the demise of the work model of action is not filled by another equally significant dimension of human relations. The disappearance of poiesis does not make room for praxis but is filled by poetics. The emancipatory hopes that once accompanied laboring activity are now transposed to the aesthetic realm. Repeatedly, Adorno destroys the myth of a collective, singular subject of history, and of a logic of the historical process. Yet this search for the non-identical leads Adorno away from the discursive realm altogether. By focusing on the concept of mimesis, which is intended to anticipate a new, non-dominating mode of relation to inner and external nature, I show that the work of art cannot fulfill what Adorno searches for through this concept. Only one that is like us and yet distinct from us, and that can coexist with us in the proximity of likeness and the distance of otherness can authenticate true otherness (see chapter 6, section 4).

The second dimension pursued in my critique of the work model of action and the philosophy of the subject concerns their implication for social theory. Chapter 4, on Marx's analysis of capitalism, chapter 6, on the Frankfurt School diagnosis of state-capitalist societies, and chapter 7, on Habermas' theory of late-capitalist societies, deal with questions of social theory.

Two social-epistemic perspectives are distinguished. The standpoint of "intersubjectivity" corresponds to that of individuals themselves qua *participants* in social life. The second perspective, that of "transsubjectivity," reflects the view of the *observer* who analyzes and judges social relations. These two epistemic perspectives are correlated with two concepts of social crisis. "Lived crisis" refers to experienced needs, demands, feelings, and dissatisfactions that the social structure generates in individuals. They manifest themselves at the motivational and attitudinal levels primarily. "Systemic crisis," by contrast, articulates from the standpoint of the observer the contradictions, malfunctioning, and disturbances of social systems that derive from their structural arrangements in distributing wealth, power, and other goods. Beginning with Marx's *Capital*, it is established that these two perspectives and their corresponding crises tendencies are endemic to this mode of production. But failure to integrate the dimension of lived crises leads Marx to privilege the standpoint of systemic crises, while early critical theorists, more and more convinced that systemic crises tendencies are blocked off, primarily concentrate on cultural and motivational phenomena which become for them the harbinger of utopian impulses. Constructing a social theory adequate to the task of elucidating late-capitalist societies, I argue, involves methodologically and empirically developing a concept of social action based on the model of communication. This entails nothing less than a paradigm shift in critical theory from production to communicative action, from the politics of the philosophy of the subject to the politics of radical intersubjectivity.

Having outlined the necessities of this paradigm shift in critical theory, in the final chapter of this book I return to the question: what can be learned from Hegel's critique of Kant in the context of developing the program of communicative ethics and autonomy? Taking as my guide Hegel's objections to the principle of universalizability, his critique of the institutional bases of Kantian ethics, and the separation of morality from affect in this theory, I develop a contemporary version of this Hegelian critique. Insofar as the project of communicative ethics is presented as an inevitable sequence of moral development, one reverts back to the philosophy of the subject, while obscuring those respects in which communicative ethics is not a rehashing but a critique of neo-Kantian ethical theories, like that of John Rawls for example. While sharing with Rawls' theory the vision of a community of rights and entitlements, communicative ethics is to be distinguished from it, among other things, through its anticipation of a community of needs and solidarity. These two moments correspond to norm and utopia respectively.

Norm and utopia are concepts referring to two visions of politics, which I also name the "politics of fulfillment" and the "politics of transfiguration." The politics of fulfillment envisages that the society of the future attains more adequately what present society has left unaccomplished. It is the culmination of the implicit logic of the present. The politics of transfiguration emphasizes the emergence of qualitatively new needs, social relations, and modes of association, which burst open the utopian potential within the old. Within a critical social theory the articulation of norms continues the universalist promise of bourgeois revolutions—justice, equality, civil rights, democracy, and publicity—while the articulation of utopia continues the tradition of early socialist, communitarian, and anarchist movements—the formation of a community of needs and solidarity, and qualitatively transformed relations to inner and outer nature. In short, while norms have the task of articulating the demands of justice and human worthiness, utopias portray modes of friendship, solidarity, and human happiness. Despite their essential tension, a critical social theory is only rich enough to address us in the present, insofar as it can do justice to both moments.

In presenting the nature and significance of the paradigm shift from the work model of action to communicative action in critical theory, considerations from such diverse spheres as action theory, social theory and methodology, practical philosophy and meta-ethics, have been brought together. This integration of concerns, usually delegated to different spheres, especially in analytic philosophy, is self-conscious on my part, and reflects my belief that questions of ethics are not separable from those of politics; that normative considerations, which are uninformed by a theory of present society, are futile; and that a vision of human agency, which is not explicit about its views on action, interpretation, and emotion, is faulty. In this, I have followed the fundamental insight of critical theory that the task of philosophy is to rethink the meaning of rationality, autonomy, and reflection under altered conditions of culture and society, and that for this task a fruitful collaboration between philosophy and the social sciences, in particular, is necessary.

There is a great deal of skepticism in contemporary philosophy toward the aims and claims of such an approach. Contemporary philosophy is once more caught between neo-Kantianism on the one hand and a new contextualism on the other. The critique of foundationalism in ethics and epistemology had led to contextualism, to an emphasis on the diversity and incommensurability of life forms, language games, cultures, and practices. Any philosophical program which still seeks to formulate minimal criteria of valid knowledge and action, which still develops concepts of normative legitimacy transcending specific language games, is accused of continuing the failed program of the Enlightenment (MacIntyre), of privileging epistemology (Rorty), or of perpetrating the fictitious meta-narratives of the nineteenth century (J.-F. Lyotard).[15] The project of critical theory presents a third alternative besides the neo-Kantianism of Rawls and Gewirth on the one hand,[16] and the contextual pragmatism of Rorty or the post-modernism of Lyotard on the other.[17]

The critique of the ahistorical, asocial, disembodied moral and epistemic subject of Kantianism is one that critical theory shares with the new contextualism and post-modernism. This insight has been a cornerstone of critical social theory ever since Hegel's *Phenomenology of Spirit*. Critical social theory also shares with these two positions an emphasis on concrete, material practices that shape the human individual both as a knower and as an agent. This, in turn, is the lesson of Marx's materialist critique of Hegel. Finally, critical theory as well rejects the search for foundational givens. The repudiation of the myth of the given in epistemology is a fundamental principle of Horkheimer's 1937 essay;[18] Adorno's critique of Husserl remains one of the most trenchant analyses of foundationalist epistemology in contemporary thought.[19] Where critical social theory departs from contemporary contextualism and post-modernism is its insistence that criteria of validity, ascertained via non-foundationalist arguments, can be formulated, and that the turn to culture brings no exemption from social analysis. Contemporary philosophy has discovered the cultural world, or the "conversation of mankind," once more only to neglect society.

Insofar as it combines their strengths without sharing in their weaknesses, the program of critical social theory can offer an alternative to the impasse in contemporary philosophy between neo-Kantianism and contextualism. With neo-Kantianism it shares the premise that philosophy cannot continue without its commitment to the dignity and autonomy of the rational subject, while agreeing with critics that this subject is one that develops in time and that is historically and socially situated. Contextualism and post-modernism destroy the illusions of pure reflection, and make us aware of those inevitable cultural, historical, hermeneutical and ontological presuppositions which form the horizon of our standpoint. Critical social theory participates in this conclusion. Insofar as contextualism and post-modernism, however, reject that criteria of validity and legitimacy can be formulated, and transform philosophy into literary criticism, aphorism, or poetry, critical social theory dissents from this result. Rather than taking as its guide the *fin de siècle* premonitions of a humanistic intelligentsia, who sees itself reduced to irrelevance in the contemporary world, critical social theory turns to those structures of autonomy and rationality which, in however distorted and imperfect fashion, continue in the lifeworld of our societies, while allying itself with the struggles of those for whom the hope of a better future provides the courage to live in the present.

PART ONE
THE ORIGINS OF CRITIQUE

Chapter 1

THE ORIGINS OF
IMMANENT CRITIQUE

In his masterful analysis of the dialectics of early bourgeois Enlightenment in the period of the absolutist state, Reinhart Koselleck reminds us of an etymological detail concerning the terms "critique" and "crisis." Both have their origin in the Greek κρίσις, which means dividing, choosing, judging, and deciding.[1] *Krisis* refers to dissent and controversy, but also to a decision that is reached and to a judgment that is passed. "Critique" is the subjective evaluation or decision concerning a conflictual and controversial process—a crisis. The connection between a process of social and natural disturbance and subjective judgment upon this process is even more striking in medical terminology, to which the terms were restricted in the Middle Ages.[2] In this context "crisis" designates a stage in the development of a disease that is a turning point and during which the decisive diagnosis concerning the healing or worsening of the patient is reached. Expressions like "a critical illness" or "the patient is in critical condition" are evidence that this original philological context has been preserved in the English language as well.

In the period of early bourgeois Enlightenment, the terms "critique" and "criticism" lose that connection between subjective judgment and objective process characteristic of both Greek and later medieval usages. "Criticism" now means the art of judgment which evaluates the authenticity, truth, validity, or beauty of a given subject matter.[3] This art of competent judgment refers to the interpretation of ancient texts in particular, but can be applied to literature and art as well as the evaluation of human beings. The critic is a good judge.

During pre–French Revolutionary Enlightenment, the art of

good judgment, exercised in the interpretation of ancient texts, is emancipated from the Church's influence; while the subject's judgment in evaluating truth, authenticity, beauty, and validity is freed from the censure of political authority. Criticism is now viewed as a private, non-political, activity. The dialectic of early bourgeois Enlightenment consists of the following: in the course of the eighteenth century the forgotten ancient etymology of "criticism" and "critique" is reestablished. For the art of the critic does not remain confined to the evaluation of private, non-public matters, but extends itself to judging reasons of state as well. As the art of criticism undermines the legitimacy of the absolutist state to which it once owed its existence, the crisis of political authority becomes visible. On the eve of the French Revolution, "criticism" means the exercise of rational evaluation which reveals the "crisis" of the absolutist state to be an objective, historical process. "Criticism, which had at the beginning distanced itself from the state, in order to be able to function freely, now on its own authority transcends the limits which it once drew for itself."[4] Koselleck is referring to Kant's 1781 Preface to the *Critique of Pure Reason*, in which it is stated:

> Our Age is the age of criticism to which all must submit. Religion through its sanctity and legislation through its majesty may seek to exempt themselves from it. But they then awaken just suspicion and cannot claim honest respect which reason only grants to that which has been able to sustain the test of its free and public examination.[5]

Were one to examine not the philological but the philosophical transformation of the concept of "critique" from Kant's *Critique of Pure Reason* to Marx's "critical analysis of the capitalist mode of production," a dialectic similar to the one examined by Koselleck would be noted. Whereas Kantian philosophy is characterized by the separation of the "subjective judgment" of the thinker from the "objective process" of history and society, Marx's *Capital* is a critical analysis in the sense of exposing the contradictory and crises-ridden nature of the social totality. This transformation in the philosophical significance of the term "critique" from Kant to Marx can only be understood in the light of Hegel's rejection of "mere criticism" as practiced by Kant and the Enlightenment. The relationship between "critique" and "crisis" in Marxian social theory requires analyzing this Hegelian turn.

1. Hegelian Origins

The first two chapters of this book trace this transformation of the concept of critique by focusing on two historical stages in the thought of Hegel and Marx. In the present chapter, Hegel's early critique of modern natural right theories in the 1802–3 period and Marx's critique of the Young Hegelians prior to 1844 are discussed. Both the young Hegel and the early Marx practice an *immanent critique* of bourgeois civil society and of theories they take to justify its standpoint. This critique is inspired by the vision of a unified ethical life that once more brings together what modern civil society has torn asunder—morality and legality for Hegel, man as bourgeois and as citizen for Marx.

The second phase in the transformation of the concept of critique begins with Hegel's discovery of labor as a social and epistemological category in the 1805–6 period, and culminates with the argument of the *Phenomenology of Spirit*. Hegel's phenomenological method is the origin of what I call "defetishizing" critique, namely, a procedure of showing that what appears as a given is in fact not a natural fact but a historically and socially formed reality. Marx's critique of Hegel in the *Economic and Philosophical Manuscripts of 1844* does not amount to a rejection, but rather to a "materialistic" continuation, of this discovery.

Hegel's 1802–3 essay on *Natural Law*, which will be discussed here, is of special importance for the problem of the normative foundations of critical theory examined in this book. Its significance for my central concerns is twofold: first, in this essay Hegel develops a methodological critique of certain procedures of normative argumentation. More specifically, he maintains that the use of contrary-to-fact thought experiments, like "state of nature" devices, is objectionable. The utilization of such procedures always results in a *petitio principii*. Such argumentations presuppose or take for granted precisely what they set out to prove.

Second, Hegel's analysis of modern natural right theories has been extremely influential on the development of Marxian critical social theory. The widespread distrust of counterfactual argumentations in the Marxist tradition, and the well-known charge that such "Robinsonades" which claim universal validity in fact only serve to justify bourgeois civil society, can be traced back to Hegel's *Natural Law* essay. The resurgence of counterfactual argumentation procedures in the work of contemporary thinkers like John Rawls, Karl-Otto Apel, and Jürgen Habermas has placed this Hegelian argument on the agenda. The question as to what might be gained from Hegel's critique is thus an actual one. In this chapter, I will argue that while Hegel's charge that the structure of such theories is based upon a *petitio principii* is irrefutable, it is important to note that his early critique of natural right theories is motivated by the normative vision of a unified *Sittlichkeit*. Underlying this ideal of ethical life is a profound ambivalence toward modern civil society, which in turn leads Hegel to underestimate the normative content of modern natural right theories, insofar as these make rational consent the basis of legitimate obligation to the modern state.

2. Hegel's Methodological and Normative Critique of Natural Right Theories

The conceptual problem addressed by Hegel in the *Natural Law* essay is continuous with concerns voiced in his *The Difference Between the Fichtean and Schellingian Systems of Philosophy* of 1801[6] and *Faith and Knowledge* of 1802.[7] In these works, empiricist and in particular transcendental philosophies are criticized for radically separating concept and intuition, form and content, unity and multiplicity, identity and difference, finitude and infinity. For Hegel, the presence of these dichotomies in philosophy is the expression of a deeper rift within cultural life. He sees the purpose of philosophy to be the overcoming of these rifts and the restoration of unity. In *The Difference Between the Fichtean and Schellingian Systems of Philosophy*, Hegel writes:

> When we observe more closely the form which philosophy assumes, on the one hand we see that it emerges out of the living originality of Spirit . . . and on the other hand we see it as emerg-

ing out of that special form which bifurcation [*Entzweiung*] assumes and from which the system proceeds. Bifurcation is the origin of *the need for philosophy* and as the cultural formation [*Bildung*] of the age, it is the unfree and given aspect of this form. . . . The opposites, which, in the form of Spirit and matter, soul and body, belief and understanding, freedom and necessity, etc., were otherwise . . . of significance and once the object of weighty human interests, in the course of cultural formation have been transformed into the opposites of reason and sensibility, intelligence and nature, and from the standpoint of the absolute concept, of absolute subjectivity and objectivity. . . . To overcome [*aufheben*] such fixed oppositions is the only interest of reason.[8]

In the 1801 "Differenzschrift," "life" and the "totality of lived conditions" out of which the need for philosophy is said to emerge, as well as the "drive for totality," which is said to be the motivation for philosophy, are romantically juxtaposed to the culture of "bifurcation" (*Entzweiung*), division, and conflict which dominate the modern world. In the *Natural Law* essay as well, the inability of modern theoretical philosophy to think the "true unity of identity and difference" (NR 438/58) is said to have as consequence that the true unity of the ethical (*das Sittliche*), named the "mover of all things human" cannot be comprehended (*ibid*). The search for the unity of "identity and difference" as a principle of theoretical philosophy, and the search for the "true unity of the ethical" in practical philosophy, are seen as two sides of the same coin. In their failure to attain such unity, empiricism and formalism are not rival philosophical doctrines, but expressions of the same problem of bifurcation. Hegel maintains that the opposition between empiricism and formalism is spurious: like the opposition between any two illusorily independent terms, this is an opposition in appearance but a unity in essence. This means that while empiricism remains formalistic, formalism—which Hegel here equates with transcendental philosophy—remains a version of empiricism. Both proceed from certain givens in knowledge and moral theory which they simply assume to be valid.

This charge is illustrated with specific reference to the methodological procedure of natural right theories. Empiricist natural right theorists—among whom are included Hobbes, Locke, Grotius, and Pufendorf—begin with an abstraction called "the state of nature" (NR, 425ff./63ff.). This abstraction is arrived at via a thought experiment, for these theorists explicitly acknowledge that men never have been, and probably never will be, in such a condition as depicted in their descriptions.[9] Nevertheless, a "time immemorial" and the condition of certain primitive peoples are appealed to as evidence that such a state of nature may at one time have existed, and is therefore humanly possible.[10] Most natural right theorists maintain that the state of nature is more than a fiction and figment of the imagination, also because it is a reality corresponding to human nature. In doing so, these theorists abstract from human life in communities those aspects and elements which seem to them to constitute human nature, while leaving aside those which they consider accidental, in virtue of originating in convention, tradition, custom, and covenant. This process of abstraction takes the form of an enumeration "of the capabilities found in men through empirical psychology" (NR 444/63). Hegel sees it as perfectly consistent that a dogmatic attitude would seek to comprehend what is necessary by separating out what it considers accidental and contingent "from the confused image of the state of right" (NR 445/64). The assumption in accordance with which this abstraction and separation is carried out is never spelled out. In fact, these thinkers are guided more by their prejudices as to what is and is not part of human nature than by philosophical principle. If not empirical psychology, then the conviction that there should be just as much in the state of nature as one needs for the recognition of what is found in actuality, leads the way. Thus Hegel says, "the guiding principle for the *a priori* is the *a posteriori*" (NR 445/64). Such contrary-to-fact theories beg the question. The normative vision of humans which they try to justify is the one they start out by presupposing. In this respect, empiricism is dogmatism because the givens from which it proceeds have been posited in accordance with a criterion, which is not explicated. When one examines this implicit criterion, it is seen to involve a reification of certain elements at the expense of others. What was supposed to portray the "natural condition of mankind" turns into an image abstracted from the condition of individuals as they are in contemporary society.

In empiricist natural right theories, "the guiding principle for the *a priori* is the *a posteriori*" (NR 445/64), because these theories eternalize the current state of society, and view it as presenting the human condition as such. Hobbes calls the state of nature "an inference made from the passions" and asks each man to look within himself to discover human nature.[11] Locke first postulates a state of nature describing what humans may and could become if guided by reason, but his whole analysis aims at explaining how a state of war, and the situation of humans as he knew them, emerge from this initial state of innocence. Locke does not hesitate to add institutions like wage labor, private property, and commercial capital to his portrayal of the second state of nature.[12]

Hegel's methodological argument against "state of nature" theories can be put as follows: if a theory begins by resorting to a counterfactual abstration, then the theorist must possess criteria in light of which certain aspects of the human condition are ignored while others are included in the initial abstraction. But any such criteria will themselves be normative, for they will depend on what the theorist considers essential or inessential aspects of human nature. When one examines the normative criteria operative in these early natural right theories, one sees that each a priori is in fact an a posteriori, or how humans are in modern bourgeois society is the guiding criterion in determining what they ought to be or might have been like in the state of nature. The initial counterfactual abstraction from which the theorist proceeds does not justify, but merely illustrates, the concept of human nature and reason that he subscribes to.

Hegel's main concern in this essay is to show that the abstractions to which these theorists resort destroy any genuine conception of ethical life. In modern natural right theories, human nature is viewed as a given from which the theorist must proceed and which he cannot aspire to transform. As long as individuals are seen to be complete and mature outside the bonds of the ethical, as long as their nature is juxtaposed to life in society, the relations between the individual and the totality remain accidental. All that arises through human interaction and togetherness is reduced instead to a necessity of human psychology, while all that belongs to "customs, history, cultural formation [*Bildung*], and the state" is regarded as accidental, and as inessential to human nature (NR 445/63). What was a turn toward human nature freezes the human condition into unalterable necessity and enslaves man to the dictates of his nature. Hegel claims that the bond between the individual and the universal should be constituted through *Bildung*, rather than through the mere force of an external harmony created by economic necessity. This presupposes that the static view of human nature as unalterable must be replaced by the ancient vision of moral education, according to which political activity was the cultivation and education of virtuous human character. Hegel quotes Aristotle: "The positive is according to nature prior to the negative, or as Aristotle said, the people [*das Volk*] is according to nature prior to the individual" (NR 505/113).

Hegel's methodological critique of Kant and Fichte proceeds likewise in two dimensions: the exposition of the conceptual failures of formalism leads him to reject the normative vision of collective life implied by these theories. The highest principle of Kantian and Fichtean philosophies is the juxtaposition of the ideal unity of the thinking and willing subject to a manifold of content given to self-consciousness or the will (NR 455/71). Since in transcendental idealism the principle of theoretical reason is identified with the activity of a transcendental consciousness which unifies such a manifold, theoretical reason is ideal. Reason does not posit the moment of difference which it finds given in the manifold of intuition. Practical reason, by contrast, should be real; it should negate the opposition of the manifold given to it and posit difference out of itself. Freedom is defined by Kant and Fichte as a causality of the will determining itself in accordance with the universal law; the task of practical reason is to generate content in uniformity with the moral law. Hegel's critique of Kant[13] and Fichte[14] aims at showing that indeed this is not the case, and that practical reason is just as ideal as theoretical reason is real. The formalism of the law of freedom cannot generate content; it is dogmatically dependent upon the content given to it. At this point, I shall postpone a detailed examination of Hegel's critique of Kant to a future point (chapter 3) and focus instead on the social and political presuppositions behind Hegel's methodological reflections.

For the young Hegel, the true subject of natural right theories is not the individual and his rights at all, but the ethical totality (NR 509/116ff.). He criticizes Kant for making into a principle what could already be found in the natural right teaching of Hobbes and Locke, namely, that whereas morality concerns the individual's relation to his own conscience, "natural rights" apply in the spheres of justice and legality which is limited to external relations among individuals.[15]

The young Hegel views this separation of ethical life into the spheres of morality and legality as its very dissolution. When the citizen confronts the life of the ethical whole in the person of the officials of government alone, the purpose of the whole has then become alien to him. Conscience and action, law and moral intention, are potentially opposed to one another. In modern natural right theories, such a conflict is viewed as a conflict between equals: legality and morality have equal power and claim over the individual. The right of the whole, as represented by the legal sphere, is not superior to the call of conscience and of the moral law felt by the individual. These two domains limit one another; neither of them is truly "positive" or genuinely ethical (NR 470/84).

In his criticism of the divisiveness reflected by modern natural right, Hegel repeats one of the predominant themes of his early writings. In the modern world, social life has become "positive"; the individual confronts institutions which simply face him like a dead husk. The inner life of the laws of the community that could only live in the spirit of its citizens have become functionless appendages which coerce individuals for ends alien to them. Hegel first suggests the theme of positivity in relation to Christianity, but eventually extends it to refer to all those institutions that are relics of a dead history.[16]

If something does not have a true and living ground in the present, this ground is to be searched for in the past. In a time, when the determination fixed by law, but now dead, was *a living ethos and in harmony with the rest of laws.* . . . This historical knowledge of the law, which can exhibit its ground in lost customs and in a life which is dead, proves precisely that now in the living present the law lacks understanding and meaning. (NR 526/130, my emphasis)

Positivity does not merely mean the continuity of a dead past in the present: it is also a function of the dead weight within present social life. Natural right theories, through their individualism and through the reduction of collective life to mere legality, simply express the real transformations that have occurred in ethical life. Within the ethical totality itself, a sphere is now constituted whose principle is that of "physical need and enjoyment" (NR 482/94). Activities guided by this principle in turn constitute a "totality, in their unending intertwining obey *one* necessity and constitute the system of universal reciprocal dependence in relation to physical needs and the labor and accumulation for these. And this system, as a science, forms the so-called system of political economy" (*ibid.*). This totality is a negative totality, first, because it merely sustains individualism—the principle of negativity; second, because it threatens the unity of true ethical life; and third, because it subjects individuals to a necessity, to the blind necessity of economic laws. Modern natural right theories develop the legal and moral principles upon which this sphere of economic activity is based: the instrumentalist view of public life exhibited by empiricism and the legalistic vision of Fichte, according to which the public sphere is but the interplay of the quasi-Newtonian forces of action and reaction (NR 471ff./85ff.), give adequate expression to this situation. In their methodological constructions, modern natural right theories merely reflect or mirror the condition of an ethical totality divided against itself and in which the "negative absolute," the sphere of economic individualism, has grown and developed.

Here we reach the problematic at the origin of Hegel's philosophical methodology and the guiding concern of his early political philosophy, namely, the *ideal* of the ancients and the *fact* of the moderns;[17] the emergence within the ethical totality of a "negative absolute"—of an economic system of property, enjoyment, and need satisfaction—and the subsequent fissure and bifurcation, *Entzweiung*, in ethical life. I use the term "origin" to define the historical situation and conceptual problem to which Hegel was responding. For Hegel modern civil society,[18] as well as modern philosophies like empiricism and transcendental idealism, were characterized by this *Entzweiung:* whereas modern civil society pitted the individual against the universal, economics against politics, morality against ethical life, the philosophy of the modern age expressed this social-historical content through the conceptual dichotomies of the senses versus the understanding, inclination versus the will, necessity versus freedom. By diagnosing both developments to be forms of *Entzweiung*, Hegel also implicitly gave the solution to this diagnosis: the overcoming of this bifurcation in society and in thought. But such an overcoming could not be attained by juxtaposing the *ideal* of the ancients to the *fact* of the moderns; only an immanent critique of modernity and of modern subjectivity could show the way.

The *Natural Law* essay states this problem without providing the solution. Instead, Hegel resorts to the image of "tragedy and comedy in ethical life" (NR 495/104) in order to explain bifurcation. This figure of thought leads even further away from an immanent solution to the historical dissolution of the ethical. The sphere of the negative absolute—of economics—is now seen as a sacrifice which the ethical, like a benevolent God, makes of itself. Allowing itself to become its other, but recognizing itself in this otherness, it returns to itself and is one with itself. Modern economics represents the comedy of the ethical, but the act of alienation through which it comes into being is the tragedy of the ethical. The standpoint of speculative philosophy allows us to understand the tragedy in the comedy of ethical life, and to see the necessity of reconciliation.[19]

The nostalgic image of the no longer existent *polis* thus leads Hegel to a stoical reconciliation with the course of history in which the tragedy and comedy of ethical life unfolds. Hegel's critique of the methodological dogmatism of modern natural right theories thereby turns into stoic resignation in the face of world history. The charge of the lack of radicality in reason's knowledge of itself, once raised against Kant, becomes a resignative wisdom that knows reason to be but an aspect of a totality divided against itself. Immanent critique is transformed into a resigned insight into a process of divine immanence—into the play of the gods of the ethical. The critique of criticism turns into dogmatism.[20]

Hegel's characterization of modern culture and society as forms of *Entzweiung*, his Platonic rather than Aristotelian emphasis on ethical unity, and his resignative appeal to the course of history lead to an underestimation of the normative force of modern natural right theories. Although he praises as the great aspect of the philosophies of Kant and Fichte that "the essence of rights and duty and the essence of the thinking and willing subject are one and the same" (NR 470/83), the analysis developed in the *Natural Law* essay does not do justice to the truth of this principle. The fact that war rather than peace, politics rather than economics, is emphasized simply means that institutions of individuation which tear the person away from the ethical totality are criticized, but the mediation of ethical institutions through the will and freedom of individuals is not explained. The normative content of natural right theories, which make the principle of *rational consent* the basis of the individual's political obligation, is reduced instead to a mere defense of the selfish pursuit of modern economic interests.

Hegel's early critique of natural right theories, therefore, is profoundly ambivalent: insofar as the procedure of immanent critique is a critique of dogmatism, revealing the presence in modes of thought of unexamined givens, and insofar as Hegel shows these dogmatic moments to be grounded in the uncritical relation of the knower to the conditions out of which knowledge emerges, critique is emancipatory. The dogmatism of knowledge is shown to be the dogmatism of a way of life. Reflection upon this dogmatism entails a critique of this way of life, and of the alienation and bifurcation generated by the presence of irreconcilable opposites within it. Hegel's critique is based upon the normative image of a life form that has become "transparent" and intelligible to the intellect, and in which individuals once again can recognize themselves as part of a "living" as opposed to a "dead" totality. But insofar as Hegel reifies the standpoint of speculative knowledge, of "the true identity of identity and difference," his argument becomes dogmatic itself. The dogmatism of this stance reflects the dogmatism and quietism of a way of life with which the thinker seeks reconciliation through insight and comprehension. The normative projection of this mode of critique is the utopia of a "self-mediating" totality in which otherness and difference assume their tragic place in the act of sacrifice which the transsubjective totality undergoes.

The two standpoints described here as the "transparent" and "self-mediating" ethical totalities correspond to a dualism of perspective which runs through not only Hegel's work but through Marx's writings as well. In fact, they lead us back to the twofold mode of viewing social life, analyzed by Horkheimer in terms of the world of autonomous individuals on the one hand, and the world of capital on the other. Whereas the first perspective emphasizes the *lived* experience of individuals and the meaning the social world has for them, the second perspective sees meaning in social life to reside in the perspective of a third, of an observer-thinker.

Now Hegel discovers that the second perspective—which I shall refer to as "transsubjectivity" from now on—is generated by transformations undergone by society in the modern world. In the *Natural Law* essay, he traces the emergence of a sphere of economic activity whose laws and functioning often escape the intentions and knowledge of social actors, as well as constraining what they can do and how they can live their lives. The logic of a modern market economy is only intelligible to an observer-thinker who, behind the often unintelligible transactions of individuals, discovers the economic laws that result from their activities. This functionalist perspective on social life, which Durkheim identifies with the sociological perspective per se, is required by the reality of modern market economies: individuals' activities, unknown to them and often unwilled by them, result in law-like regularities, which are intelligible to an observer-thinker. Hegel, less reconciled to modern civil society than Durkheim, names this sphere the "negative absolute."

Already in the *Natural Law* essay we see the problem posed by Hegel's solution: instead of analyzing how transsubjectivity can be translated back into the lived perspective of social actors, Hegel appeals to an epistemological standpoint which is as objectivistic and as remote from social actors as the negative absolute of economics. This is the view of ethical life as a positive, God-like totality, alienating itself from itself in history, and yet ultimately reaching reconciliation by taking back into its bosom what it once let go. This solution, which becomes most apparent in those passages of the *Natural Law* essay dealing with "tragedy and comedy" in ethical life, is never abandoned, as we shall see in chapter 3, it is Hegel's ultimate answer to the problems of modern civil society.

The conclusion to be drawn from this discussion of the origins of immanent critique is as follows: whatever the merits of his methodological critique of counterfactual normative theories, Hegel's early exercise in immanent critique is ambivalent. For, on the one hand, he criticizes the dogmatism of modern natural right theories in reifying present social relations; on the other hand, he himself admits that there is no moment in the present upon which to anchor the view of a unified ethical life. The ideal of ethical life is not an immanent but a transcendent ideal, in the sense that it involves looking back to the past. This means that the normative standard governing Hegel's immanent critique is a *retrospective* one, drawn from memory. If this is so, then Hegel's critique of natural right theories is not wholly immanent either, for it is unclear why the view of a unified *Sittlichkeit* should be considered any less dogmatic an assumption in the face of the realities of the modern world than the assumption of natural right theories that human nature is a static, unchanging entity.

In the following section, I will examine Marx's writings in the pre-1844 period both to show that they are indebted to Hegel's rejection of natural right theories and to indicate the characteristic Marxian transformation of Hegel's procedure. At the normative level, Marx's relation to modern civil society is characterized by an ambivalence similar to the one noted in Hegel's case.

3. Marxian Transformation: Critique of Mere Criticism in the Pre-1844 Period

It is a well-known fact that Karl Marx subtitled nearly everything he wrote "critique." Marx's pre-1844 writings, which will be examined in this section, consisted in large part in differentiating and articulating the specificity of critique, as he practiced it, from mere "criticism."[21] While criticism—as exercised prior to Marx by the French materialists and subsequently by the Young Hegelians, Bruno Bauer, Arnold Ruge, and Max

Stirner—stands outside the object it criticizes, asserting norms against facts, and the dictates of reason against the unreasonableness of the world, critique refuses to stand outside its object and instead juxtaposes the immanent, normative self-understanding of its object to the material actuality of this object. Criticism privileges an Archimedean standpoint, be it freedom or reason, and proceeds to show the unfreedom or unreasonableness of the world when measured against this ideal paradigm. By privileging this Archimedean standpoint, criticism becomes dogmatism: it leaves its own standpoint unexplained, or it assumes the validity of its standpoint prior to engaging in the task of criticism. This means that criticism is not ready to apply to itself the criteria it applies to its object. Mere criticism lacks self-reflection, for it stops short of asking itself whether its own normative standards cannot be juxtaposed to the facts by yet another critical critique, and whether its own reason cannot be shown to be equally unreasonable. Mere criticism cannot avoid an infinite regress: vis-à-vis every one of its criteria, it can be asked "by what right?" Marxian critique, by contrast, is not a mode of *criteriological* inquiry. The criteria it presupposes in its inquiry are not different from the ones by which the object or phenomenon judges itself. The Marxian method of critique presupposes that its object of inquiry is reflexive; it presupposes that what is investigated is already a social reality which has its own self-interpretation.

In a letter to Arnold Ruge written in September 1843, Marx states in programmatic terms the task of the *Deutsch-französischen Jahrbücher*, of which they were the coeditors:

> Philosophy has become worldly and the most decisive proof of this is that philosophical consciousness has been drawn into the torment of struggle not only externally but internally as well. Just as the construction of the future and becoming fit and ready for all times is not our task, so is all the more certain what we have to accomplish in the present. I mean *the ruthless critique of all that exists*, ruthless in the sense that critique does not fear its own consequences, and just as little, conflicts with existing powers.[22]

The "ruthless critique of all that exists," Marx proceeds to explain, does not mean hoisting a dogmatic flag, not even the flag of communism, as the early communists (Weitling) and utopian socialists (Cabet, Fourier, Proudhon) do. Rather, the critic must begin with existing forms of consciousness and must not "juxtapose them to some ready-made system like the *Voyages to Icary*" (MEW 1:344). For "reason has always existed, but not always in a rational form. The critic can therefore begin with each form of theoretical and practical consciousness and out of the very form of existing actuality he can develop true actuality as its 'ought' and its 'goal'" (MEW 1:345). The task of the critic is not to juxtapose an ideal, eternal standard to the existent, but through a "ruthless critique of the existent" to reveal that what is, already contains within itself what "ought" to be as a possibility. Marx advocates dissolving the existent (*das Bestehende*) into the conflict between the actual and the possible, and to show that under present conditions reason exists, but not in "a rational form."

This very formulation reveals the extent to which Marx adopts the Hegelian thesis of the unity of the actual and the rational.[23] To view the existent as a realm of possibility containing within itself what ought to be is to view the existent as actuality (*Wirklichkeit*). What is, is seen as having become. Only when the immediate is viewed as mediated, only when what is, is understood in light of the forces that have made it become, can it be seen as the unity of actuality and possibility. For what is actual is not merely the given. Actuality means an existent that has returned to its ground, i.e., an existent that is mediated, and posited such as to correspond to its concept.[24] "What is actual is rational" does not mean that the given is rational, but that when the existent is viewed in light of its process of becoming and is analyzed as the moment of difference posited by an essence, it reveals within itself the unity of existence and essence. In revealing this unity, actuality also reveals what it could be but is not. In Marx's words, out of "existing actuality" one can develop future actuality as it "ought" to be and its goal.

Marx presupposes here Hegel's critique of empiricism and formalism: while the thesis that the actual is the rational presupposes Hegel's rejection of the given, and his analysis of all that is (*Sein*) into a having been (*gewesen Sein*) and a having become (*geworden Sein*), the thesis that "reason has always existed but not always in rational form" presupposes Hegel's rejection of formalism. Reason is not a mere principle of thought; it is thought that must embody and externalize itself in the world. Reason can only be in the world as embodied in it, although this embodiment may fail to give reason its most adequate expression.[25] Marx rejects utopianism on the same basis that Hegel rejected methodological thought experiments: by postponing what ought to a beyond (*Jenseits*), these procedures also imply that what is, is devoid of reason. To view what is as non-rational is to view it as simply immediate, as a mere factum and mere given. The task of the critic is to show that the given is not a mere fact, that to understand it to be actuality is also to criticize it by showing what it could be but is not. In this context, Marx distinguishes "immanent" from "transcendent" utopia. "It will then be shown that the world already possesses the dream of something, of which it must also possess the consciousness, before it can actually take possession of it. It will be shown that the task is not to insert a line between the past and the future, but the *fulfillment* of the thought of the past. Finally, it will be shown that humans begin no new task, but consciously bring old tasks to fruition" (MEW 1:346).

The "dream" which the world possesses, but of which it has not taken full possession, is contained in contemporary religious and political consciousness. To name this dream, Marx uses Feuerbach's method of "inversion." Religious consciousness projects onto a divine being the attributes of omniscience, eternity, universality, goodness, and perfection. It is not the divine that is the subject of all these predicates, but humanity itself that is the true subject, for these predicates are nothing but theoretical and practical ideals that humans have of themselves, and which they falsely hypostatize and constitute into an existent being.[26] The inversion of predicate and subject, namely, making the divine into a predicate instead of a subject, reveals that the true subject is humanity and that divinity is its attribute. Modern political consciousness is guilty of the same inversion as religious consciousness. "Universality," "rationality," and "freedom" are considered attributes of the state. Humanity once again projects onto a separate sphere, onto the political state, its own capacities and potentials and succumbs to the power of an illusory subject.

Although they coexist side by side in Marx's writings of this period, the Feuerbachian method of inversion and the Hegelian method of immanent critique are not altogether compatible. The process of inverting subject and predicate does not explain why this inversion occurs in the first place or what its dynamics are. The reduction of a false subject to the status of a predicate and the elevation of what seems to be a predicate to the status of a subject is a fairly one-dimensional operation which shows that all human exteriorizations must be returned to, or be reappropriated by, their subjects. What is missing in this procedure is an analysis of the dynamics between exteriorization and internalization, between human cultural and political products and the human needs that are expressed through them. The Feuerbachian method cannot explain why human needs must be expressed in this alienated, topsy-turvy form. In Hegelian language, this method of inversion cannot explain why appearance is a moment of essence, or otherness a moment of a self-alienated totality. Reflections—meaning here human cultural and political products and institutions—are not reflected to their ground in the Hegelian sense. That out of which they arise, and the necessity that they manifest themselves in this form rather than another, is not explained. The essay "On the Jewish Question," written shortly after the letter to Ruge, exemplifies best Marx's attempt to reconcile both procedures.

Marx's polemic against Bruno Bauer's treatment of the Jewish demands for political emancipation in this essay is also a statement about the correct method of criticism. Against Bauer, who claims that to demand political emancipation as Jews in a Christian state is illusory because the modern state must free itself of all religion,[27] Marx argues that the post–French Revolutionary state does not presuppose the *abolition* but rather the *privatization* of religion. The distinction between public citizenship and private religiosity, between man as citizen and as bourgeois, belongs to the essence of the modern state. Bauer is a mere "critical critic" of this state of affairs, because he cannot see that the norm he juxtaposes to actuality—the emancipation of politics from religion—is contradicted by this very actuality. The modern state does not emancipate itself from religion; rather, it bans religion into the private sphere. Thus the Jewish demands for political emancipation are perfectly consistent with the internal logic of the modern political state (MEW 1:349).

The modern political state cannot abolish religious consciousness, "since the existence of religion is the existence of a lack and this lack can only be searched for in the *essence* of the state itself. Religion is for us no more the *ground* but merely the phenomenon of worldly limitedness! We explain therefore the religious bias of the free citizen on the basis of his worldly bias. We do not maintain that these citizens should get rid of their religious chains, in order to eliminate their worldly chains. We assert that they eliminate their religious chains as soon as they have eliminated their worldly ones" (MEW 1:352). In his analysis of modern religious consciousness, Marx returns to Hegel's method of criticism. Religious consciousness is a phenomenon posited by an essence that is alienated from itself. Religious consciousness distinguishes between worldly and divine existence, between the kingdom of man and the kingdom of God. This separation and bifurcation is contained in the very structure of the modern state. The modern state likewise distinguishes between a sphere of universality and a sphere of individualism, between a sphere of common, rational interest and a sphere of individual selfishness and limitation (MEW 1:356).

It is important to note that this analysis of religious consciousness is not a reductionist one. Unlike some of his later writings, Marx here is not reducing religion and the need for religion to the interests in domination of certain social groups over others.[28] Rather, he is arguing that both modern Christianity, particularly in its Protestant form, and the modern state project a distinction between universality and particularity, the general and the concrete, commonality and selfishness. Both abstract from concrete human existence certain human qualities which they project onto a separate sphere. Insofar as religion expresses this need for universality, it corresponds to a real need, itself a consequence of the limitations of worldly existence. This real need is fulfilled in a false manner, for the religious system of belief reproduces, but does not eliminate, the real life conditions out of which the need for an abstract universality arises. Just as the modern state requires bourgeois civil society as its opposite both to negate it and to be negated by it, so too modern religious consciousness requires the misery of the world which it negates but which it also confirms. The political sphere exercises an abstract domination over the social-economic sphere; religious consciousness exercises abstract domination over worldly consciousness.

Although Marx uses here Hegel's method of immanent reflection to show that the juxtaposition of two opposites—religious and worldly consciousness, universality and particularity—is due to a split, to a bifurcation within the totality of life conditions, he does not postulate that this contradiction in appearance is a unity in essence. The bifurcation within bourgeois civil society is not seen as the moment of the negative totality which the ethical whole posits as an act of self-sacrifice. In his *Critique of Hegel's Philosophy of Right*, Marx states this methodological difference between Hegel's procedure and his in the following way: "Hegel's chief mistake consists in the fact that he conceives of the *contradiction in appearance* as being *unity in essence*, i.e., *in the Idea*, whereas it certainly is something more profound in its essence, namely an essential contradiction" (MEW 1:295–96, emphasis in the text).

This methodological difference, which is of great importance for understanding the logic of Marx's *Capital* as well,[29] should not obscure the fact that Marx's early diagnosis of the antagonism inherent in bourgeois civil society clearly parallels the Hegelian one of *Entzweiung*. The principle of essential unity is denied methodologically, but it is reasserted at the normative level as the immanent utopia which Marx claims is the implicit "ought" toward which actuality must evolve. As a next step, let me examine these normative presuppositions of Marx's critique.

If the task of the critic is to "begin with each form of theoretical and practical consciousness" and to develop "out of the very forms of existing actuality true actuality as its 'ought' and its goal" (MEW 1:345), what is the true actuality toward which modern political and religious consciousness ought to evolve? What is the dream which the world possesses but of which it has not taken full possession? The essay "On the Jewish Question" names this ought and this dream: the elimination of the antagonism between universality and particularity, between the state and civil society, and between man as "citizen" and man as "bourgeois."[30] The *reappropriation* of the powers and potentialities that humanity has alienated from itself is the dream. This process of reappropriation can take two distinct forms, and Marx names both without clearly distinguishing between them. I will describe the first as "the universalization of the political" and the second as "the socialization of the universal."

In the first case, Marx criticizes the instrumentalization of the political sphere to serve the interests of the bourgeoisie alone. When the rights of the citizen merely serve the maintenance of the rights of man—property, security, equality—means and ends have been reversed.

> This state of affairs will become even more mysterious when we see that the citizenry of the state, the *political common being* will be reduced by political emancipators to be the mere means of the so-called rights of man; that the citizen will be declared the servant of the egotistical man; the sphere in which the human being behaves as a universal being will be degraded below the sphere in which he behaves as an individual being; finally when not the human being as citizen, but the human being as bourgeois will be considered the *authentic* and *true* human being. (MEW 1:366)

Marx speaks here the language of a radical democrat who sees in the degradation of the rights of the citizen below those of man the instrumentalization of the revolution in the interests of the bourgeoisie alone. In his *Critique of Hegel's Philosophy of Right*, Marx expresses this in the statement that "democracy is both form and content" (MEW 1:231), meaning thereby that it is not political democracy alone which guarantees formal rights, but that societal democracy as well is required for this task. This would imply that the juxtaposition of the common good to private interests, of the political to the social and economic spheres, would be abolished through the restructuring of the social as well as economic spheres to serve the common good.

The elimination of the antagonism between these spheres can either mean the independent subsistence and restructuring of both or their real elimination qua independent spheres. Marx expresses this latter alternative in his statement that "in a true democracy the political state disappears" (MEW 1:232). This I name the "socialization of the universal." According to this al-

ternative, social life itself would become the genuine expression
of universal and common interests and would not delegate the
representation of this universal interest to an independent political realm. Such a restructuring of social life, however, would
mean eliminating the sphere of legal and political relations altogether. It would mean the communalization (*Vergemeinschaft-
ung*) of bourgeois society. In the essay "On the Jewish Question,"
Marx expresses this in the following terms. "First when the actual individual human being reincorporates the abstract citizen
and has become a *species-being* as individual human being in his
empirical life, in his individual work, in his individual relations,
first when the human being has recognized and organized his
forces propres and no longer separates them from himself in the
form of *political* force, only then is human emancipation completed" (MEW 1:370). Human emancipation is the reappropriation by concrete human individuals in their actual, everyday
relations, and work of the forces that they have delegated to
alien structures. It is the establishment of a mode of sociality in
which relations are no longer mediated by juridical categories of
the rights of man and where individuals no longer interact as
antagonistic atoms, but reaffirm in their everyday relations
their common humanity and universality.

Whereas the ideal of the "universalization of the political"
signifies the *extension* of the democratic norms achieved by
bourgeois revolutions to other spheres in civil society, the ideal
of the "socialization of the universal" signifies the *radical transformation* of these norms themselves and the elimination of an
independent politico-juridical sphere, along with the restructuring of human relations in communal and communitarian
terms. While in the one case the "ought" that faces actuality is
the completion of a norm immanent in actuality itself—
"Democracy is both form and content"—in the second case, the
"ought" that faces actuality involves its radical negation—"In a
true democracy the political state disappears." But is this radical negation of actuality not a transcendence of actuality? Does
not Marx contradict his own claim that "humans begin no new
task, but consciously bring old tasks to fruition" (MEW 1:346)?
For according to the second interpretation, the radical transformation of the norms of bourgeois democratic revolution does
not imply their fulfillment, but their transfiguration.

It is no accident that in his own self-understanding and evaluation, Marx denies the moment of utopia, the moment of radical otherness, that his project entails. Since utopian thinking is identified with the creation of a mere wishful beyond and rejected on the same grounds that Hegel rejects the Kantian "ought," Marx does not acknowledge the radical otherness that the determinate negation of the existent brings with it. The determinate negation of the existent is viewed as the conscious bringing of old tasks to fruition, but not as the beginning of a new task which this project always also is. The difficulty I am pointing to here is not restricted to Marx's early writings alone. In the *Grundrisse* and *Capital* as well, the determinate negation of the existent does not simply mean the fulfillment and continuation of an old task but the beginning of a qualitatively different one. Furthermore, Marx himself shows that this new task emerges out of the ashes of the old, for he diagnoses the genesis of needs and demands within the capitalist system which in their radicalness transcend the existing order.

The alternatives described as the "fulfillment" and "transfiguration" of bourgeois revolutions indicate the presence of a similar ambivalence in Marx's thought, as noted above with respect to Hegel's vision of ethical life. The perspective of transfiguration—the socialization of the universal—corresponds to a view of social life as a transparent unity in which human beings have come to reappropriate their alienated powers. The perspective of fulfillment, by contrast, is less antagonistic to the differentiation of modern civil society into political, economic, and social spheres, and does not require the radical abolition of legal and political institutions which the first seems to imply. This ideal corresponds to Hegel's view of ethical life as "self-mediating totality."

Throughout this work, I will use the terms "transfiguration" and "fulfillment" to refer to two different projects of emancipation. By the term "fulfillment" I mean a view of social transformation according to which emancipation carries to its conclusion, in a better and more adequate form, the already attained results of the present. Emancipation is realizing the implicit but frustrated potential of the present. The term "transfiguration," by contrast, is intended to suggest that emancipation signifies a radical and qualitative break with some aspects of the present. In certain fundamental ways, the society of the future is viewed to be, not the culmination, but the radical negation of the present.

Let me summarize the conclusions reached through this initial examination of the origins of the method of immanent critique. Immanent critique is first and foremost a critique of dogmatism and formalism, that is, a critique of the myth of the given and of the juxtaposition to the given of a formal principle to which the former must be subordinated. Both content and form, the given and the "ought," are reflected to their ground and shown to be products of a form of consciousness embedded in a form of life that is divided, bifurcated, and alienated. Theoretical critique is also the critique of a way of life implied or projected by theories. In the *Natural Law* essay, Hegel criticizes the bifurcation of modern society reflected through natural right theories from the standpoint of a retrospective utopia. For Marx, by contrast, the critique of bifurcation is not a retrospective but a prospective task: the unification of universality and particularity is the implicit dream of the modern state. Here Marx allies himself with the radical republican tradition of bourgeois revolutions, with the citizen against the bourgeois. But the ideal of the unification of universality and particularity also points in the direction of the transfiguration of the norms of the bourgeois state altogether—it projects the image of a form of life in which the modern state and the whole sphere of politico-juridical relations disappear. While Hegel's model of "transparent ethical life" is a retrospective utopia, Marx's model of the "socialization of the universal" is a prospective one.

In both cases, however, modern civil society and natural right theories are criticized in the name of an ideal of "unity." Hegel is guided by the ancient image of the *polis*, while Marx condemns the differentiation of modern societies into antagonistic spheres like economics, politics, morality, and the family. The emphasis on unity in Hegel's case, and the emphasis on de-differentiation in Marx's, means that their methodological critique of modern normative philosophies cannot be separated at this stage from a view of ethical and political life that is antagonistic to modern civil society.

The next step in my analysis of the transformation of the concept of critique from Kant to Marx will focus on the discovery of the concept of labor. This discovery precipitates Hegel to reformulate his analysis of the normative potential of modern society. My concern, however, is not to spell out this reformulation in detail, but to show how the discovery of the category of labor goes hand in hand with the philosophy of the subject. If an ideal of a *unified ethical and political life* underlies the method of immanent critique, behind defetishizing critique lies the vision of a unified mankind collectively transforming the conditions of its existence and then reappropriating what it has externalized.

Chapter 2

THE ORIGINS OF
DEFETISHIZING CRITIQUE

Hegel's rereading of Kant and Fichte in the Jena period, subsequent to the publication of the *Natural Law* essay, his rejection of Schelling's identity philosophy, and most significant, his discovery of the emancipatory moments of modern bourgeois society in the dialectic of labor and recognition lead to a reevaluation of modern philosophy and society. This reevaluation in the 1805–6 writings precipitates Hegel's "retreat from Eleusis"[1] and sets him on the path of reconciliation with modernity. The immanent critique of modern self-consciousness is made possible with the discovery of the structure of human intersubjectivity in the *Realphilosophie* (1805–6). Hegel no longer juxtaposes the right of an ethical absolute to the claims of modern individualism, but shows that modern individualism denies the context out of which it emerges, namely, the interaction of self and other that is conceptually and genetically constitutive of human self-consciousness.[2] The work in which this new mode of criticizing modern subjectivity is most explicitly developed, and which marks the second phase in the transformation of the concept of critique from Kant to Marx, is the *Phenomenology of Spirit* of 1807.

   In tracing the transformation of the concept of "critique" from Kant to Marx, via Hegel's critique of Kant, it must first be remembered how much Hegel is indebted to Kant. Already in the *Critique of Pure Reason* Kant states that dogmatism in the exercise of reason inevitably leads to skepticism. When reason transcends its own limits, proposing to establish knowledge about God, immortality, and the world, all of which lie beyond experience, the path is paved for the skeptic's objections. Against the exercise of metaphysical arrogance, the skeptic will justifiably ask how and on what grounds one must take as certain and evident reason's claims about what transcends the limits of experience and the senses.[3] The skeptic uses criticism as a weapon to defeat the pretentions of metaphysical dogmatism. Against the mere criticism of pure reason by the skeptic, Kant proposes to undertake a "critique" of pure reason, " to undertake anew the most difficult of all its tasks, namely, that of self-knowledge, and to institute a tribunal which will assure to reason its lawful claims, and dismiss all groundless pretensions, not by despotic decrees, but in accordance with its own eternal and unalterable laws. This tribunal is no other than the *critique of pure reason.*"[4] The critique of pure reason is an activity of self-knowledge, for both the judge and the accused are one and the same. In submitting its claim to a court of its own design, reason transcends the age of mere criticism and comes of age itself.

Hegel interprets the "self-knowledge" of reason more radically than Kant, to mean the self-reflection of reason upon all its presuppositions, and among them the faculty and the act of critique itself. The radical self-reflection of reason cannot be restricted to an analysis of the presuppositions which constitute the objectivity of experience alone. Such self-reflection must be extended to the presuppositions which underlie the constitution of subjectivity, or of the subject of knowledge, as well. Precisely because the "Copernican turn" initiated by Kant places the activity of the knowing subject at the center of the process of knowledge, Hegel's analysis of the constitution of subjectivity and objectivity cannot dispense with the turn to the subject. Hegel must show that a radical critique of knowledge, or of the subjective moment, necessarily leads to an analysis whereby the unity of subjectivity and objectivity and their reciprocal relation is revealed. This is precisely the purpose of the *Phenomenology of Spirit.*

1. Hegelian Origins: The Phenomenological Method

There is by now a century-old controversy concerning the *Phenomenology of Spirit,* its intentions and place within the Hegelian system.[5] Is the *Phenomenology* a "preparation" for and an "introduction" to the system or the "first part" of the system, and thus already a "first science of philosophy"? If the latter, would this suggest that the *Phenomenology* is recapitulated within the *Logic* or perhaps within the *Encyclopedia*? If the former, does not this "introduction" to science already presuppose science in that it brings the chaotic and rich manifestations of Spirit into "scientific order in accordance with this necessity"? Furthermore, if this were the case, would it not contradict Hegel's own criticism of the circularity of epistemological theories in the Introduction to the *Phenomenology*?

The purpose of this chapter is not to resolve this controversy. From my point of view, the unclarity concerning Hegel's *Phenomenology*, namely, whether it is a critique of previous theories of knowledge or an exposition of the "science of appearing knowledge," points to the unity of *Kritik* and *Darstellung*, criticism and exposition, which we already confronted in analyzing the *Natural Law* essay. Insofar as in the *Natural Law* essay Hegel immanently analyzed the contradictions of empiricism and formalism and showed both to be dogmatic, his procedure was a critical one; insofar as the immanent analysis was at the same time an exposition of the speculative principle of "the identity of identity and difference," Hegel's procedure became dogmatic, juxtaposing to the object of examination a principle that transcended its own self-understanding. In the *Phenomenology* as well this twofold procedure is at work: on the one hand, Hegel criticizes modern epistemology for its dogmatism and circularity. The method of this critique is phenomenological. On the other hand, the transition from one form of consciousness to another, the selection and arrangement of the series of forms of consciousness and the "necessity" said to be inherent in this, point to presuppositions of the method of exposition the justification of which transcends the boundaries of the phenomenological argument and depends upon premises derived from Hegel's speculative philosophy.[6]

The hermeneutical brilliance of the first, the phenomenological aspect, of Hegel's argument consists in that Hegel conceives philosophical critique as dialogue, as a process of communication between the writer-thinker and the readers. The readers of the text are its *subject matter*, since they recognize and feel themselves addressed by the standpoint of consciousness. The readers of the text are also its *subject*, insofar as they are addressed as the "we" and urged to share in the construction and emergence of the text by being informed of the "stage directions," so to speak, that will be enacted by consciousness. The latent dogmatism of this procedure consists in the fact that the *dialogical* model which governs the experience of the *Phenomenology* as a text is replaced by a *monological* one in the course of the development of the textual argument. The unfolding of the experience of consciousness is seen as the activity of exteriorization of a transsubjective subject who then "reappropriates" and "takes into possession" what was once his. The activities of formation, possession, and appropriation come to replace the model of dialogue.

The perspectives of lived intersubjectivity and transsubjectivity, already encountered in analyzing the *Natural Law* essay, reemerge in the *Phenomenology*. While the first characterizes the standpoint of consciousness, the second corresponds to that of the philosopher-observer—the "we" that becomes an "I." It is this latter perspective that ultimately prevails, and which deeply informs Hegel's understanding of the perspective of philosophy in general.

The central argument of this chapter is that Hegel models the activity of consciousness upon labor, and first develops the thesis that history can be viewed as the activity of a collective, singular subject that exteriorizes itself and subsequently "reappropriates" what it has exteriorized. I will describe this position as the *philosophy of the subject* (section 2). The philosophy of the subject is the normative model underlying defetishizing critique: by defetishizing critique is meant a procedure of analysis whereby the given is shown to be not a natural fact but a socially and historically constituted, and thus changeable, reality.

In the latter half of this chapter, continuing the parallel exposition of Hegel and Marx, I turn to the *1844 Manuscripts* to show that Marx's critique of Hegel does not negate but rather perpetuates the premises of the philosophy of the subject (section 3).

2. The Presuppositions of the Phenomenological Method: Constitutive Activity as Labor

In the Preface to the *Phenomenology* Hegel writes: "This past being is already the acquired property of universal Spirit, which makes up the substance of the individual and, by appearing external to him, constitutes his inorganic nature. Considered from the standpoint of the individual, education consists in this, that he appropriates what is already at hand, lives off his inorganic nature and takes it into possession for himself" (PhG, 27/16).

That Hegel describes education as the "reappropriation" and "taking possession" by the individual of what is already the "acquired property of universal Spirit" is no coincidence. For the process of the education of natural consciousness to the standpoint of philosophical science is one in which externality increasingly loses its given character and is viewed by natural consciousness as its own "work" and "product." The epistemological argument which shows how the standpoint of natural consciousness is overcome presupposes the formative activity of labor through which Spirit shapes, appropriates, and transforms external nature into a second, historicized "property of universal Spirit."[7] "Spirit," says Hegel in the *Lectures on the Philosophy of History*, "essentially acts, it makes itself into what it is in itself; an act, its own work; so it becomes its own object, so it has itself as an existence before itself."[8] The education of consciousness leads to the recognition of this truth. The categories of labor, appropriation, and property are not merely specific forms of the experience of consciousness dealt with in the chapters on "Lordship and Bondage" (IV-A) and the "Fact of the Matter" (V-C). They are meta-categories that describe the essential activity of Spirit and the world-formative process which is the education of consciousness.

From the beginning, Hegel includes in the activity of consciousness doing as well as making, *praxis* as well as *poiesis*, but understands both as labor, namely, as an activity in which the subject externalizes him/herself by transforming what is given to it in such a way as to humanize it, to make it into an object that not only serves human purposes but into "a spiritualized object," one which can be understood and made intelligible only in relation to a human subject. This difference between an object of use and a "spiritualized object," i.e., one which conveys human meanings and significations without necessarily being useful, is usually overlooked. As the chapter on religion in the *Phenomenology* shows, Hegel does not conceive of laboring activity merely as producing use objects—this, it may be remembered, was the achievement of the Enlightenment (PhG, p. 411)— but as the more generic activity of humanizing and spiritualizing nature and externality. This spiritualization of nature begins with the naturalization of Spirit, with primitive religions in which nature is viewed not as an object of use, but as a source of meaning and value in whose likeness mankind conceives of its divinity. The labor of Spirit is also its progressive emancipation from its naturalistic form, or it is the disenchantment of nature.[9] Nature ceases to be a source of meaning and value when Spirit no longer conceives its divinity in its likeness to nature, but in its likeness with humanity. Paradoxically, it is this totally disenchanted nature that is also most spiritual, i.e., one whose meaning and value now wholly originate in what humans attribute to it. Nature becomes a matter of fact—a *Sache* (PhG, 523ff./455ff.).

Returning once more to Hegel's statement that "this past is already the acquired property of universal Spirit. . . . Education consists in this: that he [the individual] appropriates what is already at hand" (PhG, p. 27), I want to claim that underlying Hegel's concept of the activity of Spirit is a model of labor as the cumulative generator of wealth.[10]

Labor can be considered an activity of determinate negation in two ways: first, labor can be viewed as useful and purposive activity, as discussed by Marx in the chapter on the "Labor Process" in the first volume of *Capital*. In this process, the laborer "opposes himself to Nature as one of her own forces . . . in order to appropriate Nature's productions in a form adopted to his own wants."[11] Through this activity, the *form* of the natural raw material is transformed, but the matter is retained, only now it is shaped to serve human purposes. In the labor process human groups already find given to them the instruments and the raw material of labor as the product of past generations; their ac-

tivity in the present can only proceed via a determinate negation of this past. The recurring labor process begins with what is
handed down from the past, with givens that are themselves
already posits. The posits of the past are reposited via the activity of labor, for they are transformed in such a way as to serve
human purposes in the present; but this transformation always
presupposes a given, an object upon which it acts. Since this
given itself is already a transformed and humanized object, the
negation of its present form is a second negation, a negation of
the negation.

The cyclical process of labor, through which posits of the past
are reposited, is thus a cumulative process, one in which individuals in the present open to the future by transforming and
reappropriating the past. In this model, labor is considered a
concrete human activity which always proceeds from the accumulated product of past generations to restore them as use objects in the present. This aspect of labor is transhistorical
because it is a constant feature of all concrete human activity
directed to the creation of use values. Its basic outlines have
already been discussed by Aristotle in his considerations on
poiesis, on making.[12]

There is a second model of labor, however, according to which
labor is also an activity of determinate negation, but not in virtue of creating use objects; rather, in virtue of creating value.
Whereas in the first model labor is an activity of determinate
negation because it proceeds by continually changing the *form*
of the given while preserving the material, in the second model,
labor is an activity of determinate negation because it continually *revalorizes* the products of the past, which left to themselves
would disintegrate under the impact of the forces of nature.
Living labor "must seize upon these things and rouse them from
their death-sleep" (*Capital*, p. 183) and reintroduce them into the
cycle of production and consumption.[13] Whereas in the first
model labor is seen as a natural activity, as an activity by which
the human being acts as a force of nature, in the second model
labor is an activity that gives meaning and value to an otherwise
mute and dead nature. It transforms dead matter into a human
object, into an object that has meaning and value for humans.
Determinate negation here signifies a continuous humanization
and valorization of the dead weight of the past. The cyclical

process of labor reposits the posits of the past, making them into meaningful and value-laden objects for others. This process is the cumulative humanization of externality, of its transformation into an in-itself-for-humans.[14]

The significance of these two models of labor for Hegel's argument in the *Phenomenology* can be established by first recalling to ourselves the *epistemological argument*, and then seeing how these models of labor are presupposed by it. The course of the experience of consciousness consists in comparing truth with certainty, the *what* with the *that* of knowledge, or in Hegel's words, the *in-itself* with what is *for-consciousness*. Should these two not correspond—and the experience of consciousness is coming to see this lack of correspondence—then consciousness must change its knowledge claim. For it considered this to be a valid knowledge claim because it corresponded to the truth of its object. When this lack of correspondence is realized, consciousness drops this claim for a new one, but in this process it changes its object of knowledge as well. Consciousness first knew the object to be such-and-such, but the process of its experience shows the object not to be so. Its knowledge of its object now includes the first description under which the object falls, as well as the second description which entails that the first is false. "We see that consciousness now has two objects, the one the first *in-itself*, the second, the *being-for-itself-of-this-in-itself*. . . . This new object contains the nullity of the first, it is the experience of the first object" (PhG, p. 73).

The transition from the first object of consciousness to the second is so constructed that the knowledge of the first object, or "the being-for-consciousness of the first in-itself" (PhG, p. 73), constitutes the second object of experience. "This observation," writes Hegel, "is our addition"—*unsere Zutat* (PhG, p. 74). Usually what is meant by experience is that one moves from an old to a new and different content. But this is a facile understanding which views the old content simply as negated, and can only lead to skepticism and to the "path of despair." What distinguishes phenomenological critique from mere skepticism is that the falsehood of experience is viewed as a learning process in which knowledge of the inadequacy of previous experiences is integrated into and becomes an aspect of subsequent experiences.

It is this necessity, or the *emergence* of the new object, which takes
place without consciousness's knowing what happens to him. For
us this takes place behind consciousness's back. In this movement,
there is thus a moment of *in-itselfness* or *being-for-us*, which does
not manifest itself to the consciousness caught in the experience
itself. The *content* of what emerges for us is *for it*, and we comprehend only the form or its pure emergence. *For consciousness*,
this emergent is only an object; *for us* it is at the same time a
movement and a becoming. Through this necessity this path to
science is already itself *science*, and according to its content the
science of the experience of consciousness. (PhG, p. 74)

At each stage in the experience of consciousness, the object, the
in-itself, contains the experience of *being-in-itself-for-another*.
The second object of experience is the being-in-itself-for-another
of object 1; the third, the being-in-itself-for-another of object 2,
which is in turn the being-in-itself-for-another of object 1; etc.[15]
Hegel thus presents a successive totalization of the content of
the experience of consciousness, each Gestalt of consciousness
absorbing into itself the moments of the previous ones.

This totalization of the experience of consciousness presupposes, first of all, that there is a *unitary* principle which shines
through all contents of experience and in virtue of which experience can present itself as successive totalization. This unitary
principle, for Hegel, is both Substance and Subject. It is Substance insofar as the cumulative experience of consciousness is a
material accumulation, corresponding to the process through
which "universal Spirit" appropriates externality, the world, as
its property. Insofar as this accumulation corresponds to a process of *Erinnerung*, remembrance and interiorization, Substance becomes Subject. While the experience of consciousness
designates material accumulation and its unity is the *material*
unity embodied in the stuff of the world which humans appropriate and transform, the experience of the "we" is one of spiritual accumulation and its unity is embodied in the memory of
those for whom the tale of consciousness has *meaning* and *value*.
Thus the two models of the labor process, as transformative and
valorizing activities, find their correlates in the experience of
consciousness and of the "we" respectively. The activity of consciousness in transforming externality corresponds to the ma-

terial activity of creating use objects through a determinate negation of their past forms. The world-historical process of *Erinnerung*, by which Spirit "reappropriates" the past, corresponds to the abstract laboring activity of creating value and meaning out of the dead accumulation of the past.[16]

The statement with which we started this section now assumes full meaning: "This past is already the acquired property of universal Spirit. . . . Education [*Bildung*] consists in this: that he [the individual] appropriates what is already at hand" (PhG, p. 27). The past is the "property" of universal Spirit, in the sense that the world-historical activity of labor has humanized and transformed externality, and has created history out of nature. This corresponds to the *transformative* process of laboring activity. Now in taking possession of this heritage, the individual must recall that what appears as a given, external reality to him is in fact his work, and has meaning and significance only in relation to his activity. This process of recollection, which brings the external into relation with the subject, presupposes labor qua *valorizing* activity. And such a perspective is only possible insofar as consciousness adopts the standpoint of universal Spirit, or identifies itself with the "phenomenological we." Education consists in overcoming the standpoint of consciousness and in seeing that one is both Substance and Subject of this process.

The ultimate reconciliation of consciousness and the "we," of individual and universal Spirit, is based upon a series of reductions. Here I shall merely specify what I see these reductions to consist in. An analysis of the underlying model of activity which makes these reductions possible will first be undertaken in the following chapter. In the *Phenomenology*, Hegel reduces the different modes of human activity characteristic of the experience of consciousness to the single paradigm of externalization, *Entäusserung*, of which labor is the prime example. The experience of human plurality is reduced to the memory of a transsubjective subject called "Spirit"; history—the contradictory, incomplete, and often conflictual tales that human collectivities tell of themselves—is reduced to the univocal, cumulative sequence through which a super-subject comes to know itself. Furthermore, the path to philosophical wisdom is insight into the identity of *constituted* and *constituting* subjectivity. Consciousness overcomes the given in that it comes to know that the given was constituted by a subject which is none other than itself, i.e., Spirit. Consciousness knows that the limits of its subjectivity, the distinction between truth and certainty, the in-itself and the for-consciousness, can be dissolved, for it recognizes that these limits are ones that have been posited through a past history which is no other than the history of its own becoming.

I will name these four presuppositions, (a) the unitary model of activity, (b) the model of a transsubjective subject, (c) history as the story of transsubjectivity, and (d) the identity of constituting and constituted subjectivity, together the "philosophy of the subject." A major argument of this book is that these four presuppositions which constitute the "philosophy of the subject" together form the model of societal and human emancipation upon which Horkheimer's 1937 conception of critical theory rests. At first this may seem like a puzzling claim, for in this tradition Hegel has always been criticized for positing an abstract, speculative subject called "Spirit" and for viewing history as the becoming of Spirit. But the anthropological critique of Hegel, first begun by Marx in the *1844 Manuscripts,* simply replaces "Spirit" with "mankind" or "humanity." This replacement does not alter the fundamentals of the "philosophy of the subject," for history is still viewed as a *unitary* process of the unfolding of the capabilities of a collective subject, and social emancipation is still understood as the *reappropriation* by a specific social class of this heritage. The particular demands of this class coalesce with the universal demands of humanity to become the subject of its own history. Even when there is no social class at hand whose emancipatory demands can be viewed by the critical theorist as fulfilling this promise, the search for a revolutionary subject whose very particularity is to act in the name of universal mankind is not given up. As will be argued below, the course of critical theory from 1937 to 1947 presents the abandonment of the *revolutionary* subject, but not the abandonment of the search for the revolutionary *subject* as such (see chapter 5).

Let me state preliminarily that my critique of the philosophy of the subject is not inspired by the currently fashionable structuralist and post-structuralist searches for a philosophy without the subject.[17] My concern is not to substitute structures, forms, and binary oppositions for subjects. Rather, I want to pursue the perspective of radical intersubjectivity and plurality, and argue against the characteristic "flight of philosophy"—in Merleau-Ponty's words—away from our situatedness and embodiedness. This perspective is not alien to the tradition of critical Marxism: its beginnings can be found in Marx's analysis of sensuous finitude in the *1844 Manuscripts*, but as in the subsequent tradition of critical theory, already in this text too the philosophy of the subject was to dominate.

The purpose of the following analysis of the *1844 Manuscripts* will be to show that Marx's critique of Hegel does not dispense with, but rather entails, the presuppositions of the philosophy of the subject, and that the perspective of sensuous finitude suggested by Marx's anthropological critique is once again covered up, for the objectification model of activity is inadequate to articulate this perspective.

3. The Anthropological Transformation of the Phenomenological Method in the *1844 Manuscripts*

In the section of the *1844 Manuscripts* entitled the "Critique of Hegel's Dialectic and Philosophy," Marx criticizes Hegel for having confused objectification (*Vergegenständlichung*) with alienation (*Entfremdung*).[18] This critique obscures the modeling of the Marxist concept of objectification on Hegel's concept of externalization. For Marx as well, objectification is an activity through which what is inner becomes outer and external. The purpose of this activity is to give adequate embodiment and expression to the potentialities of the individual. Objectification is self-externalization, and ought to be, but is not always, self-realization (*Selbstverwirklichung*). Just as through action, the Hegelian self embodies its deed in the world and makes it a fact for others, so for Marx too through objectification the self embodies its potentialities and capacities in an object and becomes an object for others (M, p. 116).

The concrete, corporeal human being posits through external-ization (*Entäusserung*) his essential powers—in this case as alien objects. Objectification is the externalization of the essential powers of the individual. Since for Marx, life itself is an activity of externalization, and to be alive means to have the objects of one's needs outside oneself and to be oneself an object for others, the crucial question is the extent to which this anthropo-logically universal mode of activity is a form of self-expression and self-realization. Is objectification self-confirmation or self-denial? Marx names objectifying activity that denies and stul-tifies the powers and capacities of the self "alienated" activity.

This normative concept of objectification as self-confirming and self-enhancing activity is juxtaposed by Marx in the first half of the *1844 Manuscripts* to conditions of alienated labor in a private-property economy. Marx's critique of alienated labor is only intelligible when it is assumed that labor is a mode of self-confirming externalization, and that under the domination of private property it becomes the complete opposite. The *essence* of labor is the self-realization of the individuals through the creation of objects, but the *existence* of labor is the complete denial of its essence.

Marx writes: "Labor, the *life activity, productive* life appears to individuals only as a *means* to the satisfaction of a need, namely, the maintenance of physical existence. But productive life is species life. It is life that generates life. The entire character of the species is contained in its kind of life-activity, and free con-scious activity is the species character of humans" (M, p. 57). This argument reveals the extent to which Marx remains loyal to Hegel's philosophy of the subject: not only is objectification understood as self-expression through externalization, but the subject of this activity is said to be a collective singular, the species itself.[19] Indeed, the statement that objectification is self-expression presupposes this collective singular subject, because for concrete individuals objectification and labor can be forms of self-realization, if at all, only when in their empirical life conditions they approximate the universal attributes charac-terizing species essence. Since, however, empirical history is the birthplace of private property and the emergence of alienated labor, the activity of individuals *does not* correspond to this normative model of species activity.

Yet for Marx history is also the *becoming* of this goal. History is the self-production of man, his birthplace, the unfolding of his species capacities (M, p. 76ff.). On the one hand, history is the becoming and self-production of "man," of the collective singular subject, and on the other hand, empirical history is the alienation of concrete individuals from their essential species attributes. When viewed from the standpoint of the collective singular, history is objectification and self-expression; when viewed from the standpoint of the individual, it is self-negation and alienated objectification. The point is not that history cannot be both—a double-edged sword, as Rousseau named evolution in the Second Discourse,[20] the unfolding of certain potentials and their frustration. The point is that history can appear as such, both as the becoming of a goal and in need of attaining this goal, when its *unity* is attributed to the presence of a *collective singular* subject and its *diversity* to the life conditions of empirical individuals. This collective singular is both substance and subject: history is the process through which it becomes, its capacities unfold, and it is also what humans ought to be in the future. Empirical individuals can become the subject of the historical process only if, in their collective life conditions, they reappropriate the idealized properties of species being.

The parallels with Hegel's *Phenomenology* are obvious: the education of consciousness was also described as the "reappropriation" by a concrete individual of the "property" of collective spirit. "True communism is the 'positive' transcendence of *private property* as *human self-alienation*, and is therefore the *appropriation of human essence* through and for humans; thus it is the complete, conscious return of humans to themselves, within the limits of the entire wealth that has developed till today as social, that is humanized humans" (M, p. 75, emphasis in the text). The identity of constituted and constituting subjectivity is expressed in this statement. Communism is the *reappropriation* by *constituted* subjects of their potential and actual wealth as the *constituting* subjects of history. The very terms Marx uses to describe this process read like a parody of Hegel's chapter on "Absolute Knowledge": appropriation, return-to-self, "the true reconciliation of the conflict between essence and existence; objectification and self-affirmation, free-

dom and necessity, individual and the species" (M, p. 76).[21]
Marx's anthropological critique of Hegel's *Phenomenology of
Spirit* replaces the Hegelian formula "Spirit becomes and comes
to know itself through reflection upon its externalization in history" with another Hegelianism, "The human species becomes
and comes to know itself in the process of generating itself
[*Selbsterzeugung*] through the activity of labor in history." But
the subjects "mankind" and "species essence" are no less abstract than the subject "Spirit." The thesis that history is the
self-production of mankind is no less problematical than the
assertion that history is the unfolding of the freedom of Spirit.
The Marxian category of *Vergegenständlichung* is no less inadequate than the Hegelian category of *Entäusserung* to grasp the
varieties of human activity.

The second perspective suggested by Marx's anthropological
critique, namely that of *sensuous finitude*, can be summarized
through one formula: the human relation to nature and externality is at the same time a social relation among humans. Objectification is not merely the appropriation of objects, but a
process of interaction with other subjects for whom this externality is likewise an object. Here Marx proceeds from a model of
human activity quite different from the one implied by his anthropological adoption of Hegel's *Phenomenology*. In this latter
model, the relation to nature is a *social* bond among individuals
in a twofold sense. First, nature qua object is an object for other
humans as well; "objecthood" implies being present for a plurality of subjects. Second, these subjects who have objects outside themselves are in turn objects for others; each individual
can be related to by others as an externally existing human
being. The mode of relating to objects and to humans as objects
is not merely one of appropriation. It ranges from sensation and
perception to desire and to love. Subjectively, the individual
experiences his/her finitude as drives, needs, feelings, and passions. These affective experiences are fundamentally other-
directed. They place the individual not only in a state of thrown-
ness into the world, but also in a state of fundamental awareness
of his/her finitude and plurality. The experience of sensuous finitude is the awareness of radical insufficiency. It is the awareness
that one can be affected, as well as affective, and that this is a
bond to the world and to others: "The human being as an objec-

tive, sensuous being is therefore a *suffering* being, and because he experiences this suffering, he is also a *passionate* being" (M, p. 118).

This emphasis on finitude, suffering, and neediness gives the Marxian project of "true communism" a different accent.[22] The philosophy of the subject presented true communism as the triumph of a humanity conceived as a demiurge, shaping, transforming, and reappropriating the world as its product. According to the second perspective, true communism means the formation of *radically new needs*, the satisfaction of which requires the transcendence of the present form of society. Need satisfaction can no longer be viewed as the appropriation of objects. In order to satisfy a need, it is not necessary to possess the object of that need: "Private property has made us so dumb and one-sided that an object is first *ours*, when we have it, when it exists as capital for us or when we can immediately possess, eat, drink, wear and inhabit it, in short, when we can *use* it" (M, p. 79). Transcending private property means transcending a specific mode of need satisfaction restricted to use and to having. Marx does not specify whether this new mode will be one of aesthetic enjoyment, play, the joy of theoretical contemplation, or mimesis.[23] The project of communism is viewed as the "total emancipation of human senses and properties" (M, p. 80). It is the radical otherness of hitherto existing forms of satisfaction and enjoyment, and not the completion of existing modes.

This new mode of need satisfaction also entails a transformation of the *object* of need. "The senses," writes Marx, "relate to objects [*Sache*] for their own sake, but the object itself is an *objective human* relation to itself and to humans and vice versa. Need and enjoyment have thereby lost their *egotistical* nature and nature has lost its mere *usefulness*, in that use has become *human* use" (M, p. 80). The relation to the object of needs is now seen as the confirmation of a human bond; enjoyment loses its private, egotistical character and becomes the affirmation of mutual humanity. The object of need does not reinforce privatistic consumption but reinforces togetherness. The object of need is thus not the object at all, but the other human being and his/her qualities and capacities as reflected and expressed through the object.

The two perspectives of the philosophy of the subject and of

sensuous finitude, and the ideals of human emancipation entailed by them, confront us at the meta-theoretical level with
the same dualism we encountered in analyzing "On the Jewish
Question." The two models of emancipation discussed there
were named "the universalization of the political" and the
"socialization of the universal." Whereas the first meant a
fulfillment of the past achievements of bourgeois revolutions
in the future, the second meant a *transfiguration* of these
achievements and the creation of a new mode of association
and sociability. Likewise, the philosophy of the subject is a universalization of the labor paradigm of human activity, the deification of human productive activity first begun by bourgeois
political economy, while the perspective of radical needs requires a transfiguration of the labor paradigm of activity. The
philosophy of the subject views mankind as a demiurge, fashion-
ing nature to reflect its own image, and contemplating itself in
what it has created. This view requires a fulfillment, not a transfiguration of modern bourgeois society, for it merely carries to
its logical conclusion the deification of growth and productivity
upon which the logic of capitalism rests. The perspective of sensuous finitude, by contrast, corresponds to the transfigurative
vision of emancipation, for on this view, emancipation is said to
usher in radically *new needs* and a *new subjectivity*. Despite the
presence of these two perspectives, it is ultimately the philosophy of the subject that predominates in the *1844 Manuscripts*.
From this standpoint, the alternative vision of human emancipation, suggested by the category of "sensuous finitude," cannot even be named adequately. Before analyzing why this is so,
let me try to clarify why this dual perspective is more than a
hermeneutical curiosity and why it points to an ambivalence in
the Marxian project of critique itself.

It is the Hegelian heritage of Marxian critique that it does not
juxtapose blueprints of the future to the present. Critical philosophy, according to Marx, "is the self-clarification of the times
about its own struggles and wishes" (MEW 1:346). Critique
which seeks to clarify a given society about its own struggles
and wishes must show that these struggles and wishes, created
by current conditions, also anticipate its radical transformation. Self-clarification means understanding the dreams of the

present but also showing that these dreams cannot become a reality in the present. Critical philosophy is a philosophy of the present, but one which conceives of the present as a radical future. The present must generate its own radical negation from within itself. This insistence upon the present as a radical future necessarily vacillates between the perspectives of continuity and break, the completion of the old and its transfiguration. Since the radical future must be a task of the present, it appears as the continuation and fulfillment of the present. Since the present contains this radical future in itself, it appears as its own transfiguration and as a rupture.

Besides this dual perspective of the present, as extension of the past and harbinger of the new, there is an additional reason why Marx cannot even name this alternative model of human emancipation suggested by the perspective of sensuous finitude. This lies in that, for Marx, the category of "objectification" does not merely describe a specific kind of human activity. This category has a meta-theoretical significance in light of which all human history is to be comprehended. Marx sees history, more precisely the humanization of the species in history, as an evolutionary process whose dynamic is provided by objectification.[24] This predominance of the category of objectification in explaining the becoming of the species in history leads to the normative ascendance of the demiurge model of humanity over the vision of sensuous finitude. In other words, precisely because objectification is a category that explains the constitution of the human species, emancipation is understood in terms circumscribed by this notion of objectification.

According to Marx, history can be viewed as the unfolding of the potentialities of the *same* species, precisely because there is a cumulative logic in the material medium of the formation of objects and their successive appropriation by subsequent generations. Let us remember: objectification means that certain capacities, skills, and techniques are embodied or materialized in an object. The production of objects entails knowledge of rules pertaining to the nature of the material at hand, as well as reflecting our human capacity to shape this material. We may be more or less knowledgeable about these rules; we may be more or less skillful in applying them. At any point in time, the human species faces a world that is already the objectified product of past generations. To reproduce themselves, humans must first learn to reappropriate the given, both the rules of knowledge and the rules of know-how. The reproduction of the species through the material medium of labor entails a learning process. And at the level of the instrumental use of tools and the material of reproduction, one can claim that a continuity, a learning process, exists.

But objectification is an activity of social individuals and production is *social reproduction*. The formation of societal individuals does not take place in the medium of object production alone, but primarily through the mediums of language, culture, and social interaction.[25] What then constitutes the medium of material accumulation and a learning process in these domains? The rules for the acquisition of knowledge and know-how pertaining to the manipulation of objects and those pertaining to language, culture, and social interaction are not the same. In the former case, these rules refer to our knowledge of nature as beings capable of acting within and upon externality. In the latter case, the rules refer to our knowledge of ourselves as social, symbolical, and cultural beings. Whereas in the former case, we manifest this knowledge of these rules by *applying* them, in the latter case we manifest this knowledge by acting, speaking, and behaving in a manner *appropriate to* and *consonant with* these rules. We cannot "apply" a natural language as a whole, although we may apply certain isolated expressions, such as the use of Latin by doctors who otherwise have no knowledge of the language. We can "apply" the rules of a culture, let us say, when we *pretend* to be an English, French, German, or Chinese person. In this case, we distance ourselves from who we *pretend to be*. We act as if we were someone else, but our knowledge of the rules of this culture is first manifested by our acting *just as* a member of this other culture would act. Even in actions through which we distance ourselves from symbolic, cultural, or linguistic rules, we must be able to adopt the perspectives of the first and second persons who are members of this culture. We must know how one would act as a member of this other culture, what would have to be said under given circumstances by oneself and by others, and how this would be perceived, understood, or interpreted by others. The knowledge of such symbolic, interactive, and linguistic rules is an understanding of their meaning and of their context. It entails the competences of understanding and interpreting what we do and say, as well as how others perceive what we do and say.[26]

The Marxian category of objectification is inadequate to capture this dimension of human learning and development. By acting and speaking as cultural, social, and linguistic beings we do not "objectify" ourselves; rather, we first become subjects, that is, beings capable of initiating meaningful utterances, of acting and interacting; beings capable of revealing themselves, their intentions, purposes, desires, feelings, and moods. There is, of course, a trivial sense in which words, deeds, and gestures can become objects that can be seen, perceived, and observed by others. The very perception of words, deeds, gestures, and acts as objects is a distortion of their essence and the indication of a failure in the process of communication and understanding. The words of language we do not understand are merely "noise" for us. We perceive acts and gestures whose meaning we do not recognize as objects. We see them but we do not understand them. What Marx conflates via the category of objectification are two different kinds of human activity and the rules of acquisition and learning characteristic of each. This conflation is nowhere more evident than in the following passage. Although lengthy, it deserves quoting in full (also because it is not included in the standard English of the *1844 Manuscripts*).[27]

> Supposing we had produced as humans: each of us had through our production confirmed himself and the other. 1) In my production I had objectified my individuality and its uniqueness, and had enjoyed thereby during my activity an individual life-expression, and had experienced individual joy at the sight of the object, for I know my personality as objective, as perceivable by the senses and as raised beyond all suspicion. 2) Your enjoyment and your use of my object would give me the immediate pleasure and consciousness of having satisfied a human need in my work, of having objectified human essence and of having created an object corresponding to the needs of another human being; 3) of having been for you the mediator between you and the species, of having been known and experienced by you as a completion of your own essence and a necessary part of yourself. Thus I would know myself to be con-

firmed in your thought as well as in your love. I would know that I
created through my life-expression immediately yours as well.
Thus in my individual activity I would know that my true essence,
my human, common essence is contained and realized. Our production would be so many mirrors, in which our essence would be
mutually illuminated.

This passage from Marx's notes on James Mill shows his attempt to analyze a non-alienated mode of production as a structure of interaction guided by the norms of reciprocity and
mutuality. Production becomes an activity of self-confirmation
because it now involves a confirmation of the self for another.
Objects of production are not ends in themselves, but serve as
mediators between human beings. In a non-alienated mode of
production they would no longer be mystified carriers of value,
but would fulfill their natural function, which is to satisfy human needs. The object mediates human needs and capacities.

How plausible is this attempt to interpret reciprocity and mutuality in light of the categories of production, use, and enjoyment? First, for Marx the line between production for use and
aesthetic production seems to disappear. A mode of production
in which I could "confirm and express" my individuality could
hardly be a mechanized, automated, and standardized mode of
production. There is nothing self-expressive about machine production and the conveyor belt. A work of art as well as a crafts
object, the process of whose production is controlled by the
producer and does not depend upon automatized forces, may
be self-expressive. Second, Marx ignores that the more self-
expressive the object, the less it is grasped in light of the category of objectification. And this is the crucial point: an object
that expresses the self is one that allows the identity of the individual person to become manifest. We describe this dimension
in ethico-moral terms. Thus, brush strokes in a painting may be
"impatient," "gentle," "precise," or "angry." The paint may reflect a dark, happy, sinister, or joyful mood. The painter may
depict misery, may seek to appease the nobility, may be whimsi-
cal or indifferent. All these terms, which are used to characterize a "self-expressive" object, are in the first place predicated of
actions, emotional states, feelings, and deeds. They derive from
the domain of interaction and are then applied to objects them-

selves, insofar as these lead back from themselves to their makers and their individuality.

This conflation of categories of moral-interactional discourse with those derived from the sphere of production may become clearer if we consider Marx's claim that your enjoyment and your use of something I had produced would lead me "to be confirmed in your thought as well as in your love" (see quote above). Why should satisfying my need through an object you have produced lead me to think of you "as completing my being" and to confirm you in my thoughts and love? Apart from the fact that this is an absurd conception in an impersonal, market economy based on exchange, such an attitude would have to imply that there existed a prior context of interaction between us. I may be so desperately in need that I conceive of you as "completing my being" and as my benefactor. I may confirm you in my thoughts and love, if my acquisition of the object was an act or gift from you generating my gratitude. In the first case the relationship would no longer be one of mutuality, but one of dependence, and your act would be supererogatory, transcending the bonds of reciprocity. Or let us consider the case of mutual exchange of gifts: in enjoying the gift, I may indeed think of you and confirm my love, but not because the enjoyment of the object compels me to do so, but because I have these feelings in the first place. Likewise, for you the object may serve as a reminder of my person and qualities, but then the object is no longer one of need satisfaction alone; it is the *symbol* of a special human bond. The object as such does not express this bond. It is the context of ethico-moral relations out of which it emerges and through which it is acquired that creates this bond.

Self-confirming and self-expressive activities cannot be conceptualized through the categories of making, use, and enjoyment.[28] As soon as we try to concretize what self-expressive productive activity could mean, we think of aesthetic activity, of friendship, of love and symbolic exchange relations. Self-expressive needs drive us to show, to reveal ourselves to others and to seek confirmation in the eyes of others. These needs toward the confirmation of our mutual humanity are what guide the Marxian view of sensuous finitude and its liberation. But since the objectification paradigm is extended to apply to all forms of human activity, expressive needs and new interactional structures are reduced to appropriative needs and to forms of objectifying activity.

In Hegel's *Phenomenology*, "externalization" becomes the primary model of human activity, while in the *1844 Manuscripts*, a similar reduction of diverse forms of human activity to the "objectification" paradigm takes place. Both "externalization" and "objectification" are further claimed to be a mode of "self-realizing" activity through which the self manifests his/her identity and realizes his/her potentials. Note, however, that objectification and externalization can be said to serve self-realization only when it is presupposed that by engaging in such activities, the self in some sense reveals or manifests its own nature or essence. This can be assumed on the basis of the following premises alone. First, Spirit or the human species becomes in history; this is its nature or essence. Second, history can be viewed as a process of becoming precisely because it is the unfolding of the capacities of a collective singular subject. Third, this unfolding occurs through a process of externalization or objectification and the reappropriation of what has been alienated. It then follows that engaging in activities of externalization and objectification is a mode of self-realization for the subject whose nature and essence consists in that it creates itself through its own activity. Note, further, that we can only assume this to be so when the perspective of the *collective* singular subject is surreptitiously identified with that of the *finite*, empirical individual who produces and labors. The category of "self-realization" is based upon this confusion of an *empirical* with a *normative*, constitutive self. The empirical self realizes itself in labor in that through its activity it "becomes" the normative, constitutive, collective singular itself. The meaning of this becoming is unclear: for Hegel it seems to involve an activity of *anamnesis* or recollection; for Marx it entails both laboring activity and political struggle. Empirical selves become the normative-constitutive subjects of history insofar as they "reappropriate" it through political struggle.

In the next two chapters, it will be my task to show that this normative model of self-realization through exteriorization and reappropriation is the critical yardstick by which Hegel and Marx measure bourgeois, capitalist society. For Hegel, such self-realization is always attained at the end of a speculative process of thought; for Marx, it entails transformative struggle. But this distinction between theory and practice, and Marx's critique of Hegelian theory in the name of political praxis, should not lead us to overlook that what Hegel, through the category of exteriorization, and Marx, through that of objectification, achieve is nothing less than a subversion of the Aristotelian concept of *pratein*. Praxis no longer means ethical and moral activity, speech, and the "doing of just and noble deeds"; instead, it comes to signify a mode of *transformative activity* through which externality is shaped and appropriated for human purposes.[29]

This analysis completes the examination of the origins of immanent and defetishizing critique. It will be remembered that I claimed such an examination to be necessary for the following reason: despite its emphatic normative dimension, Marxian critical theory has an ambivalent relation to practical philosophy. On the one hand, it rejects it in the name of a science of society; on the other hand, it criticizes positivist social science in the name of emphatic normative ideals—remember Horkheimer's allusion to the "golden age of philosophy under Plato and Aristotle" (see p. 5 above). Understanding this ambivalence, I maintained, requires examing, first, Hegel's critique of prescriptive normative theories, and second, his transformation of Aristotelian practical philosophy into a philosophy of praxis. While Hegel's early critique of natural right theories is the precursor of the Marxian charge that these theories are "Robinsonades" of bourgeois society, Hegel's discovery of the constitutive activity of labor is the origin of the Marxian concept of praxis as history-shaping, transformative activity.

From a systematic point of view, my analysis has highlighted several theses. First, I established the presence in Hegelian discourse of two modes, one which I named "intersubjectivity," the other "transsubjectivity." For Hegel, philosophical discourse unfolds from the perspective of the latter. Second, I likewise noted the vacillation of the Marxian concept of emancipation between the views of "fulfillment" and "transfiguration." So far, neither the role of these concepts in my overall argument nor their relation to one another has been clarified. Here this will be done in a preliminary way only.

Let me begin by noting that the first set of concepts is social and epistemological and refers to different modes of analyzing and knowing the social world, while the terms "fulfillment" and "transfiguration" are substantive and normative, referring to different conceptions of emancipation. One of the central achievements of Marxian social theory, and one anticipated by Hegel, is the discovery that the two points of view of intersubjectivity and transsubjectivity are constitutive of modern capitalist society. In this society for the first time a sphere of activity is institutionalized which operates according to laws unintended by and unknown to social agents themselves, and which can only be analyzed from the transsubjective standpoint of the observer. The main purpose of critical social theory is to demystify the power of this domain upon individuals' lives, and to return the control over their actions and interactions to individuals themselves. The claim is that humans should "reappropriate" what orignates with their deeds. This "reappropriation" can take two different forms: it can be viewed either as fulfilling the implicit potential of the present or as transforming it in the name of the new. The central difficulty lies not with these two concepts of emancipation, nor with the ambivalencies that accompany them. The real difficulty lies with the concept of "reappropriation" and the epistemology and politics it implies. With the concept of "reappropriation," Marxian discourse once more reverts to the philosophy of the subject and denies the standpoint of intersubjectivity.

The purpose of the next two chapters is to articulate the perspectives of intersubjectivity and transsubjectivity further, and to clarify their role in Hegel's analysis of civil society and Marx's analysis of capitalism. My thesis is that because the primary model of human activity to which both resort is, in the final analysis, work and not interaction, the discourse of transsubjectivity comes to dominate. Of course, since neither Hegel nor Marx begins from a Lockean state of nature, they do not assume that work consists in the activity of an isolated individual. It is acknowledged that work takes place in the context of a human community. But the *telos* of the work model of activity is not interaction or communication, but either the formation of externality or the manifestation of the self's essence or nature to others via this process. Now this moment of the manifestation of the self to others, or self-realization, cannot be understood in terms which are restricted to the activity of work alone; such understanding requires the introduction of interactional categories. Instead Hegel and, following him, Marx resort to the perspective, not of an intersubjective plurality of communicating selves, but to the transsubjective perspective of a collective singular subject. This collective singular subject allows them to avoid the individualism of the natural rights tradition, but is wholly incompatible with the meaning of human plurality.

From a systematic point of view, the following two chapters are at the heart of the first part of this work: they try to show how the various themes of intersubjectivity versus transsubjectivity, transfiguration and fulfillment, the philosophy of the subject versus sensuous finitude, are related to what I call "the work model of activity." The work model of activity, for reasons to be explored more precisely below, is the basis of an epistemology and politics which critical Marxism has accepted rather uncritically. Since this model of activity, however, is the central, but not the only, legacy of Hegelianism in this tradition, the following chapter begins by considering Hegel's critique of Kantian ethics, in order to extricate from this critique those moments of valid insight which do not seem to me to depend upon a wholesale acceptance of the work model of activity and of the philosophy of the subject.

Chapter 3

INTEGRATING CRISIS: AUTONOMY AND ETHICAL LIFE

In the preface to this work I explained that in examining Habermas' attempt to formulate the normative foundations of critical theory by way of a communicative ethics, I asked myself whether Hegel's critique of natural right theories and of Kant did not already contain objections of such a nature as to cast doubt upon the whole enterprise of rehabilitating a universalistic, formalistic, ethical theory. The previous two chapters have looked at the methodological and normative aspects of Hegel's critique of natural right theories, and have traced the gradual evolution in his thought of a standpoint more conciliatory toward modernity. Hegel's acute observations on "state of nature" type abstractions were vitiated by his anti-modernist subscription to the idea of a unified *Sittlichkeit*. The preceding chapter has shown how this view was eventually replaced by the normative model of a collective singular subject of history, externalizing itself in time, and reappropriating again what it once let go of itself.

With this analysis I have provided a preliminary answer to my initial question concerning the fruitfulness of Hegel's normative critique of natural right theories. To repeat, this answer is that Hegel's acute methodological observations on the nature and shortcomings of counterfactual arguments rest on questionable normative assumptions. In this chapter I begin to consider the second half of this issue, namely Hegel's critique of Kant's moral philosophy. As previously, my aim will be to separate the wheat from the chaff in this matter as well by distinguishing between Hegel's justifiable critique of Kant and his equally unjustifiable subscription to the work model of action. This view, I shall argue, is wholly inadequate to articulate the standpoint of the moral agent and is not even concerned to do so. More important, it cannot even capture Hegel's own insights fully. Hegel's critique of Kantian ethics has cast a long shadow on considerations of ethics and politics in the tradition of critical social theory. Even more than the rejection of natural right theories and their questionable methodologies, this critique of Kant has shaped not only Marx's dismissal of "blueprint" utopian thinking, but Adorno's contempt for positive utopias as well. I first show that in his critique of Kant, Hegel does not reject the norm of autonomy, but its specification through the formula of the universal moral law (section 1). After an examination of his effort to situate freedom in the modern state, I conclude that for Hegel freedom becomes a transsubjective ideal (section 2). The tension between critique and dogmatism, intrinsic to Hegel's critique of Kant and the Enlightenment generally, confronts us here as well. Hegel's claim that Kantian practical reason remains dogmatic insofar as Kant fails to analyze the social and historical constitution of autonomy leads him to the dogmatic conclusion that freedom is realized in a modern state which promotes *integration* while excluding *political participation* (section 3).

1. Hegel's Critique of Kant's Moral Philosophy

Hegel's critique of Kantian moral philosophy was a lifelong preoccupation. Beginning with the attempt in his early writings to reconcile a Kantian ethic of duty with a Christian ethic of love, extending to his critique of the moral worldview (*die moralische Weltanschauung*) in the *Phenomenology*, to his comments on Kant's deduction of the private right of the household master over his wife, children, and servants in the *Philosophy of Right*, and finally to his attempt to ontologize the "ought" in the *Logic*, the confrontation with Kantian moral philosophy runs through the corpus of Hegel's writings.[1] This fact alone should serve as a warning to those who see in Hegel's position a definitive argument against formal, universalistic, and prescriptive moral theories. A serious consideration of Hegel's critique of Kantian moral philosophy will have to do justice to a number of paradoxes: while denying Kantian ethics as formalistic, Hegel provided no substantive or material theory of ethics himself. His treatment of morality in the *Philosophy of Right* does not culminate in a doctrine of virtue, but at most in an analysis of the paradoxes of moral action that is as formalistic as Kantian ethics. While rejecting universalizability procedures at best as empty and at worst as dogmatic and arbitrary, Hegel accepts universalism as a normative principle. Hegel's consideration of abstract human rights, the respect for which forms the basis of the legitimacy of the modern state, does not regress behind Kant's *Metaphysical Elements of Justice;* in fact, with regard to the analysis of the juridical basis of property rights and the family, it constitutes an advance.[2] While rejecting prescriptivism in moral theory, Hegel does not reject the principle of autonomy which makes the rational insight of the agent the basis for the validity of norms. Hegelian critique, despite its vacillation between emancipation and dogmatism, does not lead moral philosophy back from autonomy to heteronomy.

Hegel's critique of Kantian moral philosophy,[3] scattered throughout his various writings, can be grouped around three major points: (a) the *procedural* critique of the Kantian universalizability principle; (b) the critique of the *institutional deficiency* of Kantian moral theory; and (c) the critique of Kantian *moral psychology* and analysis of moral motivation.

   a. The Procedural Critique of the Kantian
   Universalizability Principle
   In two sections of the *Phenomenology,* called "Reason as Giving Laws" and "Reason as Testing Laws," Hegel develops a procedural critique of the Kantian principle which stipulates that whether the maxim of one's actions can be a moral law for all is to be determined according to the criterion of universalizability. Universalizability can be interpreted either as a procedure to *generate* moral maxims or to *test* existing ones.

According to Hegel, as a procedure to *generate* maxims the criterion of universalizability is useless. Hegel provides two examples here, neither of which *prima facie* supports his critique of Kant. I will examine the first only. Let us consider the moral law that "everyone ought to tell the truth" (PhG, p. 303). This law is only meaningful when each knows the truth. So we arrive at a second formulation, "Everyone ought to tell the truth every time in accordance with his knowledge and conviction thereof" (*ibid.*). In this formulation, whether or not the truth will be told is made dependent upon the contingent circumstances of whether I know the truth and can convince myself that what I know is the truth. "This *contingency of content* has *universality* only in the *form of the proposition* which expresses it; but as an ethical proposition, it promises a universal and necessary *content* and through contingency it contradicts itself" (*ibid.*; emphasis in the text).

What actually is Hegel's objection to this principle? Hegel is raising two issues without distinguishing clearly between them. The first concerns the principle that *ought* implies *can*. Whether or not I can in fact tell the truth is dependent upon whether or not I know what the truth is, but my moral obligation to tell the truth is not dependent upon the fact that what I tell is the truth. It suffices that I tell what I can be reasonably expected to know is the truth and what I believe to be the truth in good faith. Hegel's objection is not convincing.

A second question raised by Hegel's critique is the problem of the *contextualization* of moral principles. A moral agent, convinced of the principle that s/he should tell the truth, nevertheless faces the task of contextualizing the principle such as to act in the right way. Even when we ignore the famous problem of the clash of duties in Kantian ethics, it is the case that a moral *principle* does not yield only *one maxim* of action, and the same maxim of action can be embodied in *different performances*. Suppose I am a journalist who has discovered that government authorities in a Third World country have committed a massacre. My duty as a journalist and as a human being is to make this fact publicly known. Now should I go to an influential daily newspaper and print the news there, should I inform Amnesty International of the matter, or should I inform members of my own government first and inquire into the diplomatic implications of this news story? All three are plausible courses of action, but obviously which I choose will not depend on the principle of telling the truth alone. I accept this principle as one I should act upon; but if I choose the first option, then the maxim of my action does not simply involve telling the truth, but also the conviction that I should tell the truth to attract the greatest publicity and attention to the events which have taken place. If I choose the second option, I may do so because I am concerned for the personal fate of the victims and of their families and believe that going to Amnesty International is the best method of assuring that the interests of those immediately affected will be protected. If I choose the third option, I may be worried that in view of the already existing tension between my country and this other one, breaking the news may lead to worsening of diplomatic relations, an increase in military tension, etc.

Clearly, there is a gap between a general moral principle like telling the truth and its concretization through a specific course of action. In the example considered above, this principle alone is not sufficient to determine the maxim of my action—a number of other moral principles, from helping victims to contributing to world peace and informing world public opinion, are codetermining. What this example indicates is that there is indeed a problem of the *contextualization* of moral principles, but it does not show that the *universalizability procedure* is inadequate to generate *general moral principles* whose contextualization often requires additional considerations.

Although the arguments through which Hegel supports his critique of Kant on this point are not particularly convincing, the questions concerning the status and correct interpretation of Kant's universalizability procedure remain.[4] Hegel's general point is that this procedure cannot generate contentful moral maxims, for "what remains from giving laws is the *pure form* of *universality* or in effect the *tautology* of consciousness which juxtaposes itself to content and is a *knowledge* not of *what is*, nor of actual *contents*, but concerns the *essence* or self-equality of consciousness" (PhG, p. 305). Hegel interprets universalizability as a principle of non-contradiction or as the self-equality of consciousness (I = I). The formula "Act in such a way that the maxim of your actions can also be a universal law for all rational beings" is read by him to mean "Act in such a way that the maxim of your actions does not contradict itself." The second half of Hegel's criticism in the section on "Reason as Testing

Laws" attempts to show that this formula of non-contradiction is vacuous as well.

If universalizability is viewed as a criterion for *testing* existing moral maxims, then Kantian moral theory is open to the charge that it remains dogmatic insofar as it considers existing maxims and institutions as givens from which to proceed. To avoid dogmatism, Kantian moral theory should generate content, but since it fails to do so—at least in Hegel's view—it becomes a mere procedure for testing existing normative content; but since it cannot even arbitrate adequately between two existing normative contents, it becomes empty. "The criterion of law which reason has in it, is equally compatible with all and is therefore no criterion" (PhG, p. 308). Hegel arrives at this conclusion by considering the principle that there must be a right to property.

As will be remembered, in the *Groundwork* Kant attempts to show that loans made to one should be repaid, for otherwise the institution of promising and the right to property would be nullified.[5] Each could keep what he got his hands on, regardless of his title to do so. Hegel comments that this example does not prove anything, for the non-existence of the institution of property is as little contradictory as the principle that things remain without masters (*herrenlose Dinge*) or that property should be communal. What allows us to decide whether or not the institution of property should exist and in what form are *additional* considerations concerning human needs and distributive justice. The introduction of a principle of human needs contradicts the proposed formalism and contentlessness of the Kantian procedure. Since Kant views all material principles of morality as leading to heteronomy, the moral law cannot presuppose a contentful principle like the most beneficial satisfaction of human needs, for it is the universal *form* alone which should decide whether the most beneficial satisfaction of human needs ought to be adapted as a principle in the first place.[6]

Hegel's critique of universalizability, both as a maxim-generating and maxim-testing procedure, points to a dialectic of form and content: if the universalizability procedure is interpreted as one of non-contradiction, on this basis alone we cannot decide among different normative contents. If such a decision is reached, as is the case with Kant's defense of the right to private property, then this can only be so because certain additional principles, which are themselves inconsistent with the required formalism of the universalizability procedure, have been introduced. In one case, the theory would be so empty as to be irrelevant; in the second, contentful but self-contradictory and dogmatic.

Let me remark that the universalizability procedure need not be interpreted as a principle of non-contradiction, although several of Kant's examples in the *Groundwork* in particular conform to this. It is possible to reformulate universalizability as a collective bargaining game under conditions of the "veil of ignorance," as John Rawls has done,[7] as a procedural formalism of three stages to be supplemented by the principle of taking the standpoint of every other one, as John Silber has proposed,[8] or as a special argumentation situation aiming at consensus, as Jürgen Habermas has attempted.[9] Hegel's critique points to a dialectic of form and content in Kantian moral theory, but his manner of stating the problem alone is not sufficient to criticize contemporary attempts to develop more cogent universalizability procedures. Nonetheless, in chapter 8 I show that a similar dialectic of form and content is present in the theory constructions of Rawls and Habermas, and that to avoid this problem, the claims of universalistic moral theories need considerable modification.

b. The Institutional Deficiency of Kantian Moral Theory

The respect in which Kantian moral theory is institutionally deficient, in Hegel's view, can be seen from the example of the right of property discussed above. Hegel criticizes the Kantian tendency to consider social institutions and practices in isolation from their interdependence within a given social structure and form of life. Such practices and institutions cannot be judged simply with reference to their conformity or lack thereof with the moral law. In the first place, they must be viewed as part of a totality of relations and practices that are *functionally interdependent*. This institutional realism of Hegel's ethical theory derives from its orientation to the ancient teaching of politics, according to which not only the *polis* but the *oikos* (the

household) and various forms of *koinonia* (associations) constitute the substance of an ethical way of life.[10] The ancient
teaching of the *oikos* and the *koinonia* are incorporated into
Hegel's theory of objective Spirit. "Objective Spirit" refers to
materially embedded and objectified human practices existing
in space and time. Such practices and institutions are "objective"
not only because they exist for all, but also because their relationship to each other and their mode of functioning display a
necessity intelligible to the thinker-observer.

The concepts of "objective Spirit" and "ethical life" are in the
first place *descriptive*. Hegel often refers to ethical life as
"ethical substance," as an enduring and materially embedded
reality.[11] To be correctly described, this objective reality must
first be understood and explained. Hegel's orientation toward
the concrete explanation and understanding of social reality, at
work since his early essays on the *Spirit of Christianity*, is effec-
tive throughout his philosophical analysis. Yet "objective
Spirit" is not only *ethical substance* but *"ethical life."*[12] Ethical
life is not a descriptive, but an *evaluative* category. Hegel thereby
indicates that the objective reality of social institutions and human practices is also a normative one, and this in two senses:
first, normative rules and criteria are *constitutive* of institutional and social practices. Family life presupposes the norms of
mutual support and concern, just as the "system of needs" presupposes the right of persons to enter freely into contractual
obligations. Second, such constitutive rules and criteria have
also a *regulative* dimension in that institutions and practices are
judged as to whether or not they have fulfilled them: families
can be unified or broken, cooperative or destructive; contracts
can be valid or invalid, fraudulent or correct. When such constitutive criteria cease to function regulatively, institutions become dead. They exist, but they are also meaningless. In his
early writings, Hegel thought this to be the case with the Church
in revolutionary Europe and with the baroque multiplicity of
political formations in pre-Napoleonic Germany. "Positivity"
sets upon social life when normative principles cease to be a
convincing and lived reality for individuals engaged in the practices required by them. This can happen when individuals find
such principles *cognitively inadequate* as well as *motivationally*

implausible. One can continue to go to church just as one may remain a family member, long after one has ceased to believe either in religion or in monogamous love or be motivated by faith or affection.

The institutional realism of Hegel's normative perspective suggests a number of interesting problems for Kantian moral theory. First is the issue of *plurality of norms.* Does Kantian moral theory provide us with a procedure or perspective to judge all *relevant* norms of human action? Is the universaliz-ability procedure, however interpreted, a method for judging all forms of human action and interaction? Or is it, as Hegel argues, that Kantian moral theory has a privileged object domain, namely, the domain of juridical and quasi-juridical relations, but is blind to all else that escapes such classification—like friendship, professional duties, citizenship, or political par-tisanship?[13] Second is the question of *social identity* and *moral personality.* How are they to be mediated? What is the correct moral point of view vis-à-vis those normative rules and expecta-tions that are constitutive of my identity as a family member, as an economic and legal agent, or as a citizen?

British moral philosophers around the turn of the century thought that for Hegel, ethics consisted in evaluating "my sta-tion and its duties" (Bradley).[14] While it is true that Hegel was the first to clearly articulate what we today call "social ethics," the moral point of view forms an aspect of the right of free personality which is not simply superseded by ethical life, but remains present in it as the right of subjectivity and conscience (PhR, #132). The modern individual is entitled to demand that institutions, practices, and human relations stand the test of "moral insight" (PhR, #107, #132, and #123A). Social reality can be questioned cognitively as to its rightness or wrongness, valid-ity or invalidity, as well as being subjected to the motivational test of individual conscience. Despite his institutional realism, Hegel does not reject "the moral point of view," but shows that it emerges out of a context of lived relations and institutions and can be at odds with them. Bradley's emphasis on Hegelian social ethics, therefore, is not wrong, but it is misleading. It generates the opinion, shared by many, that with the transition from morality to ethical life, the standpoint of the former is also eliminated.

Considered from the standpoint of the methodology of transitions in Hegelian works, the claim that with the transition to ethical life the standpoint of morality is rendered futile is untenable. Ethical life presents a unification of two moments that are juxtaposed to each other without eliminating either. These are the moments of objectivity and subjectivity, separated from each other by the moral standpoint. The moral agent confronts an objective world with its own logic and regulations and seeks to *express* his or her purpose through an action in this world, as well as to *embody* his or her intention and consciousness in a *deed* recognizable by others. But since from the moral point of view, there is a discrepancy between what *is* objectively given and what *ought* to be, in acting moral agents submit to the laws of the world as they are and thus run the risk that their purpose will be frustrated, their action will lead to unintended consequences, and their intentions will be misjudged or misinterpreted. The standpoint of ethical life solves this dialectic of moral action only to the extent that within an intersubjectively shared context of institutional action, one's action and purposes become recognizable by others in accordance with socially shared rules and meaning patterns. But when a human agent ceases to recognize this shared social world as *cognitively valid* or as *motivationally meaningful,* the world is once more reduced to facticity, to what is but ought not to be. The moral point of view remains a continuing possibility even within ethical life; it is contained in it and is not eliminated by it.

This is an important conclusion for several reasons. First, it shows that despite its debt to the Aristotelian tradition, Hegelian ethics is modernist, insofar as it acknowledges the right of the individual to judge and to question norms and institutions that seek his/her compliance. Second, depending on how one interprets the interaction between the sphere of morality and that of ethical life, either the perspective of intersubjectivity or of transsubjectivity comes to dominate. If emphasis is placed on the right of the modern individual to find ethical institutions *cognitively intelligible* as well as *motivationally plausible,* then the perspective of lived experience is upheld. If, by contrast, emphasis is placed on the view that institutional life renders the demands of moral conscience meaningless, for the mere presence of organized institutional existence indicates these arrangements to be cognitively intelligible as well as motivationally plausible, then the standpoint of the thinker-observer, who judges but who does not participate in social life, gains the upper hand.

It should be clear then that the institutional realism of Hegelian ethics is a mixed blessing: it can lead to an emphasis on intersubjectivity and the perspective of participation in social life, just as it can legitimize the *objectivating* discourse of the one who views social life as if s/he were merely observing and not participating. Hegel's critique of Kantian ethics incorporates both perspectives; in Hegel's final analysis of modern society, it is the transsubjective standpoint which will dominate and which will disguise the radical implications of his position. The critique of Kantian moral psychology, which shows the conflict between *Sittlichkeit* (ethical life) and *Sinnlichkeit* (sensuality) to be empty, is a case in point. The radical implications of Hegel's position remain latent, and interestingly, it is first the psychoanalytic critique of Kant, developed by Adorno and Horkheimer, that will allow us a full view of the implications of Hegel's argument.

c. The Critique of Kantian Moral Psychology

Since his early fragment on "Love," one of Hegel's central criticisms is directed against the severity and implausibility of Kant's moral psychology. Kant views all material maxims of action as issuing from a single source of motivation called "self-love."[15] In this respect, Kant shares with Hobbes and later utilitarians the basic premise that the goal of all our voluntary actions is some good for ourselves. According to Kant's moral psychology, humans are egotists and escape this condition only insofar as they are capable of acting in accordance with formal maxims of duty. But Kant's conviction that "men are made of so crooked a wood"[16] is so great that for him the question whether humans can have an interest in the moral law which contradicts their self-interest is unsolvable, and becomes a transcendental fact of reason (*Faktum der Vernunft*). If Kant had not assumed that as finite, natural beings, humans were subject to motivational laws which directed them to act such as to realize self-love alone, then the question whether such beings would be *motivated* to act in accordance with the moral law could not become a transcendental issue.

In his critique of Kantian moral psychology, Hegel rejects the juxtaposition of morality to sensuality (*Sinnlichkeit*) and to the individual's desire for happiness (PhG, p. 426). The basic premise from which he proceeds is not that Kant has misjudged human nature, but that Kant has failed to acknowledge the educative and formative role of reason and reflection. For Hegel, reason designates the *cognitive* capacity of a human individual to comprehend necessity and universality; an *affective* and emotional ability to *act* on the basis of such comprehension, and the *practical* ability to formulate courses of action on the basis of principles of the rationality of which the individual is convinced. Reason is a self-reflexive capacity; it entails comprehending not only the object of cognition but the interaction between subject and object as well. Reason entails cognitive as well as practical rationality.[17] While acknowledging that the discovery of the reflexive moment, the awareness of the contribution of the knowing subject, constitutes the great achievement of Kantian philosophy, Hegel criticizes Kant for not viewing self-reflection radically enough. Self-reflection cannot only mean the return of self or the subject from a cognitive content that is given; it also means the repositing of the given. In the language of the *Logic,* self-reflection is a return to self from a presupposition that has been reposited.[18]

This abstract thought is to be concretized as follows. In the sphere of human individuality, the movement of self-reflection takes the following form: in the first place, reason is the capacity of a concrete, finite, embodied individual—in logical language, of a *particular*—to abstract from this given content, to distance oneself from it and to reflect upon it. This is called by Hegel the moment of *universality* (PhR, #5). This movement of abstraction and reflection does not leave the given content as is; through it, the determinate content is appropriated and reposited in accordance with its own rules—this constitutes the moment of *individuality* (PhR, #7A). We become individuals in that we shape, transform, and reappropriate the given content of our desires, inclinations, and needs by reflecting upon them and by developing the capacity to act in accordance with rational principles. The cognitive capacity of the individual to reason and the practical ability to act self-reflectively are one. Hegel writes, "Those who regard thinking as one special faculty, distinct from the will as another special faculty, and who even proceed to contend that thinking is prejudicial to the will, especially the good will, reveal at the very outset their complete ignorance of the nature of the will" (PhR, #5A). Kantian moral psychology, according to which reason is juxtaposed to inclination and morality to sensuality, does not allow for the view that rationality is not merely a cognitive capacity of abstracting from given content, but primarily one of transforming and reshaping the given. Hegel expresses this as the failure of Kantian philosophy to apprehend the "negativity immanent in the universal or self-identical" (PhR, #6A). This "negativity" refers to the capacity of reason and reflection to transform and to reshape cognitive and affective contents.

On the basis of these considerations, we reach a surprising conclusion: while Kantian moral psychology is anti-cognitivist in that it precludes the possibility of transforming inner nature through our rational, reflective faculty, Hegelian moral psychology is cognitivist in that it views the development of the human, reflective, rational faculty as the successive transformation and reeducation of inner nature. For Hegel there is rational desire; for Kant, all desire is irrational.[19] But if desire can be rational, then the Kantian juxtaposition of the drive for happiness to the call of moral duty is meaningless. For the realization of moral duty is accompanied by the rational desire that actions embody the intentions of moral consciousness and that the individual see his/her moral worth confirmed by others through such actions. "Since the subjective satisfaction of the individual himself (including the recognition which he receives by way of honor and fame) is also part and parcel of the achievements of absolute worth, it follows that the demand that such an end alone shall appear as willed and attained, like the view that, in willing, objective and subjective ends are mutually exclusive, is an empty dogmatism of the abstract Understanding" (PhR, #124). Hegel completes this with the remark that "what the subject is, is the series of his actions" (ibid.). The distinction between moral intention and worldly cleverness in the carrying out of correct action cannot be an absolute one. The moral point of view, as explicated by Kant, severs the bond between motivation and action in such a fashion that the individual's legitimate desire to have the moral worth of his actions confirmed and recognized by others is completely frustrated and postponed to a beyond (*Jenseits*) (PhG, 435/375).

Against this repression of inner nature, Hegel argues that the right of the individual to his own welfare and happiness must be recognized (PhR, #124A). Happiness is neither mere whim nor can it be simply juxtaposed to the good. Hegel names it the "right of private welfare" (PhR, #126). This right consists in the entitlement of the individual to a life plan integrating all particular interests, needs, and desires into the unity of a single existence (PhR, #127). On this view, happiness is not a state of mind nor an emotion, but a form of activity, as it was for Aristotle, that has became the projection of a single life. But the contents of this life form are left remarkably unspecified, for it is not the ultimate *goal* or the *content* of a way of life that defines its moral worth, but the capacity of the modern individual to integrate *reflectively* different goals, desires, and inclinations into a unified life history. Hegel sees in this tolerance of the plurality of life projects and modes of satisfying them the fundamental distinction between antiquity and modernity (PhR, #124A). In this sense Hegelian ethics is neither an ethics of duty nor one of conscience or even consequence. It is a social ethic of freedom, guided by the ideal of the rationally integrated personality.

In his critique of Kantian moral psychology, and particularly in his insistence that morality and the search for happiness are not mutually exclusive, Hegel reveals the continuing influence of the standpoint of lived intersubjectivity on his normative concerns. Just as the early *Natural Law* essay insisted that individuals had a right to recognize and rediscover themselves in ethical institutions, Hegel insists in the *Philosophy of Right* that moral life and self-actualization ought not to be mutually exclusive. To the contrary. Insofar as happiness involves life activity and insofar as such life activity entails manifesting one's purpose to others, social recognition and moral confirmation from others are essential to the constitution of the self.

In these considerations, Hegel appeals to a model of action

which, following Charles Taylor, I want to name "expressivist."[20]
The expressivist model of action is related to the paradigm of
externalization which was discussed in the previous chapter.
Both share a number of features: first, in both cases action is
viewed as exteriorizing an interiority; second, this process of
exteriorization is said to *express* and *unfold* a potentiality implicit in the agent; and third, the move from the interior to the
exterior is seen as a move from potentiality to actuality. I want
to claim that the model of *work* captures the essential idea behind expressivism far more adequately than *moral action* ever
can. It is also here that Hegel reverts from intersubjectivity back
to the transsubjective ideal of freedom.

2. Expressivist Action and the Transsubjective Ideal of Freedom

Hegel rejects the Kantian dualism between moral intention
and moral action because of his fundamental philosophical discovery that the materially embedded, intersubjective social
world is the medium (*die Mitte*) in which human action unfolds
and is actualized. Moral or practical reason is not a matter of
purity of heart alone, but involves the virtue of *phronesis*, of the
capacity to *choose* and to act correctly. This capacity, and not
merely what we intend to do, reveals who we are and what our
standpoint is. This insistence that moral intention be *exteriorized* and manifest itself to others is related to Hegel's view that
action is a mode of *expressing* to others who we are and what our
intentions may be. Against Kant's distinction between the noumenal world of freedom and the phenomenal world of causality,
Hegel seeks to disclose the structure of that middle which he
comes to call *Geist*.

I want to defend the thesis that precisely because he accepts
an *expressivist* model of action, Hegel cannot illuminate the
intersubjective—more precisely, the interactional—basis of
Spirit. To justify this interpretation, I will consider three discussions: first, the analysis of action (*Handeln*) and doing (*Tun*) in
the *Phenomenology;* second, the dialectic of action and consequence; and finally, the deduction of the concept of right in the
Philosophy of Right.

In the last chapter of the *Phenomenology*, Hegel writes:

> But Spirit has shown to us that it is neither the retreat of self-consciousness to its pure inwardness, nor its mere sinking into Substance and the nullification thereby of its distinction. Spirit [has shown itself to be] this movement of the self that externalizes itself to itself and sinks into its substance, but at the same time as subject it has returned from this movement to itself, and makes this into object and content, thereby eliminating this distinction of objectness and content. . . . The power of Spirit is rather to remain equal to itself in its externalization and as that which is in- and for-itself to posit *for-itselfness* just as much as moment as in-itselfness. (PhG 561/490)

Hegel's characterization of the activity of Spirit, as outlined in this passage, can be analyzed into three components: (a) the externalization of an in-itself, (b) which thereby makes itself for-itself (the externalization is the *expression* of an *interiority*); (c) when these two moments are grasped as a unity and as movement, this entails the sublation of the distinction between substance and subject. For substance is now the expression of a subject or has become the for-itselfness of an in-itself. In order for this unity of substance and subject to be achieved, substance has to be *transformed* in such a way that it becomes the expression of interiority and *corresponds* to what Spirit is in-itself. This naturally presupposes the shaping, appropriation, and transformation of externality; in short, it presupposes labor. For this movement sublates the given form of objectivity and makes objectivity into a reality that expresses Spirit.

Hegel applies this general model of the activity of Spirit in his analysis of individual action (*Handeln*) and doing (*Tun*) as well. The distinction between them is that while action refers to the state of affairs, the product or the result which an actor *intends* to bring about in the world, doing refers to the execution of this intention.[21]

The action process is differentiated into the following components. First, doing (*Tun*) is an object belonging to consciousness. It is a purpose (*Zweck*). Second is the "movement" of purpose or "the realization as the relation of purpose to the wholly formal reality . . . or as means" (*Mitteln*) (PhG, p. 286). Third, the object of the agent is "no longer a purpose of which the doer is immediately aware that it is his, but as it is outside him and is for it as

an other" (*ibid.*). Hegel distinguishes, then, among three moments of action: in the first place, purposes, intentions, and
motives are referred to as "in-itself," as contents of consciousness; in the second place, through the choice of means to realize
the action, the in-itself becomes for-itself; finally, the realization
of purpose is also its externalization; it is an in-itself that has
become for-another.

Note that this analysis can be applied both to *instrumental*
action, through which an agent intends to bring about a state of
affairs or to produce a thing, and to *expressive* action, where the
act expresses, manifests, and reveals the intentions and motives
of an agent to another. This manifestation of oneself to others
entails their comprehending my intentions and motives correctly in a process of mutual understanding and interpretation.
And it is precisely this *interpretive* aspect of expressive action
that leads Hegel to see it as an ontologically inadequate form.

For Hegel, the dialectic, even the fate, of acting and doing
consists in that, in this movement from interior to exterior, from
purpose to its realization, the self can fail to express itself. The
realization may fail to correspond to the intention; the purpose
may be frustrated by reality. This is unavoidable, for "in order to
be *for-itself*, what it is *in-itself*, consciousness must act, or action
is the becoming of Spirit *as consciousness*. What it is *in-itself*, it
only knows from its actuality" (PhG, p. 287, emphasis in the
text). Let me dwell for a moment on the phrase "Action is the
becoming of Spirit as consciousness." This means that the distinction that is characteristic for consciousness, between truth
and certainty, between the executed deed and the intention, has
not been overcome. Hegel argues that "for consciousness, therefore, the contrast between doing and being reemerges in his
work" (PhG, p. 292). It is significant that Hegel now names the
realized action the "work" of consciousness. If action is understood as the exteriorization of an interior—if, furthermore, "in
order to be for-itself as it is in-itself, consciousness must act"—
then the act must be viewed as a work which expresses or embodies the purpose of the self. It must give the self an adequate
expression that can be recognized by others as belonging to him,
as his work. If, however, reality cannot be appropriated in such a
way that the self can realize itself therein, then the dialectic of

action, the incongruence of purpose and deed, intention and execution, sets in.

The statement that "action is the becoming of Spirit as consciousness" assumes its true meaning. Since human action is still burdened with distinctions characteristic for consciousness, in the unfolding of Spirit it is a defective form. The action of Spirit is to be its own "work"; for this to be attained, reality must be appropriated in such a way that the dialectic of action, the incongruence between deed and intention, is eliminated. The remarkable aspect of Hegel's discussion is that here work—an object that unequivocally embodies the intentions of the agent—appears as the *telos* of action.[22]

This is an extremely significant conclusion; among other things, it supports the thesis of the previous chapter that, even if other modes of activity besides labor and work are discussed in the *Phenomenology of Spirit*, from the standpoint of Spirit, of the philosopher's discourse, everything appears as Spirit's "work." Human action, by contrast, remains perpetually caught in a dialectic where the discrepancy between intention and consequence is never eliminated. This must be the case because the source of this discrepancy is not simply that the world does not permit the realization of our purposes. This may well be. More significant, the discrepancy between action and consequence arises through the misunderstanding, misinterpretation, and misconstrual of our acts by others. To be an acting agent is to live in this interpreted world where one's own understanding of one's deeds is but one point of view, one interpretive framework, among others. In this sense, it is even misleading to speak of "misinterpretation," as if the standpoint of the agent, her or his interpretation of what she or he was doing, was the only relevant one.[23] Very often, we come to learn *what* we have done through others' understanding and interpretation of, and reaction to, our actions. Human actions, unlike objects and things, are not the property of their agents, or their "work." They do not embody or express a univocal meaning or purpose. Such a meaning or purpose can only be determined interpretively; in this sense, human action is fundamentally indeterminate. Hegel criticizes this indeterminacy of action in order to show the antinomies of moral consciousness. But what he reveals thereby is his profound ontological rejection of lived intersubjectivity in the name of an objectifying philosophical discourse.

The inconclusive dialectic of moral action discussed in the *Philosophy of Right* consists in two features: the incompatibility between intention and consequence, and the indeterminate reality of a deed once it has become part of the objective world.[24] Let me elaborate the first point: in acting, a human agent seeks to embody her or his purpose in the world, but the act which embodies this purpose becomes a link in a chain of other acts and assumes a life of its own. The consequences of our actions are like waves in water. Once the stone is cast, concentric waves unfold from it; upon reaching the shore these waves break, but in human affairs, upon reaching the shore our actions may boomerang and return to their original point with increased intensity. Inspired by Greek tragedies in which the dialectic of action and consequence is named "destiny," Hegel seeks to limit the force of fate by postulating the "right of intention." The right of intention stipulates that we can impute to human agents only what we can ascertain them to have willed and what we can reasonably expect them to know. The right of intention correlates with a duty to be informed of what one's action may involve before acting. This aspect of modern law protects the agent from such tragedies as killing a beggar and discovering that it was one's father, and marrying a woman and discovering that it was one's mother. Modern law protects the individual from tragedy by neutralizing fate and by reducing it to the foreseeable chain of events lying reasonably within the reaches of comprehension and competence of a human agent (PhR, #117A).

In the second place, human actions are fateful in a different way, and against this kind of fatefulness Hegel can offer no juridical guarantees. The image of waves caused by a stone in the water is inadequate to fully capture the dialectic of action and consequence, because where as a stone may be identified by means of a fairly neutral state description, act descriptions are constitutive of human actions and are essential for their correct identification. The purpose and intention of the agent, what the agent thinks he or she is doing and why, are an essential component of this identification, but they are not the only ones. The action and the intention are also interpreted by *others*, and often this is the reason why the purpose of the agent is frustrated through the misinterpretation of that deed and intention. It is interesting to note that Hegel does not include this *interpretive indeterminacy* of action as an explicit feature of its becoming a link "in the world . . . a chain of external relations" (PhR, #119A). External relations are viewed by him as causal, not as interpretive. But as an event in the social world, the act is influenced both by the necessity of natural and social laws governing the complex of actions and their consequences, and by the contingency of interpretive rules governing human action and communication.[25] In both respects, action can be less than a complete exteriorization of the individual and his or her purposes. The act is not the "work" of the subject, an objective entity in which one's purposes are unequivocally embodied and in which one can recognize oneself without the peril of being misinterpreted or misunderstood. Human action is risky, and from the standpoint of an expressivist paradigm, less adequate to capture the essential idea behind it than that of a made object. Hegel fails to explain how self-expressive action can also be interaction, and remain expressive of the subject despite misinterpretation and misperception. This is why, in the transition from objectivity to the concept in the *Logic* and from objective to absolute Spirit in the *Encyclopedia*, the paradigm of action is replaced by that of work, i.e., by an externality that univocally and fully expresses thought and concept.[26] Ontologically, work is a higher mode of being than action.

Hegel's claim that human action is a deficient mode of the activity of Spirit is based upon the predominance in his thought of the expressivist model, which interprets all action as the exteriorization and embodiment in the world of an agent's potentialities. This expressivist paradigm, along with the premise of the ontological priority of work to action, leads Hegel to suppress his discovery of human intersubjectivity and to interpret it instead as transsubjectivity. To reiterate the distinction between them, as I draw it in this work:[27] according to the standpoint of intersubjectivity, the perspective of human agents is constitutive of the validity and meaning of their interactions, whereas the standpoint of transsubjectivity locates this validity and meaning in a source external to the shared perspectives of social agents, in the standpoint of a thinker-observer. The trans-subjective standpoint does not deny the plurality and variety of human perspectives constitutive of social practices, but maintains that this validity and meaning cannot be exhausted from the first- and second-person perspective of the participants; instead, it requires the articulation of the observer perspective of the third person. As a last step, I want to examine Hegel's deduction of the concept of "right" in order to clarify his transsubjective understanding of freedom.

In the *Philosophy of Right*, Hegel defines right "as an existent of any sort embodying the free will. . . . Right therefore is by definition freedom as Idea" (PhR, #29). To unpack this extremely compact definition, it is first necessary to note that Hegel distinguishes between "right" in the formal-juridical sense as the legally recognized claim of individuals to act or to refrain from acting in certain ways, and "right" in its broader sense as what is normatively valid in general. Whereas "right" in the first sense corresponds to what is termed "abstract right," the second includes what is valid from the moral standpoint as well as from the standpoint of social institutions and non-institutional human relations. In thus distinguishing the formal-juridical from the inclusive sense of right, Hegel returns to one of his early criticisms of the natural right tradition. This tradition considers normatively binding human relations on the model of legal ones alone, and views society as an antagonistic heap of individuals held together by juridical bonds; but an adequate normative perspective does not restrict the sphere of normative validity to legality alone.

Through this definition, Hegel also indicates that the basis of normative validity is freedom. "Right is by definition freedom as Idea"[28] means that the concept and the actuality of freedom united in the Idea of right. The "concept"—in the Hegelian sense—becomes Idea by actualizing itself, by embodying itself in a world. Freedom is defined as the will "having universality, or itself qua infinite form, for its object, content and aim, the will is free not only *in* itself but *for* itself also" (PhR, #21, emphasis in the text). Freedom signifies the capacity of the will to make universality its content and aim, i.e., to determine the content of one's actions in accordance with "universality."

"Universality" is the will qua "infinite form." In this context "infinity" means perfect relation to self, and this is no other than the human capacity to abstract from a given context, to reflect upon it and to reposit it in accordance with rational principles. The free will is the will which makes this formal capacity for reflection a basis for generating its own content.

So far, this definition appears to recapitulate the Kantian claim that freedom is the capacity of humans to act in accordance with autonomous principles, or with principles deriving from humans' conception of themselves as rational beings. But whereas Kant provides a procedure for determining what such principles may be through the formula of the universal law, Hegel rejects any such procedure of universalizability. Consequently Hegel's definition of freedom is even more abstract and formalistic than Kant's; yet paradoxically, it is also richer and more contentful. Let me elaborate. The dialectic of universality, particularity, and individuality, examined in section 1, signifies that the will always has a content already present to it.[29] This may be the particular constitution of a concrete, finite individual and his or her inclinations, needs, desires, and interests. Freedom consists not in eliminating and suppressing this content, but in reshaping, appropriating, and repositing it. The natural inclinations of an individual, when they are reflected upon and consciously determined as legitimate interests to be pursued within a rationally integrated life plan, for example, come to express the moral freedom of private welfare and happiness. Hegel can accuse Kant of having generated a dialectic of form and content precisely because, for Hegel, form is always the *formation* of an already given content, a repositing of the given and not its generation anew.

Returning to the definition of right as "freedom as Idea," on the basis of these clarifications we see that right consists in the correspondence between the will's *concept* of itself as free and as the *actualization* of this freedom in the world. These are actually the same step, for a will that is free not only in-itself but for-itself is a will that has reappropriated, reshaped, and transformed externality in such a way as to make it actuality. The movement from concept to actuality is not a temporal, but a logical one, for the concept is always already embodied in the world, although it may not have found adequate expression through this embodiment.

Is there a way to make Hegel's frightfully abstract definition plausible to ourselves and to avoid the feeling that we are moving around in circles? I want to suggest that Hegel's derivation of the concept of right can be reconstructed as follows. The Introduction to the *Philosophy of Right* specifies what Hegel means by "rational agency." Hegel attributes to human individuals the capacity to act on the basis of *principles*, i.e., on the basis of general rules of whose validity the agent has been convinced through reflection and reasoning, and the capacity for *accountability*, i.e., the ability to cite reasons why one has chosen to act in one way rather than in another. This conception of "rational agency" belongs actually to the first part of the *Encyclopedia*, to the logic of subjective Spirit. For this reason, Hegel refers his readers for a demonstration that the will is free to the *Encyclopedia* in particular and to his system in general (PhR, #4). "Right is an existent of any sort embodying the free will" can now be interpreted as a formula specifying those conditions necessary for the actualization of our capacity of rational agency in the world. The actualization of this capacity means the transformation both of the world of *objects* and a certain mode of acting in the world of *subjects*. "The system of right is freedom made actual, the world of mind brought out of itself like a second nature" (PhR, #4).

But when thus reconstructed, this argument does not establish normative validity. At the most, it provides an analysis of what constitutes *necessary conditions for the exercise of rational agency*. From the fact that certain conditions are necessary for realizing my capacity for rational agency, it does not follow that they are also normatively valid. A metaphysical analysis of the free will establishes no grounds as to why we have to regard what is necessary for the exercise and actualization of the will as being valid and binding. From the proposition that it is necessary for me as a rational agent to possess certain external goods, it does not follow that I have a right, in the sense of a legitimate claim recognizable by others, to do so. When it is asked, "Why should I recognize what is necessary for the exercise of your rational agency as right?" the answer cannot be "Whatever is right for the exercise of my rational agency is right." This answer amounts to the claim that might—whatever I can bring into my power in the world—is right. There must be a suppressed premise in Hegel's argument which should allow us to distinguish between "right" and "might."

Hegel's argument needs to be reformulated as follows: 1) whatever is necessary for the exercise of my rational agency is right; 2) if you refuse to recognize 1, then you deny my freedom, for my freedom consists in my capacity to act in accordance with a conception of myself as a moral agent; 3) but if you deny my freedom, then I am not obliged to accept any rules which you postulate as legitimate and normatively binding; 4) for only those rules are binding upon my will to which I as a free agent would rationally consent.

The suppressed premise of the argument, then, is 4. In fact, beginning with this premise that only those rules are binding upon my will which I as a free agent would rationally consent to, we can move to 3, that my freedom ought not be denied if valid normative claims are to be established, to 2, that you should therefore not deny my capacity to act in accordance with a concept of myself as a rational agent, and to 1, that you ought therefore to recognize whatever is necessary for me to exercise this rational agency as valid.

There is an additional premise that is suppressed in this argument, namely, that you and I reciprocally recognize each other as beings who are *equally entitled* to accept only those rules as binding to which we give our rational consent. If the *reciprocal recognition of the equal entitlement to rational consent* is not presupposed, then the argument would still not establish normative validity. I can only be obliged to recognize you as a being entitled to rational consent if you are willing to grant me the same recognition. If this is not the case, there can be no relation of obligation between us, but only one of force, coercion, and power. You can *force* me to recognize you, but you cannot *oblige* me to do so. I may factually obey you, but deny that I am obliged to do so, and as soon as the opportunity presents itself, I can attempt to reverse this relationship and subject you to my will. Actually, the *Philosophy of Right* proceeds from the standpoint of the "resolution of the struggle for recognition." Reciprocal recognition is the second suppressed premise of Hegel's deduction of the concept of right. In fact, it is the only one, for the principle of rational consent (premise 4) is entailed by it. If you and I recognize each other as rational beings equal in this capacity, then we accept that only those rules of action are right to which we would both freely consent.

It may be objected to this analysis that Hegel does not suppress the premise of reciprocal recognition, but has already included it in his definition of right. The struggle for reciprocal recognition is discussed in the section of the *Encyclopedia* called "Phenomenology of Spirit" in the transition from individual to universal self-consciousness.[30] Therefore the moment of "universality" of the will, from which the section on Abstract Right proceeds, can be supposed to include a principled recognition of the equality of all as rational beings. This objection is not unjustified, but it disregards several points. First, the deduction of the concepts of the free will and of right excludes systematic reference to the standpoint of the individual as a willing being. Hegel criticizes the popular way of looking at right since Rousseau, "according to which what is fundamental, substantive, and primary is supposed to be the will of a single person in his own private self-will, not the absolute or rational will, and mind as a particular individual, not mind as it is in its truth" (PhR, #29). Second, Hegel's definition of "right as an existent of any sort embodying the free will" is a category mistake which suppresses the standpoint of intersubjectivity from the beginning. Even when we interpret "right" in its comprehensive sense as what is normatively valid, it cannot be an *existent* as Hegel assumes; it is a *claim* addressed to others that they *ought* to recognize certain rules of acting and doing as legitimate.

It is no coincidence that Hegel interprets "right" as an "existent." This interpretation once more reveals his tendency to view human activity as work. Just as Spirit reveals its freedom in history through its work, in the sphere of human relations as well the embodiment of freedom as idea is an "existent." But the very logic of the term "right" indicates that this is an *intersubjective claim* specifying what is to be considered normatively valid and worthy. The suppression of intersubjectivity and the "work" paradigm of human activity are two sides of the same coin. From the standpoint of transsubjectivity, validity need not be defined through the intersubjective perspective of actors. Hegel's deduction of the concept of right wholly fulfills this condition. Here normativity is established from the standpoint of the thinker-observer, whose analysis of the conditions necessary for the actualization of free will leads him to the conclusion that these conditions constitute the "abstract right" of individuals. No appeal need be made in this procedure to what acting agents themselves may be motivated by or entitled to regard as binding and valid.

The will discussed by Hegel in the opening sections of the *Philosophy of Right* "is related to nothing except itself and so is released from every tie of dependence on anything else" (PhR, #23), "because its object is itself and so is not in its eyes an 'other' or a barrier; on the contrary, in its object this will has simply turned backward into itself" (PhR, #22). This perfect relation to self through which Hegel defines freedom is not an intersubjective, but a transsubjective ideal.[31] From the standpoint of intersubjectivity, "otherness" is constitutive. Of course, the human person can overcome "immediate otherness" and not view the will of the other simply as a barrier and as a limit juxtaposed to one's own, but not being related to anything "except itself" and being "released from the tie of dependence on anything else" is for concrete human beings a non-sensical ideal. The human will which has only itself as its object would be solipsistic. From the standpoint of the third, of the observer, Hegel is led to deny the "otherness" constitutive of the perspectives of the first and second person.

3. Integrating Crisis: Healing the Wounds of the Ethical

The suppression of intersubjectivity, present since Hegel's deduction of the concept of right, attains systematic significance at one point in the *Philosophy of Right*. This occurs during the discussion of the "system of needs" (*System der Bedürfnisse*). The system of needs presents the moment of "appearance" within ethical life (*Sittlichkeit*) in the sense that this sphere destroys the unity of ethical life and creates the illusion of self-interested

individuals, each pursuing his or her own goals and private interests in isolation from each other (PhR, #189). This is an illusion (*Schein*), for "each man in earning, producing, and enjoying
in his own account is *eo ipso* producing and earning for the
enjoyment of everyone else" (#199). Through his analysis of the
social constitution of needs (#190ff.) and the *social* constitution
of work, Hegel attempts to show that the individualism of the
system of needs is in fact mediated by universality, by a system
of social interdependence. However, an illusion (*Schein*) is not a
delusion (*Täuschung*), but a semblance through which essence
itself appears.[32] The individualism of civil society indeed presents only the *appearance* of universality. The mediation of individualism by universality occurs through a "dialectical
advance" (#199); it is a "compulsion" proceeding behind the
back of individuals and not willed and comprehended by them.
The "complex interpendence of each on all" (#199) is not apparent from the standpoint of individuals engaged in these activities. This is only revealed to the eye of the *observer* who sees
the unity and the logic behind individuals' activities. In the
"system of needs," the third-person perspective of the observer
is constitutive of social practices. Like Adam Smith's "invisible
hand," the standpoint of the social whole is not apparent to
social individuals, but to the thinker-observer.

Hegel's transsubjective ideal of freedom has its origin in this
fact constitutive of modern societies. The "system of needs"
means the emergence of *contexts* of action in which the coordination of their activities with one another takes place behind
the backs of individuals and through the dialectical advance of
unintended consequences.[33] In this sphere, the individuals
themselves are not aware of the systematic interdependence
of their activities and of the social context in which these are
embedded. The laws of political economy, like the laws of as-
tronomy, are not apparent to the naked eye.[34] They are the non-
appearing laws of appearance. The system of needs constitutes a
"system" precisely for this reason: the individual's activities are
governed by laws whose meaning remains hidden from them;
but from the standpoint of the observer analyzing this process,
the whole presents a necessity and a logic.

The system of needs institutionalizes, at the heart of ethical life, the bifurcation (*Entzweiung*) lamented by Hegel since the *Natural Law* essay. While being in conformity with the right of particularity, economic freedom does not represent freedom in the Hegelian sense. Although the satisfaction of her own needs and interests constitutes the goal of the agent's activity in modern economic transactions, this form of activity is subject to laws not willed by the agent. The will does not have itself "qua infinite form as its content and aim." Economic activity presents the submergence of the will in the particularism of individuality; universality is not willed and consciously aimed at, but results from a "dialectical advance."

This loss of freedom is accompanied by a loss of meaning. There is a distinction between the meaning imputed by individuals to their own activities—the satisfaction of their own needs—and the *social* meaning of what they do—the satisfaction of the need of others. Despite the moment of education and the civilizing influence which Hegel attributes to the system of needs, universality in this sphere is a consequence of "abstraction," not of willed insight. Needs become abstract in the sense that they are more and more refined and dependent for their satisfaction upon the work of others. Work becomes abstract in that it is increasingly fragmented and subdivided into details, thus making the individual dependent upon others for the completion of his task. In the system of needs, universality presents itself as an abstraction.

Hegel's main effort in the *Philosophy of Right*, following the discussion of the "system of needs," is to render the universality of social interdependence more transparent. Justice is administered by the public organs of the law, while the corporations have the task of protecting their own members' welfare against the blind impact of economic laws. In making the welfare of their members the principle of their existence, corporations represent a "familial" moment in the system of needs: they protect their own against the rage of the abstract universal and motivate the individual to consider others' welfare along with his own. The task of the corporation is to make the abstract universal more concrete. The concretization of the universal signifies that the loss of freedom characteristic of the system of needs will be mitigated by the individual's engagement in realms of

activity having the concrete universal—the public good—as
their aim. The concretization of the universal also means the
recovery of meaning by the individual who, in this process, ori-
ents his or her actions more and more toward a *willed* universal.
The concrete universal is embodied in the state.

The irony of Hegel's theory of the state, disputed since the
time of the Left Hegelians, cannot be overlooked. Here, as well,
the concrete universal is not *willed* by the citizens of the state,
but is *administered* for them by a "universal class." Whatever the
merits in hindsight of Hegel's theory of bureaucracy and of the
civil service—and they are many—the fact that the "universal"
is *administered* while the citizens sink to the moment of mere
"representation" in the estates cannot be ignored. Willing the
concrete universal means revolution for Hegel; its administration, by contrast, removes the rationality of the universal into a
realm of professional expertise immune to the whims and mere
opinion of the "rabble" (*der Pöbel*). The well-known authoritarianism of Hegel's theory of the state, therefore, is not a matter of
mere political preference. It is perfectly consistent with a transsubjective ideal of freedom which assigns insight into the meaning and validity of individuals' activities of a "third" who
observes and comprehends, while excluding the standpoint of
intersubjectivity. The bureaucrat is the philosopher himself,
analyzing, comprehending, and transforming into a rational
language the confused opinion articulated by the masses. Social
agents are the *object*, not the *subject*, of this rational discourse
shared by the bureaucrat and the philosopher.

This discourse unfolds through the distinction between concept and actuality. There is always a contradiction between the
structure of the concept and of the real.[35] It is this failure of the
real to give complete and adequate expression to the Idea that
propels the Hegelian exposition forward. This distinction between the real and the concept means that in the modern state,
universality is established behind the backs of individuals, and
never through their doings. The concept which represents the
moment of universality never finds adequate embodiment
through the reason and will of individuals themselves. The
structure of the transitions in the *Philosophy of Right* are most
revealing in this respect: the transition from abstract right to

morality occurs because crime and wrong are endemic to juridical relations; the transition from morality to ethical life takes
place because the individual's attempt to realize the moral universal through her own actions is frustrated; the unity of the
family dissolves into the individualism of the system of needs,
for family members are dependent upon the market for their
subsistence; the system of needs realizes "universality" only by
a dialectical advance.

At each point, the disjunction between the concept and the
real also signifies a disjunction between *lived experience* and its
systematic significance. What individuals experience as lived
crises—as wrong or punishment, as the antinomies of moral
conscience, or as the conflicting demands between family and
civil society, or civil society and the state—remain. These lived
crises have a systematic meaning only for the thinker: they reveal the contradictions of the whole and propel the exposition
forward. The logic of the exposition demands that a point be
reached when concept and actuality completely correspond to
each other or when crises are completely integrated into the
system. The elimination of crises would mean the transformation of the conditions generating them, whereas the integration
of crises requires that the social system *function* well enough to
neutralize the possibly disturbing effects of such crises on the
whole. If crime cannot be eliminated, then at least punishment
must be correctly administered. If the pangs of moral conscience
cannot be stilled, then at least institutions should neutralize the
distinction between the "is" and the "ought." If poverty cannot
be eradicated, then the public system of welfare and the corporations should alleviate its disastrous consequences; if the class
divisions of civil society tend to polarize the estates, then it is
the task of the bureaucracy to assure that their polarization can
be kept under control. In short, crises must be managed and the
wounds of the ethical healed. Although ethical life can never
again be rendered transparent, it can be reintegrated.

The ideal of a unified ethical life, guiding Hegel's critique of
the modern natural right tradition since the *Natural Law* essay,
becomes transformed in the *Philosophy of Right* into a model of
the integration and management of crises. The reconciliation of
autonomy and ethical life in the modern state requires crises

management, and the philosopher contributes his share to this task by making the contradictions of the whole visible and intelligible to the bureaucracy—the "universal class." We must insist upon this ambivalent legacy of the Hegelian critique of the Kantian standpoint. Insofar as philosophical exposition reveals the contradictions of the whole, it delivers the possibility of explaining the emergence of crises and of diagnosing their necessity. But insofar as philosophical exposition privileges the standpoint of the whole over and against the experience of lived crises, and refuses to acknowledge the rational potential for transcending the present expressed by the latter, it becomes quietistic and conciliatory.

Hegel's solution in the face of the bifurcation characteristic of modern societies, in the face of the loss of universality caused by the appearance of a system of needs within the ethical totality, is ironic. His model of crises integration and management does not alleviate the consequences for citizens of their loss of freedom, but encourages the emergence of a second sphere of social relations, which are as omnipresent via-à-vis the citizens as the laws of the market are vis-à-vis the bourgeois. This second sphere is the bureaucratic system of justice and administration. It is essential for their proper functioning that they not be interfered with by the particularistic interests of civil society. The modern legal and administrative systems follow the principle of formal rationality.[36] The right and privileges of these functionaries are defined through general legal norms stipulated publicly through due legal process. The formal correctness of the legal process, and the publicity of legal proceedings, assure the right of subjective freedom that one can only be obliged by such rules as are well known by all and apply equally to all. But Hegel does not view the condition of *publicity* as the formation of a system of *public participation*. It suffices that citizens know what they can be held accountable for; it is not necessary that they participate in its formulation. The latter remains the task of the executive and of the bureaucracy. The citizens' estates act as a mere channel for the conveyance of information and opinion, which is then translated into knowledge and insight by state functionaries.

The mature Hegel departs in two ways from the model of

transparent social relations guiding his early critique of modernity: the separation between the private (intimate), economic, and legal-political spheres is institutionalized; but the demand that both the economic and legal-administrative spheres reconcile public rules with private moral principles is abandoned. The institutional differentiation characteristic of modern societies is seen ambivalently, both as causing a loss of freedom and as doing justice to the right of the modern individual to self-determination in the moral and economic spheres. In viewing this process of institutional differentiation within ethical life in all its ambivalence, Hegel is undoubtedly correct. Yet the trans-subjective ideal of freedom does not permit him to exhaust the ambivalent gains of modernity further by extending the right of self-determination to the political sphere. The classicistic bias does not allow Hegel to see in modern societies more than an antagonistic and potentially explosive grouping of interests whose coexistence has to be administered by others. Precisely this biased search for unity leads him to substitute ethical integration for political participation, and reveals him to be an anti-modernist after all.

The Platonist ideal of unity present since the *Natural Law* essay is at work in the *Philosophy of Right* as well; only, the unity of the individual and universal is not attained through a caste-like ordering of public function and individual competence, as it was in the *Natural Law* essay, but through the therapeutic efforts of the philosopher. The philosopher's therapeutic efforts reveal the *necessity* behind the whole to the thinker and to the reflective observer. The insight into this necessity is not formed by citizens themselves in and through their deliberations; it is handed to them top down. But a recognition of necessity that does not result from their collective deliberation is not binding for those whose rational consent is the basis for normative legitimacy. Rather, this insight into necessity becomes a manual for those in positions of public office to "manage" the whole and to integrate crises. The significance of Hegel's transformation of the Kantian concept of autonomy into a transsubjective ideal of freedom is now clear: to protect modernity against its own revolutionary excesses by limiting the communicative evaluation of political legitimacy by citizens themselves.

Chapter 4

CRITIQUE AS CRISIS THEORY: AUTONOMY AND CAPITALISM

The previous chapter has examined Hegel's critique of Kant's moral philosophy, and his transformation of the concept of autonomy into a transsubjective ideal of freedom. I argued that such a move on Hegel's part to a transsubjective concept of freedom was necessary, for this ideal of freedom was the only one compatible with the "expressivist" concept of action. As will be remembered, my claim was that an expressivist concept of action does not allow interpretive indeterminacy in the definition of action; rather, human action is viewed as expressing, manifesting, unfolding, and revealing the implicit essence or nature of the agent. The essence of action is not at all its place in a world shared by other acting and interpreting agents, but its capacity to bring to actuality what is implicit as the agent's essence. The expressivist model of action views action as a process of self-actualization. For this to be successfully attained, however, interpretive indeterminacy, which gives or imputes a meaning to action often different from and contradictory to the one intended by the agent, must be excluded. To actualize itself, the self must not be frustrated, misunderstood, or misinterpreted by others. Yet if such interpretive indeterminacy belongs to human action, then action can be regarded as self-actualization only when its meaning and validity is removed from interpretive contention and placed under the auspices of an observer-thinker. In other words, the expressivist paradigm of action ne-

An earlier version of sections 1 and 3 of this chapter have appeared as "The Marxian Method of Critique: Normative Presuppositions," *Praxis International* (October 1984), 4(3): 284-299.

cessitates the transsubjective perspective of the third person, who has insight into the "potentiality," "essence," or "nature" that the agent is to manifest or reveal.

My final argument in the preceding chapter was that this model of human action, and the transsubjective perspective on which it rests, led Hegel to offer an integrationist rather than a participatory solution to the problem of modern society. It is clear why this must be the case. If, for social agents, the meaning and validity of their actions reside in their understanding of these actions, then the agents can only solve the problems of their collective life insofar as they participate in processes which define the problem as well as the answer. If we assume from the outset that the meaning and validity of social actions reside in the perspective of a third person, then it is not necessary that social agents themselves participate either in framing the appropriate questions or in answering them. The transsubjective standpoint which Durkheim and Hegel share is the perspective of the social therapist, or, less flatteringly, of the social engineer and the systems theorist, but not that of social actors themselves.

The aim of the present chapter is to show that the Marxian method of critique, unlike the Hegelian one, does not aim at crisis integration but at crisis diagnosis, such as to encourage future transformation. The fundamental achievement of Marx's critical theory of capitalism is the view that the two perspectives of intersubjectivity and transsubjectivity are constitutive of capitalist society, and that the task of the theorist is to indicate how concrete individuals can come to "reappropriate" what is justifiably theirs. The task of criticism is to show how transsubjectivity can become intersubjectivity.

Throughout *Capital*, two strains of analysis are followed: whereas the first proceeds from the interpersonal perspective of individuals-in-social-relations whose activity of production is also one of social reproduction, the second level of analysis depicts the movement of capital as self-valorizing value from the perspective of a third person, of the thinker-observer. This second discourse, through which Marx exposes the transsubjective logic of capitalism, is not affirmative but critical. Unlike Hegel,

Marx does not reify the logic of transsubjectivity, but shows it to be the consequence of a form of life dominated by the law of the valorization of capital.

The model of emancipation guiding this critique is the view that what faces individuals currently as the law of value of capital must be reappropriated by them and made to serve their ends. Under capitalism, social wealth presents itself as the wealth of capital, as an accumulation of commodities. The future task is to reappropriate this social wealth for human ends. My claim is that this model of emancipation, which emphasizes the "reappropriation" by humans of their own alienated social wealth, vacillates once more between the perspective of the philosophy of the subject and that of individuals-in-social-relations. Ultimately the politics implied by the model of reappropriation is incompatible with the perspective of individuals-in-social-relations, for the concept of reappropriation (*Wiederaneignung*) as an emancipatory norm only makes sense if we assume the presence of a collective singular subject that actualizes itself in history. At the *normative* level Marx, following Hegel, resorts to the expressivist model of action and denies the dimensions of *plurality* and *indeterminacy* which are constitutive of social action. The consequences of this view are not, as in the case of Hegel, an integrationist solution to the problems of modern society, but a bureaucratic and anti-democratic view of socialism that considers it to accomplish only more perfectly what capitalism has left undone, namely, economic growth and technological advancement. This view is not the only one that follows from Marx's analysis, but it is the one which most consistently articulates the ambivalencies of the reappropriation model. My purpose in this chapter is not to offer an interpretation which does justice to all the readings, rereadings, and misreadings of Marx, but to show why the predominance of the work model of activity in his thought could in practice justify the various distortions of the ideal of socialism.[1]

Within the context of the argument of this book as a whole, the present chapter has several purposes. First, I intend to show how the various modes of critique, whose origins in Hegel's works I have analyzed above, come together concretely in Marx's critical analysis of capitalism. The following chapter then shows how all three dimensions of the critical method are transformed in the work of the Frankfurt School. Second, the two epistemic perspectives, defined as intersubjectivity and transsubjectivity, are shown to be correlated to the twofold concept of *systemic* and *lived* crisis which Marx utilizes in *Capital*. These two perspectives, I want to argue, are not mutually exclusive but complement one another in a critical social theory. What I criticize in Marx's procedure is not that he utilizes both points of view but that he fails to integrate them into a coherent social theory, and in his normative considerations reverts instead to the standpoint of transsubjectivity and the philosophy of the subject.

I begin by outlining the three levels of critique in Marx's *Capital* and pose the question why a normative critique of the bourgeois paradigm of legitimacy could be developed through a critique of political economy (section 1). In section 2, I examine Marx's argument in the famous chapter on the fetishism of commodities to show the ambivalence of the normative model of reappropriation. The subsequent discussion indicates how this ambivalence is also at work in Marx's dual crisis theory, the first dimension of which brings to light functional-systemic crisis and the second, lived crisis, under capitalism (section 3). I conclude this chapter with systematic considerations on the model of self-actualizing activity and the philosophy of the subject (section 4).

1. The Three Levels of Critique in Marx's *Capital*

At one level, Marx's *Capital* unfolds an immanent critique of capitalism. There are two aspects of immanent critique. I shall name the first *categorial* and the second *normative* critique. Let me first explicate the categorial aspect. Proceeding from the accepted definitions and significations of the categories of political economy, in *Capital* Marx shows how these definitions and significations turn into their opposites. For example, political economy postulates the unity of labor and property, and claims that labor provides the only title to property. However, the capitalist mode of production is based upon the radical separation of the property of labor power from the ownership of the means of production. Labor provides no title of property to the products of labor; the only property that the laborer acquires as a consequence of selling his labor power is its cash equivalent— the wages of labor power.[2]

In this procedure, Marx does not juxtapose his own categorial discourse to that of political economy, but through an internal exposition, elaboration, and deepening of the already available results of classical political economy, he shows that these concepts are self-contradictory. This self-contradictoriness does not amount to a logical inconsistency. The categories of classical political economy are self-contradictory in the sense that when their implications are thought through to their end, they fail to explain the phenomenon which they intend to explain, i.e., the capitalist mode of production.

To cite another example: if capital is defined as self-expanding value, and if the reason for the increase in the value of capital is sought in the sphere of the exchange of commodities, then either the exchange of commodities violates the principle of equivalence or the self-expansion of the value of capital becomes unintelligible. The violation of the principle of equivalence means that one commodity in the marketplace always commands less or more exchange value than it is worth. This is a nonsensical claim, for exchange value is precisely the measure of the value of a commodity in relation to others. If one accepts the classical definition of exchange value, one cannot explain the increase in the value of capital. In fact, Marx accepts this definition and shows that the increase in the value of capital cannot be analyzed in light of the exchange process alone, but that one must consider the process of the production of commodities, and the unity of exchange and production as moments of the self-realization of capital.[3] Since Marx does not measure the achievements of political economy against external criteria but confronts the claims of this science with the thought-out consequences of its own categories and assumptions, this aspect of his procedure presents an *immanent critique* of political economy. The categories of political economy are measured against their own objective content. It is this discrepancy and inconsistency between categories and their objects, or concepts and their actual content, which reveals how these categories turn into their opposites.

There is a second dimension to Marx's procedure. Immanent critique is not only categorial critique, but also *normative critique*. In the transition from the exchange of commodities to the labor process in *Capital*, Marx writes: "This sphere that we are deserting, within whose boundaries the sale and purchase of labor power goes on, is in fact a very Eden of the innate rights of Man. There alone rule Freedom, Equality, Property, and Bentham. . . . On leaving this sphere of simple circulation or of exchange of commodities . . . he, who before was the money owner, now strides in front as capitalist; the possessor of labor power follows as his laborer."[4] The normative ideals of bourgeois society—the right of all to freedom, equality, and property—are expressed in social relations of exchange between individual property owners, who are equal in their abstract right to voluntarily dispose of what belongs to each. Social relations of exchange in the marketplace actualize the norms of equality, freedom, and property.

With the transition from exchange to the sphere of production, Marx shifts the perspective from the surface appearances of capitalist society to its deep structure. This shift in perspective amounts to a *normative* critique. In the sphere of the exchange of commodities, the *genesis* of the social relations between commodity owners is unexplained. But when the process by which individuals become commodity owners, or the process of production of commodities, is drawn into consideration, the social-existential meaning of the norms of freedom, equality, and property changes. Freedom for some now simply means the social necessity they face to recurrently sell their labor power; equality means the social dependence of one class upon the members of another, and property, the right of some to appropriate the products of the labor of others. When the *norms* of bourgeois society are compared with the *actuality* of the social relations in which they are embodied, the discrepancy between ideal and actuality becomes apparent. This juxtaposition of norm to actuality is the second aspect of Marx's method of immanent critique. Marx contrasts the normative self-understanding of this society to the actual social relations prevailing in it, with-

out appealing to a different set of norms from the ones immanent in bourgeois society.

On a second level, the critique of political economy is both a
critique of a specific mode of theoretical and social *consciousness*, and a critique of a specific social reality whose theoretical
expression takes the form of political economy. *Capital* is a critique of the social reality articulated by the discourse of political economy, as well as a critique of this discourse itself. This
dimension of Marx's procedure will be named *defetishizing critique*. The theoretical expression of capitalist social relations in
the discourse of political economy assumes a specific conceptual form to which Marx gives the name "fetishism." This form is
characterized by the following: social relations between humans appear as a relation between things. "It is a definite social
relation between men, that assumes in their eyes the phantastic
form of a relation between things."[5] The categories of political
economy, and specifically the category of value, present economic reality as if it were an objective, law-governed reality
encompassing various abstract quantities and entities. In this
presentation, the social process of production which lies behind
the product, and the social relations among humans that assume an objective, mystified quality in their eyes, are not analyzed. Political economy proceeds from social givens, as if they
were natural ones, and cannot uncover the social constitution of
its own object domain.

Through the method of defetishizing critique, the social constitution and historical development of theoretical and everyday
forms of consciousness is analyzed with reference to a future
actuality. This future manifests itself in moments of crisis. The
capitalist mode of production cannot reproduce itself eternally:
it has *systemic* as well as *social* limits. The systemic limits of
capitalism are analyzed by Marx as a series of contradictions
between the socialization of the mode of production and the
continuing private ownership of capital, between the diminishing significance of labor in the production process and the law
that socially necessary labor time remains the measure of value.
The social limits of capitalism are manifested as class conflicts,
struggles, and antagonisms fighting against the social hegemony of capital. In the historical chapters of *Capital*, Marx ana-

lyzes the struggles against the lengthening of the working day, the intensification of production, and child labor. Whereas the systematic limits of capital give rise to dysfunctionalities in the economic sphere—the falling rate of profit, unemployment, bankrupties—the social limits of capital express themselves as conflicts, struggles, and antagonisms of social groups and classes in the fight against the hegemony of capitalist relations. In such moments of crisis, both the irrationality of the system and its transitoriness reveal themselves. The irrationality of the system manifests itself as a discrepancy between the *potential wealth* of society and the *actual misery* of individuals, while its transitoriness becomes apparent to individuals who struggle for its transformation.[6]

This third aspect of Marx's procedure reveals the unity of critique and crisis theory. The critique of capitalism, which brings to light the internal contradictoriness of the system, has the purpose of explaining how and why this internal contradictoriness gives rise to oppositional demands and struggles which cannot be satisfied by the system as it is at present. The function of critique is not therapy and healing the wounds of the ethical as in Hegel's case, but "crises diagnosis" enabling and encouraging future social transformation. The aspect of Marx's procedure described as "defetishizing" critique will be analyzed in detail in the next section. Here I want to focus on the dimensions of categorial and normative critique.

Marx's categorial critique of political economy is also a critique of a mode of social production, the self-understanding of which is reflected in this discourse. The figure of thought which most frequently provides political economy with a methodological principle and bourgeois political philosophy with a counterfactual legitimation procedure is that of the "state of nature." In the Introduction to the *Grundrisse*, Marx writes: "The individual and isolated hunter and fisherman, with whom Smith and Ricardo begin, belong among the unimaginative conceits of eighteenth century Robinsonades which in no way express merely a reaction against oversophistication and a return to a misunderstood natural life as cultural historians imagine."[7] Marx views "state of nature" abstractions, not as retrospective utopias, but as anticipatory legitimations of "civil society."

These ideals do not express a nostalgia for past forms of life; rather, they project images of an already existing present. "In this society of free competition, the individual appears detached from the natural bonds, etc., which in earlier historical periods make him the accessory of a definite and limited conglomerate."[8] The illusion of free and autonomous individuals, coming together through their own consent to found the political commonwealth, is not a delusion of natural right theorists but expresses adequately a truth about civil society. Civil society is the first social formation in history which derives its legitimation from *immanent* as opposed to *transcendental* norms.

By contrast, precapitalist social formations were articulated into hierarchical wholes in which activities in all life spheres received their meaning with reference to a transcendent norm—naturally, cosmologically, or metaphysically grounded. The institutional framework of these societies, relations of production as well as relations of domination, were grounded in an unquestioned structure of legitimation provided by mythical, religious, or metaphysical interpretations. These communities assured themselves of their identity and unity, by positing a transcendent norm which gave cohesion to their self-interpretation and which legitimized the organization of relations of production and domination. There was no clear distinction between production and domination, between the economy and the political sphere.[9] More important, in all these social formations "the *reproduction* of *presupposed* relations . . . of the individual to his commune . . . of his relations both to the conditions of labor and to his co-workers, fellow-tribesmen, etc. . . . are the foundation of development."[10] Here the goal of social life is not the production of commodities, but the reproduction of social relations of domination. In general, in such societies wealth is never considered an end in itself, but a means to the perpetuation of the good life of the community. "Thus the old view, in which the human being appears as the aim of production, regardless of his limited national, religious, political character, seems to be very lofty when contrasted to the modern world, where production appears as the aim of mankind and wealth as the aim of production."[11]

The development of capitalism destroys these social formations. Their dissolution also signifies the disappearance of the transcendent point of view. Capitalism destroys the communal relation of the laborer to the earth as his inorganic means of subsistence. The laborer is separated from the ownership of his means of production, but also from relations like slavery and serfdom, in which individuals themselves appear to belong among the objective conditions of production. The *free*, independent individual is, in fact, one who has been *freed* from the organic relation to the land and to the human community. Such an individual can only be thought of as an abstraction, but this abstraction corresponds to a real historical process. The free, autonomous individual is the product of a real process of historical abstraction.[12]

This shift from transcendent to immanent legitimation is thematized by natural law and contract theories from Hobbes to Kant. The constitution of civil society is presented as an act of consensual union among free and autonomous subjects; the justification of this union is that it corresponds to a necessity of human nature or human reason. Not a transcendent source, whose dictates remain unintelligible to human reason, but the needs, desires, and enlightened self-interest of an emancipated subjectivity provide the legitimizing instance of the new social formation. The ideology of just exchange institutionalizes the principle that individuals are entitled to the pursuit of their own good as long as this does not conflict with the right of others to do the same. Political authority must guarantee all subjects their right to participate in just exchange relations. Respect for the natural rights of individuals to the pursuit of life, liberty, property, or happiness—as listed by contract theorists—is essential if political authority is to be considered legitimate. Political domination is legitimized "from below," with reference to the activities of individuals in civil society, and not with reference to a transcendent norm from above. Since capitalist civil society does away with the transcendent point of view, and since the legitimizing norms of this society, like equality, liberty, and property, are embodied in activities of exchange, the critique of political economy becomes a critique of the normative self-understanding of this society.

In criticizing political economy, Marx is also criticizing its normative force of legitimation. Marx's critique of the normative self-understanding of capitalist civil society does not replace the immanent by the transcendent point of view. Rather, this critique aims to show that this society contains within itself an unrealized potential for expressing "the most developed social relations." Under conditions of capitalist production, this unrealized potential appears through the oppositions of poverty and wealth, exploitation and accumulation, individual impoverishment and social enrichment. Commenting on the lofty view of the ancients, which seems to make wealth a means and not the end of individual and collective development, Marx writes:

> In fact, however, when the limited bourgeois form is stripped away, what is *wealth* other than the *universality* of individual needs, capacities and pleasures, productive forces, etc., created through universal exchange? The full development of human mastery over the forces of nature, those of so-called nature as well as humanity's own nature? The absolute working out of his creative potentialities, with no presuppositions other than previous historical development, which makes this totality of development, i.e., the development of all human powers as such the end in itself, not as measured on a *predetermined* yardstick.[13]

Capitalist civil society has the potential to develop the "universality" of individual needs, capacities, and pleasures; to allow the full unfolding of the human mastery over nature as well as over humanity's own nature, and to bring forth the total individual. This process is not to be measured by a *predetermined yardstick* but the "development of all human powers as such is an end in itself." The potential immanent in capitalist civil society is to allow self-actualization through the unfolding of human capacities and powers. Self-actualization is thus an end in itself, a process the sole legitimation of which is its own unfolding: "the *absolute working out* of his creative potentialities . . . not as measured on a *predetermined* yardstick," Marx writes (emphasis added).

This passage expresses in a nutshell the normative ideal underlying Marx's critique of capitalism. Marx's vision is that of an active humanity, dynamic, enterprising, transforming nature and unfolding its potentials in the process. The bourgeoisie, which can be named the first social class in history to derive its legitimation from an ideology of change and growth rather than one of order and stability, is on Marx's view not to be rejected but sublated (*aufgehoben*). For in bourgeois society the "true universality of individual needs, capacities, and pleasures" is identified with a *limited* form, namely, with wealth in the sense of the mere accumulation of material objects. What is required in the society of the future is to make this wealth, not an end, but rather a precondition for the development of real human wealth, i.e., true universality and individuality. Marshall Berman correctly observes that in this respect

> Marx is closer to some of his bourgeois and liberal enemies than he is to traditional exponents of communism, who, since Plato and the Church Fathers, have sanctified self-sacrifice, distrusted or loathed individuality, and yearned for a still point at which all strife and striving will reach an end. Once again we find Marx more responsive to what is going on in bourgeois society than are the members and supporters of the bourgeoisie themselves. He sees in the dynamic of capitalist development—both the development of each individual and of society as a whole—a new image of the good life: not a life of divine perfection, not the embodiment of prescribed static essences, but a process of continual, restless, open-ended, unbounded growth.[14]

Of course, a second reading of this passage, one which does not emphasize the Enlightenment ideal of humanity as a demiurge, but one which focuses on the meaning of the "true universality" of individual needs, capacities, and pleasures, is possible. Such universality could not mean quantitative abundance, but rather the *qualitative* transformation of needs and pleasures, and the reeducation of our capacities. Such a qualitative transformation and reeducation would not perpetuate the Faustian image of man; if anything, it would come closest to an "aesthetic education" of our sensibilities. Through such reeducation and transformation, the objects of needs and pleasures would be redefined. What one needs, what gives one pleasure, and the capacities one chooses to develop would all change. But change according to what criterion and in light of what norms? Remaining true to Hegel's method of immanent critique, Marx does not say, and maintains that the historical process will generate its own critical standards. The task of the critic is not to provide reality with utopian blueprints for the education of mankind.

But this appeal to the historical process is pointless, for among other things, it does not help us arbitrate between the two visions of transfiguration and fulfillment which are also part of the Marxian concept of history, but which entail *different* politics and different normative standards. Let me name the fulfillment model of historical development "progressivism" and the transfigurative conception "utopianism." As emphasized previously, according to the first model emancipation consists in fulfilling and completing the implicit potentials of the present. The transfigurative or utopian conception, by contrast, envisages a radical break between present and future, and sees the future as ushering in a radically new principle of human togetherness and subjectivity.

To show that both progressivism and utopianism are intrinsic to Marx's method of critique, and that ultimately the disparities of the project of socialism are rooted in the ambivalence of the concept of "reappropriation," I now turn to Marx's analysis of the "fetishism of commodities." The Enlightenment conception of scientific-technical progress as leading to emancipation, and the view that emancipation presents a break in the continuity of history, are present side by side in that famous passage with the interpretation of which critical Marxism in the twentieth century begins.

2. Fetishism and Emancipation

The phenomenon described by Marx as "fetishism" designates a structure of everyday as well as theoretical consciousness, summarized in the statement that "it is a definite social relation between men, that assumes in their eyes the phantastic form of a relation between things" (*Capital*, p. 72). This phenomenon is characterized by a number of inversions or category mistakes. First, social *relations* appear as natural *properties* of things; second, the *social content* of human labor appears as a *formal aspect* of the products of labor; third, the confusion of relations with properties, and of social content with form, has the consequence that what is *mediated* appears as *immediate;* and fourth, what is a *socio-historical* arrangement presents itself as if it were the *natural* order of things.[15] I now want to outline four possible readings of Marx's critique of the fetishism of commodities. Each of these readings has a certain hermeneutical plausibility and I will not attempt to choose among them, for my purpose is to show that the various interpretations of Marx's position are all compatible with the normative ideal of the reappropriation by associated producers of their alienated wealth.

a. The Myth of the Self-Transparent and Self-Identical Collectivity

Marx's critique of fetishism, it may be argued, rests on the myth of a self-transparent and self-identical collectivity.[16] Even if we reject the category mistakes which reduce social relations to properties of things and the market to a natural, ahistorical order, it does not follow that we can eliminate the objectivity of the laws of the market or prevent individuals from engaging in exchange relations. Wherever monetary exchange is institutionalized, individuals will abstract from the quality of labor that went into producing commodities and will seek to buy or sell them in virtue of their formal value-bearing characteristics. If the institution of monetary exchange obeys the laws of supply and demand, then it is meaningless to demand that this cease being the case. These laws have an objective logic and can never simply be subject to conscious planning decisions. Certainly it is possible to reform the injustices and inefficiencies of the market through certain policy measures, but a complete elimination of the laws of the market can only lead to worse inefficiencies and to bureaucratic nightmares.

In his critique of fetishism Marx posits a myth, the myth of a self-transparent and self-identical collectivity, in which human activities are not mediated by exchange relations and by the market. Such a collectivity can only be thought of as a small utopian commune that is perfectly self-sufficient. Any large human society operating with the level of productive and technical knowledge available to us will involve a high degree of specialization, division of labor, and exchange relations. Such a society will inevitably produce objective spheres of exchange, production, and expertise, each with its own laws. It is impossible to think that in a complex society all the consequences of human activities can ever be rendered perfectly transparent.[17] We certainly do not have to believe that these spheres are governed by natural laws, but we cannot deny their objective logic, which cannot be reduced simply to the intentions of social agents. The critique of fetishism may have been a useful method for demystifying the myths of classical political economy, but it itself is based upon the myth of a self-transparent and self-identical collectivity.

b. The Reconstitution of the Social Sphere

Against this interpretation which reduces the Marxian critique of fetishism to a longing for a mythical, self-transparent utopia, it can be objected that the *specific* nature of capitalist exchange relations is ignored thereby. Marx does not object to relations of exchange *tout court*, but to a mode of social life in which monetarized exchange relations seem to form the only significant social bond among independent individuals. Marx's criticism is directed against the *reduction* of the sphere of sociation (*Vergesellschaftung*) to exchange relations, and against the definition of social interconnectedness in terms of monetarily mediated transactions.

Indeed, capitalism signifies the dissolution of the ethical and of all fixed personal relations of dependence. As Hegel already saw, a "system of needs," a universal system of objective dependencies, is established.[18] Each individual can only earn a livelihood insofar as his or her work can command a certain value in the marketplace. Each individual can satisfy his or her needs insofar as he or she possesses a quantity of the universal medium of exchange, of money. As opposed to personal relations of dependence characterizing ethical life and precapitalist economic formations, capitalism institutionalizes an impersonal and objective (*sachlich*) sphere of dependence. Individuals standing under the laws of this sphere are indifferent to one another and yet dependent on each other. Their only social bond is exchange value. Each individual must produce a general product—exchange value—and must have money to command exchange value. "The individual carries his social power, as well as his bond with society, in his pocket."[19] In capitalist society, writes Marx, "the social character of activity, as well as the social form of the product and the share of individuals in production . . . appear as something alien and objective, confronting the individuals not as their relation to one another, but as their subordination to relations which subsist independently of them and which arise out of collisions between mutually independent individuals."[20] Fetishism is the expression of a mode of social life in which social relations and the social content of activity are completely "thingified," reified and treated as abstract, exchangeable, indifferent units. The critique of fetishism aims at *restructuring* social life by transforming the social mode of production into one which does not "exist outside individuals as their fate." The goal is not to "return to an original fullness" but to develop a future society of "universally developed individuals, whose social relations, as their own communal [*gemeinschaftliche*] relations, are hence also subordinated to their own communal control."[21]

c. The Transcendence of the Law of Value

The restructuring of the social sphere such as to return to individuals control over their own social relations is only possible, it may be argued, through a transcendence of the law of value.[22] As Marx points out, the fetishism of commodities has its origin in the particular *social* character of the labor which produces them.[23] The mutual exchangeability of all commodities with one another presupposes that the private, useful labor of each producer is ranked equally with that of all others. Such an equalization can only be the result of an abstraction or the result of reducing all forms of concrete human labor to their common denominator, namely, to the expenditure of human labor power in the abstract. Once this abstraction is carried out, the only commensurable measure between the labor power of different individuals is their expenditure in time units. Abstract human labor is measured in time. Thus, although individuals may not be aware of it, whenever through exchange they equate as values different products, by that very act they also equate different forms of human labor with one another. "We are not aware of this, nevertheless we do it" (*Capital*, p. 74). "In the midst of all the accidental and ever-fluctuating exchange relations between the products, the labor time socially necessary for their production asserts itself like an overriding law of Nature" (p. 75).

The determination of value by the socially necessary labor time expanded in the production of commodities is the "objective," nature-like necessity facing individuals. All human activity and products are reduced to abstract homogeneous units of time whose commensurability consists in their being units of embodied value. But the law of value governs the activities of this sphere because it governs the capitalist mode of production in general. Capital is self-expanding value; it is value which begets value. The expansion of capital requires that the socially necessary labor time invested in the production of commodities be continuously decreased, or that relative surplus value be increased by diminishing the labor time necessary for the reproduction of living labor itself. The increase in relative surplus value or in the productivity of labor means simply increasing the subjection of the producers and of their way of life to the tyranny of accelerated production. On the one hand, then, capitalism attempts to render living labor increasingly more obsolete in order to increase relative surplus value; on the other hand, as long as socially necessary labor time remains the measure of the value of human activities and products in society, individuals will need to work more and more efficiently in order to attain the necessary means of survival.

> Capitalism itself is the moving contradiction [in] that it presses to reduce labor time to a minimum, while it posits labor time, on the other hand as a sole means of wealth . . . on the one side, then it calls to life all the powers of science and of nature, as of social combination and of social intercourse, in order to make the creation of wealth independent (relatively) of the labor time employed in it. On the other side, it wants to use labor time as the measuring rod for the giant social forces thereby created.[24]

Capital thus increases disposable time and reduces labor time to a social minimum, but since labor time remains the measure of value, disposable time does not appear as free time, but as surplus labor and as unemployment that is not socially compensated. "The means of wealth is then not any longer, in any way labor time, but rather disposable time. *Labor time as the measure of value* posits wealth itself as founded on poverty and disposable time as existing *in and because of the antithesis to surplus labor time;* or the positing of an individual's entire time as labor time and his degradation therefore to mere worker, subsumption under labor."[25]

The overcoming of the logic of fetishism requires a new mode of production in which the expenditure of socially necessary labor time is no longer the measure of value and value no longer the unit of social wealth. Marx adds that although "labor cannot become play, as Fourier would like . . . it remains his great contribution to have expressed the suspension, not of distribution, but of the mode of production itself, in a higher form, as the ultimate object."[26]

d. The Rationalization of the Law of Value

This utopian vision outlined by Marx in the *Grundrisse* envisages the transition to socialism as eliminating the law of value and as creating free time for all through the reduction of socially necessary labor time to a minimum. When socially necessary labor time ceases to be the measure of value, the realm of necessity is left behind and the realm of freedom begins. In the section on the "Fetishism of Commodities" in *Capital,* Marx develops yet a second model of the emancipated society, which he contrasts to the distortions caused by fetishistic consciousness. According to this model, the law of value is not *eliminated;* it is fully *rationalized.*[27]

"Let us picture to ourselves," writes Marx, ". . . a community of free individuals, carrying on their own work with the means of production in common, in which the labor power of all the different individuals is consciously applied as the combined labor power of the community" (*Capital,* p. 78). In such a community, one portion of the total social product serves as fresh means of production and is reinvested in new means of subsistence. Although the rules of the distribution between new investment and consumption will vary, it is assumed that the share of each individual producer in the means of subsistence will be determined by the labor time he has expended. "Labor

time would, in that case, play a double part. Its apportionment
with a definite social plan maintains the proper proportion between the different kinds of work to be done and the various
wants of the community. On the other hand, it also serves as the
measure of common labor borne by each individual and of his
share in the part of the total product destined for individual
consumption" (*Capital*, p. 79). Labor time no longer defines their
activities behind individuals' backs, but individual labor which
is considered social from the start is distributed among various
sectors of production. The law of value is rendered perfectly
transparent according to a definite "social plan." This model
indeed presupposes the transparency of a rationalized, planned
economy. Fetishism is overcome because individuals no longer
confront a sphere of nature-like, objective necessity; instead,
they confront the "transparent" logic of collective planning. A
bureaucratic elite is needed to determine the magnitude of socially necessary labor time and to apportion the share to be
reinvested and the share to be consumed, and to determine the
level of wages. Wages are still measured according to the necessary labor time contributed by an individual to the collectively
necessary social labor time. Whereas in capitalism the law of
value asserts itself via the law of supply and demand, including
the demand for labor power itself, in this model of bureaucratic
socialism, the laws of the market are suspended and the law of
value becomes the object of conscious, rationalized planning.
But socially necessary labor time remains the measure of value
and value the unit of social wealth. In the *Grundrisse*, it was
maintained that "labor time as measure of value posits wealth
itself as founded on poverty."[28] The model of "transparent" social relations offered in the first volume of *Capital* makes this
"wealth founded on poverty" the basis of socialist planning.

The four readings of Marx's critique of fetishism offered above
can now be identified more closely. While the first presents a
liberal rebuttal of Marx's critique, the second and third are utopian depictions of the future socialist society, and the fourth a
legitimation of bureaucratic central planning and of "really existing socialism." The tension between the progressivist fulfillment of the potentials of capitalist society, and the utopian
transfiguration of this potential into a new and as yet histor-

ically unknown form, analyzed above with respect to Marx's early writings and the *1844 Manuscripts*, confronts us here as well. On the one hand, the overcoming of fetishism means that the laws of the market will be rationalized according to a central plan. Socially necessary labor time will be used as the standard in distributing the work force among the various sectors of production; furthermore, the determination of an individual's share in social wealth will also be based upon his or her contribution to the socially necessary labor-time pool. Instead of the chaotic and often unintelligible workings of the market, socialism will introduce a rational and predictable plan. On the other hand, Marx views the overcoming of fetishism in utopian terms, as ushering in a *new* form of human sociation (*Vergesellschaftung*). Here, the emphasis is on a mode of sociality and togetherness that is not based upon exchange relations and the juridical norms embodied in them. In the passage from the *Grundrisse* cited above, Marx writes of a society of "universally developed individuals, whose social relations, as their own *communal* (*gemeinschaft-lich*) relations, are hence also subordinated to their own communal control" (see p. 162; emphasis mine). The use of the term "gemeinschaftlich" in this context is not accidental. Marx means to invoke images of solidarity and togetherness that are no longer characteristic of the *bürgerliche Gesellschaft* which is held together by exchange relations and juridical norms.

By emphasizing the contrast of *Gemeinschaft* and *Gesellschaft*, I do not want to suggest that Marx, like Ferdinand Tönnies and others after him, was a traditionalist.[29] Clearly, he never ceased to emphasize that the kind of "communality" of the future he envisaged could only be attained on the *basis* of the already achieved stage of development of capitalism. Marx defended this view not only because capitalist development was a fact that could not be denied, but primarily because capitalism ushered in a normative potential which was to be the basis of all future socialist sociality. Marx expresses this normative potential in the following passage: under capitalism, "this complete working out of the human content appears as a complete emptying out, this universal objectification as total alienation and the tearing down of all limited, one-sided aims as sacrifices of the human end-in-itself to an entirely external end."[30] The "complete working out of the human content" is the complete unfolding of human potentialities in history, the development of human productive forces, but also the education and refinement of needs and desires through capitalist luxury and wealth. This process cannot be measured by an external yardstick; it itself generates its own standards of evaluation. Capitalism unleashes human wealth, yet continues to measure wealth according to the standard of socially necessary labor time. The real transfiguration of capitalism begins with the rejection of necessary labor time as the measure of wealth. The real measure of human wealth is, rather, disposable time. The utopia suggested by Marx here is that of a society of abundance in which, in Hannah Arendt's provocative formulation, "leisure from labor" has been attained.[31]

Whether one interprets the Marxian utopia as enjoining a new form of *sociality*, or *leisure from labor*, or emphasizing that socialism must rationalize the irrational waste of human potentials under capitalism, it is clear that the texts can be made compatible with all three readings. However, the utopian conception of leisure from labor and the progressivist notion of the rationalization of the law of value share one element in common. In both cases, it is the nature and restructuring of laboring activity that defines the society of the future. But in Marx's emphasis in the *Grundrisse* on a new form of *sociality*, it is human relations of interaction that are made pivotal for the society of the future. Although running through the corpus of Marx's writings, this conception of a new sociality, of a new intersubjectivity, is never explicitly developed. The issue here is not whether a new vision of labor may not also be necessary to the project of a new mode of sociality. I rather think the two tasks are complementary, not exclusive. The issue here is that the alternative of a *new sociality* presupposes an understanding of human action and politics which, in the final analysis, has no room in the Marxian framework. This is so, I want to argue, for the Marx of *Capital* as well reverts to the philosophy of the subject. From the standpoint of the philosophy of the subject, there is no room for reconceptualizing new forms of interaction and togetherness, for, as I will explicate below, this position is based on two presuppositions which preclude this alternative. These are the myth of a collective singular subject, and the model of action as self-actualization.

In the following section, I first want to elaborate Marx's synthesis of the standpoints of intersubjectivity and transsubjectivity in his analysis of capitalism as a crisis-ridden social system; in the second place, I want to show how, in mediating these two perspectives, Marx once more reverts to the philosophy of the subject, incorporated now by the proletariat.

3. Systemic and Lived Crisis: The Unresolved Tension

Throughout *Capital* two strands of analysis, corresponding to two distinct social epistemologies, are followed: the first is the interpersonal perspective of individuals-in-social-relations, while the second depicts the movement of capital from the perspective of a third, of the thinker-observer. These two modes of analysis correspond to two types of crisis theory. Whereas the first presents crises as the *lived* phenomena of alienation, exploitation, and injustice, the second regards crises as the failure of the *functional logic* of the system from the perspective of the thinker-observer. Lived crises and systemic-functional crises are the two points of view from which Marx observes the internal contradictions of capitalism. Marx himself thought he could reconcile these two perspectives by focusing on the dual character of labor power as a commodity. I now want to turn to Marx's attempted reconciliation and show why this is a synthesis we can no longer accept.

For Marx, capitalist social relations begin when labor power can be bought and sold in the marketplace as a commodity. Yet labor power is unlike any other commodity in three ways. First, it is not *separable* and distinct from its owner. There can be no labor power without the one who labors. Through the wage-labor contract, the worker alienates to the owner of the means of production his capacity to perform a concrete form of labor over a period of time. Second, not being separable from its owner, labor power is not *reproducible* at will either. The reproduction of labor power is identical with the reproduction of those individuals who sell their labor power as a commodity. Third, unlike a machine, labor power can only be set into motion when its owner *consents* to labor, i.e., when the individual agrees to perform the activity involved. Labor power is a subjective capacity whose employment depends upon the subjective will of the laborer.

Now, the ideological kernel of capitalist social relations is that what in all previous societies was a *direct relation of domination* between immediate producers and those appropriating their surplus product or labor appears in capitalism as an objective (*sachlich*) relation between things: labor power is a commodity whose value is likewise one, i.e., monetary wages. In all human societies the distribution of social wealth entails a set of power relations, while under capitalism the power relations inherent in the distribution of social wealth appear as laws of the market, as consequences of an automatically determined process. This complete objectification or "thingification" of labor power does not and cannot succeed. The purchase and sale of labor power is unlike that of any other commodity, although the internal logic of capitalism is based upon a denial of this fact.

The purchase and sale of labor power entails a social struggle, a conflictual social relation. In the historical discussions and digressions of *Capital* (chapters 10, 15, 25, and 26–31), Marx narrates the development of capitalism from the standpoint of those who *live through* these developments and suffer their consequences. The struggle of the workers against the lengthening of the working day and against child labor; their resentments and outbursts against machinery; their strikes, and the gradual emergence of a collective consciousness that transforms the wage-labor contract from a private act into a collectively negotiable power relation are narrated.[32] These struggles set objective limits upon the functioning of capitalism: absolute surplus value cannot be attained via the lengthening of the working day, for the political struggle prevents it. The extraction of relative surplus value through an increase in the productivity of labor, and the rationalization and scientification of production, also have limits, as expressed by the resistance of the workers—ranging from machine storming to absenteeism to the sabotage of production or to lowering levels of productivity.

There is by now a long debate on the methodological significance of the historical observations and digressions in *Capital*.[33] Whereas the main analysis itself proceeds from a systematic abstraction called "*the* capitalist mode of production," the historical digressions rely primarily on the English case and the development of the English working class. Are these historical digressions *illustrations* of the systematic analysis, or is there a sense in which the analysis itself is *historically* specific and expresses the development of capitalism in one particular case only? For the purposes of my argument, I need not get involved in this debate. The dual perspective displayed in *Capital* through historical narrative on the one hand and systematic analysis on the other corresponds to the dual quality of labor power as a commodity. In the historical passages, the subjects are the laborers themselves as owners of concrete labor power, whereas according to the systematic analysis, capital itself is the subject; from the standpoint of capital, labor power is simply what is paid in the form of wages, i.e., variable capital. This dual perspective of the text reflects the unresolved struggle between laborers as subjects and capital that objectifies them.

To illustrate this dual perspective at work, let me give an example from Marx's discussion of the "Working Day" in chapter 10 of *Capital*. Marx writes: "But capital has one single life impulse, the tendency to create value and surplus value, to make its constant factor, the means of production, absorb the greatest possible amount of surplus labor. . . . The capitalist then takes his stand on the law of the exchange of commodities. He, like all other buyers, seeks to get the greatest possible benefit out of the use value of his commodity" (*Capital*, p. 233). This passage explicates the rationality of the capitalist's action from the *systemic* perspective of capital as ever-increasing wealth. When presenting the consequences that this systemic law of capitalism to increase surplus value has for the working class, Marx abandons the language of analysis and proceeds to let the workers speak for themselves. The shift in perspective is most vividly illustrated in the text as a shift in *narrative voice* from that of the social analyst to the voice of the participant.

> Suddenly the voice of the laborer, which had been stifled in the storm and stress of the process of production, rises: The commodity that I have sold you differs from the crowd of other com-

modities, in that its use creates value, and a value greater than its own. This is why you bought it. . . . To you, therefore, belongs the use of my daily labor power. But by the means of the prices that you pay for it each day, I must be able to reproduce it daily, and to sell it again. Apart from natural exhaustion through age, etc., I must be able on the morrow to work with the same normal amount of force, health, and freshness as today. . . . I will each day spend, set in motion, put into action only as much of it as is compatible with its normal duration, and healthy development. By an un-limited extension of the working day, you may in one day use up a quantity of labor power greater than I can restore in three. What you gain in labor I lose in substance. (*Capital*, p. 234)

These two perspectives, illustrated by Marx most vividly through different narrative voices, correspond to different con-ceptions of crisis:[34] in the historical chapters, the development of capitalism is presented as it causes *lived crises* for real his-torical actors. By "lived crises" in this context I mean radical transformations in work, living, and domestic conditions: the emergence of feelings of exploitation, injustice, resentment, malaise, and the like. In these passages, the domination and brutalization of the workers, but also their struggles and re-sistance against exploitation and domination, are narrated. The main argument of the text, by contrast, presents the *functional* or *systemic* crises of capitalism: the tendency of the rate of profit to fall; bankruptcies; concentration of capital; blockages in the realization and circulation of capital; and unemployment are discussed. Sociologically, lived crises signal the breakdown of norms, values, and meaning structures incorporated in social actions. Functional crises signal the "malfunctioning" of objec-tive contexts of relations. "Stagflation," for example, is a func-tional crisis of late-capitalist economies, but it becomes a lived crisis for individuals only when, through inflation and lack of gainful employment, their material life-basis is destroyed—e.g., the aged—and their belief in the values and norms of the society are called into question and phenomena of disorientation, anomie, meaninglessness, appear—e.g., ghetto youth. What is missing in Marx's analysis is the *mediation* between these two points of view. The text weaves in and out of both without an explicit guidance as to what is involved. The lack of mediation between these two points of view has significant theoretical as well as normative implications. Let me explicite the theoretical problem first.

The two points of view, which I have described as the internal one of the lived experience of social actors and the external, objectified one of a thinker-observer, correspond to two fundamental categories of modern social theory. Modern social theory distinguishes between *system integration* and *social integration*.[35] System integration takes place through the functional interconnection between the consequences of social actions. From Adam Smith's notion of the "invisible hand" to Hegel's concept of a "system of needs," Durkheim's notion of the organic division of labor, and Parsons' notion of the "generalized media," modern social theory has emphasized this aspect of modern societies, according to which large domains of social life become *functionally* dependent upon one another without this being willed, desired, or even known to anyone. Social integration, by contrast, refers to the coordination of social actions through the harmonizing of action orientations. Individuals orient their actions to one another because they understand the meanings, social rules, and values in question. System integration occurs despite the *discrepancy* between said intention and consequence, but in social integration, the coordination of social action takes place through the orientation of social actors to the rules and meanings governing their social life. Whereas action systems can be analyzed from the perspective of the third person, of the *observer*, social integration needs to be analyzed from the *internal* perspective of the first and second person.

Commenting on these two perspectives, Claus Offe observes: "All social systems reproduce themselves through the normatively regulated and meaningful action of their members on the one hand, and the effectiveness of objective functional contexts on the other. This differentiation between 'social integration' and 'system integration,' between followed *rules* and *rule-like regularities* that assert themselves beyond subjects is the basis for the entire sociological tradition."[36] We certainly cannot take Marx to task for not having developed the social-theoretical means of analysis by which to integrate these two perspectives, but it is no coincidence that as a social theory, Marxism seems to vacillate between economistic objectivism on

the one hand—emphasizing the moment of functional crisis—
and culturalist or psychological perspectives of alienation on
the other—corresponding to the moment of lived crisis. The theoretical problem left unresolved by Marx's analysis is the relationship between action contexts out of which lived crises
emerge and objective-functional interconnections among action
consequences that lead to systemic malfunctioning.

I will not develop the implications of this problem for Marxian social theory in this chapter.[37] Suffice it to say that beginning with the early efforts of the Frankfurt School to integrate
psychoanalysis and family and culture sociology with Marxian
political economy, the tradition of critical social theory has had
to come to grips with this problem. As contemporary capitalist
society moved further and further away from the model discussed by Marx, and as the nature of the protest movements in
these societies took an increasingly different character from the
one diagnosed as the "wage labor-capital" conflict, it also became necessary to distinguish between systemic and lived
crises. To elaborate these issues further will be the task of future
chapters (5 and 7).

This unresolved theoretical problem has normative consequences. The reader of the historical excursus in Marx's *Capital*
cannot avoid the impression that in these passages the workers
are not the subjects of their struggles, but become so only to the
extent that they are made into subjects by capitalism itself, i.e.,
only insofar as their misery is collectivized and their living conditions so homogenized that they become members of a single,
unified class. Marx's evaluation of this process of the constitution of the workers into a "class" is positive.[38] The formation of
class consciousness is seen as a step toward autonomy, as a step
in the direction of becoming true subjects. Collective actors
whose struggles cannot be subsumed under the concept of
"class" are not subjects at all. Yet the concept of "class," as Marx
himself also points out, is only a meaningful social category for
analyzing those social systems in which stratification is not
ascriptive; in which birth, age, blood lineage, and profession no
longer determine social rights and privileges; and where social
integration is achieved primarily through the free market of
wage labor.[39] In such social systems, class formations are not

subjective, but objective means of identification by which the observer-thinker can determine the functional regularities and statistical qualities that come to characterize the living conditions, actions, and thought patterns of large masses of the population.

At the subjective level, what is supposed to "bind" members of a class together is their "objective interest," i.e., the preservation of their material and power status within the sytem of production. Class interests are "ascribed" *(zugerechnet)* in the true sense of the word, for one can determine what is or is not in the interests of a class only through an "objective" analysis of the social system itself. There is, however, no such purely "objective" analysis; the determination of so-called "class interests" requires us to specify what we see as just or unjust, as exploitation or domination in social relations. If the concept of a class interest is to designate more than a statistical regularity of the behavior of large human groups and is to be used as a *normative* measure as to how real groups *ought* to act, then one's normative standards must be identified previously and not subsequently to "objective" class analysis.[40] Social classes are specific historical forms of *collective actors*. They are not the only ones. Struggling collectivities may be formed around other normative concerns besides class interests, and relations of exploitation and domination may be based upon other characteristics like sex, race, ethnic and linguistic identity, and even age. Marx was correct in diagnosing the manner in which capitalist society seemed to render previous modes of collective identification irrelevant, but he was wrong in ascribing a normative status to the only mode of collective identification that capitalism seemed to create. In ascribing such a normative status to the concept of class, Marx adapted exclusively the point of view of thinker-observer, ignoring the very social experiences of *collectivity* and *plurality* which are fundamental to struggling social actors. As the final step in this section, let me elaborate why this concept of class rests on the philosophy of the subject.

The four presuppositions of the position which I describe as the "philosophy of the subject" are: first, that there is a unitary model of human activity which can be defined as "objectification" or "production"; second, that history is constituted by the activities of this one subject—humanity or mankind; third, that human history presents the unfolding of the capacities of this one subject; and fourth, that emancipation consists in our becoming conscious of and acting in accordance with the knowledge that the constituting and constitutive subjects of history— the subject of the past and the subject of the future—are one. Insofar as we in the present can see our identity with this subject whose past "work" is our present, we can either attain reconciliation with an objectivity which we know to be our doing (Hegel) or we can attain emancipation by reappropriating those forces and achievements of the past which we know to be products of our activity (Marx). In his 1841 Introduction to the *Critique of Hegel's Philosophy of Right,* Marx summarizes his vision of emancipation in the following terms: "The formation of a class with *radical chains,* a class of bourgeois society, which is none; an estate which is the dissolution of all estates; a sphere that possesses a universal character in virtue of its universal suffering and claims no *particular right* for itself because it claims no *particular wrong* . . . a sphere . . . which in one word is the *total loss* of humans and which can therefore gain itself by *completely regaining humanity.*"[41] Let me first explicate the normative consequences of this early view of Marx's, returning subsequently to the philosophy of the subject in *Capital.*

In Marx's theory, the proletariat represents a *universal* interest because it acts in the name of the collective singular subject of history. The emancipation of the proletariat amounts to the emancipation of humanity, precisely because the specific interests of this class correspond to the universal interests of humanity. Note, however, that this equation of proletarian with universal human interests *tout court* rests on two assumptions: first, it is assumed that there is a real subject of history to whom we can ascribe a "universal" interests; in the second place, it is maintained that one social group or class must be capable of representing *the* universal interest as such. Both assumptions are faulty.

The claim that there is a *subject* of history to whom we can ascribe an interest rests on a confusion of empirical and normative categories. For Marx, empirically, humanity is the subject of history, in the sense that history develops as a consequence of human activities. But humanity is an abstraction, for it is the concrete activities of specific individuals in certain times and places that drive the historical process. The subjects of history, in the sense of *agents* of history, are human beings in the *plural*, not humanity in the singular as such. In the second place, what allows Marx to shift from the plural to the collectively singular, from humans to humanity, is the assumption that lets him view humanity as a normative category. History is the condition of the possibility of becoming a subject, not in the sense of agency, but in the sense of a goal and a *telos*. Humanity here appears as the goal of history, as that toward which history tends.

Having inherited this dual perspective of humanity as an *empirical* subject and as a *normative* goal from classical German idealism and its philosophy of history,[42] Marx often conflates the two principles and writes as if what is a regulative ideal in history—the ideal of humanity—is also operative in history as an agent—humanity as an empirical subject. It is this conflation of empirical and normative perspectives which drives Marx to the equally questionable assumption that one can impute an "interest" to it. But if humanity is a normative category alone, its interests would have to be defined in the course of struggle and could not be specified beforehand, for humanity itself would only be a *telos* of struggle and would not refer to a preexistent subject. Not what the theorist claims to be *the* human interest, but what struggling social actors themselves would come to recognize as their own common goals and desires, would constitute human interests. If human interests cannot be defined theoretically and a priori, then it also follows that it makes no sense to view one social class alone as representing *the* universal interest. In Marx's work, the proletariat is ascribed a normative role that follows from the theoretical conflation I have been attempting to outline. As Jean Cohen astutely observes in *Class and Civil Society: The Limits of Marxian Critical Theory*,

> The concept of a universal class and the identification of one historically produced, empirically existent group as the bearer of universality rests on the problematic attempt, derived from Hegel, to present history as positive and rational. The universal class, the subject/object of history, the negation of the negation, are concepts

in Marx's thought that imply a return to Hegel's absolute through
the substitution, first of species for *Geist*, second, of the class as the
general representative of society for the species. The concept of the
universal class subjugates the contingencies of historical praxis
and the plurality of potential actors to the demands of "reason"—
to the demands of a logic that seeks to discover its own operations
on the level of human praxis.[43]

Certainly, in *Capital* Marx is no longer operating with a conception of species essence that is an empirical version of Hegel's
concept of *Geist*. Nonetheless, as I have stressed above, the conception that what has been alienated under capitalism and in
the course of human history must be *reappropriated* by the producers is the normative model that continues throughout Marx's
oeuvre. The privileged normative status of the concept of "class"
allows Marx to avoid specifying more closely the social and political form this "reappropriation by associated producers of
their alienated wealth" would take. If it is assumed that the
wealth of human history is produced by a collective singular
subject, then it is not necessary to specify what such reappropriation would or could mean in concrete social and political
terms. The collective singular subject does not behave as a
collectivity that has decided to act together, but as a *singularity*
that reappropriates what is legitimately its own. In this respect,
Marxian social theory faces a dilemma: either the proletariat is
one social actor among others whose struggles we choose to
support on diverse ethical and political grounds, or the proletariat is *the* privileged social actor whose struggles must be
supported on systematic-theoretical grounds. If one chooses the
first alternative, then as a future emancipatory theory Marxism
cannot justify the privileged status it ascribes to the proletariat.
If one chooses the second alternative, then one can uphold the
special role of the proletariat but cannot explain why its interests equal universal human interests as such, except by a series
of equations and reductions based on the philosophy of the
subject.

I have been suggesting that questioning the privileged status
of the concepts of class, reappropriation, and the position I
name the "philosophy of the subject" is essential for clarifying
the normative foundations of Marxian social theory. I do not

want to suggest thereby that one may not be able to find in Marx's critique of capitalism other concepts, like exploitation, equality, fairness, and self-determination, which are also operative in his normative vision. Only it seems to me essential in developing an alternative conception of ethics and politics that one dispense with the assumptions I have identified as the model of self-actualizing activity and the reduction of human plurality to collective singularity.

4. Concluding Systematic Considerations to Part I: Self-Actualizing Activity and the Philosophy of the Subject

Hegel's critique and rejection of modern natural right theories in his early writings presupposes the nostalgic ideal of a unified ethical life. Against both empiricist and formalist natural right theories, Hegel maintains that the juxtaposition of morality against legality, of economics against politics, of the individual against the social, and of reason and will against the inclinations reflect the bifurcation at the heart of modern society. To overcome this bifurcation and to render one what critical reason and modernity have torn asunder is the task of philosophy and of speculative knowledge. Hegel's discovery of the constitutive activity of labor in the *Phenomenology* sets him upon the path of reconciliation with modernity and provides him at the same time with a critical method which can show that the social-historical world is not only *positive*, in the special sense of being a mere given, but is *posited*, in the sense of being the work of a transsubjective subject called Spirit. The activity of Spirit in history is defined as self-externalization; through self-externalization in history, Spirit actualizes itself.

Marx's anthropological critique of Hegel in the *1844 Manuscripts* replaces "Spirit" with "mankind" or "humanity." This replacement does not alter the fundamentals of the philosophy of the subject, for history is still viewed as the unfolding of the capacities of a collective subject, and social emancipation is still understood as the reappropriation of this heritage by a specific class. The particular demands of this class coalesce with the universal demands of humanity to become the master of its own history. This normative model of the reappropriation of the alienated wealth of humanity, which now masquerades as "capital," is at work in Marx's critical analysis of this mode of production. Of course, there are fundamental differences between the philosophical anthropology of the early writings and the model of individuals-in-social-relations from which Marx proceeds in *Capital*. This change in social theory and in the fundamentals of social analysis from the *Manuscripts* to *Capital* does not alter the normative model. As the dual perspective of lived versus systematic crises shows, Marx's normative model of emancipation still is that the products of the mystical subject of this process—capital—should be *reapproriated* by the true subjects, by concrete individuals in whose name the proletariat acts. This reappropriation of an externalized social essence can be construed either as a *utopian* transcendence of capitalism, or as the *progressive* fulfillment and perfecting of the incomplete rationality of capitalism. Both utopian and progressivist readings of this normative presupposition are possible; but neither reading questions the fundamentals of the reappropriation model and the philosophy of the subject which underlie it. But why is it necessary to question this model and the philosophy of the subject? In order to answer this question, let me begin by considering the shortcomings of the model of self-actualizing activity.

The inadequacies of the Marxian category of "objectification" to characterize communicative activities (see chapter 2, section 3) and the failure of the Hegelian paradigm of externalization to explain the interpretive indeterminacy of human action (chapter 3, section 2) have been discussed. Both "objectification" and "externalization" are based upon an intentional-teleological model of human action. It is assumed that the human agent is a being seeking to bring about in the world a product or a state of affairs corresponding to his or her intentions. As Marx notes in *Capital*, what distinguishes even the worst human architect from the most skillful bee is that the former projects beforehand in his mind what he intends to construct in the world, whereas the activity of the bee is instinct-guided.[44] Human action is not only teleological but intentional, or intentionality is what constitutes the teleology of human action.

This model of action is certainly not wrong. In contemporary language, the truth it contains can be stated as follows: all act descriptions which do not entail reference to the subjective intentions and purposes of human agents are underdetermined. The explanation of action requires that the intentional, first-person perspective of the agent be a constituent of any such explanation regardless of what other theoretical models of description and explanation are also employed.

Yet this model of action is a monological one. It privileges the subject-object relation and abstracts from the dimension of subject-subject relations and from the social context of action. In the first place: purposeful or intentional activity is described with the help of a *prelinguistic* model. One proceeds from a reflecting consciousness formulating its intentions and goals. While Hegel describes this activity of reflection as "the repositing of contents of consciousness," Marx resorts to the metaphor of "the image which the architect has before the eyes of his mind."[45] Goals, intentions, and purposes are described in mentalistic language as "contents" of consciousness, as "images," as what is "before the eyes of the mind." One abstracts from the linguistic mediation of these goals, purposes, and intentions through a propositional form. But the answer to the question "What do you intend, wish, want to do?" is not "I want to bring about a content of my consciousness called X or an image Y," but a reply of the sort "I intend to get an education," "I wish to help her," "I want to build a bridge or a private home in the Bauhaus style," etc. The contents or images of consciousness are linguistically mediated propositional expressions. This is not to imply that all contents of consciousness are linguistically mediated—pains, itches, tastes, and sensations may or may not be—but the kind of intentional activity we are considering in this instance most certainly is. The demonstration for this is to pose the rather simple question "What do you want to do?" Teleological-intentional activities are by definition those which we assume are performed by an agent for the reasons s/he cites in answering the question "What do you want/intend/wish to do?" The categories of objectification and externalization are so constructed as to imply that the private, prelinguistic contents of consciousness—"the images before the eyes of the mind"—

become *first* public and *shared* when one moves from "inner" to "outer," from "potentiality" to "actuality." In this sense the model privileges the subject-object relation and abstracts from the shared, social world in which humans attain their identity as persons through linguistically mediated socialization.[46] Despite his discovery of the structure of human intersubjectivity, Hegel in particular continues to describe this phenomenon in prelinguistic, mentalistic terms.

This emphasis on a prelinguistic, mentalistic model of action which treats intentions as if they were the furniture of the storehouse of our consciousness leads further to a disregard of the interpretive indeterminacy of action. By the "interpretive indeterminacy of action" I mean that human actions and the intentions embedded in them can only be identified by a process of social interpretation and communication in the shared world. This identification of the "whatness" of an action and the "whoness" of the actor is a social and communicative process, intrinsically liable of disputes of interpretation, misconstrual, and misidentification. Both what has been done and who it is that has acted emerge from such essentially contestable interpretive practices and as a consequence of the communicative give-and-take between self and other(s). Human action is linguistically mediated in a twofold sense: first, not only are what we as agents see as our purposes or wishes in the world linguistically formulated, but in the second place, others can understand what we do and who we are insofar as our actions can be retold by them as a story, as a narrative. Action unfolds within a "web of intepretations."[47]

From the standpoint of Hegelian ontology, this interpretive indeterminacy of action is a mark of its inferior status. Action is subject to an unending dialectic of "bad infinity." That moment of "being-by-oneself-in-otherness," the self-regained repose and tranquillity of Spirit, can never be achieved in the human domain. Such reconciliation is the ultimate goal of Spirit, and this can be more adequately attained if we think of action as "work," as making and shaping externality. Spirit returns to itself by reappropriating the object or externality in which it had once embodied its potentialities, faculties, and essence. This model of an interiority which empties itself out to the external world and then reabsorbs or takes back to itself what it once let go is an attempt to escape the dimension of interpretive indeterminacy. It is for this reason that to explain the meaning of self-actualization, be it of Spirit or of humanity, Marx and Hegel resort to the work model of action. To claim that an agent has actualized him/herself through an act is to claim that the potential, essence, and faculties of an agent have been unequivocally revealed in what s/he has done. This model tends to deny the linguisticality of action in the twofold sense of discussed above. First, the model of self-actualization operates with the assumption of an epistemologically transparent self, who seems to possess unequivocal knowledge for determining what would "actualize" him/her. Second, it is assumed that what this agent accomplishes in doing is fundamentally independent of what others think or claim s/he is doing. In this respect, communication is not viewed as an essential feature of the process of self-actualization. A self-transparent individual reveals, manifests, his/her essence in work.

Such activity is often described through terms as "embodiment," "transformation," or "appropriation" of externality. Whereas an object or externality may or may not "embody" the purpose of an agent—the material may be resistant, we may not know how to go about reshaping it, we may not be skillful enough in applying the rules—another subject can never "embody" a purpose. They either act or refuse to act consonant with our intentions, desires, and purposes. They are not "embodiments," externalizations, or objectifications of our will, but other subjects with whom we have to *communicate* and to whom we have to *justify* our purposes and intentions. Self-actualizing activity does not capture this dimension of human action.

Following Habermas,[48] I want to distinguish between four types of human action. These are indicated in table 4.1. This table gives an analysis of the relevant elements of each action type. Modes of analyzing these action types with other theoretical means are certainly possible. It should also be remarked at the outset that these action types are in a certain sense "ideal types." Concrete social actions or a series of social actions may involve one or more of these types: factory work, for example, can combine instrumental and strategic modes, just as a conver-

Table 4.1

Action Type	Purpose	Modality	Structure of Self/Other Relations
Instrumental	Making; bringing about a state of affairs	Subject-object relation	Technique Skills
Communicative	Communicative understanding	Multiple, but primarily subject-subject relation	Symmetry Reciprocity Understanding
Expressive	Self-realization Self-actualization	Subject-object Subject-subject	Recognition Confirmation Self-enhancement
Strategic	Command	Subject-subject	Non-symmetrical Non-reciprocal Instrumentalized human relations

sation may entail communicative and expressive action types. But an action cannot be communicative or expressive *and* strategic. These modes exclude one another.

By the "modality" of an action type, I understand the characteristic subject-object relation for each. Modality can also be described as a form of "world reference." It indicates which sphere of reality is of primary importance in each case, i.e., to which sphere the propositional expressions accompanying each action type refer. The *instrumental* type of action—under which we can include opening a beer can and repairing a bicycle, as well as constructing a nuclear power plant—has as its primary reference the objective, external world in which something is made, a state of affairs brought about. The modality of *communicative* action—speech and discourse—is the social world and the subject-subject relation; but communicative action is also meta-action. When communication breaks down in instrumental, strategic, or expressive modes of action, and one assumes a reflexive state toward the referential claims of these action types, one engages in communicative action, seeking to come to a mutual understanding.[49] In this sense, the world reference of communicative action is multiple; it can concern the object world, the world of other selves, or the inner world of the self. *Expres-*

sivist action can have two modalities: either the communication to others of our inner states, feelings, and emotions or manifestations of our capacities for their own sakes—playing the violin; painting; drama or dance. *Strategic* action is, like communicative action, primarily subject-oriented. The purpose is not to reach mutual understanding, but to have others act or speak in ways which fulfill our purposes and ends. Examples of strategic action would be dealing in the stock exchange; advertisements; military planning; and taxation and political propaganda.

By the structure of "self-other" relations is meant the kinds of norms and rules defining social interaction. In the case of *instrumental* action these are technical rules and rules of skill, corresponding to our knowledge of the external world and of its functioning.[50] In the case of *communicative* action, these rules and norms—always counterfactually anticipated by empirical speech—are symmetry and reciprocity between the participants. Agent A cannot deny certain rights in speech and argumentation to agent B without denying them to him- or herself. A and B are equally entitled to all the rights and privileges of discursive argumentation. The rules and norms of *expressivist* action are the recognition and confirmation of the uniqueness of oneself and capabilities by others, or in the case of performative-expressivist actions like dance, music, and singing, the enhancement of the self. The rules and norms of *strategic* action are characterized by non-mutuality and non-reciprocity. I can convince you through political propaganda, brainwash you through advertising, force you into deterrence through military planning, as long as you and I do not share equal chances, opportunities, resources, and knowledge.

On the basis of these action types, I want to suggest that the work model of activity discussed so far corresponds to expressive action. As can be noted from the table, expressive action can be both subject- and object-related. The dual world-reference of this type of action allowed Marx and Hegel to criticize both *instrumental* and *strategic* action types. Marx's main critique of capitalist civil society is that labor is reduced to *instrumental* activity and human relations are reified, reduced to non-reciprocal, non-mutual, *strategic* relations alone. Whereas industrial wage labor robs the worker of his or her capacity to view his or her life activity as self-enhancing and self-confirming, monetarized exchange relations institutionalize strategic social action. Hegel's critique of the bifurcation characteristic of modern societies, of their individualism, legalism, and formalism, is likewise a critique of the reduction of ethical relations to strategic ones. Although the concept of "ethical life" would seem to imply action types of the communicative sort, in Hegel's transsubjective view, freedom becomes not a mode of reciprocal, mutual action, but a form of self-confirmation and self-enhancement. In the first part of this work, I have claimed that the work model of activity, and the expressivist paradigm it relies on, both lead away from a politics of intersubjectivity to the politics of collective singularity. This has the consequence that the alternative vision of human relations, also intended by the expressivist model, is never clarified.

While the work model of activity is a fundamental premise of the position I describe as the "philosophy of the subject," it is not the only one. As will be remembered, the other two assumptions are that there is a single, collective subject called mankind or humanity, as whose activity history unfolds, and emancipation consists in "reappropriating" the legacy of this humanity. In this chapter, I have tried to clarify the relationship between the work model of activity and the politics of reappropriation in Marxism, as it substitutes humanity for *Geist*, and the working class for humanity. Whereas for Hegel the work model of activity leads to the standpoint of transsubjectivity, to that of the thinker-observer, for Marx the work model of activity leads to the politics of class, to the politics of the subject as a collective, singular entity. In both instances, this results in a denial of human *plurality*.

By plurality I do not simply mean that we are distinct bodies in space and time, but that our embodied identity, and the narrative history that constitutes our selves, give us a unique perspective on the world. Commonality and community arise and develop among us not only because we are thrust into similar life conditions, but because we create a common perspective together, and build a space of appearance from which to view the world. Plurality is the condition of embodied beings born of others like themselves.[51] The experience of becoming an "I" necessarily entails the experience of learning to distinguish one's perspective from that of others, and this entails learning to see how the world might look through the eyes of the other. It is essential to the condition described as plurality that one reaches one's perspective only as a result of the cognitive and moral process which teaches one also to recognize the presence of other perspectives in the world. Paraphrasing Aristotle, only a god or a beast has no need of the perspective of others to constitute its own.[52]

Marx's concept of class tends to deny the condition of plurality. He assumes that the likeness of the objective social conditions under which one lives is what constitutes class; yet the very distinction between a class-in-itself and a class-for-itself betrays a certain recognition that the objective determinants of action are not sufficient to generate the shared meaning of collective action as well. The process of the *formation* of collective consciousness, while being the subject of Marx's and Engels' more directly political treatises,[53] is not given a predominant place in their history of the crises of capitalism.

It should be clear that what I name "plurality" is incompatible with the transsubjective standpoint and the social epistemology implied by it. This, however, leads to a problem. Can one assume that only the *lived* perspective of social actors themselves is the locus of social truth and knowledge; can such a view be reconciled with a critical social theory that also criticizes aspects of everyday consciousness as ideological? Indeed, an exclusive emphasis on the standpoint of intersubjectivity and plurality runs the risk of wanting to construe the social world from one perspective alone. While being a healthy antidote to sociological functionalism, which happily disregards the meaning of lived experience of social actors, a single-minded emphasis on lived experience can also be distorting. A critical social theory must incorporate both perspectives. In this sense, Marx's twofold conception of crises in *Capital* remains exemplary, and what I have criticized here is not that Marx adopts this dual perspective, but the manner in which he mediates—rather, fails to mediate—between the functionalist logic of capital and the lived experience of proletarian misery and suffering, as well as resistance and struggle. Social critique must show crises not only to be objectively necessary but experientially relevant as well. In the final analysis, it is the success of the theory in translating the functional language of crisis into the experiential language of suffering, humiliation, oppression, struggle, and resistance, which bestows upon it the name of "critical theory."

I shall refer to these two dimensions of critical theory in the second half of this work as the "explanatory-diagnostic" and "anticipatory-utopian" moments of critique. The explanatory-diagnostic function of critical theory corresponds to the epistemic viewpoint of the observer, of the third (even if not exclusively). Here the social system is viewed as having internal contradictions, limitations, and crises. The anticipatory-utopian dimension of critique addresses the lived needs and experiences of social agents in order to interpret them and render them meaningful in light of a future normative ideal. Without an explanatory dimension, critical theory dissolves into mere normative philosophy; if it excludes the dimension of anticipatory-utopian critique, however, it cannot be distinguished from other mainstream social theories that attempt to gain value-free knowledge of the social world.

With this clarification, let me return to the remaining assumptions of the philosophy of the subject, namely, that history is the work of a collective singular subject and that emancipation consists in "reappropriating" this legacy. Clearly, the assumption that history is the "work" of any subject rings hollow when the work model of activity is shown to be *one* and not necessarily *the* fundamental human activity. Likewise, once we have seen through the empirical and normative equivocations of the concept of humanity—humanity as agent and as goal—this concept of history is no longer tenable.

But it would be misleading to think that twentieth-century Marxism readily gave up both presuppositions. Since the thesis of the social-historical constitution of reality through praxis is a fundamental thesis of all Marxist theory, even when the concept of a subject of history appeared dubious to most, they were unwilling to give it up altogether, and sought instead to rebuild the normative dimensions of Marxism on some modified version. This is Hokheimer's strategy in the 1937 essay on "Traditional and Critical Theory." This essay, which has given its name to an entire tradition, most clearly reveals the tension between the normative and empirical senses of the subject of history while also documenting Horkheimer's unconvincing attempts to mediate them. In fact, this essay is the beginning of a mode of theorizing in the Frankfurt School that increasingly shows that the classical Marxist paradigm of critique, and its immanent, defetishizing, and crisis-theoretical dimensions, are no longer adequate to deal with the reality of twentieth-century capitalism.

The work of Adorno, Horkheimer, and Marcuse in particular is the best demonstration of how feeble the philosophy of the subject has become. Yet they never abandon it altogether; even when the historical process seems to destroy all hope in the *revolutionary* subject, the search for *a subject* whose needs and interests might represent those of humanity as such continues. Through his emphasis on the discontinuous, refractory, and ruptured nature of social reality, Adorno, in my view, came closest to exploding the myth of the revolutionary subject from within. But these insights did not lead him to the standpoint of radical intersubjectivity and plurality; instead, the work model of activity is replaced by that of mimesis. Poiesis became poetics.

The second part of this book traces this transformation of the concept of critique from Horkheimer to Habermas. As in the first half of this work, my goal is to reconstruct the history of this theoretical shift from a systematic point of view. My concern is to uncover the systematic relationship between a certain model of activity and the conception of the subject(s), and to show once more the prevalence of the philosophy of the subject in the thought of Horkheimer and Adorno. My argument culminates in chapters 7 and 8, where I turn to examine Habermas' contribution to the question of the normative foundations of critical theory. My claim is that, despite the shift from the work model of action to that of communicative interaction, to which I am indebted, Habermas as well does not altogether dispense with the philosophy of the subject. I will try to demonstrate this with specific reference to his program of a communicative ethics.

PART TWO
THE TRANSFORMATION
OF CRITIQUE

Chapter 5

THE CRITIQUE OF
INSTRUMENTAL REASON

The red thread of ambivalence running through the corpus of Marx's writings is the tension between the "fulfillment" of capitalism on the one hand and its "transfiguration" on the other. Since his early critique of the Young Hegelians, Marx conceived the project of an emancipated society both as *fulfilling* the legacy of bourgeois revolutions via the establishment of radical democracy and as the *transfiguration* of this legacy via the elimination of the distinction between state and civil society. These two alternatives were named the "universalization of the political" and the "socialization of the universal," respectively. In the *1844 Manuscripts* a similar tension was noted between the positions described as "the philosophy of the subject" and "sensuous finitude." Finally, the two perspectives of "systematic" and "lived" crises in Marx's *Capital* were analyzed. Whereas the first terms of these sets of concepts correspond to a perspective which views emancipation as resolving the immanent contradictions of the existing order, the second terms stand for a perspective that anticipates the radically new and the radically other. What distinguishes the utopian strand of Marxism from romantic and anarchist utopianism is the insistence that the radically new and the radically other be nonetheless viewed as the "determinate" and not merely as the "abstract" negation of the existent. Utopia means "nowhere" in Greek. For critical Marxism, utopia does not have a spatial but a temporal meaning: it signifies the "not as yet," "that which can be but is not in the present."

Members and affiliates of the Institut für Sozialforschung, Max Horkheimer, Theodor Adorno, Herbert Marcuse, Leo

Löwenthal, Friedrich Pollock, and Walter Benjamin, developed their theory at a time when the "determinate negation" of the existent and the fulfillment of capitalism could only mean perpetrating the misery, suffering, and insanity of the present.[1] The disillusionment with the first experiment of socialism in the Soviet Union, and especially the experience of European fascism and the destruction of European Jewry, seemed to make insistence upon the "determinate negation" of the present futile if not immoral. Critical theory was confronted with the task of thinking the "radically new" and the "radically other."

In his 1971 Foreword to Martin Jay's *The Dialectical Imagination*, Horkheimer wrote: "The appeal to an entirely other [*ein ganz Anderes*] than this world had primarily social-philosophical impetus. . . . The hope that earthly terror does not possess the last word is, to be sure, a non-scientific wish."[2] In this extremely compact formulation, Horkheimer appears to be drawing a distinction between philosophical and scientific truth, and ascribing to philosophy the task of thinking "the entirely other." In response to the discussion generated in the *Zeitschrift für Sozialforschung* by the 1937 publication of Horkheimer's "Traditional and Critical Theory" essay, Marcuse formulates this point even more poignantly:

> When truth is not realizable within the existent social order, for the latter it simply assumes the character of utopia. . . . Such transcendence speaks not against, but for truth. The utopian element was for a long time in philosophy the only progressive factor: like the constitution of the best state, of the most intense pleasure, of perfect happiness, of eternal peace. . . . In critical theory, obstinance will be maintained as a genuine quality of philosophical thought.[3]

Neither formulation captures adequately that unique blend of philosophical reflection and social-scientific research known as "critical theory" which members of the Frankfurt School developed in the 1930s. Applying "historical materialism to itself" (Korsch), they were able to analyze the historical conditions of the possibility of Marxian political economy, and were thus confronted with the task of articulating a "critical theory of the transition" from liberal-market capitalism to a new social formation which they ambiguously named "state capitalism." The purpose of this chapter is not to explore the breadth and depth of this contribution, nor is it to trace the history of the intellectual development of the Frankfurt School; such comprehensive analyses have been undertaken by others, notably by Martin Jay and David Held.[4] Its purpose is to explore the transformation of the project of "critique" via the work of the Frankfurt School. Using the concepts of immanent, defetishizing critique and of critique as crisis diagnosis, I want to analyze how the work of Horkheimer, Adorno, and Marcuse transforms these modes of inquiry.

I shall begin with a general characterization of the transition from the critique of political economy to the critique of instrumental reason (section 1). Horkheimer, Adorno, and Marcuse develop the theory known as "the critique of instrumental reason" with the help of categories drawn from Max Weber's account of rationalization and disenchantment in the West. Their reception of Weber's work is highly ambivalent: on the one hand, they agree with Weber about the self-destructive dynamics of processes of rationalization; on the other hand, they insist that it is possible to conceive of a non-instrumental reason. They thus accept Weber's diagnosis of societal and cultural rationalization in the West, while juxtaposing to instrumental reason a utopian reason. The aporetic nature of their project is examined in section 2.

1. From the Critique of Political Economy to the Critique of Instrumental Reason

It is customary to consider the essay written by Horkheimer in 1937 on "Traditional and Critical Theory" as paradigmatic for the mode of philosophical and social inquiry developed by the Frankfurt School. Yet this essay expressed a significant reformulation of the early research program of the Institut für Sozialforschung. As the recent work of H. Dubiel, W. Bonss, and A. Söllner documents, the evolution of the research program of the Institut für Sozialforschung can be divided into three separate phases: the "interdisciplinary materialism" phase of

1932–1937, the "critical theory" approach of 1937–1940, and the "critique of instrumental reason" characterizing the period from 1940 to 1945.[5] Each of these shifts takes place in the wake of the historical experiences of this turbulent period: the prospects of the working class movement in the Weimar Republic, the appraisal of the social structure of the Soviet Union, and the analysis of fascism give rise to fundamental shifts in theory. These developments lead to reformulations in the self-understanding of critical theory: the relation between theory and practice, between the subjects and addressees of the theory, are redefined, while the interdependence of philosophy and the sciences, critical theory and Marxism, are reconceptualized. Let me begin by outlining the changing nature of the theory-practice relationship which takes place between the "materialism" and "critical theory" phases.

The essay on "Traditional and Critical Theory" was written in a period when the defeat of the German working class movement and of its parties by fascism appeared complete, and when the open Stalinist terror and the ensuing "purges" in the Soviet power apparatus had destroyed all illusions concerning this first experiment of socialism. These experiences were reflected in a reformulation of the theory-practice relation, as well as in a fundamental redefinition of the addressees of the theory.

Whereas in the period preceding 1937, truth was defined as "a moment of correct praxis,"[6] which nonetheless had to be distinguished from immediate political success, in "Traditional and Critical Theory," the relation between theoretical truth and the political praxis of specific social groups begins to appear increasingly remote. In 1934 Horkheimer could still write:

The value of a theory is decided by its relationship to the tasks, which are taken up [in Angriff genommen] at definite historical moments by the most progressive social forces. And this value does not have immediate validity for all of mankind, but at first merely for the group interested in this task. That in many cases, thought has truly estranged itself from the questions of struggling humanity, justifies, among other things, the mistrust against the intellectuals. . . . So this charge against the apparently non-committed [unbedingte] intelligentsia . . . is insofar correct, as this free-floatingness [Beziehungslosigkeit] of thought does not mean freedom of judgement, but a lack of control on the part of thinking with respect to its own motives. ("Zum Rationalismusstreit in der gegenwärtigen Philosophie," ZfS 1934:26–27)

In "Traditional and Critical Theory," by contrast, Horkheimer emphasizes not the *commonality* of goals, but the possible *conflict* "between the advanced sectors of the class and the individuals who speak out the truth concerning it, as well as the conflict between the most advanced sectors with their theoreticians and the rest of the class" (ZfS 1937:269; 215). The unity of social forces which promise liberation is a conflictual one. In place of an alliance with the progressive forces in society, in relation to whose tasks the "value" of the theory would be determined, Horkheimer now emphasizes the value of the critical attitude of the thinker whose relation to such social forces is seen as one of potential conflict and aggressive critique. "This truth becomes clearly evident in the person of the theoretician: he exercises an aggressive critique against the conscious apologists of the status quo but also against distracting, conformist, or utopian tendencies within his own household" (*ibid.*). Between the theory of society with emancipatory intent and the empirical consciousness of the social class or group who would be the agents of emancipatory transformation, there is no necessary convergence.

In "Philosophy and Critical Theory," written in response to the discussion generated by Horkheimer's essay, Marcuse expresses the existential situation which isolates and forces the intellectual "back upon himself": "What then, when the developments outlined by the theory do not take place, when the forces which should have led to the transformation are pushed back and appear to be defeated? The truth of the theory is thereby so little contradicted, that instead it appears in a new light and illuminates new sides and parts of its object. . . . The changing function of the theory in the new situation gives it the character of 'critical theory' in a more poignant sense" (ZfS 1937:636–37, my translation). "This changing function of theory" signals the growing gap between the critical truth of Marxism and the empirical consciousness of the proletariat, which the theory nonetheless continues to designate as the objective agent of the future transformation of society.

The essay on "Traditional and Critical Theory" reformulates the early materialism program of the Institute in two additional respects. The relation of philosophy to the specialized sciences, as well as the "critical" truth content of Marxism, is now redefined. In "Materialism and Metaphysics" (1933), Horkheimer had maintained that "materialism requires the unification of philosophy and science. Of course it recognizes that work techniques differ between the more general tasks of philosophy and those of the individual sciences, just as it recognizes the distinctions of method in research and the presentation of research. But it does not recognize any difference between science and philosophy as such" (ZfS 1933:23, 34). This unification of philosophy and science means that neither the specialized results nor the prevailing self-understanding of the sciences is to be uncritically accepted. They are to be reintegrated from the perspective of a materialist science of the historical totality. The materialist theory of society integrates the achievements of the specialized sciences in order to construct a picture of the societal process as an evolving dynamic totality. Such a theory knows itself to be a moment of this totality and recognizes the "conditioned" character of all thought.[7]

By contrast, in "Traditional and Critical Theory," Horkheimer no longer advocates an integration of science and philosophy, but develops a philosophical critique of the epistemological bases of the sciences.[8] He now claims that the findings of the specialized sciences cannot be integrated with philosophy without the latter exercising a critique of the foundations upon which the sciences are based. Both the specialized sciences and those philosophical theories which consider their achievements to be the only valid model of knowledge perpetuate an epistemological illusion: the object of cognition is presented as a ready-made, ahistorical reality, and the relationship of the knowing subject to this object is presented as one of passive cognition or limited experimentation. Horkheimer calls this position the standpoint of "traditional theory." Traditional theories question neither the historical constitution of their own object, nor the purposes to which the knowledge they produce is put in society. Horkheimer no longer rests satisfied with the general thesis that all thought is conditioned through life processes; instead, he analyzes the *categorial structure* of traditional scientific theories to show how the objectivist illusion of a contemplative relation to the object of knowledge is perpetrated by the very structure of this mode of thinking. Horkheimer moves from an "externalist" to an "internalist" critique of science and theory: the primary object of his attack is not the uses to which science and theory are put in society, but the manner in which the concepts, constructions, and scientific operations of traditional theories reproduce a distorted image of social reality.[9] The question can no longer be a unification of philosophy and science, nor a mere utilization by critical theory of the results of the specialized sciences. Philosophy asserts its right against the sciences in its capacity as "critique."

Horkheimer maintains that the critical theory of society has continued to be a philosophical discipline even when it engages in the critique of the economy (ZfS 1937:627/247), and names the three aspects which constitute the "philosophical moment" of the critique of political economy. First, the critique of political economy shows the "transformation of the concepts which dominate the economy into their opposites" (*ibid.*). Second, critique is not identical with its object. The critique of political economy does not reify the economy. It defends "the materialist concept of the free, self-determining society, while retaining from idealism the conviction that men have other possibilities than to lose themselves to the status quo or to accumulate power and profit" (ZfS 1937:628/248). Third, the critique of political economy regards the tendencies of society as a whole and portrays "the historical movement of the period which is approaching its end" (ZfS 1937:627/247). Horkheimer names these the "philosophical moments" in the critique of political economy, for each conceptual procedure aims at more than the empirical comprehension of the given laws and structures of society, but judges and analyzes what is in the light of a normative standard, namely, the "realization of the free development of individuals" through the rational constitution of society. For Horkheimer, it is the critique of the given in the name of a utopian-normative standard that constitutes the legacy of philosophy. The first aspect named by Horkheimer corresponds to what I have called "immanent critique" in Marx's procedure; the second to "defetishizing critique." The third aspect emphasized by Horkheimer is that of crisis diagnosis (see chapter 4, section 3). Let me elaborate each of these aspects further.

1. With the claim that the *critique* of political economy shows the "transformation of the concepts which dominate the economy into their opposites," Horkheimer draws attention to the following aspect of Marx's procedure: beginning with the accepted definitions of the categories used by political economy, Marx shows how these turn into their opposites. Marx does not juxtapose his own standards to those used by political economy, but through an internal exposition and deepening of the available results of political economy, he shows that these concepts are self-contradictory. This means that when their logical implications are thought through to their end, these concepts fail to explain the capitalist mode of production. The categories of political economy are measured against their own content, i.e., against the phenomenon which they intend to explain, and are shown to be inadequate in this regard. I have previously named this aspect of Marx's procedure immanent "categorial critique." In the second place, by claiming that "critique is not identical with its object," Horkheimer emphasizes the dimension of defetishizing critique.

2. The purpose of defetishizing critique is to show that the social reality of capitalism necessarily presents itself to individuals in a mystified form. Spontaneous, everyday consciousness, no less than the discourse of classical political economy, proceeds from the assumption that social reality is an objective, law-governed, nature-like sphere. Neither the social relations nor the human activities which give rise to this appearance of a nature-like objectivity are taken into account. "The materialist concept of a free, self-determining society" emphasized by Horkheimer (ZfS 1937:628/248) is only possible on the assumption that individuals are the *constitutive* subjects of their social world. Rather than "losing themselves in the status quo," they can reappropriate this social reality and shape it in such a way as to make it correspond to human potentials. The "idealist conviction that men have this possibility" (*ibid.*) is demonstrated for Horkheimer by Marx's procedure of defetishizing critique. In this sense critique is not identical with its object domain—polit-

ical economy. By analyzing the social constitution of this object domain and its historical transitoriness, it also brings to light the contradictory tendencies within it which point toward its transcendence. The critique of political economy aims at a mode of social existence *freed from the domination of the economy.*

3. The Marxian critique of capitalism exposes the internal contradictions and dysfunctionalities of the system in order to show how and why these give rise to oppositional demands and struggles which cannot be satisfied by the present. Critical theory diagnoses social crises such as to enable and encourage future social transformation. As Horkheimer formulates it, "Of central importance here is not so much what remains unchanged as the historical movement of the period which is now approaching its end" (ZfS 1937:647/247). He adds: "The economy is the first cause of wretchedness, and critique, theoretical and practical, must address itself primarily to it" (ZfS 1937:628/249). Yet "historical change does not leave untouched the relations between the spheres of culture. . . . Isolated economic data will therefore not provide the standard by which the human community [*Gemeinschaft*] is to be judged" (ZfS 1937:629/249).

The qualification added in these last two sentences means two things: first, although Horkheimer and Marcuse, the coauthor of the epilogue to "Traditional and Critical Theory," perceive "the economy to be the first cause of wretchedness," they are well aware of the fact that an economic crises theory alone is no longer sufficient to analyze the contradictions of the period between the two world wars; second, as historical change has a cultural dimension, crisis phenomena will not be experienced merely as economic dysfunctionalities, but also as *lived* crises. Thus the two dimensions of crisis diagnosis analyzed in the preceding chapter as "systemic" and "lived" crisis are reformulated by Horkheimer and Marcuse in light of the relation between economy and culture. Cultural and psychological relations are already singled out as domains in which individuals *live through* the crises generated by the economy. Although caused by the economy, these phenomena are not economic in nature. As their early efforts to integrate Erich Fromm's psychoanalytic studies into the research program of the institute show, Horkheimer and his co-workers are well aware of the need to develop a new social-scientific crisis theory to deal with the historical events confronting them.[10]

Even this brief analysis of Horkheimer's 1937 essay and the epilogue on "Philosophy and Critical Theory" coauthored with Marcuse reveals the unresolved tension in these formulations: on the one hand, it is acknowledged that not only is there no convergence between the standpoint of the theorist and that of working class movements, but, in fact, there is an ever-widening gap. Although critical theory names certain sectors of the working class its "addressees," the latter are viewed less and less as an empirical social group; increasingly, all individuals who share a "critical sense" are designated as the addressees of the theory. On the other hand, Horkheimer holds fast to the critique of political economy as a research paradigm and insists upon the emancipatory interests inherent in this kind of critique. The social world—indeed, objectivity as such—is said to be *constituted* by the "social praxis" of producing individuals. By "social praxis" Horkheimer in the first place understands the labor process through which the species reproduces its existence by transforming external nature. In the second place, he defines "social praxis" as the "critical human activity" corresponding to the reflective-moral attitude of the thinker who views society as a "possible object of planful decision and rational determination of goals."[11]

By referring to both objectivity-constituting labor and to critical-political activity as "social praxis," Horkheimer shows the extent to which he remains true to the philosophy of the subject. In the first place, two different kinds of activity are conflated via a single concept, whereas the transformation of externality by labor and critical-political activity which entails communication, interpretation, dispute, and organizing are clearly not the same. As has been emphasized previously (chapters 2 and 4), both the rules and the developmental dynamic of laboring activity are different from those of interpersonal communication. Whereas in the one case these rules pertain to our knowledge of nature and of nature's forces, and their development proceeds through the material accumulation of products, skills, and modes of mastery of nature, the rules pertaining to communication are constitutive of the self-identity of individuals, and these do not accumulate *in res* but only develop as *competencies* of individuals who are socialized in a linguistic and cultural community, and who become thereby certain kinds of persons. The term "praxis," which for Aristotle meant the "doing of fine and noble deeds," is used by Horkheimer in this essay equivocally to refer both to its older sense as political, moral action and to the new sense it acquires after Hegel's discovery of the emancipatory moment of labor in his Jena writings of 1805–6 (see chapter 2).

Underlying this conflation in the concept of praxis is the further assumption that these are activities of the *same* subject; here the empirical and normative senses of humanity as agent and as goal are once again collapsed into one another. Humans who are the *constituted* subjects of the historical process become its *constitutive* subjects insofar as they recognize that it is their labor, their world-transforming activity, which has shaped and formed external reality. This ideal of a constitutive subject underlies Horkheimer's critique of the "objectivism" of the sciences. Horkheimer transforms the Kantian concept of the constitution of our objects of experience via epistemic activity into the Marxian doctrine of the historical constitution of our shared, social world via the activity of labor. Once humans realize that they are the makers of history, i.e., its agents, they can take the normative step toward becoming its goal, i.e., to set self-consciously the purposes and goals which ought to govern the future course of history.

Ironically, after Georg Lukács in *History and Class Consciousness*, Horkheimer gives one of the clearest expositions of the philosophy of the subject, at a time when his own social and historical analyses show that there is no identity but rather an increasing distance between the consciousness of the working class and the critical individuals who act in its name. In view of the growing gap between the consciousness of producing individuals and those of critical intellectuals, the subjects of social praxis can no longer be assumed to be the same—if indeed they ever were. In partial recognition of this, Horkheimer maintains that the truth of the theory is to render not only the working class but all those with a "critical awareness" conscious of the fact that past history is their work. By recognizing their identity in the present with this collective, fictive subject of the past, individuals can once more reappropriate their history in the name of a better future. In these formulations the productive subject is slowly replaced by the critical one, but again a present subject acts in the name of the collective one in the past.

The precarious balance that Horkheimer brilliantly sustains in his "Traditional and Critical Theory" essay is upset by historical developments. In view of the realities of World War II, the entire Marxian paradigm of the critique of political economy appears to be thrown into question. The paradigm shift from "critical theory" to the "critique of instrumental reason" occurs when this increasing cleavage between theory and practice, between the subjects and potential addressees of the theory, leads to a fundamental questioning of the critique of political economy itself. The transformation in the nature of liberal capitalism between the two world wars and the consequences of this for the Marxian critique of political economy are developed by Friedrich Pollock in an article published in the last issue of the institute's journal, now appearing as *Studies in Philosophy and Social Science.*

In "State Capitalism: Its Possibilities and Limitations," Pollock describes the transformations in the structure of political economy that have occurred in Western societies since the end of the First World War as "transitional processes transforming private capitalism into state capitalism" (ZfS 1941:200). Pollock adds that "the closest approach to the totalitarian form of the latter has been made in National Socialist Germany. Theoretically, the totalitarian form of state capitalism is not the only possible result of the present form of transformation. It is easier, however, to construct a model for it than for the democratic form of state capitalism to which our experience gives us few clues" (*ibid.*). The term "state capitalism" indicates that this formation is "the successor of *private* capitalism, that the state assumes important functions of the private capitalist, that profit interests still play a significant role, and that it is not socialism" (ZfS 1941:201).

State capitalism radically transforms the functions of the market. The market no longer acts as the coordinator of production and distribution. This function is now assumed by a system of direct controls. "Freedom of trade, enterprise and labor are subject to governmental interference to such a degree that they are practically abolished. *With the autonomous market the so-called economic laws disappear*" (*ibid.*). If free trade, enterprise, and freedom to sell one's labor power—in short, the exchange market—are becoming a thing of the past, then the critique of the emergent social and political order can no longer take the form of the critique of political economy. First, *the institutional structure* of this new social order can no longer be defined in relation to the laws of the marketplace, and to the impersonal administration of the rule of law by the state. The increasing etatization of society, and the new prerogatives of the state, create institutional structures whose sociological significance requires new categories of analysis besides those of political economy.[12] Second, if with the "autonomous market" the so-called economic laws disappear as well, then the dynamics and crisis potentials of the new social order cannot be presented as contradictions immanent in the functioning of the economy alone.[13] Under state capitalism, economic crises are either suspended or transformed. Third, if freedom of exchange in the marketplace once actualized the *normative ideals* of liberal bourgeois society—individualism, freedom, and equality—with the disappearance of the market behind a system of direct controls, the normative ideals of liberalism also disappear. The critique of political economy alone can no longer offer access to the institutional structure, normative ideologies, and crisis potentials of the new social order.

It was emphasized in chapter 4 that the Marxian critique of political economy was at the same time a critique of the capitalist social formation as a whole. In the period of liberal capitalism, a critique of this social formation could be presented via a critique of political economy for two reasons: first, according to Marx, social relations of production defined the *institutional* backbone of liberal capitalism by legitimizing a certain pattern of the distribution of wealth, power, and authority in the society. Under capitalism, the economy was not only "disembedded" from the restraints of the social and political domain, but this "disembedded economy" in turn provided the mechanism for the redistribution of social power and privilege. Second, exchange relations in the capitalist market supplied *normative legitimation* for this society to the extent that ensuing differentials of social power and privilege were viewed as consequences of the activities of freely contracting individuals. The "autonomous market" embodied the ideals of freedom, consent, and individualism which provided the legitimation of this social order. "With the disappearance of the autonomous market," as hypothesized by Pollock, the critique of political economy can no longer serve as the basis for a critique of the new social formation.

To put it differently, *a critical social theory of state capitalism cannot be a critique of the political economy of state capitalism,* for two reasons: in the first place, with the disappearance of the autonomous market under a system of direct state controls, the social distribution of wealth, power, and authority becomes "politicized." This distribution is no longer a consequence of the laws of the market but of political directives. To analyze the social structure of state capitalism, one needs not a political economy but a political sociology. In the second place, with the "politicization" of the once autonomous market, the normative ideals and ideological foundations of liberal capitalism are also transformed. The forms of legitimation in state capitalism need to be analyzed anew: with the decline of the autonomous market, the "rule of law" also declines; liberalism is transformed into political authoritarianism and eventually into totalitarianism.[14]

The core of what has come to be known as the "critical social theory of the Frankfurt School" in the English-speaking world since the late 1960s is this analysis of the transformation of liberal nineteenth-century capitalism into mass democracies on the one hand and totalitarian formations of the national socialist sort on the other. Between 1939 and 1947, members of the Frankfurt School devoted themselves to analyzing the economic, social, political, psychological, and philosophical consequences of this shift. While Pollock's work centered around political economy, Franz Neumann[15] and Otto Kirchheimer[16] concentrated on political sociology and political theory; Horkheimer, Adorno, and Marcuse focused on developing the sociological, psychological, and philosophical consequences of this transformation. In this chapter, I will concentrate on their analysis, for it is in their writings that the philosophical consequences of the shift from the critique of political economy to the critique of instrumental reason were most poignantly worked out.

In their writings between 1939 and 1947, Adorno, Horkheimer, and Marcuse claim that under national socialism as well as in industrial mass democracies, changes in the structure of political economy have led "to the primacy of the political-administrative state apparatus over the economy."[17] The institutional organization of both social formations is characterized by the primacy of the political apparatus over the economy, the society, and the family. In a passage that correlates the transformations of the economy and of social organization with transformations in the psychic structure of the individual, Horkheimer writes:

> Today the individual ego has been absorbed by the pseudo-ego of totalitarian planning. Even those who hatch the totalitarian plan, despite and because of the huge mass and capital over which they dispose, have as little autonomy as those they control. The latter are organized in all sorts of groups, and in these the individual is but an element possessing no importance in himself. If he wants to preserve himself he must work as part of a team, ready and skilled in everything, whether in industry, agriculture or sport. In every camp he must defend his physical existence, his working, eating and sleeping place, must give and take cuffs and blows and submit to the toughest discipline. The responsibility of long-term planning for himself and his family has given way to the ability to adjust himself to mechanical tasks of the moment. The individual constricts himself. (ZfS 1941:377)

Although differences exist in this period between Marcuse on the one hand and Horkheimer and Adorno on the other, concerning the appropriate political-economic definition of National Socialism,[18] the following describes the implicit sociological model which all three utilize:

—liberal capitalism and free market competition is correlated with the liberal state, patriarchal bourgeois family, rebellious personality type, or strong superego
—state capitalism (Adorno and Horkheimer) or monopoly capitalism (Marcuse) is correlated with the fascist state, author-

itarian family, and authoritarian personality type
—or, the same economic phenomena are correlated with mass
democracies, the disappearance of the bourgeois family, the
submissive personality type, and the "automatization" of the
superego

Within the framework of this sociological model, which establishes functional relationships between the level of the organization of the productive forces, the institutional structure of
society, and personality formations, the concepts of "rationalization" and "instrumental reason" are used to describe the
organizational principles of social formation as well as the *value
orientations* of the personality, and the *meaning structures* of the
culture.

By "social rationalization" Adorno, Horkheimer, and Marcuse
mean the following phenomena: the apparatus of administrative and political domination extends into all spheres of social
life. This extension of domination is accomplished through the
ever more efficient and predictable organizational techniques
developed by institutions like the factory, the army, the bureaucracy, the schools, and the culture industry. The efficiency and
predictability of these new organizational techniques is made
possible by the application of science and technology, not only
to the domination of external nature, but to the control of interpersonal relations and the manipulation of internal nature as
well. This scientifically and technologically informed control
apparatus functions by fragmenting processes of work and production into simply homogeneous units; this fragmentation is
accompanied by social atomization within and outside the organizational unit. Within organizations, the cooperation of individuals is subject to the rules and regulations of the apparatus;
outside the organizational unit, the destruction of the economic,
educational, and psychological function of the family delivers
the individual into the hands of the impersonal forces of mass
society. The individual must now adapt him/herself to the apparatus in order to be able to survive at all.

Already the fact that the categories of "rationalization" and
"instrumental reason" are extended equivocally to refer to societal processes, dynamics of personality formation, and cultural

meaning structures indicates that Marcuse, Adorno, and Horkheimer collapse the two processes of rationalization, the societal
and the cultural, which Max Weber had sought to differentiate.[19]
This conflation on their part leads to a major problem: while
accepting Weber's diagnosis of the *dynamics* of societal rationalization in the West, they criticize this process from the standpoint of a non-instrumental paradigm of reason.[20] Yet this non-
instrumental reason can no longer be anchored immanently in
actuality and assumes an increasingly utopian character. With
this step, a fundamental change in the very concept of "critique"
takes place. This theory paradigm, known as "the critique
of instrumental reason," leads to a radical alteration of the
procedures of immanent and defetishizing critique, while the
third function of a critical theory—namely, crisis diagnosis—
disappears.

2. The Critique of Instrumental Reason and Its Aporias

The text in which this new paradigm of critical theory is most
explicitly developed and which contains *in nuce* much of the
theoretical position of the Frankfurt School after World War II
is *Dialectic of Enlightenment.* As has often been remarked,
Dialectic of Enlightenment is an elusive text:[21] a substantial part
of it was composed from notes taken by Gretel Adorno during
discussions between Adorno and Horkheimer. Completed in
1944, it was published three years later in Amsterdam and re-
issued in Germany in 1969. More than half the text consists of an
exposition of the concept of the Enlightenment, with two Excursuses, one authored by Adorno on the *Odyssey* and the other,
authored by Horkheimer, on the Enlightenment and Morality.[22]
Although in their 1969 Preface, Adorno and Horkheimer write
that "no outsider can easily imagine the extent to which we are
both responsible for every sentence" (DA, p. ix), a careful reading
of the two Excursuses reveals a tension, if not an incompatibility, between them. Whereas in the Excursus on the

Parts of section 2 have appeared previously as "Modernity and the Aporias
of Critical Theory," *Telos* (Fall 1981) no. 49, pp. 39–59.

Odyssey it is argued that the structure of Western reason as such is one of domination and sublimation, the Excursus on Enlightenment and Morality defends the weaker thesis that it is not Western reason as such which is incompatible with autonomy, but the specific instrumental form it assumes in the service of self-preservation. For Adorno, reason is governed by an identity logic, by a drive to make unlikes alike; Horkheimer criticizes reason which is in the service of the self-preservation of the individual and which is thereby instrumentalized as a means to attain ends which themselves are not rationally justified, but acknowledges that "the difficulties of the concept of reason . . . that the subjects, the carriers of this one and the same reason stand in contradictory relations, have been covered up in the Western Enlightenment behind the apparent clarity of its judgements" (DA, p. 76). In other words, Horkheimer sees in the concept of reason standards and norms which would be incompatible with its reduction to an instrument of calculation in the service of selfish ends. Nonetheless, it is more plausible to analyze the vacillations of the text between these two theses—that of Adorno, which views reason to be inherently an instrument of domination, and that of Horkheimer, who acknowledges that reason had an emancipatory force which it has since lost under current conditions—not in light of the theoretical differences between Adorno and Horkheimer, which are real,[23] but to see them as expressing the aporetic nature of the project called "the dialectic of the Enlightenment."

In the *Dialectic of Enlightenment*, Adorno and Horkheimer maintain that the two moments which constitute the legacy of cultural rationalization for Weber, namely, the value of the autonomous personality and the radical separation of nature from culture—the dualistic ontology—are mutually incompatible. The promise of the Enlightenment to free man from his self-incurred tutelage cannot be attained via reason that is a mere instrument of self-preservation. "The worldwide domination of nature turns against the thinking subject himself; nothing remains of him but this eternally self-identical 'I think' that should accompany all my representations" (DA, p. 27). These two aspects of cultural rationalism are not only incompatible but antagonistic. Their antagonism unfolds both as a dialectic of culture and as a dialectic of personality, the final consequence of which is the self-destruction of reason and the disappearance of the autonomous personality.

In order to ground this thesis, Adorno and Horkheimer investigate the psychic archaeology of the self. The story of Odysseus discloses for them the dark spot in the constitution of Western subjectivity: the fear of the self from the "other"—which they identify with nature—is overcome in the course of civilization by the domination of the other. Since, however, the other is not completely alien, but the self as nature is also other to itself, the domination of nature can only signify self-domination. The Homeric self, who distinguishes between the dark forces of nature and civilization, expresses the original fear of humanity in being absorbed by otherness. Myth, relating how the hero constitutes his identity by repressing the manifoldness of nature, also expresses the obverse side of this story. Humanity pays for overcoming the fear of the other by internalizing the victim. Odysseus escapes the call of the Sirens only by subjecting himself willingly to their torturing charm. The act of sacrifice repeatedly enacts the identity of humans with the darker forces of nature, in order to allow them to purge the nature within humanity itself (DA, pp. 51, 167). Yet as the regression from culture to barbarism brought about by National Socialism shows, Odysseus' cunning (*List*), the origin of Western *ratio*, has not been able to overcome humanity's original fear of the other. The Jew is the other, the stranger; the one who is human and subhuman at once. Whereas Odysseus' cunning consists in the attempt to appease otherness via a mimetic act by becoming like it—Odysseus offers the Cyclops human blood to drink, sleeps with Circe, and listens to the Sirens—fascism, through projection, makes the other like itself. "If mimesis makes itself like the surrounding world, so false projection makes the surrounding world like itself. If for the former the exterior is the model which the interior has to approximate [*sich anschmiegen*], if for it the stranger becomes familiar, the latter transforms the tense inside ready to snap into exteriority and stamps even the familiar as the enemy" (DA, p. 167). Western reason, which originates in the mimetic act to master otherness by becoming like it, culminates in an act of projection which, via the technology of death, succeeds in making otherness disappear. "'Ratio' which suppresses mimesis is not simply its opposite; it itself is mimesis—unto death" (DA, p. 53).

In one of the notes appended to the text, "The Interest in the Body," Adorno and Horkheimer write that "beneath the familiar history of Europe runs another, subterranean one. It consists of the fate of those human instincts and passions repressed and displaced by civilization. From the perspective of the fascist present, in which what was hidden emerged to light, manifest history appears along with its darker side, omitted both by the legends of the national state no less than by their progressive criticisms" (DA, p. 207). This interest in the subterranean history of Western civilization is no doubt the guiding methodological principle for the subterranean history of Western reason which the main body of the text unfolds. The story of Odysseus and that of the Holocaust, the myth which is Enlightenment, and the Enlightenment which become mythology are milestones of Western history: the genesis of civilization and its transformation into barbarism.

Yet Adorno's and Horkheimer's relentless pessimism, their expressed sympathy for the "dark writers of the bourgeoisie"—Hobbes, Machiavelli, and Mandeville—and for its nihilistic critics—Nietzsche and de Sade—cannot be explained by the darkness of human history at that point in time alone. As they themselves acknowledge in their 1969 Preface, "We no longer hold unto everything that had been said in this book. This would be incompatible with a theory which ascribes to truth a temporal kernel, instead of juxtaposing it as immutable to the movement of history" (DA, p. ix). Yet they insist that the transformation of Enlightenment into positivism, "into the mythology of what the facts are," as well as the thoroughgoing identity of intellect with hostility to spirit, continues to be overwhelmingly the case. They conclude that "the development towards total integration, acknowledged in this book, has been interrupted but not terminated" (*ibid.*). The concept of "total integration" already echoes Adorno's diagnosis of the "wholly administered society" and Marcuse's "one-dimensionality" thesis.[24] The critique of the Enlightenment becomes as totalizing as the false totality it seeks to criticize.

This "totalizing critique" of the Enlightenment rests upon several premises that initiate a radical break with the 1937 conception of critical theory. Let me expand: the history of humanity's relation to nature does not unfold an emancipatory dynamic, as Marx would have us believe. The development of the forces of production, humanity's increased mastery over nature, is not accompanied by a diminishing of interpersonal domination; to the contrary, the more rationalized the domination of nature, the more sophisticated and hard to recognize does societal domination become. Laboring activity, the act in which man uses nature for his ends by acting as a force of nature (Marx), is indeed an instance of human cunning. As the interpretation of Odysseus reveals, however, this effort to master nature by becoming like it is paid for by the internalization of sacrifice. Labor is indeed the sublimation of desire; but the act of objectification in which desire is transformed into a product is not an act of self-actualization, but an act of fear which leads to control of the nature within oneself. Objectification is not self-actualization but self-denial disguised as self-affirmation.

These two theses—labor as the domination of nature and as self-denial—taken together mean that the Marxian view of the humanization of the species through social labor must be rejected. Social labor, which for Horkheimer even in 1937 contained an emancipatory moment as well as a kernel of rationality, is no longer the locus of either. Both emancipation and reason have to be sought in another instance. The totalizing diagnosis of *Dialectic of Enlightenment* does not tell us where. This transformation of the activity of labor, from one of self-actualization to one of sublimation and repression, creates a vacuum in the logic of critical theory. It is unclear which activity, if any, contributes to the humanization of the species in the course of its evolution, and furthermore, which activity, if any, critique itself speaks in the name of. It is as if to compensate for the revolutionary optimism implicit in the philosophy of the subject, Adorno and Horkheimer have to swing to the quite opposite extreme of denying the emancipatory potential of labor altogether. The rather extensive use of psychoanalysis to "deconstruct" the history of Western subjectivity in the *Dialectic of Enlightenment* also shows the undiscriminating polemic to which this traditional Marxist assumption concerning human-ization through labor is subjected.

In *Dialectic of Enlightenment*, Adorno and Horkheimer inte-grate Freudian psychoanalytic theory into social theory in order to analyze the dynamics of civilization. This contrasts with the early institute interest in psychoanalysis in the context of a more sociologically specific inquiry.[25] In *Dialectic of Enlighten-ment* categories like repression, projection, and sublimation lose their historical specificity and are used to explain the genesis of a self whose very constitution they presuppose. In other words, the interpretation of Odysseus already presupposes a self in fear of losing itself in otherness, a self aware of the dangers to his continuing identity posed by the urges within.[26] Yet this self is one whose identity formation already reveals a pathological re-sistance against the blurring of boundaries. Odysseus fears mer-ger and seeks autonomy, and attains autonomy only at the expense of self-repression. Humanity's original fear from nature is already viewed by Horkheimer and Adorno as a fear of merger and a pathological resistance to otherness. They project back to the beginnings of human subjectivity pathologies which they themselves diagnose as belonging to its historical development, for the fear of otherness becomes pathological only in the case of the rigid authoritarian personality whose ego boundaries must be violently asserted. It is as if Odysseus prefigures the authori-tarian personality. The extension of psychoanalytic categories to the beginnings of Western civilization thus leads to a profound ahistoricism which greatly reduces the plausibility of this gene-alogy of the modern self.

According to Adorno and Horkheimer, the task of culture is to establish identity of the self in view of otherness, and reason is the *instrument* by which this is accomplished (DA, pp. 62–63). Reason, *ratio*, is the cunning of the name-giving self. Language separates the object from its concept, the self from its other, the ego from the world. Language masters externality, not like labor by making it work for humans, but by reducing it to an identical substratum. Whereas in magic, the name and the thing named stand in a relationship of "kinship not one of intention" (DA, p. 13), the concept which replaces the magical symbol in the course of Western culture reduces "the manifold affinity of be-

ing" to the relation between the meaning-constituting subject
and the meaningless object (DA, p. 13). The disenchantment of
the world, the loss of magic, is not primarily a consequence of
the transition from premodernity to modernity. The transition
from symbol to concept already means disenchantment. *Ratio*
abstracts, seeks to comprehend through concepts and names.
Abstraction, which can grasp the concrete only insofar as it can
reduce it to identity, also liquidates the otherness of the other.
With relentless rhetoric, Adorno and Horkheimer pursue the irrationality of cultural rationalism to its sources, namely, to the
identity logic which is the deep structure of Western reason.[27]

> When it is announced that the tree is no longer simply itself but a
> witness for another, the seat of mana, language expresses the con-
> tradiction that something is itself and yet at the same time another
> beside itself, identical and non-identical. . . . The concept, which
> one would like to define as the characterizing unity of what is
> subsumed under it, was much more from the very beginning a
> product of dialectical thinking, whereby each is always what it is,
> in that it becomes what it is not. (DA, pp. 17–18)

Here the aporetic structure of a critical theory of society, as
conceived by Adorno and Horkheimer, becomes apparent. *If the
plight of the Enlightenment and of cultural rationalization only
reveals the culmination of the identity logic, constitutive of reason,
then the theory of the dialectic of the Enlightenment, which is
carried out with the tools of this very same reason, perpetuates the
very structure of domination it condemns.* The critique of Enlightenment is cursed by the same burden as Enlightenment
itself. This aporia, which is acknowledged by Adorno and
Horkheimer themselves (DA, p. 3), is not resolved, but redeemed
through the hope that the critique of Enlightenment can nonetheless evoke the utopian principle of non-identity logic, which
it must deny as soon as it would articulate it discursively. The
end of Enlightenment, the end of the "natural sinfulness of humanity," cannot be stated discursively. If Enlightenment is the
culmination of identity logic, then the overcoming of Enlightenment can only be a matter of giving back to the non-identical,
the suppressed, and the dominated their right *to be*. Since even
language itself is burdened by the curse of the concept that re-

presses the other in the very act of naming it (DA, pp. 16–17; EoR, p. 181; KiV, p. 156), we can evoke the other but we cannot name it. Like the God of the Jewish tradition that must not be named but evoked, the utopian transcendence of the history of reason cannot be named but only reinvoked in the memory of men.

This search for a non-identitary, non-discursive reason fundamentally alters the relation of critical theory to the sciences. As opposed to the interdisciplinary materialism program of 1932–37 and the critique of scientism announced in 1937, Adorno and Horkheimer now abandon all efforts to synthesize the achievements and conclusions of the specialized sciences within a philosophical program. The abandonment of the hope that critique could proceed via an immanent analysis of the sciences to reveal the kernel of reason contained therein is accompanied by a turn to the aesthetic realm. In particular, Adorno's aesthetic theory is formulated in order to reveal the non-discursive moment of truth still contained in art.[28] This turn to aesthetics is already announced in *Dialectic of Enlightenment*. The recovery of the non-identical is the task of the true work of art: "That moment in the art work by means of which it transcends reality . . . does not consist in the attained harmony, in the questionable unity of form and content, inner and outer, individual and society, but rather, in those traces, through which discrepancy appears, and the passionate striving toward identity is necessarily shattered."[29]

The most far-reaching consequence of the project called the "dialectic of the Enlightenment" is the transformation of the very concept of critique itself. The "dialectic of the Enlightenment" is also meant to be a "critique" of the Enlightenment. When it is maintained, however, that autonomous reason is only instrumental reason in the service of self-preservation, then the Kantian project of critique in the sense of "the self-reflection of reason upon the conditions of its own possibility" is radically altered. As Baumeister and Kulenkampff rightly observe,

> Classical rationalist philosophy practiced criticism against the dogmatic assumptions and untrue contents of reason in the form of reflection upon its own pure concept. However, philosophical thought thereby remained blind to the true essence of reason and

to the defect deeply hidden in its fundamentals. It follows thereby
that critical theory, which remains true to this *claim* of reason, can
no longer assume the form of transcendental reflection and cannot
rely upon the available forms of traditional philosophy. Critique is
only possible from a standpoint which allows one to question the
constituents of the dominant concept of reason, above all, the fixed
universal contrast between reason and nature. A critical concept of
reason cannot be gained out of the self-preservation of reason, but
only from the more deeply seated dimension of its genesis out of
nature.[30]

The self-reflection of reason upon the conditions of its own possibility now means uncovering the *genealogy* of reason, disclos-
ing the subterranean history of the relationship between reason
and self-preservation, autonomy and the domination of nature.
Since, however, genealogy itself is supposed to be critique and
not a mere exercise in historical knowledge, the question returns: what is the standpoint of a critical theory that allows it to
engage in a genealogical reflection upon reason by using the
very same reason whose pathological history it itself wants to
uncover?[31]

Thus, the transformation of the critique of political economy
into the critique of instrumental reason, examined so far, signals not only a shift in the *object* of critique, but more signifi-
cantly in the *logic* of critique. The three aspects described
previously as immanent critique, defetishizing critique, and critique as crisis diagnosis are each thrown into question. It is
important to emphasize that the position named as the "critique
of instrumental reason" does not characterize the works of the
Frankfurt School in the period of the Second World War alone,
but in the post-war period as well. I will describe this transformation in the logic of critique as follows: immanent critique
becomes negative dialectics, defetishizing critique becomes the
critique of culture, and crisis diagnosis is transformed into a
retrospective philosophy of history with utopian intent.

Immanent Critique as Negative Dialectics

According to Adorno, the task of immanent critique is to
transform "the concepts, which it brings, as it were, from the
outside, into what the object, left to itself seeks to be, and con-

front it with what it is. It must dissolve the rigidity of the tem-
porally and spatially fixed object into a field of tension of the
possible and the real."[32] As Hegel had already analyzed in the
dialectic of essence and appearance, what is, is not mere illusion
(*Schein*), but the appearance (*Erscheinung*) of essence.[33] Appearance discloses and conceals its essence at one and the same time.
If it did not conceal essence, it would be mere illusion, and if it
did not reveal it, it would not be appearance. Conversely, essence is not a mere beyond. It is embodied in the world through
appearance. It is "the as yet non-existent actuality of what is."
Dissolving the rigidity of the fixed object into a field of tension
of the possible and the real is to comprehend the unity of essence
and appearance as actuality. Essence defines the realm of possibilities of what is. When the reality of appearance is understood in light of essence, i.e., in the context of its latent
possibilities, reality becomes actuality. It no longer simply is; it
becomes the actualization of a possibility, and its actuality consists in the fact that it can always transform an unrealized possibility into actuality.[34]

Undoubtedly, the immanent critique of political economy also
aimed at transforming the concepts which political economy
brought from the outside "into what the object, left to itself,
seeks to be." By revealing how the categories of political economy transformed themselves into their opposites, Marx was also
dissolving the existent "into a field of tension of the possible and
the real." In Hegelian terms, immanent critique is always a critique of the object as well as of the concept of the object. To
grasp this object as actuality means to show that what the object is, is false. Its truth is that its given facticity is a mere
possibility, which is defined by a set of other possibilities, which
it is not. Negating the facticity of what is means acknowledging
that "das Bekannte überhaupt ist darum, weil es bekannt ist,
nicht erkannt"—"The well-known is such because it is well-
known, not known."[35] This implies that a mode of knowing
which hypostatizes what is, is not true knowledge. True speculative knowledge, the standpoint of the concept, is grasping the
unity of appearance and essence, and comprehending that the
actual, because possible, is also necessary, and because necessary, also a possibility.

Adorno transforms immanent critique into negative dialectics precisely in order to undermine the speculative identity of concept and object, essence and appearance, possibility and necessity, which Hegel postulates.[36] Negative dialectics is the unending transformation of concepts into their opposites, of what is into what could be but is not. Revealing what could be does not mean postulating that it has to be. Quite to the contrary, negative dialectics strives to show that there is no end point of reconciliation and of insight into the necessity of the possible. In fact, Adorno's task is to show the superfluity of what is; to show that the object defies its concept and that the concept is bound to fail in its search for essence. Adorno undermines the very conceptual presuppositions of immanent critique which he practices. Negative dialectics becomes a dialectics of pure negativity, of a perpetual defiance of the actual. The discourse of negativity rejects precisely what Marx could still presuppose: that an insight into the necessity of what is would also lead to an understanding of what could be, and that what could be was worth striving for. Negative dialectics, by contrast, denies that there is an immanent logic to the actual that is emancipatory.[37] Negativity, non-identity, demystifying that passion with which thought strives after identity, guarantee no emancipatory effects. Or, to speak with Adorno, they guarantee that these consequences will be emancipatory, precisely because they refuse to guarantee them at all. Adorno rejects the *logic* of immanence, while preserving immanent critique. Insofar as the method of immanent critique presupposed an immanent logical development toward a growing transparency or adequacy between concept and reality, critique became dialectics, a mythology of inevitability guided by a belief in the identity of thought and being. Adorno insists upon the *mediation* between thought and being while denying their *identity*. "Totality is a category of mediation, not one of immediate domination and subjugation. . . . Societal totality does not lead a life of its own over and above that which it unites and of which it, in turn, is composed. It produces and reproduces itself through its individual moments."[38] The task of negative dialectics is to reveal the mediated nature of immediacy, without thereby falling into the illusion that all immediacy must be mediated. This could only be the case when the totality would become totalitarian, when all moments of non-identity, otherness, and individuality would be absorbed into the whole.

The second aspect of Marx's method of immanent critique was described above as "normative critique"—the juxtaposition of norm and actuality, of the self-understanding of bourgeois society to the reality of its social relations. But with the transformation of the liberal market economy into organized capitalism, the economic basis of bourgeois individualism is also destroyed. The individual, who through his own efforts and activities realized his freedom and equality in exchange relations in the marketplace, is now a historical anachronism. The normative critique of bourgeois ideology can no longer be carried out as a critique of political economy. The development of bourgeois society has destroyed its own ideals. The critique of ideologies can no longer juxtapose given norms to actuality; rather, it must demystify an actuality that is in the process of obliterating the norms that once provided its own basis of legitimation. The critique of norms must be carried out as a critique of culture, both to demystify culture and to reveal the latent utopian potential within it.[39]

Defetishizing Critique as Critique of Culture

Although Marx's analysis of the fetishism of commodities continues to provide the model for the critique of culture, this paradigm undergoes serious revisions in the work of Adorno and Horkheimer. As will be remembered, the metaphor around which the analysis of the fetishism of commodities is constructed is the reification of the social and the historical as the "natural." Since the exchange of commodities conceals the process of the production of commodities, and since the laws of the market conceal the constitution of law-likeness through concrete human activities and relations, defetishizing discourse juxtaposes production to exchange, use value to exchange value, the constitutive activity of humans to the appearances in culture. The disappearance of an autonomous sphere of exchange relations transforms the ontological priority accorded by Marx to production. The sphere of production does not stand to the sphere of circulation as essence to appearance. With the increasing rationalization of the productive sphere and the increasing integration of production and exchange, monopoly capitalism begins to develop into a social reality where all contrasts disappear and alternatives to the present become inconceivable. Horkheimer describes this transformation of social reality as reflected in the language of culture as early as 1941 as "the semantic dissolution of language into a system of signs" (ZfS 1941:377). The individual, according to Horkheimer, "without dreams or history . . . is always watchful and ready, always aiming at some immediate practical goal. . . . He takes the spoken word only as a medium of information, orientation, and command *(ibid.).* "With the decline of the ego and its reflective reason, human relationships tend to a point wherein the rule of the economy over all personal relationships, the universal control of commodities over the totality of life, turns into a new and naked form of command and obedience" (ZfS 1941:379).

This totalization of domination, the totalization of a system of signs in which human language disappears, no longer manifests itself as a sphere of quasi-naturalness that denies its own historicity. Rather, the very contrast between culture and nature, between second nature and first nature, begins to disappear.[40] The totalization of domination means the increasing manipulation of nature itself. The antagonism between nature and culture now turns into the revenge of nature upon culture. Whereas Marx had demystified the naturalization of the historical, critical theorists seek to demystify the historicization of the natural. It is the revolt of suppressed nature against the totality of domination which fascism manipulates, and it is the revolt of suppressed nature which mass industry recirculates in images of sex, pleasure, and false happiness. The repression of internal and external nature has grown to such an unprecedented proportion that the rebellion against this repression itself becomes the object of new exploitation and manipulation. Under these conditions, the "fetishism" of commodities does not distort history into nature, but utilizes the revolt of suppressed nature to mystify the social exploitation of the nature within and without us. In Adorno's language, exchange value no longer conceals the production of use values; quite to the contrary, commodities now compete with each other to present themselves in the immediacy of use values and to fulfill the nostalgia for the work of one's hands, for virgin nature, simplicity, and non-artificiality. Whereas in liberal capitalism, use value was a carrier of exchange value, under organized capitalism, exchange value is marketable insofar as it can present itself as the carrier of an unmediated use value, into the enjoyment of whose "spontaneous" qualities the advertising industry seduces us. The brutalization of nature under fascism, the seductive exploitation of nature by the mass media and culture industry, and the nostalgia for the natural and the organic, expressed by conservative culture criticism, have this in common: they manipulate the revolt of repressed nature into submission, oblivion, and pseudo-happiness.[41]

Crisis Diagnosis as Retrospective Philosophy of History with Utopian Intent

If organized capitalism has eliminated the autonomous market, if the irrationality of competing individual capitals has been replaced by a system of monopolistic state controls, what then becomes of economic crisis tendencies and potentials in such societies? In his 1941 article, Pollock had already claimed that the capacities of the system to manage and to control crises were unpredictably large.[42] In the post-war period, critical theorists emphasize that organized capitalism has eliminated crisis potentials without eliminating the irrationalities of the system. The systematic irrationalities of capitalism no longer articulate themselves as social crises. For this phenomenon, it is not the economy alone but the transformations in culture as well that are responsible.

In *Eros and Civilization*, Marcuse formulates the impossibility of social crises under conditions of industrial-technological civilization as follows: the very objective conditions that would make the overcoming of industrial-technological civilization possible also prevent the subjective conditions necessary for this transformation from emerging.[43] The paradox of rationalization consists of the fact that the very conditions that could lead to a reversal of loss of freedom cannot be perceived by individuals under conditions of disenchantment. In industrial-technological civilization, the real possibility of ending the loss of freedom is provided by the transformation of science and technology into productive forces and by the subsequent elimination of immediate labor from the work process. Labor is no longer experienced by the individual as the painful exertion of organic energy to accomplish a specific task. The labor process becomes impersonal and is increasingly dependent upon the organization and coordination of collective human effort. The diminishing significance of immediate labor in the work process, already analyzed by Marx in the *Grundrisse*, does not result in a corresponding decline of socio-cultural control over the individual.

Quite to the contrary, the impersonalization and rationalization of authority relations brings with it a corresponding transformation in the dynamics of individual identity formation (TuG, pp. 80–81). With the decline of the role of the father in the family, the struggle against authority loses its focus: the self cannot achieve individuation, for, bereft of personal figures against whom to struggle, he can no longer experience the highly personal and idiosyncratic processes of individuating identity formation. Aggression that cannot be discharged in the Oedipal struggle against a human figure is subsequently internalized and generates guilt (TuG, pp. 88–89).

The most far-reaching consequence of the disappearance of the autonomous personality is the weakening of the "living bonds between the individual and his culture" (TuG, p. 93). Ethical substance disappears. The disappearance of ethical substance in industrial-technological civilization dries up the cultural sources of group revolt which had hitherto been carried out in the name of the memories of past rebellions. The loss of culture as a repository of collective memory threatens the very dynamic of civilization itself: revolt, repression, and renewed revolt. When culture ceases to be a living reality, the memory of unfulfilled and betrayed promises in the name of which the revolt of the repressed was carried out ceases to be a historical possibility in the present.

The transfiguration of modern industrial-technological civilization must begin with an act of *Erinnerung* which sets free the forgotten, repressed, denied meanings, and utopian hopes and aspirations of past revolts. Instead of a critique of Western ontology and identity logic, Marcuse undertakes to reconstruct the latent utopian dimension of Western ontology. By revealing the polarities of Logos and Eros, of the endless passage of time and the wish to transcend all time, of the bad infinity of the existent (*die Seienden*) and the fullness of being (*die Vollkommenheit des Seins*), to be the dual structures within which Western ontology unfolds, Marcuse upholds the redemptive function of memory (TuG, pp. 198–99).

But this redemptive memory cannot be reactivated within the continuum of history, precisely because history now unfolds in such a way as to deny its own past, its own history. The one-dimensional society created by the industrial-technological world obliterates the ontological horizon within which it has developed and in which it unfolds. This means that the critical theory of society, which speaks in the name of redemptive theory, is itself outside the historical continuum; in an effort to negate the domination of time, it appeals to the memory of the wish to end all time from a point outside time.[44] Reviving the primordial polarities between Eros and Logos, Narcissus and Orpheus, Marcuse seeks to disclose the revolutionary potential of an emancipated sensuality (*Sinnlichkeit*). Narcissus emerges as the messenger of a new ontological principle (TuG, pp. 146–47). To be transformed into a new ethics (*Sittlichkeit*), the subversive potential of this new sensuality must be reimmersed in the tissues of history; but according to the one-dimensionality thesis, there can be no collective historical carriers of this process.

If, however, the subversive potential of the redemptive memory evoked by the theory remains outside the historical continuum, then has not critical theory acknowledged a fundamental aporia, namely, the conditions of its own impossibility? Critical theory analyzes a subsisting society from the standpoint of the possible transformation of its basic structure, and interprets emerging needs and conflicts in light of this anticipatory transformation. But if it is exactly the continuum of history that critique must reject, then the vision of the emancipated society which it articulates becomes a privileged mystery that cannot be related to the immanent self-understanding of needs and conflicts arising from within the continuum of the historical process. Critical theory must either revise the one-dimensionality thesis or it must question its own very possibility. This was recognized by Claus Offe in 1968: critical theory "must either limit the argument concerning all-encompassing manipulation and must admit the presence of structural leaks within the system of repressive rationality, or it must renounce the claim to be able to explain the conditions of its own possibility."[45]

This critique applies not only to Marcuse's analysis, but to the theoretical paradigm defined as "the critique of instrumental reason" in general. If it is assumed that societal rationalization has eliminated crises and conflict tendencies within the social structure, and that cultural rationalization has destroyed the autonomous personality type, then critical theory no longer moves within the horizon of *prospective* future transformation, but must retreat into the *retrospective* stance of past hope and remembrance. Critical theory becomes a retrospective monologue of the critical thinker upon the totality of this historical process, for it views the lived present not through the perspective of possible future transformation, but from the standpoint of the past.

The aporias of the mode of analysis developed under the heading of "the critique of instrumental reason" arise from the fact that by accepting Weber's diagnosis of societal rationalization, Adorno, Horkheimer, and Marcuse could no longer show society to be a contradictory totality. This means that the utopian concept of reason, in the name of which they spoke, could no longer be anchored in the present. One can interpret this outcome in two ways. First, one could claim that critique once again becomes mere criticism in the sense ridiculed by Marx in his early works, and that the critical theory of society must justify its explicit normative commitments. Second, one could argue that critical theory does not become mere criticism, for it still appeals to norms and values immanent to the self-understanding of late-capitalist societies, but that the *content* of the norms appealed to have been transformed. I will briefly elaborate each of these interpretations.

According to the first interpretation, critique becomes mere criticism for the following reasons: if crises and conflict potentials in late-capitalist societies have been eliminated; if this social structure has destroyed the very norms of rationality, freedom, and equality to which the critique of political economy could implicitly appeal; if, furthermore, the very boundaries between history and nature, culture and non-human nature have become unrecognizable; then where are the normative standards to which critical theory could appeal and how are they to be justified? The critical theorist must either speak in the name of a future utopian vision to which he alone has access, or he must play the role of memory and conscience in a culture that has eliminated its own past. Neither this utopian vision nor retrospective remembrance are based upon norms and values derived from the self-understanding of this culture and social structure. The standpoint of the critic transcends the present and juxtaposes to the existent what *ought* to be or what *could* have been had the past not been betrayed. Critique itself, then, is a mode of explicit criteriological inquiry. Marx's commentary on mere criticism can now be applied to the position of the Frankfurt School itself: "The reflection of the critical subject, who believes to have preserved for himself a truly free life and the historical future in the form of an appeal, remains self-righteous over and against all instances; Marx, who had already recognized this privilege to be the case of the Bauer brothers, therefore spoke ironically of the 'holy family.' "[46]

Against this interpretation, which reduces the position of the Frankfurt School to that of the "holy family," it can be argued that while the critique of political economy no longer serves as a paradigm for the Frankfurt School, there are still norms and values immanent to the culture of late-capitalist societies that have an emancipatory content. However, these norms and values are no longer provided by rationalist natural law theories, whose embodiment in the institutions of liberal-capitalist society Marx could take for granted. It is no longer the norms of a bourgeois public sphere, of the liberal marketplace and of the liberal state, practicing the rule of law, to which critique can appeal. With the transformation of political domination into rational administration, the rational and emancipatory content of the natural law tradition has been emptied out. Emancipatory norms are no longer immanent in public and institutional structures. Instead, they have to be searched for in the unredeemed utopian promise of culture, art, and philosophy (Adorno), or in the deep structures of human subjectivity that revolt against the sacrifices demanded by an oppressive society (Marcuse).

Adorno, who insists upon the unredeemed utopian potential of absolute Spirit, could therefore begin *Negative Dialectics* with the following sentence: "Philosophy, which once seemed to have been overcome, remains alive, for the moment of its actualization has been missed."[47] Since the promise of philosophy to be one with a rational actuality (Hegel) or to be a material weapon of the masses who are about to actualize reason (Marx) has failed, it must engage in ruthless self-criticism. This self-criticism of philosophy must reactivate the illusion to which philosophy owes its continued existence—the illusion, namely, that philosophy could become actuality. On the other hand, this illusion must be demystified, for it betrays the arrogance of conceptual thinking that considers its other, that which is not thought, to be a mere vehicle for the actualization of thought. Actuality is not the vessel into which thought empties itself, although it is this striving toward the unity of thought and actuality that gives philosophy its *raison d'être*. This aporia must not be abandoned, but continually practiced and revived through negative dialectics. Adorno himself names his critique one of "dissonance." It is the dissonance between thought and actuality, concept and object, identity and non-identity, that must be revealed.[48] The task of the critic is to illuminate those cracks in the totality, those fissures in the social net, those moments of disharmony and discrepancy, through which the untruth of the whole is revealed and glimmers of another life become visible. In an essay on the possibilities of social conflict in late-capitalist societies, Adorno can thus advance the otherwise astonishing claim that the conflict potentials of society are not to be sought in organized, collective protest and struggles, but in everyday gestures like laughter: "All collective laughter has grown out of such scapegoat mentality, a compromise between the pleasure of releasing one's aggression and the controlling mechanisms of censure, which do not permit this."[49] When one demands a strict sociological definition of social conflicts, then one blocks access to such experiences which are ungraspable, but "whose nuances contain likewise traces of violence and ciphers of possible emancipation" (*ibid.*).

Through his method of emancipatory dissonance, Adorno becomes an ethnologist of advanced civilization, seeking to reveal those moments of implicit resistance and suffering in which the human potential to defy the administered world becomes manifest. It is unclear, however, that these "ciphers" of possible emancipation to which Adorno appeals can justify the normative standpoint of critical theory. The charge that the critique of instrumental reason articulates the privileged discourse of a "holy family" is still left unanswered. Thus the transition from the critique of political economy to the critique of instrumental reason, examined in this chapter, alters not only the content criticized but the very method of critique itself. Through this transformation, the validity of the standpoint of critique is put into question.

APPENDIX

Lukács, Weber, and the Frankfurt School

The reception of Weber's work by Adorno, Horkheimer, and Marcuse was primarily influenced by Lukács' synthesis of the Weberian category of "rationalization" with the Marxian category of "reification" in *History and Class Consciousness* (pp. 83–110). Restricting himself to Weber's claim that processes of Western modernization and industrialization led to the increasing predominance in all spheres of life of a *formal-rational* orientation, Lukács claimed that such an orientation was required by the predominance of the commodity form. For Weber, "formal rationality" signifies a cognitive as well as a practical orientation toward reality. As a cognitive attitude, formal rationality means the attempt to comprehend reality by means of "increasingly precise and abstract concepts" ("The Social Psychology of World Religions," p. 293), enabling prediction and the instrumental control and organization of phenomena. This cognitive attitude is accompanied by a practical-instrumental attitude, according to which social action is increasingly oriented to the attainment of given ends by "means of an increasingly precise calculation of adequate means" (*ibid.*) on the basis of "universally applied rules, laws or regulations."[50] This mode of action is characterized by Weber as "purposive-rational" (*Zweckrational*). Instrumental action subordinates both the technical control of outer nature and the strategic control over other humans to predictable, homogeneous, calculable, and impersonal rules. It is this aspect of Weber's analysis of rationalization processes that Lukács synthesizes with the Marxian analysis of the commodity form.

For Lukács, the commodity is the "cell" of capitalist social relations: it reveals a structure which is reproduced in all spheres of life, from the organization of the work place to law to bureaucratic administration, and even to cultural products.[51] The secret of the commodity form is the establishment of abstract equivalence: not only can all sorts of goods be equated and exchanged with one another in virtue of being commodities, but human activities and relations as well are commodified, i.e., reduced to abstract equivalence. The establishment of equivalence among qualitatively different things and human activities requires that one abstract precisely from those substantive, concrete characteristics that distinguish them from one another. This process of abstraction is a societal one: it is not a mental act performed by individuals, but corresponds to a real social process. As monetarily regulated exchange relations spread with the rise of the modern marketplace, and as capitalist social relations get established via the purchase and sale of labor power as a commodity, abstract equivalence becomes socially institutionalized. Concrete objects and activities, which are different from one another, are equated by means of their equivalence to a third—money. What can be made equivalent can also be measured in light of this equivalence; it can be quantified into homogeneous units each of which is considered identical in value. In a capitalist economy, it is the magnitude of socially necessary labor time that serves as the measure of value. Human labor power is bought and sold in the marketplace as a certain quantity of labor time, while commodities are viewed as congealed forms of labor time.

According to Lukács, the spread of formal-instrumental rationality and the commodity form are two sides of the same coin. A formally correct technical and strategic orientation to the world, governed by predictable and calculable rules, requires the reduction of social reality to divisible, abstract, homogeneous, and equatable units. Such an "ontological reduction"[52] of social reality takes place under capitalism via the logic of the commodity form, the secret of capitalist production. Lukács thus claims that the spread of formal rationality in the spheres of law, social organization, and state bureaucracies, analyzed by Weber, is only possible on the basis of a thoroughly capitalist economy. The commodity form is the mechanism by which formal rationality is produced and reproduced in the social world.

This analysis by Lukács, who had been a member of the Max-Weber Kreis in the 1920s, can be supported by reference to Weber's own work. Weber himself acknowledged that capitalism, which is "identical with striving toward profit in the continuous, rational business organization," "requires the rational-capitalist organization of [formally] free labor."[53] Neither rational bookkeeping nor the spread of monetary exchange relations is sufficient for the long-term institutionalization of the profit motive in society. This is only achieved when free labor, sold as a commodity in the marketplace, is organized into "industrial" wage labor in the modern factory. Weber also acknowledges that the bureaucratic organization of the law and state administration in a formally rational manner is only possible in the long term if a capitalist economy based on wage labor persists. Although not unsupported by Weber's own work, Lukács' brilliant synthesis of Weber nonetheless diverges from the main intention of Weber's *oeuvre*.

Lukács' own phenomenological social analysis, which sees in the commodity form a "cell" that gets reproduced in all spheres of life, is incompatible with Weber's methodological nominalism. As Merleau-Ponty has observed, in his complex analysis of the genesis of rationalization processes in the West, Weber neither attributes causal predominance to some element over others, nor does he point to a single logic of rationalization that forces its way into different spheres of life. "Each of these elements," writes Merleau-Ponty, "acquires its historical significance through meeting others. History has often produced one of them in isolation (law in Rome, elements of calculation in India). . . . But their meeting strengthens in each the pattern of rationality it contains. . . . But at the beginning it is not an omnipotent idea, but a sort of *imagination of history* that gathers together here and there elements that are capable of being integrated one day."[54] Lukács' methodological orientation is hardly compatible with what Merleau-Ponty calls "the imagination of history" at work in Weber's writings, but it has been decisive for the subsequent reception of Weber's work by the Frankfurt School: behind the discontinuous, contradictory, and sometimes inconclusive strands of rationalization processes analyzed by Weber, they have searched for a single logic of explanation, be it the commodity form or the predominance of identity logic or instrumental reason.

Chapter 6

AUTONOMY AS
MIMETIC RECONCILIATION

In the first part of this book I have argued that the development of the Kantian critique of pure reason into a critique of political economy by Marx presupposed the following contribution by Hegel: Hegel criticized Kant for not being radical enough in the critique of pure reason, for leaving unexamined the genesis and the constitution of the subject, of the knowing and thinking self. According to Hegel, the self-reflection of reason upon the conditions of its legitimate employment has to include a self-reflection upon the genesis and constitution of the very subject of critique. For Hegel, the critical attitude is the product of a culture and society divided against itself and in which the individual is juxtaposed to the community, morality against legality, and inclination against duty. Grasping the social totality out of which critique emerges means transcending critique by recognizing the actualization of reason in the present. Reason has to be situated in a totality of human relations. Hegel no longer views autonomy as an act of individual self-legislation, but as the process of self-actualization of the collective subject. The bond between critique and autonomy, between the self-reflection of reason and the realization of freedom, is nonetheless maintained.

Marx remains true to Hegel's critique of Kant insofar as for him as well, the promise of autonomy cannot be a mere "ought" but must be fulfilled in historical reality. Autonomy is an ideal which capitalist society itself brings forth but which cannot be realized under it. The autonomy of the individual is a necessary illusion of the capitalist mode of production, for this system develops in such a way as to rob humans of collective control over their conditions of existence. Under the imperatives of the accumulation of capital, the real human wealth implicit in this society is reduced to the mere accumulation of material wealth. On the one hand, capitalism generates real human wealth, needs, and dispositions transcending the system; on the other hand, it limits and stultifies these by defining wealth, not in human terms, but in terms of the ever-intensified production of commodities. Autonomy can only be realized when human beings appropriate the social essence of their activities, an essence which now faces them as the law of capitalist development. For Marx, then, the critique of the capitalist mode of production serves the realization of collective autonomy insofar as it makes individuals aware of the internal contradictions of a system which posits autonomy as an ideal while negating it in practice.

This relation between the method of critique and the ideal of autonomy undergoes a transformation in the work of the Frankfurt School. If, as the *Dialectic of Enlightenment* announces, domination is not simply the consequence of a rationality whose potentials capitalism frustrates; if, in fact, reason itself is an instrument of domination, then the ideal of self-legislating reason is also an ideal of domination: autonomy does not mean self-actualization but self-repression, the repression of the nature within and without us. Autonomy, which for Kant ultimately required the realization of a "Kingdom of Ends" among free and equal subjects, is in reality the ideal of subjects who pursue their own ends at the cost of dominating others and repressing themselves. If relations of domination are part of the natural history of reason, of its emergence as a species-specific capacity, then the critique of instrumental reason must go beyond mere self-reflection. Between the content reflected upon—the natural history of reason—and the faculty of reflection there is no mirroring, but a tension and a struggle. The critique of the Enlightenment can only be written as a "dialectic" of the Enlightenment in which the tension between content and procedure, the object and the subject of critique is revealed.

The dialectic of the Enlightenment does not present the phenomenology of reason, but its archaeology.[1] What one learns from Hegel is not that reason can only reach self-knowledge when it recollects or remembers itself in all its instances, but

that the history of reason is based upon forgetfulness and repression. Consciousness does not know its own genesis; furthermore, it develops its own experience only insofar as it forgets
what it once had been. Similarly, to develop into the subject of
instrumental reason, to become autonomous in this traditional
sense, the self must forget and repress those impulses and needs
which intimate another mode of being, a reconciliation with
otherness. The dialectic of the Enlightenment is critique in the
sense of "psychoanalytic reflection": what is forgotten cannot be
recalled at will; all forgetting originates with a trauma. The
forgotten can only be recalled, made present to oneself, in the
effort to relive the trauma and break the spell of the past upon
the present. The access to this traumatic content brings one
closer to those repressed wishes and desires whose memory is
painful precisely because they had to be repressed. Likewise, the
dialectic of the Enlightenment requires reason to face its own
traumatic content and to recollect what it has forgotten—a possible mode of otherness, a recollection of the nature within the
subject, a reconciliation with otherness. Only through such a
process of psychoanalytic reflection can one gain access to the
true meaning of autonomy. The traditional ideal of autonomy is
simply the ideal of a reason which remains unknown to itself
because it cannot confront the history of reason's own self-
denial. "Of ourselves," wrote Nietzsche, "we are not knowers."[2]

In their psychoanalytic reformulation of the concept of autonomy, Adorno and Horkheimer ironically return to one of Hegel's
main criticisms of Kantian morality, that is, to the contradiction
between duty and inclination, between the moral law and the
affective-emotive constitution of the individual (see chapter 3).
This contradiction between duty and inclination reveals to them
the secret bond between autonomy and self-repression, between
the ideal of a community of reason and the egoistical practices
of individuals. The disjunction between virtue and happiness,
the postponement of their reconciliation to the Kingdom of
Ends, shows at once Kant's profound honesty and his blindness.
Indeed, as Kant saw, under conditions of domination and repression, virtue and happiness cannot be reconciled; but this lack of
reconciliation does not derive from the pure structures of practical reason, as Kant thought, but from certain specific historical

and material arrangements. Particularly in his pre-1937 writings, Horkheimer analyzes the antinomies of Kantian moral philosophy in light of the antinomies of bourgeois society. These early essays of Horkheimer practice the method of immanent critique, and they must not be confused with the psychoanalytic turn of the *Dialectic of Enlightenment*. What is interesting is that the problem of duty and inclination, which later lends itself to such a powerful psychoanalytic critique, is already at the center of these early essays as well.

The goal of this chapter is to examine the concept of autonomy in the writings of Adorno and Horkheimer such as to clarify the alternative normative model of human activity and subjectivity upon which they base their critique of instrumental reason, and of the society and culture of twentieth-century capitalism. Hegel and, following him, Marx view autonomy as self-actualizing and expressive activity. For Adorno and Horkheimer, autonomy becomes *mimesis*. This model of mimetic activity, I want to argue, is a reversal but not a true negation of the work model of activity discussed in the first part of this work. I shall first examine Horkheimer's early critique of Kant (section 1). Subsequently, I shall look at Adorno's analysis of Kantian moral philosophy in *Negative Dialectics*. Finally, I will discuss the presuppositions of the philosophy of the subject underlying their understanding of autonomy (section 2). My conclusion is that the question concerning the normative foundations of critical theory, posed in the preceding chapter, remains unanswered.

Before proceeding, let me explain why Marcuse's concept of autonomy will not be included in this discussion. Despite all theoretical convergence with Adorno and Horkheimer about the role of psychoanalytic theory, and agreements at the empirical level about the changing role of the family and developments in self-formation, Marcuse grounds autonomy not in the aesthetic realm, but in a theory of needs. In this respect, he remains much closer to the project of philosophical anthropology than do either Adorno or Horkheimer, and gives the longing for "the wholly other" a more immanent, subjective grounding. This emphasis on the felt and lived truth of the individual distinguishes Marcuse's project from that of mimetic reconciliation, despite the fact that the ideas of the "resurrection of nature" and

"reconciliation with the other" are no less significant in his
work. For Marcuse, such reconciliation is rooted in the individual longing for happiness. The difficulty with Marcuse's concept
is not his faithfulness to the philosophy of the subject, but his
monological model of need interpretations (see chapter 8).

1. Autonomy and Self-Preservation (*Selbsterhaltung*)

The fundamental concept through which Horkheimer characterizes the moral vision of early bourgeois philosophical
anthropology—the theories of Machiavelli, Hobbes, Locke, and
Mandeville—is that of "self-preservation." The concept of "self-
preservation" has an empirical as well as a normative dimension: as an empirical concept, it describes a mode of activity the
goal of which is the "preservation" or maintenance of the self.
What lends this concept its peculiar force in early bourgeois
philosophical anthropology is the normative assumption that it
is "right" or "reasonable"—in the moral sense—for the self to act
in such a way as to "preserve" itself. Horkheimer's effort in two
of his major pre-critical-theory essays, "Materialismus und
Moral" (Materialism and Morality) of 1933,[3] and "Egoismus und
Freiheitsbewegung: Zur Anthropologie des bürgerlichen Zeital-
ters" ("Egoism and the Movement for Emancipation: On the Anthropology of the Bourgeois Period") of 1936, is to analyze the
antinomies of bourgeois philosophical anthropology and moral
theory in light of the concept of self-preservation.

By choosing the concept of self-preservation to characterize
the moral views of bourgeois philosophical anthropology,
Horkheimer draws attention to a fundamental ambivalence in
these theories. This ambivalence is rooted in the twofold, empirical and normative, connotations of the concept; more precisely,
in the transition from its descriptive to its evaluative uses, in the
course of which the concept acquires a moral status in these
theories. The concept of self-preservation has a long history in
ancient and medieval thought.[4] In the Aristotelian as well as in
the Stoic traditions, "self-preservation" meant primarily the
preservation of the species and the conservation of the individual through species-specific activities. Characteristic for this

early usage of the concept was the assumption that the activity of self-preservation could be defined in the context of a theory of natural kinds: those activities which are species-specific are those which promote self-preservation. Admittedly, as even Aristotle saw, for a species like the human one, a simple cataloging of species-specific modes of behavior would not suffice to determine the goal of self-preservation. Nonetheless, there was no principal incompatibility between the teleology of self-preservation and the ethical-political activity of praxis, insofar as praxis was also species-specific and was the mode in which humans actualized themselves. For the tradition, self-preservation was a teleological concept.[5] Both components of the term—the self and the activity of preservation—could be defined univocally by means of a teleology of reason, the task of which was to help humans realize the correct order of nature in their lives.

That the modern use of this concept stood in an uneasy relation to the traditional one is nowhere more evident than in chapter 14 of Hobbes' *Leviathan*.[6] On the one hand, echoing premodern, particularly Stoic traditions, Hobbes writes that the law of nature is a rule of reason which dictates "that every man, ought to endeavor Peace, as farre as he has hopes of obtaining it; and when he cannot obtain it, that he may seek, and use, all helps and advantages of warre."[7] On the other hand, the fundamental right of nature, which is that of self-preservation, means that every individual is entitled to all the means through which he can preserve himself, and this reduces to "the right of all against all."[8] The "right of self-preservation" and the "law of nature" are no longer in harmony. The goal of individual self-preservation does not lead to peace, but to the universal war of all against all. As Hobbes remarks, "jus" and "lex" are opposed concepts: the one signifies liberty, the other, restrictions upon this liberty.[9]

The fact that the goal of individual self-preservation and the attainment of peace dictated by the law of nature contradict one another means the following: neither the self nor the activity through which such a self seeks to preserve itself can be univocally defined by reference to a theory of natural kinds. The Hobbesian self in search of preservation is motivated by the goals of gain, ambition, honor, and diffidence. Each defines the good as what is pleasing to him. The task of reason is precisely to overcome the state of nature by indicating how the attainment of self-preservation requires a civil order in which competition, conflict, and property relations can be contractually regulated. Self-preservation is a goal for Hobbesian individuals: they cannot act otherwise, but this teleology of their actions can no longer be defined in light of a natural order. Reason is required to control and to master nature, primarily human nature.

Hobbes' analysis contains many of those elements which are of significance for Horkheimer's reconstruction of early philosophical anthropology: the destruction of a teleological conception of natural kinds as a morally orienting vision; the assumption that humans are motivated by drives and interests which place them in conflict with one another; and the thesis that the civil order is based upon reason, the task of which is to control human nature and to neutralize the destructive consequences of its unleashed development. In "Egoismus und Freiheitsbewegung," Horkheimer draws attention to one additional aspect of these theories: the reduction of the characteristics of human nature to mere "matters of fact." The "realism" of the natural right theories, criticized by the young Hegel for its purportedly "objective," "empirical" view of human nature, is criticized by Horkheimer as well:

> What humans are should no longer be demonstrated via an exegesis of revelation or by appeal to other authorities, but in the last instance by reference to immediately accessible matters of fact. Knowledge of humans becomes a special problem for the natural sciences. (ZfS 1936:162)

According to theories of self-preservation, human nature as it is must be viewed as a given fact, and reason must be regarded as a means by which to protect individuals against the destructive consequences of the untrammeled pursuit of self-interest. Horkheimer uses the term "subjective reason" to designate this conception and contrasts it to the "objective reason" of the tradition according to which the goals and norms of human life were embedded in a general conception of the world. In a later essay, "On the Concept of Reason" (1951), Horkheimer describes the transition from "objective," premodern reason to the "subjective," modern one as follows: "The latter—the concept of subjective reason—constitutes a moment of Enlightenment in the traditional sense, the philosophical expression of demythologization, of the disenchantment [*Entzauberung*] of the world, as Max Weber has described this process."[10]

According to Horkheimer, when considered against this background, Kantian moral philosophy originates not only with human search for normative standards in a disenchanted universe, but in its deepest formulations remains true to the demands of subjective reason in the service of self-preservation. The opposition between human nature and reason is transformed by Kant into a metaphysical dualism between the phenomenal and noumenal realms. Caught between the laws of human nature which dictate that the goal of our voluntary actions be "some good to ourselves" and the dictates of reason which demand a world in which none shall be treated as a means but always as an end, Kantian moral philosophy reveals the profound antinomies of idealism. These antinomies derive from the fact that the idealist conception of reason, which also points toward a negation of the existing order, nonetheless remains faithful to the so-called "facts" of human nature discovered by subjective reason.

Viewed in this light, the truth expressed by Kantian moral theory is that human actions which are dominated by the law of economic self-advantage are not also rational. The *metaphysical dualism* between the phenomenal and noumenal realms in Kantian theory is regarded by Horkheimer as reflecting the *social dualism* of bourgeois society: on the one hand, there exists a sphere of economic activity in which individuals are motivated by self-interest and the search for profit; on the other hand, there is posited a realm of the public, rational, common good. Horkheimer sees the strength of Kantian moral philosophy precisely in that Kant, unlike utilitarian moral theorists, does not attempt to derive morality from the principle of self-interest, but insists upon the antagonism between actions governed by self-interest and actions performed out of respect for the moral law. Nonetheless, in eternalizing the conflict and in giving it a metaphysical basis, Kant conceals the real historical situation out of which his moral theory emerges.

Following Marx's analysis of exchange processes under capitalism (see chapter 4), Horkheimer claims that under conditions where social life is produced by individuals through the
pursuit of property and profit, the mediation between individual activity and the common good, between the individual and
the universal, appears unintelligible (ZfS 1933:167). In this period, economic advantage is the natural law to which individual
life must submit. The conflict between duty and inclination,
between desire and reason, in Kantian moral theory is not based
upon psychology, but upon an implicit sociology. Instead of
seeking a solution to this conflict via a teaching of "rational
desire" like Hegel, Horkheimer insists upon facing the dichotomy and tracing it back to its origins. His question is: what
social conditions make it necessary for individuals to experience the moral law as an "imperative," as an "ought" from which
they are all selfishly inclined to escape? What social forces
shape the human psyche which the moral imperative should
control?

In this context, Horkheimer suggests a distinction which is of
great importance for understanding his concept of autonomy:
the distinction between *moral reflexivity*, the capacity of individuals to distance themselves from their own needs and inclinations and to reflect upon them critically, and the Kantian
assumption that such reflexivity can only be realized when individuals adopt a "universal law" as the maxim of their actions.[11]
At the beginning of the "Materialism and Morality" essay, Horkheimer values the moral reflexivity ushered in by the modern
period in a thoroughly positive light: "That humans try to decide for themselves whether their actions are good or bad is
evidently a late historical development. . . . The capacity to subject instinct-like reactions to moral criticism and to change
them on the basis of individual considerations, could first develop with the increasing differentiation of societies" (ZfS
1933:162; also 1934:190). The increase in moral reflexivity must
not be confused, however, with an authoritarian model of moral
imperatives. As long as the conflict between individual interests
and the struggle for self-preservation on the one hand, and the
common good on the other, is not resolved, moral reflexivity
cannot be truly attained. For, in a competitive society based

on property and profit, social necessity will continue to frustrate the decision powers of individuals. If the process of self-reflection which bourgeois society initiates is to be fulfilled in truly autonomous fashion, then those social conditions which drive individuals to behave as if they were governed by blind natural laws must be altered. Autonomy presupposes moral reflexivity; but this capacity, in turn, requires certain social preconditions to develop fully.

Although in the last instance Horkheimer analyzes the issue of moral reflexivity in light of the Marxian categories of political economy, he touches upon a question which is essential to an ethics of autonomy. In Kantian moral theory, the ability of the subjects to act reflectively on the basis of general moral principles is identified with their ability to act on the basis of the categorical imperative alone. Kant assumes that the capacity for moral reflexivity is fully captured by acting on the basis of the moral law. But the Kantian subject does not reflect upon the moral law; rather, the moral law is said to present a priori the only content which can oblige such an agent. In Kantian ethics, moral reflection is not an aspect of the *generation* of moral principles, but of their *application* only. Kant proceeds deductively in his moral theory and presents moral subjects with a categorical imperative which, he claims, is the only one compatible with the principle of autonomy. But is it necessary that an ethics of autonomy be identified with the a priori content of the law of morality as formulated by Kant? Although I am thereby expanding the problem in a somewhat different direction from the one followed by Horkheimer, I think this interpretation allows us to see more clearly what Horkheimer only intimates in this essay—namely, that the norm of autonomy and the ideal of moral reflexivity may have a content which go beyond the traditional formulations of Kantian moral theory.

A second issue suggested by Horkheimer's critique of Kant is the following: it astonishes many readers of Kant that the law of autonomy, of self-legislation, is often constructed in analogy with the "natural law." "Act in such a way that the maxim of your actions can become a universal law of nature through your will," reads one of the formulations of the categorical imperative in the *Groundwork*.[12] Through this formulation, Kant may have wanted to express the idea that the moral law, like laws of nature, forbids exceptions and is valid at all times and in all places.[13] Horkheimer's analysis illuminates the *rigidity* and *compulsiveness* implicit in this formulation, by tracing it back to its social origins. The moral law, which represents reason, and which expresses the societal as opposed to the individual point of view, is presented as if it were a law of nature. This means, according to Horkheimer, that universality or the standpoint of the social is identified by Kant with a nature-like compulsion. This is perfectly consistent with the standpoint of a social order where society is reduced to economic exchange relations, to a "system of needs."

> Due to the lack of a rational organization of the social whole, . . . the individual cannot recognize himself in his true relation to the whole and knows himself only as an individual, who is also concerned for the whole, without it ever becoming clear to him what and how much he actually affects in this whole through his self-intrested actions. (ZfS 1933:167)

The *moral point of view*, which necessarily entails the perspective of others who constitute the social whole,[14] cannot be realized as long as the basis of their *social togetherness* remains a mystery for the individuals, as is necessarily the case in a "system of needs." Conversely, it holds that the more opaque the context of social relations in which individuals stand becomes for them, the less likely that they can realize the moral point of view. Toward the end of the essay, Horkheimer sounds a theme which is to build a cornerstone in the later analyses of fascism by the institute:

> The world appears to be driving towards a catastrophe or rather to find itself in one. . . . The meaninglessness of the individual's fate, which was determined in earlier phases through the lack of reason, through the mere nature-likeness of the process of production, has become in this period the most urgent feature of existence. . . . Each is a victim of blind chance. The course of his existence stands in no relation to his inner possibilities, his role in current society has in most cases no relation to what he could reasonably achieve. (ZfS 1933:183)

Under such social conditions, the ideal of autonomy is threatening to become a historical chimera. "We no longer see humans as the subjects of their fate," continues Horkheimer, "but as objects of a blind natural process and the answer of moral feelings in face of this situation is pity [*Mitleid*]" (ZfS 1933:183–84).

The transformation of liberal, individualistic capitalism into the competition of supra-individual economic units like cartels and monopolies in the period between the two world wars alters the basis of moral feelings among individuals.[15] For Kant, the dominant moral feeling was *respect*—respect for the moral law and respect for others as rational beings capable of morality. Such respect was possible, argues Horkheimer, because there was a commensurability between the activities of the individual and his or her social fate, or at least this had been the case for the propertied middle classes. As the world economic crises of this period continue, the material basis of the social achievement of autonomous individuals is destroyed. The more helpless individuals become in the face of economic pressures and impersonal economic organizations, the more they lose the basis of self-respect and respect for others. Under such conditions, the feeling of pity replaces that of respect. For Horkheimer, our moral feelings have a social history. Moral feelings are called forth and shaped by social realities: when the social bases of reciprocity are destroyed, when social achievement and individual effort no longer bear a relation to one another, the moral feeling of respect is also weakened—when not eliminated.

These considerations suggest that for Horkheimer the moral point of view indeed entails universality, but a social, not metaphysical, universality. In Kantian moral philosophy, by contrast, it is assumed that empirically distinct individuals qua moral selves are all identical. The moral law which articulates the content of practical reason is valid for all in virtue of being valid for one. From the standpoint of the moral law, the "I" is a "we" and the "we" is an "I." This tautological identity of moral selves is contradicted by their empirical plurality and societal antagonism. The moral universal in Kantian moral theory, therefore, is an apparent, not a genuine, one. Horkheimer suggests that the universality entailed by the moral point of view has to be viewed as social. Here the task is not to establish the tautological identity of the "I" and the "we," but to bring about genuine universality by reconciling the standpoint of the "I" and the "we" socially. As with the problem of moral reflexivity, once we expand Horkheimer's categories beyond their restriction to the perspective of political economy, they offer suggestions for a more fundamental critique of Kantian moral theory. But ultimately Horkheimer's suggestions are circumscribed by a set of assumptions which render them implausible. Let me expand.

Horkheimer's discussion of justice, which anticipates some of Marcuse's later formulations concerning "necessary" and "surplus repression,"[16] points to a fundamental limitation in his analysis. He suggests that in a just order "the inequality in the life-conditions of individuals should only be so great as is necessary for societal economic processes to function at a given stage of their development" (ZfS 1933:187). All modes of social inequality which do not originate in the necessary limitations imposed upon society through the developmental stage of the forces of production, but which exist because of relations of social domination, are unjust. "This is the universal content of the concept of justice" (ZfS 1933:188). Horkheimer believes that it would be possible to determine which modes of social inequality are required at a given stage of the development of the forces of production and which are products of "superfluous domination." In this respect, like Marx, he assumes that questions of justice are ultimately technical ones: once the ownership of the means of production is changed, then it should be possible to calculate what modes of inequality are *objectively* required in society, on the basis of an assessment of the development of the forces of production.

Now it is certainly true that when justice is understood as a problem of the distribution of social wealth and certain primary goods—as Horkheimer implies in this discussion—then the social-structural limitations created by a society's level of material development must be taken into account.[17] Horkheimer assumes, however, that with the socialization of the mode of production, decisions concerning justice can become purely technical and administrative ones.[18] But it can be seen from a simple consideration that questions of distributive justice are not technical questions, although they entail technical information: even if it is assumed that scarcity of resources is not a problem—a big assumption and an implausible one—distributive justice entails a pattern of social organization in accordance with which the right of social groups to the production, employment, and utilization of certain kinds of "basic goods" is regulated.

Now both the definitions of these "basic goods" and the interests and needs in light of which social groups formulate their claims to certain kinds of entitlement involve normative issues, not technical ones. What is or is not regarded as a "basic good" in society depends upon the value systems and cultural conditions of a given society, as well as on the functional limits of its organization. Whether or not "education," for example, is regarded as a basic good whose distribution must also be regulated socially is a value question; its resolution would entail a discussion of what different social groups view as necessary for the development of individuality, as the responsibility of society, etc. Education is also a social-structural question insofar as every society requires that its individuals appropriate a certain level of skill, knowledge, and information to be able to function properly. Such an issue cannot be resolved via technical information alone.

Similar considerations apply to the definition of social "needs" and "interests." Social groups define their needs and interests both in light of what they consider to be their right or legitimate claim, and in light of what they perceive as possible or feasible in society. Horkheimer assumes that the socialization of the mode of production eliminates all conflict of needs and interests. In this respect he follows Marx, who had already reduced social interest conflicts primarily to class conflicts and who had excluded the possibility of sources of conflict which do not have their origin in class relations but in sexual, racial, ethnic, and even age differences.[19]

The traditional Marxist assumptions which govern Horkheimer's discussion of justice influence some of his reflections on morality as well. At one point, Horkheimer argues that morality, which postulates the conflict between the individual and the social, can only originate in bourgeois society and will disappear when this social order is transcended. Nonetheless, he admits that moral considerations are likely to continue because

the suffering and pain which humans experience as natural beings will not cease, even if they can be alleviated. He writes:

> Morality belongs to a certain form which human relations have
> assumed on the basis of the economic organization of the bour-
> geois order. With the transformation of these relations through
> their rational regulation, morality steps into the background. Hu-
> mans can then fight together against their own suffering and sick-
> ness . . . but in nature, however, misery and death reign. Human
> solidarity is nonetheless an aspect of the solidarity of the living in
> general. Progress in the realization of the first will strengthen our
> sense for the latter. Animals need humans. (ZfS 1933:184)

These remarks contain thoughts which may be very suggestive
today for efforts to develop an ecological ethics.[20] Nonetheless,
what is striking about them is that for Horkheimer, with the
transition from capitalism to socialism, morality disappears
from the domain of human relations and interactions, and continues in the sphere of nature, in that sphere which subjects us
to suffering and to death. On the surface, this is such an implausible assumption that one must ask what really drives
Horkheimer to make such a claim. For it is one thing to claim
that the morality of the future socialist society will no longer be
characterized by the conflict between duty and inclination, the
individual and the universal, but another to maintain that in the
future society morality will continue in that domain alone
where we all, qua living beings, are subject to the forces of
nature.

I want to suggest that Horkheimer's argument can only be
understood in light of his faithfulness to the work paradigm of
human activity. For him as well, the fundamental human relation is that between humans and nature. Once this activity is
regulated rationally, morality continues only in that domain of
nature which we can never master and of which we continue to
be a part. Horkheimer has an inadequate concept of interaction
and communicative action as an equally essential dimension of
human life. Morality and moral controversy—dispute about
what is right, good, desirable, and just—is a constitutive aspect
of communicative action. Even though the social content of morality is historically contingent, and although the definition of
moral disputes, as well as modes of resolving them, change his-

torically and socially, to assume that human societies, whether socialist or capitalist, could reproduce themselves without communication, discourse, and disputation concerning the right, the just, the good, and the desirable is only plausible when relations of social interaction are reduced to relations of objectification. The course of critical theory after the *Dialectic of Enlightenment* shows that the Marxian optimism attached to the model of work and objectification, and the faith placed in the development of the forces of production, is rejected, but the basic premises of the work model of human activity and of the philosophy of the subject are retained (see section 3). Let me now summarize the results of this discussion of "self-preservation" and "autonomy" in Horkheimer's early writings.

First, the concept of "self-preservation" implies a mode of self-relation, according to which the given impulses, needs, and desires of the self are viewed as ahistorical and unchanging. The self acts, and indeed, cannot help but act in such a way as to fulfill these impulses, needs, and desires. Idealist moral philosophy, particularly the Kantian one, on the one hand acknowledges the reality of self-preservation, and on the other hand juxtaposes to it a "law of reason" in the form of a moral imperative. Inclination and duty, the goal of self-preservation, and a morality of reason contradict one another.

Second, for Horkheimer autonomy, like self-preservation, implies a mode of self-relation. Only, the self must not be viewed as a given entity, but as a social and historical individual whose psychic condition evolves historically. Autonomy entails a morally reflexive attitude, the capacity to judge one's own impulses as well as the commands of authority in accordance with principles. These principles are not derived from the categorical imperative, but are social principles of justice and equality. Autonomy is not a moral condition alone, but a future social goal to be striven for. The moral point of view, the perspective of universality, can only be realized socially.

Third, what distinguishes "materialism" from idealist moral philosophy is the assessment of the freedom of the individual. Whereas idealism proceeds from the premise of an autonomous subject, shaping norms and values through an act of reason and will, "materialism by no means traces back the interests and goals influencing the subject to his independent creative activity, to his free will, but views them as results of a development in which subjective and objective moments participate" (ZfS 1933:194).

Fourth, the critique of the idealist conception of the subject does not lead Horkheimer to criticize Kantian ethics for being *formalistic* and *empty*. In fact, Horkheimer defends Kantian formalism against efforts like Max Scheler's to develop a "material ethics of value." Horkheimer views such late theories of philosophical anthropology and phenomenology as attempts "to find a norm which should lend meaning to the life of the individual in the world as it is" (ZfS 1935:5). Such efforts may be more or less specific—they may name concrete ideals which have a meaning-creating value, or they may rest satisfied with projecting only the most general picture of humans as they ought to be. Yet whatever their theoretical procedure, these philosophies fall into a twofold error: on the one hand, they reveal a certain dogmatism, a search for certainty, for a formula or *Weltanschauung* that should create cognitive orientation and motivational meaning. The obverse side of this dogmatism is a certain empiricism. Since the search for moral absolutes ignores the very concrete conditions under which individuals exist in society, one falls into the attitude either of ignoring the given or of justifying it. When one's eyes are turned toward heaven, the depravity of earthly existence can be ignored. The search for metaphysical sources of meaning and the justification of earthly egoism go well together (ZfS 1935:10).

Fifth, even in these early writings, Horkheimer views the process of cultural differentiation analyzed by Weber to be irrevocable. Philosophical attempts to create meaning in what is otherwise perceived as a meaningless universe are viewed as dogmatic and empiricist at once. In their attempt to transcend the present, they only end up reifying it.[21] Reason in the service of autonomy is not substantive, but critical. Its task is not to generate new absolutes for individuals, but to stimulate processes of reflection in them about the real nature of the social world they inhabit. In this respect, the critical theorist has no privileged monopoly over meaning and insight which he seeks to transmit to individuals he considers less insightful than the theorist. It is precisely respect for the autonomy of individuals which forbids the theorist to act as a meaning giver.[22]

The turn to the "critique of instrumental reason" after 1937 changes the above picture in important ways. The sources of the contradiction between "subjective" and "objective" reason are no longer located in social processes alone, but increasingly in the natural history of reason and in the genealogy of bourgeois subjectivity. In particular, Adorno's critique of Kant turns upside down many of the positive elements in Kantian philosophy which the early Horkheimer praised. Horkheimer's 1936 essay on "Egoism and the Movement for Emancipation" already announces the turn to psychoanalytic theory which characterizes Adorno's later critique of Kant.

In this essay, Horkheimer examines the conflict between duty and inclination, between freedom and happiness, in bourgeois moral philosophy no longer exclusively in light of political-economic categories but in psychoanalytic terms. The critique of egoism, of the instinct for self-preservation, is particularly prominent in the words and deeds of those bourgeois heroes who, from the Italian city-states of the fourteenth century to the French Revolution, juxtapose a morality of "virtue" and "sacrifice" to the mere interest in self-preservation. Horkheimer analyses this contradiction between the social reality of egoism upon which bourgeois society is based and its ideological denunciation in light of a theory of internalization (ZfS 1936:169). Egoism and virtue do not simply reflect the disjunction between the market and the public sphere in bourgeois society, but have a complementary function. The assertion of virtue, and particularly its ascetic interpretation, allows individuals to control the drive for self-preservation in such a way as to make it compatible with a puritan work ethic. Untrameled egoism could lead to hedonism, to an uncontrolled search for individual happiness, and this would threaten the basis of the social order which promises happiness without being able to fulfill that promise. The real function of bourgeois morality is to provide an ideological justification of sublimation.

> Since the egoism of the masses led by the bourgeois leader may not be satisfied, since their demands are pushed back to inner pu-

rifications [*Läuterung*], obedience, submissiveness and readiness
for sacrifice, since the love and recognition of individuals is directed towards the leader . . . to elevated symbols and big concepts
and the individual with his own claims is thereby nullified—idealist morality tends to this—the alien individual will be experienced
as a nothing and the individual as such, his enjoyment and happiness, will be despised and denied. (ZfS 1936:217)

The real significance of the disjunction between egoism and
duty, virtue and inclination, is to justify the internalization of
repression. Whereas earlier Horkheimer saw in this disjunction
the truth that the moral point of view had to transcend the mere
inclinations of the individual, here he views this transcendence
as sublimation. Presumably, however, there is a distinction between the mere assertion of egoism and the legitimate search
for happiness, for Horkheimer himself acknowledges that not all
processes of the denial of individual pleasure are repressive. He
writes: "Not only the unheard-of perfection of technique, the
simplification of the labor process, in short the increase of human power over nature, but the human presuppositions for a
higher form of society can hardly be conceived of without processes of spiritualization and interiorization" (ZfS 1936:190). If
such processes of spiritualization and interiorization are also
socially necessary, what would allow us to distinguish between
"illegitimate sublimation" and "socially necessary interiorization"? Horkheimer again introduces a distinction between necessary and superfluous repression on the basis of the functional
logic of the labor process. He writes: "In the case of an organization as well in which not social relations but only the external
nature which has not been dominated limits freedom, these naturally defined limits constrain one to internalize a part of external wishes and needs, and contribute to the transformation of
energies" (ZfS 1936:219). This criterion will not help us to specify the distinction between socially necessary and superfluous
sublimation, for the very same reasons I cited in examining
Horkheimer's concept of justice. How can "natural necessities"
alone enable us to specify what level of repression is socially
necessary and what illegitimate? Once again, Horkheimer assumes that with the disappearance of capitalist class relations,
we will enter a society where the logic of natural necessity

alone, and no longer relations of social domination, will constrain social organization.

Against this background, Adorno's contribution can be summarized as follows: Adorno radicalizes the critique of instrumental reason to such a point that the implicit functionalism of the Marxian paradigm of emancipation—to which Horkheimer continues to appeal in this period—becomes transparent. For Adorno, the distinction between "socially necessary" and "superfluous" domination disappears. The source of sublimation in individuals is not merely the class-specific controls of every society, but the fact that to constitute itself, society must continue to dominate nature, inner as well as outer nature. Marxism justifies the domination of nature and can therefore offer no solution. Whereas Horkheimer uses psychoanalytic theory to distinguish superfluous from socially necessary repression, Adorno maintains that social repression cannot cease as long as the domination of nature continues. Adorno's treatment is admirable for its consistency, yet it pushes back the genesis of repression to such a primordial level that critical social categories can no longer be derived from his analysis. If Horkheimer's difficulties arise from his continued Marxist functionalism, Adorno's difficulties originate with the radicalness of his diagnosis.

2. Autonomy and Reconciliation with the "Other"

The gist of Adorno's critique of Kant in the *Negative Dialectics,* which spans some eighty pages, is contained in the following statement:

> The I (ego) . . . is not immediate but mediated; in psychoanalytic terms, one that emerges, one that is split off from the diffuse energy of the libido. It is not only the specific content of the moral law that depends upon factual existence, but its presumably pure, imperative form does as well. This imperative form presupposes the internalization of repression, as the I which remains self-same develops into a steady instance; Kant absolutizes this I as the necessary condition of ethical life.[23]

Whereas in his 1936 essay on "Egoism and the Movement of Emancipation," Horkheimer locates the repressive aspects of

Kantian morality in the authoritarian character of the moral
law, Adorno views the moral law as expressing the "steady instance of the I which remains self-same."[24] The source of repression lies deeper: it is located in that compulsion to self-identity
which Adorno, in psychoanalytic terms, views as the "split-off
energy of the libido."[25]

In one respect, Adorno echoes the Kant critique of the young
Hegel, who traced the moral law back to the "empty" formula of
the "I = I." Both the early Hegel and Adorno see in the categorical imperative the compulsive search for self-identity. "Act in
such a way that the maxim of your actions can always also be a
universal law" is interpreted by them to mean "Act in such a way
that you—the moral subject—never contradict your will." This
identification of "universalizability" with the principle of non-
contradiction is questionable and implausible. Neither aspect of
Hegel's criticism—the one which considered the moral imperative as *generating* maxims and the one which viewed it as *testing*
maxims—was successful in demonstrating that the categorical
imperative was simply a tautological principle (chapter 3).
Adorno's concern, however, is different. He repeats the charge
raised by the early Hegel, not like him to ridicule the vain
claims of a moral conscience juxtaposed to the given plurality of
norms in ethical life, but to uncover the pathology of a subject
that identifies morality with the compulsion to self-sameness of
the "I."

Adorno's thesis in this respect is so radical that one can no
longer distinguish between two different claims: does Adorno
mean that the "I" as such, the ego, is an instance of repression—
for it develops by sublimating the split-off energies of the libido? Or does he mean that the model of ego identity implied by
Kantian moral theory is repressive—for in this model a cognitive search for self-sameness is made a moral virtue. The explication which follows does not help us decide the issue: "Even in
its most external abstraction the law is one that has become; the
most painful aspect of its abstraction is a sedimented content,
domination which has been brought to its normal form, identity."[26] Adorno praises the Freudian school in its heroic period
for its "unrestrained criticism of the superego as an aspect
strange to the I, as heteronomous."[27] He attacks "revisionist"

psychoanalysis precisely for wanting to distinguish between the "ego" and the "superego" at all. He writes: "The unreflected domination of reason, that of I over the id [Es], is identical with the repressive principle which, psychoanalysis whose critique becomes dumb in view of the reality principle of the I, postpones to the unconscious levels [Walten] of the latter."[28] Both the "I" and the superego have their origin in the "internalization of the father figure,"[29] and Kant, who sees in the moral law an "irresistible" imperative, is more consistent than revisionist psychoanalysts who seek to distinguish between "healthy" and "non-healthy" superego controls. The "superego" represents for Adorno the "unreflected domination of reason, that of the I over the id."

Upon a first reading of this discussion, the problem seems to be that of distinguishing between ego identity as such and a non-repressive ego ideal; but now one is faced with the problem of distinguishing between the ego and the superego in general. The two problems are related, for Adorno implies that a non-repressive ego ideal would have no room for the superego at all. This is the basis of his critique of Freud's early student, Ferenczi.[30] Yet if both "ego" and "superego" develop via the internalization of the "father figure" and are sublimations of the split-off energies of the libido, can there ever be an ego identity that is non-repressive and not bound up with a superego? Or does the "I," the "self," the "subject" as such, originate with repression? If so, would Adorno's model be that of subjectivity without the subject, of a self that was not self-same, of an "I" whose "pure apperception need not accompany all our representations"?[31]

Yet for Adorno, the dissolution of the self can only be regressive. "If under the immeasurable pressure which weigh upon it, the subject, as schizophrenic, falls into the condit_n of dissociation and ambivalence, of which the historical subject has divested itself, so the dissolution of the subject is equal to the ephemeral and condemned image of a possible subject. If its freedom once demanded that myth stop, so now it emancipates itself from itself as from a final myth."[32] The historical subject, in whose constitution the emancipation from myth is sedimented, cannot realize the non-regressive ego ideal. Under present social and historical circumstances, "ego weakness," "the transition of the subject into passive and atomistic, reflex-like behavior," and not a non-repressive ego ideal, is the norm.[33] The continued appropriation of nature, the drive for self-preservation, leads civilization to a point when the self-identical ego, this hero of civilization, threatens to disappear into a series of reflex-like acts. The Kantian self contains the potential of reflection within it which, in the course of civilization, becomes a "reflex." Compared with the weak ego of the present, whose virtue is its submissiveness, the Kantian self represents a moment of independence which, even if repressive, entails a certain strength.

However, the dissolution of the autonomous self is implicit in the very idea of the autonomous self. For such autonomy presupposes the repression of nature; the more this repression is developed, all the more does the self become nature-like and cease to be autonomous. "In this dialectic, the more unscrupulously reason constitutes itself as the absolute opposition of nature and forgets this in itself, all the more self-preservation that is gone wild regresses into nature."[34] The continued domination of nature renders the subject nature-like. The price of civilized sublimation is the threat of regression to the archaic. On the one hand, Adorno juxtaposes the Kantian moral self, capable of reflection, to the "passive and atomistic" individual of the present who is only capable of reflex-like behavior; on the other hand, the autonomous Kantian ego is already said to contain the seeds of its own destruction within itself, insofar as its reflective strength rests upon the domination of nature. The more the latter increases in the course of civilization, the more does the threat of regression back to nature increase.

At the center of these paradoxical considerations, which set up an ideal of ego autonomy only in order to destroy it in the very next sentences, is an antinomy which has been clearly analyzed by Jessica Benjamin:

> According to Adorno and Horkheimer, those dimensions of consciousness which contain the potential for resistance against domination—critical reason, individuation, integrity, and finally, the capacity for resistance—are inseparable from the processes of the internalization of authority. Therefore, emancipation from author-

ity can only result after it has first been recognized, for the subjective dimensions of domination, that is, accommodation to domination, is measured by how authority has been internalized, but the condition of the possibility of resistance in general is contained in this process.[35]

This analysis refers to the *Dialectic of Enlightenment* and not to the *Negative Dialectics*, but on this point I see no fundamental disparity between the two texts. The paradox of autonomy—namely, that the same process of the internalization of authority, which means sublimation, also contains the potential for the subversion of authority—is common to both analyses. A further thesis is that with the destruction of the autonomous ego-identity characteristic of early liberal capitalism, the sources of such resistance dry up. The destruction of the role of the father in the family and in the economy, the replacement of fatherly superego controls by the impersonal mechanisms of the apparatus, all generate a weak, passive, and atomized self.[36]

Although it is perfectly consistent with the program of *Negative Dialectics* to reveal the antinomical and self-contradictory character of positive concepts like "autonomy" rather than attempt to develop affirmative utopias, it is not illegitimate to ask what intimations of otherness, of other modes of being, such negative dialectics can offer. In his critique of Kant, Adorno, like Horkheimer, evaluates "reflexivity" as a positive moment of the autonomous ego and contrasts it to "reflex-like" regression. We know from the analysis of the *Dialectic of Enlightenment* that "reflex-like" behavior contains traces of that original act of mimesis, through which a fearful self sought to master nature by becoming like it. Under conditions of civilization, mimesis does not reveal the affinity of the self with nature; the natural condition to which the self regresses is corrupted by civilization itself.[37] But if so, can reflection offer any promise of healing, any promise of otherness?

Adorno is more relentless than Horkheimer in this regard. Whereas Horkheimer attempts to replace the Kantian model of the authoritarian moral law by a process of "social reflection"—the moral universal is, for Horkheimer, a social one—Adorno criticizes reflection based upon identity logic, while leaving it ambiguous whether there ever can be any other mode of reflection that does not presuppose identity thinking.

Western philosophy offers two models of reflection, neither of which is useful. The first is what Hegel names "external reflection"[38] and which has been developed by empiricist philosophy under the heading of "relations of ideas."[39] According to this model, the knowing subject abstracts certain elements from the given content presented to it and thereby brings the concrete instances under a common category. Empiricist philosophy regards this as the process through which concepts—abstract ideas in general—are generated. This model of reflection is indeed one according to which the activity of the mind consists in the establishment of abstract principles of identity and equivalence.

The second model of reflection, common to the idealist tradition, is that of the mind thinking itself, of the knower knowing itself. Here, reflection is considered not as abstraction, but as an act of self-relation. For Kant, "self-reflection" and "self-knowledge" are distinct, for knowledge implies that a given object be brought under concepts.[40] For Fichte, both acts become one: the self is not there prior to thinking itself; the self originates in the act of self-relation.[41]

From Adorno's perspective, the interest of the subject in self-reflection and freedom would seem to be equivalent to "narcissism," to pathological self-love. The world and otherness disappear, are "posited" by the ego, as Fichte claims; what remains is the self-identical ego. Against this narcissistic interest in reflection, Adorno appeals to the therapeutic effects of a nonidentitary logic.

> According to the Kantian model, the subjects are free, insofar as, conscious of themselves, they are identical with themselves; and in such identity they are once more unfree, insofar as they stand under its compulsion and perpetrate it. They are unfree as nonidentical, as diffuse nature, and as such free, because in the stimulations that overcome them—the non-identity of the subject with itself is nothing else—they will also overcome the compulsive character of identity.[42]

Autonomy is the capacity of the subject to let itself go, to deliver itself over to that which is not itself, to remain "by itself in otherness." Adorno once more reveals his ambivalent relation to Hegel. The critique of both empiricist and idealist models of reflection, and the search for a model of "self-relation" that entails a relation to otherness within it, guided Hegel's philosophy from its beginnings. But Hegel's definition of freedom as "being-by-oneself-in-otherness" is, according to Adorno, inadequate insofar as the World Spirit reduces otherness to a mere vehicle in which it can actualize itself.[43] "Otherness" for Hegel is simply the narcissistic mirror in which the World Spirit contemplates itself. What, however, could be a genuine being-by-oneself-in-otherness? How can the self find itself in otherness, without losing itself in it? For the young Hegel, love is such a relation.[44] Hegel distinguishes *love* from *recognition* precisely because love cannot be universalized and is inextricably bound up with particularity, with this *this-ness* of the other. Relations of reciprocal recognition, on which justice and freedom rest, abstract from the "this-ness" of the other and are based upon the acknowledgment of the abstract identity between self and other.

Adorno opts neither for love nor for justice. Indeed, it is fascinating that the one model of human togetherness which could have offered itself as a form of being-by-oneself-in-otherness is never discussed by Adorno. Undoubtedly, the orthodox Freudian view of desire, upon which Adorno relies, plays a role here. This sort of desire is not love, a desire for the other, but a blind quanta of libidinal energy that seeks release, and whose fixation upon love objects seems rather accidental. From such a perspective, Hegel's early concept of love may appear like a romantic rhapsody.[45]

"Utopia," writes Adorno, "would be the non-identity of the subject that would not be sacrificed" ("Utopie wäre die opferlose Nichtidentität des Subjekts").[46] For Adorno, this non-sacrificial non-identity is not a social ideal, but an aesthetic one. The ability of the subject to be by-oneself-in-otherness is equivalent to the ability of the subject to forget oneself in the aesthetic experience of the "Naturschöne"—"the naturally beautiful."[47] The "naturally beautiful" is "allegory," a "cipher," a "sign" (*Zeichen*) of reconciliation. One must not think of this in essentialist categories, as an eternally given and unchanging substratum of beauty. The "naturally beautiful" is antithesis, the antithesis of society[48] and as undetermined, the antithesis of determination.[49] It is a mode in which the mediation between humans and nature, between subject and object, can be thought of. It is not a state of affairs, a final condition, but a suggestion that is present ever anew. Even an image of an enduring state of reconciliation would be false. One must think of the "other" as that utopian longing toward the non-identical which can only be suggested as "allegory" and as "cipher."[50] From the standpoint of conceptual thought, the "naturally beautiful" is deficient, "but for the critique of dialectical reason and its medium, discursive language, this deficiency is a source of truth, which justifies the interest of radical Enlightenment in the naturally beautiful."[51] Art seeks to compensate for this deficiency, and to transcend it, but its truth is to recreate the naturally beautiful even in the effort to overcome it. The utopia of a non-sacrificial non-identity of the subject is intimated in that non-compulsory relation to otherness which forces the subject to forget him- or herself and to catch a glimpse of the moment of reconciliation. What distinguishes this appeal to the aesthetic, it must be emphasized, from a romantic theory of the flight into nature is precisely the ambivalence of the concept of nature. Nature, for Adorno, signifies not a given entity, state, or medium, but "otherness," the "otherness" of society, civilization, and reason. The semantic content of this otherness changes historically, and must be recreated again and again.

It would be trivial to criticize Adorno, as is often done, for reducing critical theory to aesthetics. The more fundamental question is the following: why is it not possible to conceive the "non-sacrificial non-identity of the subject" as a social, interpersonal condition? Why is the ideal of a non-repressive and non-regressive autonomy not a moral and political, but an aesthetic one?[52] Adorno, who probably more consistently than any of the critical theorists saw the deficiency and the demise of the philosophy of the subject upon which Marxist philosophy rested, could nonetheless offer no alternative to it. Let me expand this conclusion by first going back to the premises of the philosophy of the subject which, I maintained, underlay the Hegelian-Marxist concept of autonomy as "self-actualization."

3. Concluding Systematic Considerations: The Critique of Instrumental Reason and the Philosophy of the Subject

The four presuppositions of the position described as "the philosophy of the subject" were: (a) a unitary model of human activity defined as "externalization" or "objectification"; (b) a transsubjective subject; (c) the interpretation of history as the story of transsubjectivity; and (d) the identity of constituting and constituted subjectivity. Beginning with the *Dialectic of Enlightenment*, Adorno and Horkheimer reject the claim that the human mastery of nature reveals the humanization of a transsubjective subject—Spirit or Mankind—which develops its potentialities by "externalizing" or "objectifying" them in an other. In retrospect, the human mastery of nature appears not as humanization but as dehumanization, not as the unfolding of the potentialities of the species, but as their distortion and sublimation. But neither the thesis that history is the story of transsubjectivity, nor the presence of a collective singular subject as whose story history can be told, is rejected in the *Dialectic of Enlightenment*. The revolutionary hopes that once accompanied this model are increasingly transformed into a relentless pessimism. The moment of emancipation is no longer located in the concrete activities of social and historical individuals, but in the realm of absolute Spirit—art and philosophy—or in Marcuse's case, in the realm of subjective Spirit—the rebelling psyche.

In *Negative Dialectics*, Adorno goes one step further. He criticizes both the philosophy of history and the premise of transsubjectivity as instances of identity thinking. What is juxtaposed to them is not an alternative concept of intersubjectivity, nor another mode of comprehending the past, but what Adorno names the "priority of the objective."[53] This is a materialist category according to Adorno insofar as through it, the priority of historically accumulated conditions over and against the illusions of a completely self-determining subject is maintained. The "priority of the objective"[54] means, first, the contingent but nonetheless compelling course of historical events, which often reveal a "causality of fate"; second, the priority of nature to all subjectivity that presupposes nature; third, the suffering of the subject through the accumulated residue of its own unconscious history; and finally, epistemologically, the concept implies that no claim to absolute knowledge is possible. The function of this category is to show the limits of identity thinking, by juxtaposing otherness to identity.

This categorial shift does not present a real alternative to the philosophy of the subject. What it shows are the limits of revolutionary, optimist thinking and of concepts like the world spirit. It shows that thought remains determined by non-thought, the subject by the non-subject, and necessity by contingency. Negative dialectics remains the abstract negation of the philosophy of the subject without showing how it can be transcended. But this negation does not allow us to thematize what this philosophy really precluded: above all, plurality and being-with-the-other in the sense of being-with-an-other-like-myself.

At one point in the *Negative Dialectics*, with unmatched rhetoric and contempt, Adorno dismisses philosophies which seek to go beyond the Kantian concept of the person via a turn to intersubjectivity. He writes: "The concept of the person and its variations, like the I-Thou relationship, have assumed the oily tone of a theology in which one has lost faith."[55] To show that such a position is not mere wishful theological thinking, one would have to establish that the discussion of intersubjective relations points to a genuine lacuna in the projects of negative dialectics and the critique of instrumental reason. To do this, let me begin by returning to the concept of self-preservation.

From the perspective of the *Dialectic of Enlightenment*, one can establish the affinity between the concepts of "self-preservation" and "self-actualization" as follows. Both concepts signify an intransitive relation:[56] the self to be actualized and the self to be preserved do not act to realize a system of preestablished goals and values. The goals and values of both modes of activity are immanent to the wishes and desires of the thinking and laboring subject. What distinguishes the concept of "self-actualization" from the utilitarian one of "self-preservation" is the assumption that the activity of objectification carries with it an essential dynamic through which the immediate, empirical individual is led to transcend itself. This dynamic is referred to by Hegel as "Bildung," by Marx as "humanization." It signifies an educational process in which the capacity for reflection and autonomy are developed. It is assumed that the historical process does not merely bring with it the accumulation and increase of man's material powers, but that it is a process of self-education and self-transformation as well. The normative content of this concept is then derived in light of two further assumptions.

The first is that behind, beneath, or within the empirical activity of producing individuals, one detects an "essence" of humanity. This essence is not a goal in the Aristotelian sense, for it is not external but immanent to the empirical activity of individuals; but it is a goal in the sense that at any point in time, individuals may be more or less aware of the implicit and immanent logic of their doings and act accordingly. This position can be described as "philosophical anthropology." Regardless of how the empirical and the essential self are to be mediated and brought into harmony with one another, one assumes that such a distinction is cognitively meaningful.

A second theory through which the concept of "self-actualization" can be rendered meaningful is the philosophy of history. Philosophical anthropology and the philosophy of history do not preclude one another. When it is assumed that the "essence" of humanity unfolds through the "material reality" or the "immanent meaning" of history, philosophical anthropology becomes a philosophy of history. The goal of self-actualization is then said to be implicit in the cumulative logic of the historical process. Since, however, neither the empirical activity of individuals nor a particular moment of time can wholly reveal this hidden potential in history, one assumes that the goal of self-actualization is approached by the transsubjective subject whose doings empirical individuals can become aware of only dimly.

Horkheimer's critique of philosophical anthropology in the 1930s and Adorno's later critique of the philosophy of history indicate that, for them, the normative content of the concept of autonomy cannot be captured via the category of "self-actualization," interpreted in two of the possible ways suggested above as implying a philosophical anthropology or a philosophy of history. Furthermore, the destruction of the "objective reason" of the ancients is irrevocable. No ontology of the Platonic or Aristotelian kind can be reinstated. How then is one to distinguish between "autonomy" and "self-preservation"? What could be the normative content of an intransitive self-relation which, nonetheless, would allow us to criticize relations of domination and oppression in the present?

Actually, the question suggested is a twofold one: first is the problem of giving an adequate *content* to a concept of autonomy that transcends self-preservation; second, and more significant, if the relation between reason and self-reflection is so reversed that the natural history of reason is one of domination and not emancipation, how can the link between self-reflection and autonomy be *justified* at all? Adorno and Horkheimer, on the one hand, claim that reason is an instrument; on the other hand, they continue to appeal to the healing process of rational reflection. The solution to both problems would be to base the relation between autonomy and self-reflection in the one medium which Adorno and Horkheimer consistently ignore, namely, that of linguistically mediated communication, and to lend content to the concept of autonomy on the basis of an analysis of human interaction. This first step would entail a number of assumptions that radically break with the legacy of German idealism and, above all, with the idealist concept of the subject. Let me explain here why such a step is necessary.

As discussed above (chapters 3 and 4), both Hegel and Marx operate with a prelinguistic view of consciousness and view its contents imagistically, as what is before the eyes of the mind; posited by Spirit, etc. Reflection and self-reflection are considered as activities through which a thinking ego establishes connections between such prelinguistic contents of consciousness. Marx expands this model of reflection insofar as, for him, the capacity of the subject to know itself entails the capacity to objectify such knowledge in a material medium. Beginning with the unity of the mind and body in the concrete self, Marx emphasizes that an objective being must first objectify itself and develop its cognitive capacities in the medium of life. Above all, such a being must act such as to appropriate the material conditions of its existence. The transition from idealism to philosophical anthropology, first carried out by Feuerbach, substitutes for the idealist model of the *thinking subject* that of the *acting, living, and producing subject*.[57] This is the critique of idealism to which Horkheimer returns in his 1937 essay on "Traditional and

Critical Theory." He shows that the Kantian thesis that objectivity is constituted through the act of the self-conscious ego must be interpreted materialistically. Constitution is not an epistemological act but a social and historical activity. The subsequent criticism of reason by Adorno and Horkheimer continues this perspective. It is shown that reason does not develop out of an act of self-reflection; rather, it grows out of the material process of the species' relation to nature.

Yet the transition from the idealist model of the *thinking* and *knowing* self to that of the *making* and *producing* one is inadequate to establish the relationship between reflection and autonomy which is severed in the *Dialectic of Enlightenment* and *Negative Dialectics*. If, as Adorno and Horkheimer show, making makes the subject like what it makes, then the traditional Marxian criticism which once served to demystify the illusions of an absolute spirit does not go far enough. Marx could appeal to the process of "real material life-conditions" to refute the idealist claim that the self could, via an act of self-reflection, emancipate itself from all contingency and situatedness. Neither such an act of absolute self-reflection nor the complete transcendence of contingency and situatedness are possible, according to Marx. The Marxian critique of absolute self-reflection not only serves to demystify the illusions of idealism; it also maintains that the root of human emancipation is to be searched for in this material sphere of production. But if, as Adorno and Horkheimer assume, production no longer contains an emancipatory moment, then the materialist critique of idealism will not lead us out of the quandaries of the critique of instrumental reason. It no longer suffices to point out that reason develops in a material context and, more specifically, in the context of expanding human mastery over external nature. For by becoming conscious of this fact, one does not also recover an emancipatory hope embedded in the natural history of reason. In this respect, the materialist concept of the subject can no longer play the same role for Adorno and Horkheimer as it did for Marx. Nonetheless, in explicating the genesis of subjectivity, Adorno and Horkheimer consistently follow the Marxian concept of the subject and focus upon the medium of the domination and appropriation of nature.

By tracing the genesis of the self back to the history of its interaction with nature, they also assume that they can explain the genesis of social relations of domination and the self-relation of sublimation. The premise upon which they base their assumption is that the domination of nature inevitably leads to domination over others and over the self. It is unclear what kind of causal or other sort of connection is being established here: do they mean that social relations are secondary to the primary relation of production, and that we have to show the emergence of the social out of the sphere of production; or do they mean that there is an analogy, or maybe even stronger, a necessary link between the domination of external nature and intersubjective domination and intrapersonal sublimation? I believe both assumptions to be operative. As was shown in the previous chapter, the category of "instrumental reason" referred to a certain mode of scientific-technical production, a pattern of impersonal, bureaucratic organization, and certain kinds of meaning and value systems. The connections between the spheres of society, culture, and personality were never clarified adequately. It was assumed that these were subordinated to the functional logic of a system reproducing itself via the domination of nature. The Freudian theory of internalization provided the missing link between the function of the economy and that of culture: to translate economic imperatives into internal sanctions of the self for whom these imperatives then constituted superego controls.

But this model is sociologically deficient, for the individual dynamics of the various spheres—society, culture, and personality—and the logic of their reproductions are left unexplained. More precisely, a homology or "functional fit" is claimed between the domination of nature, social domination, and the dynamics of personality formation. But social domination and the dynamics of personality formation cannot be explained via such a fit. This can be seen more clearly, I think, when we focus upon the one word which cuts across all three levels—domination (*Herrschaft*). The concept suggests an *illegitimate* exercise of power bordering on force and perhaps even violence. Adorno and Horkheimer use the domination of nature as an explanans and social domination as the explanandum, whereas even to develop a concept of what the domination of nature could mean, we would have to think of the illegitimate exercise of power, inequality, and lack of reciprocity among human subjects. I am not addressing here the sociological question of how the human relation to nature influences or determines social interaction, but rather the conceptual question: what meaning can the phrase "the domination of nature" have if we do not thereby imply the opposite of reciprocal, symmetrical, and equal relations, as they would exist among humans? The concept of "mimesis" is so fuzzy precisely because it cannot suggest a real alternative to relations of domination. Adorno distinguishes between "mimesis" and "mimicry," between a relation to otherness that acknowledges otherness and a relation to otherness that imitates without acknowledgment.[58] We know what it is to mimic someone; yet what would it mean to mimic nature as opposed to developing a mimetic relation to it? I am suggesting that in order to be meaningful, the concept of "domination" must first be specified in the context of interpersonal relations. To reverse the order of explanation, as Adorno and Horkheimer do, only confuses the matter, since a term which originates in the sphere of interpersonal relationships is then projected onto our relation to nature in order to explain subsequently social relations.[59]

If, as suggested here, the category of "domination" has its origin and proper place in the sphere of interpersonal relations, then the model of "autonomy" which Adorno and Horkheimer aspire to must be sought in this domain as well. As my discussion in this chapter has attempted to show, although it is difficult to specify a positive concept of autonomy particularly for Adorno, for him as well as for Horkheimer autonomy entails a form of *reflectiveness* on the part of the moral subject; furthermore, both argue that the autonomy of the subject is incompatible with the domination of nature but requires some form of reconciliation with otherness, with the otherness within and outside the self. Whereas in the *Negative Dialectics* the concept of reflection culminates in that of mimesis, in Horkheimer's early writings a different model of reflection, one we can call a "social" model, is already present. However, Horkheimer cannot develop the positive implications of this model both for relations among selves and for self-relation, for, following Marx, he too suggests that with the end of class relations, domination will be replaced by "administration," and ethico-political relations will become administrative ones. In the classless society of the future, the "rule over men" will be replaced by the "administration of things." After 1941 it is suggested that even the "administration of things" implies "domination over others." The only sphere that can then intimate images of an other, an emancipated mode of interaction, becomes the aesthetic one.

By seeking the alternative to identity logic and to the domination of internal and external nature in the aesthetic realm, Adorno and Horkheimer still remain faithful to the objectification paradigm of activity. The rejection of the emancipatory significance of work and objectification does not lead them to develop an alternative model of social action. In their interpretation, *poiesis* becomes not *praxis* but *poetics*. I referred to such actions as "expressive" (chapter 4) and suggested that it was the dual world-relation of expressive action—its subject-subject and subject-object reference—that allowed Hegel and Marx to use this paradigm in criticizing both the reduction of labor to mere instrumental activity and the reduction of communicative action to strategic behavior. For Adorno and Horkheimer as well, this mode of expressive action suggests both a new relation to externality—mimetic reconciliation—and a new mode of self-relation—non-repressive ego identity. The use of the concept of "nature" to refer both to material externality and to the inner, psychic constitution of individuals facilitates the suggestion that the alternative to the domination of nature in both realms must be an expressive act. Such an expressivist orientation implies a new mode of being with the other within and outside the self. The subject recovers an authentic self-relation by giving itself to the other: self-confirmation and enhancement come via an act of losing and recovering oneself in the other.

What is so astonishing in this turn to the aesthetic, particularly in Adorno's philosophy, is that the aesthetic realm offers no real negation of identity logic. The "non-sacrificial non-identity of the subject," which Adorno describes as "utopia," is identified with giving oneself over to the other via an act of contemplation.

Yet what distinguishes this act of giving oneself to the other from an act of narcissism? How can we ever establish that this act of contemplative giving into the other is not merely a *projection* on the part of the self onto the other attributes that the self would gladly acknowledge to be its own? Why cannot the art work become a narcissistic mirror of self-contemplation? Are there immanent constraints in the work of art itself that would bring the self back from its boundless self-adoration to the acknowledgment of the other?[60] Why isn't mimesis a form of narcissism?

The true negation of identity logic would imply a relation to an "other" who could at every point remind the self that it was not a mere projection or extension of the self, but an independent being, another self. The limits of the compulsion to identity are revealed when the object of identification is itself capable of acting in such a way as to differentiate between identity and difference, between self and other. If identity logic is the attempt to blur limits and boundaries, then those limits can be re-established via the act of an other self who is capable of rejecting the narcissistic self-extension of the other. The true negation of identity logic would be an epistemological relation in which the object could not be subsumed under the cognitive categories of the self without that it—the object—could also regard these categories as adequate to capture its own difference and integrity. Identity logic can only be stopped when difference and differentiation are internal to the very self-identification of the epistemological object and subject, and this is only the case when our object is another subject or self.

We have a foreknowledge of such relations which precedes our relation to the aesthetic. Our capacity to use a language properly, to know that every speaker of a language is an "I" and a "you," one that is at once like us and distinct from us, is predicated on such foreknowledge. In the sphere of linguistically mediated communication, the other cannot simply be subsumed under our epistemic categories; rather, what develops is a horizon of mutual self- and other-interpretations. Our understanding of the other is always also contested by the other; similarly, our self-understanding rests on our foreknowledge, and contestation of the knowledge that the other has of us. In previous chapters, I have referred to such conflicts of understanding and contestations of knowledge as the "interpretive indeterminacy of action." This interpretive indeterminacy results precisely because in this sphere the identity of acts as well as of actors can only be established via the communicative exchanges between them. Such identity entails difference as an essential aspect. The compulsion to identity logic is broken in this sphere of communication. The epistemological logic of this sphere is never that of the subsumption of a lifeless object under general categories. The epistemology of mutual understanding and communication is narrative and interpretive, not subsumptive. Our categories are meaningful insofar as they are also categories of self-interpretation and -understanding, and insofar as they can be contested by both parties in terms of their own plausibility, adequacy, and authenticity. The utopia of the "non-sacrificial non-identity of the other" must be searched for in this sphere in which identity can only be attained via difference, and where it is sustained via the continuous redefinition of the boundaries between self and other. Such a step implies nothing less than an "epistemological break" in critical theory—a break with the premises of the work model of activity and a turn to the sphere of communicative intersubjectivity.

The development of the critical theory of Horkheimer and Adorno, which has been examined in this and the preceding chapter, leaves unanswered a crucial question: what is the normative standpoint of critical theory? For, if neither the self-reflective subject of German idealism, nor the productive subject of Marxism, incorporate that link between reason and emancipation, reflection and freedom, in the name of which critique is exercised, then critical theory can find no immanent basis for its utopian ideal of reason. In the previous chapter, I examined how Adorno becomes an ethnologist of advanced civilization, seeking emancipation in those traces and moments of otherness, in those cracks in the crust of the totality of the administered world. *Negative Dialectics* shows how this search for otherness, for a non-identitary logic, leads to the aesthetic realm. This turn to the aesthetic, however, can hardly secure the basis of a critical analysis of society. In a somewhat different vein, Horkheimer's early critique of Kant and his attempt to give the ideal of autonomy a more social content suggest an alternative reformulation of the relation between reflection and emancipation. These suggestions, however, ultimately bear no fruit, for the predominance of the work paradigm of activity leads Horkheimer to the conclusion that with the transition to the socialist society of the future, moral interaction will continue in the sphere of our relation to nature alone.

It has been the purpose of the critical theory of Jürgen Habermas to rethink the problem of the normative foundations of critical social theory under the altered conditions of the relationship between philosophy and the social sciences in the post–World War II period, and to initiate the paradigm shift in critical theory from the work model of activity to that of communicative interaction. In his 1969 article "Theodor Adorno: The Primal History of Subjectivity—Self-Affirmation Gone Wild," Habermas quotes Adorno: "The reconciled state would not annex the alien with a philosophical imperialism, but would find its happiness in the fact that the alien remained distinct and remote within the preserved proximity, beyond being either heterogeneous or one's own."[61] Habermas comments:

> Whoever meditates on this assertion will become aware that the condition described, although never real, is still most intimate and familiar to us. It has the structure of a life together in communication that is free from coercion. We necessarily anticipate such a reality, at least formally, each time we want to speak what is true. The idea of truth, already implicit in the first sentence spoken, can be shaped only on the model of the idealized agreement aimed for in communication free from domination. To this extent, the truth of propositions is bound up with the intention of leading a genuine life. . . . Adorno might just as well have not assented to this consequence and insisted that the metaphor of reconciliation is the only one that can be spoken, and not only because this satisfies the prohibition not to draw images of God [*Bilderverbot*] and, as it were, cancels itself out. The wholly other may only be indicated via determinate negation; it cannot be known.[62]

This passage captures quite precisely the turn from utopian to communicative reason, from the work model of action to that of communicative interaction in critical theory initiated by Habermas. The last two chapters of this work will analyze the significance of this paradigm shift.

Chapter 7

THE CRITIQUE OF
FUNCTIONALIST REASON

Since his early essays on "The Classical Doctrine of Politics and Its Relation to Social Philosophy," "Natural Right and Revolution," and "Hegel's Critique of the French Revolution,"[1] one of Jürgen Habermas' major concerns has been to revive the normative tradition of ethics and politics in order to suggest what freedom from domination could mean in a scientific-technological civilization and in late-capitalist societies. Orienting himself in this early period to the work of neo-Aristotelians like Hans-Georg Gadamer and Hannah Arendt, Habermas pointed out that the transition from the Aristotelian concept of praxis to a Marxian philosophy of praxis had resulted in our losing sight of the specificity of normative problems. The Frankfurt School's critique of "instrumental reason" was an aporetic project precisely because once the identification of emancipation with the increased technical mastery of nature was rejected, there seemed no other instance of human rationality to appeal to besides aesthetic reason. Habermas maintains that the critique of instrumental reason need not appeal to a utopian reconciliation with nature;[2] the true negation of instrumental reason is not utopian but communicative reason.[3]

It is this aspect of Habermas' project which will concern me in the next two chapters. More specifically, I am interested in analyzing the reformulation of the normative foundations of critique as a theory of communicative action and communicative ethics. Let me first dissipate the impression that may arise, however, that my method of exposition follows a Hegelian logic, in the sense that what is last in time is also the most fully developed and the most adequate. To the contrary: this work arose precisely out of the suspicion, discussed in the preface, that the turn from Hegel to Kant, already announced in *Knowledge and Human Interests*, may have been ill-founded. In the first part of this book, I examined Hegel's critique of modern natural right theories and of Kantian ethics precisely in order to answer the question whether there were aspects of Hegel's reflections that still could be useful today for developing the normative foundations of critique. As I argued in chapter 3, whatever insights we gain from Hegel in this respect, we can no longer rest satisfied with his model of transsubjective freedom and expressivism. The question now is: how can this Hegelian critique be made fruitful within the framework of a communicative model of action and rationality?

I intend to discuss this question in two steps: in this chapter I outline aspects of Habermas' critical theory of late capitalism and of his diagnosis of the pathologies of the lifeworld. I turn to the more specifically normative conceptions in the next chapter. My reasons for proceeding from Habermas' critical social theory to his normative one are as follows. Despite his attempt to revive normative questions within the Marxist tradition, Habermas remains true to the transition from the ancient doctrine of politics to the study of society as initiated by Marx, Durkheim, and Weber. A purely normative theory of ethics and politics is viewed by him to be just as illusory as Horkheimer himself considered philosophical anthropology and philosophies of life to be in the 1930s. Even when we cannot take for granted that historical progress itself will guarantee the normative ideals in the name of which social actors struggle, a normative theory which cannot show how the "ought" and the "is" are to be *mediated* is useless from a critical standpoint. The task of critical social theory is not to develop Kantian imperatives, but to show the potential for rationality and emancipation implicit in the present.[4] I have questions about the extent to which Habermas succeeds in mediating the "ought" and the "is," and about the extent to which the intentions of his critical social theory can be met by his normative framework. Primarily for this reason, it will be important to consider his social-critical theory first.

Let me explicate more precisely the relationship between the two dimensions of critical theory which have been referred to in the above paragraph as the "social-critical" and the "norma-tive." A critical social theory has two aspects:[5] first is the *explanatory-diagnostic* aspect through which the findings and methods of the social sciences are appropriated in such a way as to develop an empirically fruitful analysis of the crisis potential of the present. The purpose of this aspect of the theory, which has been referred to as "crisis diagnosis" in chapters 4 and 5, is to analyze the contradictions and dysfunctionalities of the pres-ent, and to explicate the protests or pathologies—as the case may be—which they give rise to in the population.

The second dimension of critical theory is its *anticipatory-utopian* one; this constitutes the more properly normative as-pect of critique. When explicating the dysfunctionalities of the present, a critical social theory should always do so in the name of a better future and a more humane society. The purpose of critical theory is not crisis management, but crisis diagnosis such as to encourage future transformation. A critical social theory views the present from the perspective of the radical transformation of its basic structure, and interprets actual, lived crises and protests in the light of an anticipated future. In its *anticipatory-utopian* capacity, critical theory addresses the needs and demands expressed by social actors in the present, and interprets their potential to lead toward a better and more humane society.

This twofold aspect of a critical social theory allows us to see more precisely the significance of the dual concept of crisis which was introduced in chapter 4. In its *explanatory-diagnostic* capacity, critical theory utilizes a *systemic* notion of crisis. Such a social theory must be able to locate the problems of the pres-ent in the macro-sociological constraints of the economy, the political-administrative system, and the like. However, the con-cept of *systemic* crisis must be complemented by that of *lived* crisis. For unlike its functionalist counterpart, a critical social theory is not exclusively interested in impersonal forces that act behind the backs of social agents, but in showing how such forces generate certain experiences of suffering, humiliation, ag-gression, and injustice, which in turn can lead to resistance, protest, and organized struggle. While systemic analysis expli-cates the roots of the crisis in the present, to focus on experiences of lived crisis and to evaluate them is the task of anticipatory-utopian critique.

With this clarification, we are in a better position to assess the aporias of previous critical theory. After the *Dialectic of Enlightenment*, the critical theory of the Frankfurt School lost its explanatory-diagnostic dimension. It could no longer analyze the contradictions of the period. Of course, in all fairness one must say that the realities of the Cold War, the moral and political horrors of Stalinism, and the conservative-restorationist tendencies of some Western democracies in the aftermath of World War II did not leave much room for hope.[6] With its explanatory-diagnostic dimension blocked off, critical theory continued as anticipatory-utopian critique alone. Since the ideal of utopian reason in the name of which Adorno and Horkheimer spoke could not be anchored in the present, or mediated with it, however, their critical theory became an increasingly aporetic project. In this respect, it is one of the great merits of Habermas' critical social theory to have restored that moment of genuine collaboration between philosophy and the social sciences, and to have developed an empirically fruitful explanatory-diagnostic theory of late-capitalist societies.

As I will outline in section 1, Habermas has not only initiated a philosophical critique of the work paradigm of action, but equally significant, he has shown how the communicative model of action is more fruitful from a social-scientific standpoint. This in turn entails a rejection of the *Marxist functionalism* of early critical theory which sought to establish undifferentiated correlations among the organization of production forces, personality structures, and cultural meaning patterns.

These considerations should place the preceding chapters of this work in a new light. In my reconstruction and analysis of the theories of Hegel, Marx, Adorno, and Horkheimer, I tried to disclose the various models of social action which they presupposed, and sought to uncover the link between these and various visions of autonomy. The concept of communicative action was already introduced in chapter 4, section 4. At that point, however, it was not explicitly developed; rather, it was suggested that the domain of linguistically mediated human interaction could not be explained in light of objectification, self-actualization, and, as the preceding chapter has made clear, mimesis. The present chapter intends to develop the full implications of this suggestion by placing the concept of communicative action in a philosophical and social-theoretic context. Since in this respect I follow Habermas, my initial concern will be to highlight those aspects of his paradigm change in critical theory which are central to my concerns in this book. I shall begin my immanent critique of his theory first in section 2 of this chapter.

1. Communicative Action and the Paradoxes of Rationalization

If one were to express the differences between Habermas' analysis of the crisis potentials of late capitalism and that of the Frankfurt School through a philosophical analogy, one could say the following: whereas Marcuse, Horkheimer, and Adorno agree with the young Hegel in seeing modernity as a "tragedy and comedy in ethical life," Habermas shares the sobriety of the older Hegel, who saw in the *Entzweiung* of ethical substance into a system of needs on the one hand and ethical life on the other irreversible gains in freedom and autonomy.[7] Of course, this is more than an analogy. Since *The Structural Transformation of the Public Sphere* (*Strukturwandel der Öffentlichkeit*) and the early essays on the unfulfilled utopian content of modern natural right theories,[8] Habermas has focused on the inconsistency between the utopian kernel of the early bourgeois political tradition—the consensus of all as the basis of a just order—and the institutional contradictions of capitalism which constantly violate this utopian promise through relations of exploitation based on race, class, status, and gender differences. However, until the *Legitimation Crisis* this difference in orientation did not lead Habermas to revise the one-dimensionality thesis shared by Marcuse and Adorno alike.

Yet already in "Technology and Science as 'Ideology,'" Habermas introduced certain distinctions which later amounted to a radical revision of Max Weber's diagnosis of societal rationalization, and of the Frankfurt School theory of late-capitalist societies which was based on this diagnosis. As opposed to Weber, who saw social rationalization in terms of the expansion of purposive-rational action systems, in this essay Habermas argued that a categorical distinction needed to be made between the rationalization of communicative action on the one hand, and of purposive-rational and strategic action on the other.[9] Whereas the rationalization of the latter meant the development of productive forces and the increase of technical mastery over nature as well as over certain social processes, the rationalization of communicative action would entail a decreasing degree of repressiveness and rigidity, increasing role distance, and the flexible application of norms; in short, socialization without repression.

This new mode of *socialization* would correspond at the institutional level to a new principle of *social organization*, according to which action-orienting norms and principles would be generated in processes of public and unlimited discussion. The new principle of social organization would be that of discursive will formation through communication freed from domination. Nonetheless, the claim that social rationalization could lead to new modes of socialization and social organization remained a hypothetical projection, not adequately corresponding to any concrete social development.[10] Habermas could point to no dialectic that would reverse the distortions caused by the one-sided rationalization of purposive-rational action in the direction of an emancipatory rationality. Critique and crisis remained disjointed in his social theory as well.

It is first in the *Legitimation Crisis* that Habermas attempts to reveal the immanent crisis tendencies of rationalization processes. This now constitutes one of the central theses of the recent *Theory of Communicative Action*. Let us recall that for Weber as well as for the Frankfurt School, societal rationalization meant the subjection of increasing domains of action and interaction to formal, abstract, uniform, and predictable rules and regulations. The subjection of social action to such rules was perfected in particular by the organizational model of a hierarchical and bureaucratic structure, occupied by functionaries and experts trained to obey. According to Horkheimer, Adorno, and Marcuse, such rationalization generated an epistemic illusion. The more efficient, planned, scientific, and direct administrative control became, the more general, impersonal, and anonymous did it seem. The more direct domination became, the less could it be seen as domination. They agreed with Weber that by increasingly diminishing the cognitive as well as the practical capacities of individuals to defy orders and regulations, and to define for themselves a meaningful and right course of action, societal rationalization generated an irretrievable "loss of freedom."[11] In order to show that societal rationalization was not the seamless web that Weber and the Frankfurt School assumed it to be, Habermas had to revise this analysis at the methodological and empirical levels. Let me briefly outline here the contributions of the *Legitimation Crisis* in these two respects before proceeding to a more extensive analysis of the argument of *The Theory of Communicative Action*.

At the methodological level, Habermas rejects the implicit functionalism of the Frankfurt School model. According to this model, rationalization is an all-encompassing process in which the organization of the productive forces, societal institutions, cultural meaning patterns, and personality structures all submit to the same logic of ever-increasing fragmentation, atomization, efficiency, and formalism. Habermas introduces a more differentiated sociological model which in the first instance distinguishes between "social" and "system" integration and which denies that there is a "functional fit" between the economy on the one hand and culture and personality on the other.[12] Briefly explicated, the distinction between "system" integration and "social" integration is the following: by the former is meant a mode coordinating social action through the functional interconnection of action consequences, whereas "social integration" refers to the coordination of action through the harmonizing of action orientations. The institutional differentiation of modern societies into the polity, the economy, and the family meant that in two domains in particular—the economy and state administration—the coordination of social action was functionalized. Both the capitalist economy, mediated through monetarized exchange in the marketplace, and the modern state, relying on the medium of money as well as formal, juridical power, generate a series of social actions that influence one another through their unintended consequences. Behind the back of individuals and unintended by them, their actions give rise to other actions and reactions such that a domain of quasi-self-regulating mechanisms arises. But for Habermas, system integration refers only to *one* of the modes in which modern societies coordinate the action of individuals. The system perspective must be complemented by the perspective of social integration.

Social integration means that individuals orient their actions to one another because they cognitively understand the social rules of action in question. For example, to wish well to relatives on a festive occasion, or to debate the appropriateness of a particular policy, is a social interaction that can only take place when and if at least two individuals know the pertinent action context and orient themselves to it. Whereas system integration can occur even when there is a *discrepancy* between intention and consequence, social integration cannot take place unless action consequences are compatible with the intentions of social actors. It follows that whereas action systems can be analyzed, and in fact can *only* be grasped from the external perspective of the third, of the *observer,* social integration must be analyzed from the *internal* perspective of those involved, of alter and ego, as Habermas names them in *The Theory of Communicative Action*.[13] In the one case the consequences of social action proceed "behind the back of individuals"; in the latter case the occurrence of social action needs to be explained via a reconstruction of its meaning as grasped by social actors.

The distinction between system and social integration is accompanied by the twofold concept of crisis. The economy, world market, and administrative mechanisms can be viewed as *self-regulating* systems which enter into crisis when they become dysfunctional. Blockages in world trade, worldwide inflation, default on international loans, administrative inefficiency, and the like are dysfunctionalities of such systems. Only those dysfunctionalities, which derive from social integration and which generate crises of identity in individuals and collectives, can be called crises in the emphatic sense. "Thus, only when members of a society experience structural alterations as critical for continued existence and feel their social identity threatened can we speak of crises. . . . Crises states assume the form of a disintegration of social institutions" (*LC*, p. 3). Individuals and collectivities constitute and reproduce their identity in relation to values, norms, and meaning structures which define a sociocultural system. Individual and collective identity crises emerge when new motives and values are generated in the culture, which lead to the formation of new needs and interactional patterns that cannot be satisfied within the established framework of a given society.

The distinction between systemic and lived crises was already introduced in chapter 4. Since I developed the need to make such a distinction on the basis of an internal analysis of some aspects of Marx's *Capital*, I shall not repeat these arguments here. Only, it is important to note two points. First, according to Habermas, the concept of an identity crisis or lived crisis presupposes the following: individuals interpret their needs, desires, and wishes, which constitute the motives of their action, in the light of values and norms available to them in their culture. No matter how private and idiosyncratic the needs and desires of an individual may be, they are only meaningful if we also interpret them socioculturally.[14] As opposed to social and economic theories, particularly of the utilitarian sort, which presuppose that an individual's needs and desires are givens, fixed aspects of some immutable human nature, Habermas views inner nature as the product of linguistic socialization of the human child. Here he joins hands with symbolic interactionism as well as psychoanalysis and cognitive developmental theories.[15] There is no individuation without sociation. We are not individuals prior to society, we only become so within society. It is important to recall this point both to see why Habermas views a motivation crisis as a socially relevant phenomenon, and to evaluate the role of need interpretations in his ethical theory (which will be discussed in chapter 8).

The second important point in connection with the notion of a lived crisis is the following. As will be recalled, in my concluding considerations to chapter 4, I raised the question whether my emphasis on the concept of a lived crisis could be made compatible with a Marxian social theory which also criticized the consciousness of individuals and their self-understanding as being ideological in certain respects. I pointed out that an adequate crisis theory would have to integrate both moments: an analysis of systemic as well as lived crisis phenomena would have to come together. Habermas in *Legitimation Crisis* points to the danger of "idealism" inherent in a one-sided emphasis on the notion of lived identity crises and proposes the following:

> Crisis occurrences owe their objectivity to the fact that they issue from unresolved steering problems. Although the subjects are not generally conscious of them, these steering problems create secondary problems that do affect consciousness in a specific way— precisely in such a way as to endanger social integration. . . . A social-scientifically appropriate crisis concept must grasp the connection between system integration and social integration. (*LC*, p. 4)

Applying this methodological caveat to late-capitalist societies, and particularly to their social-welfare state policies, Habermas at the *empirical* level put forward the following hypothesis.[16] In order to safeguard the continuing private appropriation of capital, the capitalist state must assume an increasing number of functions such as to guarantee mass loyalty. These functions of the state lead it to intervene in certain domains of social existence in such ways that the consequence of state-interventionist and regulatory policies may not at all result in guaranteeing the continuing allegiance of the population to the capitalist system: quite to the contrary, the actions of the state may demystify the power relations in the name of which it acts, thus leading to increased demands for legitimation and political participation.

Habermas' argument hinges on three premises which I will discuss in detail. First, he claims that the dynamics of late-capitalist societies can be analyzed via a four-tiered crisis theory, distinguishing among economic, administrative, legitimation, and motivational crisis. The established pattern of the social welfare state is to absorb the dysfunctionalities of the economic system via administrative measures and reforms. The state acts both to *subsidize* capitalism—e.g., via the construction of the necessary infrastructure, through investment in economically significant science and technology research—and in those areas where the market fails, the state *replaces* it—as for example in health policy, housing, education, and transportation. In seeking to both subsidize and stabilize the capitalist economy, the state must subject certain domains of life to increased regulation.

Second, this increased role of the state can generate unintended consequences. Whether it acts to subsidize the continuing private appropriation of capital, or to replace the market, the state extends its administrative-bureaucratic apparatus into family and educational life, the health care system, city and neighborhood development.[17] The entry of the state into these domains has two consequences: first, new issues now become subject to public policy and controversy—take for example the issue of benefits for the elderly or the reforms associated with guaranteeing equality of opportunity to minorities in education. Entire domains of social relations become politicized and enter the public consciousness as contestable claims. Second, this increase of public contestation and controversy over certain domains means that the role of tradition, as well as the meaning of tradition in these spheres, is challenged. What is the role of the state, for example, in guaranteeing elderly citizens health and old age benefits? Should this be left to the action and conscience of their family members instead? Both consequences may result in a legitimation crisis, i.e., in an increased demand for public justification of the action of the state in the eyes of its citizens.

In the third place, the repoliticization of such relations through state-interventionist and reformist measures generates an additional dynamic which may exacerbate the legitimation crisis of the state. The state must not only generate mass loyalty by delivering certain economic and social goods and services, but it must also secure the continuity of certain motivational patterns[18]—like the ethic of work, achievement and belief in the family, both of which are necessary for the continuing cultural horizon of capitalism. But the manipulative production of meaning is destroyed as soon as the mode of its production becomes visible. "There is no administrative production of meaning" (*LC*, p. 70). Values and meanings cannot be called forth at will in a culture; they have their own obstinate logic. These provide individuals with shared horizons of expectations and with plausible patterns for need and motive explication. They cannot be reproduced via administrative logic.

Habermas' conclusion in the *Legitimation Crisis*, therefore, is that the welfare state is caught in a dilemma. The dilemma is that in order to compensate for the steering problems that arise from the continuing capitalist control of the economy, the state has to assume an increasingly active role. Yet this active role of the state can lead to an increased demand for legitimation, thereby augmenting the pressures on the state and its agencies to justify publicly the reasons and rationale behind their actions; these processes, in turn, may result in demystifying the power of capital. Such a legitimation crisis becomes more likely when the state fails to generate values and meaning patterns in the culture such as to guarantee continued allegiance to capitalism. In the last instance, whether a legitimation crisis occurs depends on the availability of cultural and evaluational patterns which would counteract the civic, religious, and familial privatisms that are also part of the culture of late capitalism.[19] These privatisms can block the emergence of participatory demands and can compensate for dissatisfaction via a retreat into privacy. Legitimation crisis depends then on a motivational crisis, that is, on the emergence of needs and motives which can only be satisfied by transcending the present.

Of the three premises examined above, the one that is least satisfactorily established is the last. It is unclear what the phrase "there can be no administrative production of meaning" means; it is also obscure why values and meaning patterns have an irreversible "internal logic of development" that resists such manipulation (*LC*, p. 84). Neither the first nor the second premises of this argument are all that controversial. From Claus Offe to Christopher Lasch and Daniel Bell, other critics of late capitalism have also pointed to the contradictions and legitimation deficits of the welfare state. What distinguishes Habermas' analysis from that of Offe is his effort to bring motivational crises into the picture.[20] Unlike Daniel Bell, Habermas does not see the solution to the problems of our societies in the appeal to a transcendental system of values which would counteract the new culture of narcissism and the ethos of "entitlement."[21] Instead, he tries to reveal how late-capitalist development undermines traditional value systems like the work ethic on which it itself rests while obscuring in people's consciousness the real causes behind the destruction of certain values.

Habermas' two-volume *Theory of Communicative Action* does

not alter but expands the dynamic theory of late capitalism first suggested in the *Legitimation Crisis*. The thesis that late capitalism requires an integration of the economic and administrative systems, and the repoliticization of the relations of production, is retained.[22] What this work succeeds in making clear is the interaction between economic and administrative systems of action on the one hand, and domains of social life, which Habermas had previously referred to with the category of "social integration," on the other. In this work Habermas contrasts system integration to three functions which must be fulfilled if societies are to maintain their identity as collectivities that are culturally and symbolically constituted. These are the functions of *social integration, cultural reproduction,* and *socialization.* The one-sided rationalization of economic-administrative systems under the imperatives of capitalist growth creates a dynamic such as to undermine the rationality of the lifeworld in which alone these three functions can be carried out.

> Only with the conceptual framework of communicative action do we gain a perspective from which the process of societal rationalization appears as contradictory from the start. The contradiction arises between, on the one hand, a rationalization of everyday communication that is tied to the structure of intersubjectivity of the lifeworld, in which language counts as the genuine and irreplaceable medium of reaching understanding, and, on the other hand, the growing complexity of subsystems of purposive-rational action, in which actions are coordinated through steering media such as money and power. . . . The paradox of rationalization of which Weber spoke can then be abstractly conceived as follows: the rationalization of the lifeworld makes possible a kind of systemic integration that enters into competition with the integrating principle of reaching understanding and, under certain conditions, has a disintegrative effect on the lifeworld. (ThCA 1:34)

Put in a nutshell, this is the thesis of *The Theory of Communicative Action:* rationalization processes are paradoxical because they undermine the very rationality of the lifeworld which first made societal rationalization possible. The rationalization of the lifeworld, initiated by modernity, contains an emancipatory potential which is constantly being threatened by dynamics of societal rationalization spurred on by capitalist growth.

In what follows, I will focus only on two aspects of this rich and complex work.[23] First, as with the previous analysis of the *Legitimation Crisis*, I will emphasize those methodological additions which serve to clarify the complex framework of social analysis which Habermas utilizes. This emphasis should serve to bring out the break with the Marxist functionalism of the Frankfurt School more sharply. In the second place, I will discuss how, when applied to late-capitalist societies, this complex framework yields the diagnosis that the crises of our societies are likely to manifest themselves not as organized class struggles but as "pathologies of the lifeworld" to which a multiplicity of new social movements respond.

The distinction between "system" and "social integration" in the *Legitimation Crisis* is the forerunner of the distinction between system and lifeworld in the *Theory of Communicative Action* (see ThdkH 2:348–49). As in the *Legitimation Crisis*, in the new work as well, by "system" Habermas means that social life can also be viewed as a quasi-purposive whole, where the unintended consequences of social actions come together to yield functional interdependencies. Such functionally interdependent systems of action can regulate themselves, adapt to the environment, assume capacities of problem solving, and the like. Habermas maintains that the systemic perspective on society, which is always developed from the point of view of an observer, of a third, must be supplemented by the internal perspective of social actors. The lifeworld can only be comprehended from the "performative" perspective of the alter and ego, whereas society as system can only be comprehended from the point of view of the observer.[24] The real methodological contribution of *The Theory of Communicative Action* consists, however, in the introduction of the concept of the lifeworld as the correlate of the concept of communicative action, and in the explication of how communicative action can carry out the three functions of social integration, cultural reproduction, and socialization. Let me begin with the concept of the lifeworld.

Although the concept of the lifeworld was first introduced into philosophy and social theory by Husserl and the phenomenological tradition, Habermas' reconstruction of it diverges considerably from these earlier explications. Habermas agrees with the phenomenological tradition that the lifeworld designates the horizon of unthematized, intuitive, and "always already" assumed expectations, definitions, and modes of orientation.[25] Social action always occurs against the background of such a horizon; in each case, it is only a specific and limited segment of the lifeworld which is drawn into the relevant action situation. Elements and aspects of this lifeworld are only thematized when they become relevant to the action situation at hand. The lifeworld signifies both a context of reference and a repository of intuitive knowledge and know-how for social actors.

The main drawback of the phenomenological explication of this concept is that it relies upon a philosophy of consciousness and perception. The difficulties encountered by Husserl in explicating "intersubjectivity," in reconciling the perspective of the transcendental ego with that of "alter," are well known.[26] Although the "lifeworld" refers to a shared, social horizon, it is unclear how, when one accepts the thesis of the transcendental constitution of the world via an ego, one can gain access to forms of intersubjectivity. In subsequent hermeneuticist reinterpretations, the lifeworld is conceived of as a culturally transmitted and linguistically organized repository of meaning patterns.[27] Speech and culture are viewed to be constitutive of the lifeworld. Although accepting this reformulation (ThdkH 2:190ff.), Habermas warns against the reductionism of much hermeneuticist *sinnverstehende* sociology, which tends to view the lifeworld in culturalist terms alone. This leads to the neglect of the *structural* properties of the lifeworld which do not originate with culture, but which define the institutional framework within which culture is appropriated. The "culturalist abridgment" of the lifeworld neglects both the structural conditions of the formation of group identities and the development of *individual competencies*. The idealism of *sinnverstehende* sociology focuses on the domain of cultural reproduction alone, while ignoring the dimensions of social integration through norms and values, and socialization through motive formation. In Habermas' construction, the horizon of the lifeworld does not consist of cultural meaning patterns alone, as it does for Winch and Gadamer,[28] but it entails norms and subjective experiences, practices, and individual skills as well. "Not only culture but also institutional orders and personality structures are basic components of the lifeworld."[29] Only the framework of communicative action can do justice to the three-dimensionality of the lifeworld. Habermas explicates:

> Under the functional aspect of *reaching understanding*, communicative action serves the transmission and renewal of cultural knowledge; under the aspect of *coordinating action*, it serves social integration and the establishment of group solidarity; under the aspect of *socialization*, it serves the formation of personal identities. The symbolical structures of the lifeworld reproduce themselves via the continuation of valid knowledge, the stabilization of group solidarity, and the formation of accountable actors. (ThdkH 2:208)

This means that in the first place, the lifeworld is the domain of cultural reproduction, social integration, and socialization. Second, the lifeworld must not be viewed as *transcendentally* constituted, but as one that is *reproduced* over time and whose structures change. Against the atemporality of phenomenological analysis, Habermas insists that "symbolic reproduction" must be understood as a dynamic and temporal process. Both theses are grounded in a third: linguistically mediated communicative action can fulfill all three functions of symbolic reproduction. Communicative action serves the transmission of cultural knowledge, of action coordination, and identity formation.[30] The concept of the "lifeworld" is complementary to that of communicative action. It is only through communicative action that the lifeworld is reproduced. The lifeworld remains that background horizon of unthematized assumptions, implicit expectations, and individual know-how within which communicative action unfolds. If one does not interpret the term "constitution" as the achievement of a transcendental ego but as symbolic reproduction, one could say that in this sense the lifeworld is both constitutive of, and constituted by, communicative action.

Communicative action unfolds against this background of a semantically interpreted social lifeworld. It is the uniqueness of language, however, that it can constitute its own reflective medium. In speaking, any of the validity claims which we take for granted can be challenged. When this background consensus breaks down, it can only be reestablished via special argumentation procedures. It is possible to reach an understanding (*Verständigung*) only by giving reasons to reestablish the validity of criticizable claims. Such reasons can be cited with reference to three domains of external reality, which first become clearly differentiated from one another in modernity: these are the objective, the social, and the subjective worlds.[31] In speaking, we make reference to the world about us which we conceive of as the arena in which to carry out our action plans; to the social world, the rules and norms of which constrain us to act in certain ways rather than in others; and to our own subjective world of feelings, desires, and intentions. Communicative action has a threefold world-reference. These frameworks of reference, named the "world," "society," and "self," are the pragmatic presuppositions of our speech acts. The lifeworld contains all three frameworks of reference: a cognitively interpreted external reality, a normatively interpreted social one, and an individually interpreted subjective sphere. In each of these domains agreement, once lost, can be reestablished by argumentation processes. We can thematize the validity claims of the *truth* of propositions which refer to the external world, the *rightness* or correctness of the norms which are invoked by them, and the *authenticity* or *sincerity* of a speaker's reference to his or her inner world. Language can serve as a medium of action coordination only because it allows us to continue and reestablish, via argumentation, a background consensus which breaks down.[32]

The key to Habermas' notion of "reaching understanding" (*Verständigung*) is the possibility of using reasons or grounds to gain intersubjective recognition for criticizable validity claims. In fact, Habermas' claim is even stronger: he maintains that not only reaching understanding (*Verständigung*) but understanding (*Verstehen*) as such is only possible if we would know hypothetically what it would mean to redeem the claims to validity of certain utterances.[33]

> Thus the interpreter cannot become clear about the semantic content of an expression independently of the action contexts in which participants react to the expression with a "yes" or "no" or an abstention. And he does not understand this yes/no position if he cannot make clear to himself the implicit reasons that move the

participants to take the positions they do . . . reasons are of such a nature that they cannot be described in the attitude of a third person. . . . One can understand reasons only to the extent that one understands why they are or they are not sound. (ThCA, 1:115–16)

This claim has been correctly named the "cognitivist" or "rationalist" core of Habermas' concept of action.[34] For Habermas maintains that the linguistic achievements of ordinary social actors presuppose a core of communicative competence, the essential aspect of which is the ability to continue and reestablish a lost consensus via argumentative processes in which reasons are advanced, debated, and evaluated. Even more, this communicative competence is said to be the essential medium through which the coordination of social action, the reproduction of cultural meanings, and individual socialization take place. This is no less than saying that social individuals can accomplish all three functions because they are able cognitively to judge the validity of certain claims on the basis of reasons advanced to back them up.[35] Habermas seems to have pulled the rug from under the feet of hermeneuticists like Winch and Gadamer in arguing that to "understand" another culture means to be able to take a stance in relation to the reasons which agents in those cultures would consider "good" or "appropriate" to justify certain claims. Understanding for the observer entails participation in the same universe of argumentative discourse as that of participants.[36]

This strong claim of Habermas' is important for several reasons: first, the development of reflexive argumentation procedures are seen by him to be continuous with everyday linguistic practices, and are viewed as part of the same communicative competence that makes us competent speakers of a language. Language is its own medium of reflection. This thesis is particularly significant in the context of Habermas' attempt to ground ethics in communication, and will be examined further in chapter 8.

Second, in the following chapter I will also argue that the "cognitivist" and "rationalist" bias of Habermas' concept of communicative action is not rooted in the role he attributes to argumentation or to the use of reasons to generate agreement; this rationalistic bias is rooted in the assumption that such argumentation processes also have a *motive-shaping* and *action-determining* quality. Habermas is too quick in translating the rationality intrinsic to argumentation procedures into the rationality of action and life conduct.

Third, in the context of *The Theory of Communicative Action*, the explication of the conceptual relationship among communication, argumentation, and reaching understanding through reasons serves Habermas empirically to explicate the meaning of the rationalization of the lifeworld in modernity. By the rationalization of the lifeworld is meant nothing other than the increase in argumentative practices within the everyday world in the three crucial domains of action coordination, the reproduction of cultural tradition, and socialization. Before exploring the empirical aspects of Habermas' thesis, let me pause here to place this concept of communicative action in relation to the action models of self-actualization and mimesis discussed previously in this work.

In developing the model of communicative action, Habermas finally intends to break with the paradigm of "philosophy of consciousness."[37] From Descartes to Husserl, from Feuerbach to Adorno, the philosophical tradition has offered two models of the self: either the thinking, cogitative self or the active one appropriating and transforming nature. Either a lonely self cogitates upon an object, or an active self shapes the world. At least since Hegel's revival of Aristotle, attempts have been made in the modern tradition to understand intersubjectivity and the relation between selves as well. But the focus has been on consciousness, not on language-in-use. As Hegel put it, "a consciousness faces another consciousness."[38] Habermas maintains that neither the approach of continental philosophy which reduces interaction to a form of inter-consciousness, nor the debates concerning "other minds" predominant in analytic philosophy, can grasp the integrity of *social* interaction. Both approaches proceed from *my* mind to *your* mind, from *my* consciousness to *your* consciousness. Following an insight of G. H. Mead, Habermas claims that ontogenetically, the self becomes an "I" by interacting with other selves.[39] The philosophy of consciousness puts the cart before the horse: it attempts to ground sociation (*Vergesellschaftung*) on individuation, whereas individuation proceeds under conditions of sociation alone.[40]

The concept of communicative action and the complementary one of the lifeworld allow us to see the shortcomings of previous action models relied upon by Hegel and Marx, as well as by critical theorists. Hegel ultimately views human action as a deficient mode of "work." The model of work, according to which an actor changes externality by appropriating it, is the essential one for Hegel, for it is more appropriate to capture the meaning of "self-actualization" than interaction. In acting, an agent is said to unfold, enhance, manifest, or express certain implicit potentialities. The object of work, of for that matter the work of art, can be viewed more readily as the "embodiment" of the potentiality of the agent. But in the case of moral and political action, or human interaction, this is hardly the case. Our actions are subject to an "interpretive indeterminacy" in this sphere. What we do is never unequivocally the "embodiment" of our potentialities, for the definition of our actions and the identification of our motives are subject to the interpretation of others. Hegel sees in this problem the "dialectic of action and consequence" and maintains that human action exemplifies a "bad infinity," a never-ending series of interpretations and contingencies (see chapter 3, section 2). He thereby does injustice to one of the fundamental features of our social lifeworld. Human action is linguistically mediated, both for the actor and for others, who formulate their intentions and the definitions of what they do in linguistic terms. Such formulations are essentially contestable, by ego as well as by alter. The interpretive indeterminacy of social action is not an ontological shortcoming, but its constitutive feature. The model of communicative action, by contrast, emphasizes that social action always entails linguistic communication, and that interpretive indeterminacy is a constitutive feature of social action.

A second shortcoming of the work model of action and of the emphasis on self-actualization is the undervaluation of the dimension of *human plurality*. This problem can be most clearly observed in the case of Marx's continuing reliance upon the Hegelian model. As I have noted before, although one of Marx's main criticisms of Hegel is that the latter has mythologized a super-subject called "Spirit," Marx himself never does justice to the dimension of human plurality. He emphasizes repeatedly that "objectification" is an activity which occurs in the context of a human community and that the first relation of nature is the sexual relation to other humans. But he never analyzes the experience of human plurality and reduces it instead to one of the conditions of the social *context* of action. This reduction is most noticeable in those passages where Marx speaks of socialism as initiating the "reappropriation" of alienated human powers, of ushering in the time when human potentials will return to individuals themselves. In such passages, a super-subject appropriating once more what it has once externalized enters the picture. Plurality becomes transsubjectivity.

The communicative model of action does justice to the experience of human plurality as well. For communication is the medium through which *plurality* is revealed. In acting and speaking we show who we are and our difference from others. The interpretation of our actions in light of our utterances and of our utterances in light of our actions, and our capacity to explain both when questioned, is what establishes our distinctiveness from others. Whereas in the work model of action, this experience of plurality is viewed simply as the "context" of action, according to the theory of communicative action it is constitutive of acting from the very start.

Finally, the model of self-actualization does not allow us to thematize social integration or the relation of human actors to the norms governing their social world. This was particularly emphasized in my analysis of Adorno and Horkheimer. Their reinterpretation of self-actualization as mimesis suffered from the shortcoming that the human relations of domination they sought to criticize, and the new concept of autonomy they sought to develop, were modeled on the human relation to nature. Emancipation was understood as "reconciliation" with the other. It was left fundamentally unclear what such reconciliation could or should mean in social-interactional terms. Adorno's critique of the "oily theology of intersubjectivity" offered little comfort in view of the ambiguities of his own concept of "mimesis."

By allowing us to view social integration as a communicative process of norm interpretation and revision, the model of communicative action corrects this deficiency of early critical theory. Although I have not yet analyzed the concept of communicative autonomy that follows from this model, it should be clear that from the standpoint of communicative action, the "other" is the social other, and reconciliation with this other can only come about through mutual understanding (*Verständigung*) which itself, however, is permanently open to revision and reinterpretation. Ego and alter coordinate their actions through the understanding they reach with respect to their cultural traditions and social norms, as well as subjective experiences. With these methodological and conceptual clarifications, we are now in a position to turn to the more properly empirical aspects of Habermas' theory of communicative action.

Habermas' main goal in introducing the methodological distinction between system and lifeworld, and in developing the complementary concept of communicative action, is to build the tools of analysis such as to enable him to make good a criticism of Weber which was voiced as early as his essay on "Technology and Science as 'Ideology.'" This criticism, examined above, was that the rationalization of *systems* of purposive-rational and strategic action had to be distinguished from the rationalization of communicative action, and according to the terminology of the new work, from that of the lifeworld itself. Habermas locates Weber's and, following him, the early Frankfurt School's mistake in the conflation of these two types of rationalization:

> The concept of instrumental reason suggests that the rationality of knowing and acting subjects is expanded to the purposive rationality of a higher order. The rationality of self-regulating systems, which with their imperatives go beyond the consciousness of those integrated into them, thus appears as a totalized instrumental rationality. This conflation of system- and action-rationality prevents Horkheimer and Adorno, as already Weber, from sufficiently distinguishing between the rationalization of action orientations in the sphere of a structurally differentiated lifeworld on the one hand, and the growth of the steering capacity of differentiated societal spheres on the other. (ThdkH, 2:491)

The rationalization of systems of action must be sharply differentiated from the rationalization of the lifeworld. The former means the following: increasing complexity, the development of a self-steering capacity, and adaptability to crises.[41] In the course of the development of modern societies, these systems of action become increasingly complex, autonomous, and appear as an impersonal "iron cage," dominated by an intrinsic logic, and impervious to the wishes and desires of social individuals. The rise of such a reified, semi-autonomous sphere out of the lifeworld itself is one of the paradoxes of rationalization, for such systems of action, as dominate the modern economy and administrative-bureaucratic mechanism, themselves have been made possible by transformations in values and motives which emerge in the wake of the rationalization of the lifeworld. The rationalization of the lifeworld takes place via three interrelated processes. In the first place, the decentration of the modern worldview and the emergence of a dualistic ontology sharply distinguish nature from culture, the external from the social world. In the second place, this decentration of the worldview is accompanied by an increasing *differentiation* of the once-unified *value spheres* of science, morality, religion, law, and aesthetics, and by the institutionalization of discourses aiming at working out the internal logic of these spheres. Finally, the rationalization of the lifeworld results in an increase in *reflexivity*. Whereas in describing the first two processes, Habermas critically appropriates Max Weber's analysis as outlined in particular in his *The Social Psychology of World Religions*,[42] to explicate the increase in reflexivity in the lifeworld Habermas turns to Durkheim's analysis of the transformation of the sacred.

Max Weber rightly saw that cultural modernity meant the emergence of a dualistic ontology, the emphasis on the value of the autonomous personality, and the differentiation from one another of value spheres like science, religion, ethics, and aesthetics. Habermas names the first two aspects of cultural modernity "elements of the decentered world view," while preserving the term "cultural differentiation" for the third.[43] The "decentration" of the worldview in modernity occurs when, through the rise of modern natural science, the universe is reduced to a mechanical space-time sequence; when, via modern natural right theories, the normative basis of the social order is increasingly dissociated from a cosmological worldview, and when an autonomous literary and aesthetic culture frees the subjectivity of the modern individual from societal constraints. Like Weber, Habermas is concerned to analyze how such transformations in worldview lead to moral-motivational changes which, in turn, stabilize action orientations compatible with the requirements of modern economy and law. Here developments in moral and legal spheres are pivotal. Relying upon Parsons' concepts, Habermas emphasizes processes of "motive" and "value" generalization.[44] Motive generalization implies the growth of the reflexive capacity of individuals to adjust to new environments through the self-generation of reasons for action; value generalization means, again, a reflexive growth of patterns of meaning creation. These become diffuse as opposed to specific, abstract as opposed to concrete, and are increasingly subject to argumentative procedures for their acceptance. Motive and value generalization are necessary for individuals to develop action orientations required by modern economy and law.[45]

Processes of cultural rationalization then, which initiate cognitive, motivational, and evaluative transformations, have three characteristics: they generate a decentered worldview, and lead to increased reflexivity and to the differentiation of value spheres. How do these characteristics of cultural modernity contribute to the "rationalization of the lifeworld"?

Relying on Durkheim's reconstruction of the transition from mechanical to organic solidarity, Habermas suggests that the cultural achievements of modernity which destroy the legitimizing power of theological, metaphysical, and religious worldviews also initiate the "linguistification of the sacred" (*die Versprachlichung des Sakralen*) (ThdkH, 2:118ff.). The declining power of the sacred in cementing social solidarity is eventually transformed into the "rationally binding force of criticizable claims to validity" (*die bindende Kraft kritisierbarer Geltungsansprüche*) (ThdkH, 2:133ff.). The reproduction of cultural tradition, the establishment of social integration, and the formation of individual identity, are now increasingly affected by the medium of linguistic communication. Tradition is constantly subject to questioning; disputes about the interpretation of norms and their reasoned justification increase; individual self-histories become more and more differentiated, and are sustained by the efforts of individuals themselves in ordering their life narratives into a coherent whole. The "rationalization" of the lifeworld brings with it an increase in reflexive, argumentative modes of coming to grips with the contents of the sociocultural universe as well as a reflexive reappropriation of the resources of the lifeworld.

Making this distinction between the rationalization of systems of action and of the lifeworld allows one to see that the "iron cage" of modernity is not as sturdy as it might first appear, and that late-capitalist societies contain many contradictions. As in the *Legitimation Crisis*, in *The Theory of Communicative Action* as well Habermas emphasizes that the social-welfare state faces a dilemma. Reforms that were instituted to correct the dysfunctionalities of capitalist growth have the consequences that they serve the disintegration of the very lifeworld contexts which they sought to protect (ThdkH, 2:531ff.). But whereas in the earlier work he had emphasized the paradoxical consequences of state activism, now he emphasizes the disintegrative effect of such statist measures upon the lifeworld itself.[46] As a consequence of political demands and concrete economic problems, the late-capitalist state tries to regulate education, housing, transportation, health care, job retraining, family planning, etc. Its means for carrying out these reforms are formal-administrative regulations. Such regulations subject the life histories of individuals, as well as the network of social relations in which they are embedded, to certain constraints. More often than not, such well-intending reforms have the consequence that the lifeworld context disintegrates even further, and becomes impoverished via the control of experts.

It would be wrong to read Habermas to mean that state regulation does not compensate for injustices also inherent in the lifeworld of our society.[47] But he emphasizes that a state which is pushed into political reformism in order to compensate for the structural inequalities and dysfunctionalities of capitalism is faced with certain paradoxes. This paradoxical logic means that the competition between two types of integration—systems and social—is intensified. The monetary-bureaucratic complex intervenes in the lifeworld to regulate the lifeworld and to generate motives as well as meaning patterns it requires for its own legitimation—the work ethic, the defense of the nuclear family, material sacrifice, and postponed gratification. Through processes of regulation and intervention, the lifeworld context is subject to monetary and legal measures. But the communicative structures of the lifeworld can fulfill the functions of cultural reproduction, social integration, and socialization when individuals themselves can generate motives and reasons for action via argumentative processes. There can be no "administrative production of meaning," for meaning and motives can only be recreated through the power of conviction as experienced by participants themselves. Cultural traditions cannot be revived at will (as neo-conservatives would like to think);[48] individuals have to be convinced that such traditions still have an orienting force in their lives, and they can only be so convinced via reasons. Similarly, motives have to be both cognitively meaningful and personally plausible. In the attempt to generate such meaning and motives, the agencies of the monetary-bureaucratic complex are themselves inevitably drawn into the internal logic of argumentations as they unfold in the lifeworld. This implies a certain risk. In this process, both political authority and economic power can lose their opaqueness. The mechanisms and methods of generating legitimation can become subject to increased argumentation and debate. Domination does not mean reification alone; processes of establishing domination are themselves caught in paradoxical situations which can generate their demystification.

Whether the consequences of this process are the demystification of power or modes of retreat and reaction cannot be determined a priori. The pathologies of the lifeworld arise in three domains: in the sphere of culture reproduction, the consequence is a loss of meaning; in the sphere of social integration, anomie emerges; and as regards personality, we are faced with psychopathologies.[49] Since each of these spheres contributes to the reproduction of the other two, the crises phenomena are in fact more complex: loss of meaning in the cultural domain can lead to the withdrawal of legitimation in the sphere of social integration, and to a crisis of education and orientation in the person. Anomie can imply increasing instability of collective identities, and for the individual, growing alienation. Psychopathologies bring with them the rupture of traditions, and in the social sphere, a withdrawal of motivation (ThdkH, 2:215ff.).

This diagnosis of the possible pathologies of the lifeworld shows that Habermas does justice to one of the main insights of early critical theory—the claim, namely, that in our society since World War II, crises have assumed an increasingly cultural and psychological character.[50] With the pacification of class struggles, a number of new social actors have appeared on the scene. From the ecology movement to the movement for "limits to growth," from the women's to the gay liberation movements, from consumer-protection groups to citizens' committees and to the anti-nuclear movement, a change in the *social identity* of struggling actors, the *issues* around which they mobilize, and their *patterns of struggle* have taken place. Habermas tries to capture this new logic of protest movements with the phrase "from the paradigm of distribution" to the "grammar of forms of life."[51] He maintains that these movements arise precisely at the juncture of system and lifeworld and represent the resistance of social actors to the "colonization of the lifeworld." These movements attempt to uncouple themselves from the system of monetary-bureaucratic control and produce within the lifeworld a network of communes, health collectives, ecologically organized communities, neighborhood associations, alternative schools, bookstores, restaurants, and cultural and youth centers. The theory of the "colonization of the lifeworld" claims to be able to explain such phenomena more fruitfully than alternative diagnoses available at the present, as well as helping us evaluate their ambivalent potential.[52]

Of course, many questions remain: first, one can ask, as some have,[53] whether Habermas is not conceding too much to system-functionalist theories by shifting the center of social crises and contestation from "system" to the boundary between "system" and "lifeworld." Are the economy and administrative systems as capable of adaptation and self-regulation as these theories and, following them, Habermas seem to imply? Does the new world-

economic crisis not prove the opposite in many ways? Second, is
it really the case that welfare-state reforms pose such a threat to
lifeworld contexts? Why does state intervention via juridical
means impoverish the lifeworld and aid in its further disintegration?[54] Third, can this theory really explain the rise of
new social movements? For, oddly enough, the proponents of
new social movements often come from a socioeconomic background rather different than that of those social groups who are
most subject to the advance of the monetary-bureaucratic complex—the poor, the aged, the unemployed, and minority groups.
As Claus Offe has observed in a manuscript on "New Social
Movements as a Meta-Political Challenge," "Much of what is
known about the structural composition of the new social movements as the bearers of the paradigm of "new politics" suggests
that it is rooted in major segments of the new middle class. . . .
Structural characteristics of the new middle class core of activ-
ists and supporters include high education status, relative economic security, and employment in personal service occupa-
tions."[55] Offe also points out that there is a convergence between
this group and members of the "peripheral" or "decommodified"
groups like housewives, students, the retirees, and marginally
unemployed youths. But at this stage this alliance in new social
movements has not been sufficiently analyzed to explain the
paradox that the *victims* of crises in the welfare state and the
carriers of social change do not appear to be the same. Can the
theory really account for this discrepancy and explain why the
victims of the welfare state—the poor, the aged, and the unemployed—fight for its restoration, while those who in many ways
possess the social resources to avoid it—members of the new
middle class—seek to transcend it?

Finally, in presenting the advance of modernity as the encroachment of system upon the lifeworld, is not Habermas ne-
glecting the complementarity between system and lifeworld
which emerges in the very early stages of capitalism? This question becomes particularly acute with respect to the role of the
family.[56] Habermas subsumes the family under the lifeworld; in
this respect he echoes some of the more conservative diagnoses
of the Frankfurt School and, following them, of Christopher

Lasch on the changing nature of the family. Such diagnoses are oblivious to the fact that the monogamous nuclear family historically has been the arena for the oppression of women.[57] Furthermore, the interaction between state and family is not as recent as some of these theorists lead us to believe: from the poor laws and child labor legislation of the early nineteenth century down to the Victorian crusades against prostitution, and the increasing attention paid by doctors and health experts in the last century to the reproductive and psychic health of women, the family has always interacted with systems of action either in the form of market forces or in the person of state, health, and education officials.[58] Habermas' treatment in *The Theory of Communicative Action* makes it seem as if this development is peculiar to the social-welfare state alone, whereas its beginnings extend to the previous century. Furthermore, when it is also recalled that the lifeworld of the modern family was not a "heaven in a heartless world" for women, then the question arises: can the theory of communicative action really explain the emergence of one of the most significant social movements of our times, namely, the women's movement?

The fact that the theory of communicative action has not provided the answer to all these questions is not an argument *against* it, but *for* it. Let me explain. With the turn in the 1940s to the "critique of instrumental reason," a previous phase of critical social theory in which extremely fruitful empirical research had been generated in social psychology, political sociology, and cultural theory came to an end. That unique blend of philosophical reflection and social-scientific research known as "critical theory" seemed to have dried up. The diagnosis of societal crises and their philosophical evaluation were increasingly disjointed. Abstracted from the context of social crises and struggles, critical theory lost its *raison d'être* and threatened to become the discourse of a "holy family."

Since *Legitimation Crisis*, Habermas has sought to restore the link between "critique" and "crisis" which had been ruptured with *Dialectic of Enlightenment*. Both this early work and his latest one bring back an explanatory-diagnostic dimension to critical theory. This constitutes the social-scientific potential of a critical theory. Therefore, it is no argument against such a theory that it does not answer all the questions it raises. The issue is: does it succeed in generating future research hypotheses which are fruitful and subject to refutations? It seems to me that the answer at the present stage to this question must be positive.

Yet it would be inadequate to leave the evaluation of Habermas' theses in *The Theory of Communicative Action* to the future fortunes of empirical research alone. For neither the choice of concepts nor of explanatory paradigms is value-neutral, and this is particularly so in the case of a critical social theory which always analyzes the social world from the standpoint of its future emancipatory potential. Critical theory is a social science with practical intent. This practical intent is the commitment to render humans the autonomous subjects of their actions. A critique of "functionalist reason" seeks to destroy the pseudo-objectivity of social processes and of theories defending them by showing that this objectivity is not a law of nature, but a result of the uncomprehended and unmastered action of social individuals. Just as Marx's critique of fetishism sought to demystify the laws of capitalism in order to render social subjects masters of their life processes, the purpose of the theory of communicative action is to demystify the functionalist cage of late-capitalist societies. For this reason, a critical social theory not only *diagnoses* social crises, but also *evaluates* the present in light of its future emancipatory potential.

In the following section I will analyze those respects in which Habermas claims his presentation in *The Theory of Communicative Action* not just to be an empirically fruitful way of analyzing the problems of the present, but also to fulfill the intentions of a critical theory with emancipatory intent. This requires, first and foremost, understanding the role of communicative reason in this theory.

2. Communicative Reason and the Integrity of Modernity

Since his early essays on *Theory and Practice*, one of Habermas' chief concerns has been to show that the project of modernity entailed a moral and political potential which could not be exhausted by the achievements of a primarily technical reason. In breaking with the utopian project of reconciliation with inner and outer nature as postulated by Adorno, Horkheimer, and Marcuse, Habermas turned to this practical legacy of modernity. The thrust behind the distinction between the rationalization of systems of action on the one hand and that of the lifeworld on the other is to suggest that the latter contains processes and achievements whose normative potential we have not yet exhausted.

Put in a nutshell, Habermas' question is the following: how can the "loss of freedom" caused by the encroachment of systems upon the lifeworld be reversed under conditions of "loss of meaning"—itself a consequence of modernity—without giving up, however, the cognitive gains implied by the rationalization of the lifeworld? His answer is that the project of an emancipated society does not entail the rejection of the cultural legacy of the moderns, but its completion. One must distinguish the distortions caused by the one-sided rationalization of the economy and the administration under capitalism from the rationalization of the lifeworld. It is the destructive dynamics of capitalism and not the rationalization of the lifeworld which must be reversed. The constituents of cultural modernity—decentration, reflexivity, and the differentiation of value spheres—are binding criteria of rationality. The project of an emancipated society implies the fulfillment of communicative rationality, not its transfiguration.[59]

This, of course, is a far stronger claim than the thesis that rationalization does not imply reification alone. While one may concede the latter, should one also concede the former? How can such a strong thesis be established and defended? Two lines of objection suggest themselves: first, it may be argued that the process *described* by Habermas as the "rationalization of the lifeworld" can be described in other terms as well. Whereas for him, modernity implies the increase of reflexivity, for Michel Foucault it means the increase in the power of domination;[60] whereas for Habermas the decentering of the worldview is indispensable for the growth of moral rationality, for Alasdair MacIn-

tyre exactly the opposite seems to be the case. The Copernican
universe undermines moral rationality.[61]

Second, it may be maintained that Habermas' analysis of
modernity as rationalization *begs the question* concerning the
validity of these criteria. Since these criteria constitute features
of *our* rationalized lifeworld, we first presuppose their validity
and subsequently reconstruct all previous development as leading to their emergence. What we extract from this account is
what we have already put into it. To take the anatomy of humans
as the key to the anatomy of the ape, as Marx suggested,[62] is no
proof that human anatomy is to be preferred to that of the ape.
Why not view this process as a contingent one, without falling
into the pathos of universal history, at the end of which the
conceptual structures of our world emerge as constituents of
rationality *tout court*? Unless we see *The Theory of Communicative Action* against the background of this contemporary struggle over the "soul of modernity,"[63] we are likely to miss its
philosophical import.

I want to approach these questions by turning to Max Weber;
for Weber as well, despite his oft-noted decisionism and cultural
perspectivalism, attempted to establish that the legacy of cultural modernity was not a contingent but a binding one. The
famous Introduction to *The Protestant Ethic and the Spirit of
Capitalism* begins with the following question:

> The son of the modern European cultural world [*Kulturwelt*] will
> examine the problems of universal history, unavoidably and justifi-
> ably, from the perspective of the following question: which chain of
> circumstances has led to the fact that exactly in the West, and in
> the West alone, cultural phenomena have appeared, which nonethe-
> less—or at least as we like to think—lie in a line of development hav-
> ing universal significance [*Bedeutung*] and validity [*Gültigkeit*]?[64]

The ambivalence in Weber's manner of posing the question
can hardly be overlooked: on the one hand, he qualifies the
"unavoidable and justifiable" nature of this query with the pa-
renthetical remark that "we," the children of the European
Kulturwelt, "would like to think" that these developments have
universal significance and validity. He thereby suggests that this

query is very much the consequence of *our perspective*, that it is only our "cultural interest" which motivates us to pose this question. On the other hand, this *perspectivalism* sharply contrasts with the *universalism* expressed in the main body of the text: it is "unavoidable and justifiable" that problems of universal history be examined in this light. The tension between the perspectivalist and universalist positions betrayed by this question runs through the corpus of Weber's reflections on modernity and rationalization. While regarding them very much as the fate of the West, Weber nonetheless insists that this fate is one that affects all humanity. If one were to ask whether Weber ever justified the claim that cultural phenomena that emerge at the end of cultural rationalization have universal validity, the answer must be negative. Taking the dualistic ontology, the principle of value autonomy, and the plurality of competing value spheres as the main achievements of this cultural legacy, I want to reconstruct three possible argumentations in Weber's writings concerning the universal significance and validity of the cultural legacy of the West. Each of these falls short of establishing a universal validity claim, and each will enable us to see Habermas' own intentions, as opposed to those of Weber, much more clearly.

a. The Transcendental Validity of the Standpoint of the Moderns

The dualistic ontology and the principle of value autonomy have a "transcendental" status for Weber, for they form the conditions of the possibility of understanding the social and cultural world.

> The transcendental presupposition of every *cultural science* lies not in our finding a certain culture or any "culture" in general to be valuable, but rather in the fact that we are *cultural beings* endowed with the capacity and the will to take a deliberative attitude towards the world and to lend it significance.[65]

Only if we assume that culture is a realm of meaning while nature has become radically meaningless; only if we presuppose that the meaningfulness of culture is constituted by "the capacity and will of individuals to take a *stance* towards the world and to lend it meaning" can there be a science of interpretive (*verstehende*) sociology. Since the object domain of this science—meaning (*Sinn*)—and human actions embodying meaning are not reducible to natural events, an independent methodology and conceptual apparatus such as to distinguish this science from the sciences of nature are required and justified.[66]

This mainly epistemological argument is insufficient to establish a transcendental claim, for not every presupposition of a theoretical investigation can be described as "transcendental." In a transcendental argument it is maintained that certain cognitive principles are *necessary* and *cannot* be otherwise.[67] In order to justify this, it is necessary to show that these presuppositions constitute the unavoidable deep structures of human self-consciousness, the universal anthropological givens of the species, or the a priori conditions of a community of communication. Weber can justify neither the necessity nor the inevitability of a dualistic ontology and the principle of value autonomy in this strict sense, and in many respects is not even concerned to give such a strong justification of the legacy of modernity.

b. The Epistemological Reflexivity of the Standpoint
of the Moderns

A second argument for the universal validity of the modern worldview which can be reconstructed from Weber's writings concerns its reflexivity. In comparison with premodern worldviews, the one that has emerged as a result of cultural rationalism is "self-reflexive." This modern worldview questions the basis of its own commitments, critically examines their validity, and is aware of itself as a worldview. From the modern perspective, the view that nature is the source of culture, and the belief that the true, the good, and the beautiful have a common origin, is an illusion. The modern perspective is *dis*illusioned, for it questions its own commitments and their rationality. According to Weber, it is only with the disenchantment accompanying modernity that we recognize that every monotheism is a polytheism, and that the only possible religion for us is one in which we *choose* our own gods. The scales are off our eyes: we know that we must *choose* to believe, whereas previous epochs simply *had* to believe. Weber writes, "Many old gods ascend from their graves; they are disenchanted and hence take the form of impersonal forces. They strive to gain power over our lives and again they resume their eternal struggle with one another."[68] In this respect Weber identifies reflexivity with the awareness that one's cognitive and value commitments can no longer be grounded in objective structures, but must be chosen by individuals themselves.

The increasing reflexivity of the standpoint of the moderns is for Weber primarily a consequence of the analysis of the axioms of independent value spheres by specialists. When the fundamental presuppositions of these individual value spheres are clarified, their plurality and incompatibility can be seen clearly. For Weber, this increase in reflexivity resulting from the "scientization" of values is not an unequivocal gain, precisely because the *scientization of values* cannot answer the question concerning the *value of science* itself.[69] At the heart of the increased reflexivity of the modern standpoint remains a dogmatism: this is the dogmatism necessitated by the urgency to take a position. Despite its increased sophistication in value analysis, modernity cannot eliminate the burden and dogma of an ultimate choice facing the individual.

c. The Existential Irrevocability of the Standpoint of the Moderns

The last argument can be viewed as a corollary of the second. Here reflexivity is seen as generating an epistemological paradox which no attempt to overcome the standpoint of the moderns can escape. Once disenchantment has taken place; once the world has been reduced to a chain of meaningless facts; once truth, goodness, and beauty no longer have a unifying source; then all attempts to reenchant the world encounter the following paradox: spheres which have become deeply meaningless are to be rendered meaningful again through a *subjective decision* or act of *will*. But when belief systems become capable of questioning and doubting themselves, all efforts to eliminate this dimension carry the marks of an unavoidable subjectivism.

The world must be reenchanted through an act of will and decision; the difference between an enchanted and a *reenchanted* universe is that the validity and meaningfulness of the latter do not derive from *objectivity*—from the facts themselves—but from the *subjective* act that lends objectivity meaning.[70]

This argument as well cannot establish the universal significance and value of cultural rationalization. Even if all future value and belief systems bear unavoidable subjective marks, this would be of significance for us—children of the West; but what is of significance for us need not be of equal significance and value for other cultural standpoints.

Nonetheless, among all the arguments examined above, I believe this last one to be the most consequential in the sense that with these observations, Weber uncovers a cultural tendency of undeniable significance. In his considerations on this question, he exposes the danger inherent in attempts to "reenchant" the world. Since the cognitive unity of nature and culture, of facts and values, has been destroyed, such unity cannot be reestablished through reason; it must now proceed via an act of will. As Nietzsche saw well, when the will questions itself, when reason, doubt, and skepticism are the primary values to which the will must be subordinated, the "sickness" of the moderns sets in. On this view, the "will to life" must not be allowed to question itself; an affirmative relation to life is only possible if the Cartesian spirit is defeated; the will must learn to will itself and to ground itself via its own manifestation.[71] Questioning, doubt, and reflexivity do not lead to an affirmation of existence; they cannot recreate that reenchanted universe in which Zarathustra can once more discover the unity of beauty and truth, of appearance and essence. Such philosophies of will and existence, from Nietzsche to Heidegger and to Sartre, are the desperate attempts of the modern soul to create meaning in a silent universe, abandoned by the gods. Precisely because such meaning is not *pre-found* but must be recreated by the individual, such philosophies and outlooks stop short of the rational questioning which would threaten to expose the arbitrariness of the will itself. Since reason divides, the will must unite; to succeed in this task, the will must silence reason.

It is to Max Weber's credit to have seen so clearly that moment when the will would attempt to break out of the "iron cage" of modernity by a defiant act of transcendence or despair.[72] It is also to his credit to have cautioned against the authoritarian ramifications of the politics of the will in his analysis of modern charisma.[73] Yet in the final instance it is unclear whether Weber himself does not betray a certain sympathy toward such defiant acts of will; whether in fact he does not have more respect for those passionate outbursts of despair than the humbug of modern utilitarian existence. In this sense, although not a subtle reader of Weber, Leo Strauss was not altogether wrong in detecting a profound nihilism in Weber's dictum that the modern soul had to choose between God and the Devil.[74]

Habermas' fundamental concern in developing a theory of communicative action and rationality is to warn against the nihilism which may result from this ambivalent relation to the legacy of the moderns. This ambivalence is not unique to Weber: in the tradition of critical theory as well, the reduction of the legacy of modern reason to instrumental rationality has created deep vacillations. In the *Dialectic of Enlightenment*, the analysis of the inconsistencies of Enlightenment rationality brought Adorno and Horkheimer dangerously close to a nihilistic rejection of the legacy of the Enlightenment altogether. Habermas would like to claim that this legacy is binding on us in some modified version of all three claims outlined above.

To avoid confusion, let me first note the differences between Weber's and Habermas' characterizations of the cultural legacy of modernity. One of Habermas' central theses in *The Theory of Communicative Action* is that Weber's analysis of modernity as a rationalization process was restricted on two counts. In the first place, in his analysis of the emergence of the modern worldview, primarily in the light of the evolution of world religions, Weber focused on the dimension of the *ethical* transformation of such world religions and overlooked developments in the *scientific-cognitive* and the *aesthetic-practical* spheres (ThCA 1:214–15). Habermas strongly emphasizes that the decentration of the worldview in modernity results not primarily in the dualistic ontology which juxtaposes a normatively regulated social life—

a sphere of values—to a meaningless objectivity—a sphere of facts—but in the differentiation of three realms. These are world, society, and self. These categories are not ontological but referential ones: they designate an *objective* domain of facts, a normatively regulated *intersubjective* sphere, and a *subjective* domain of the self's inner experiences. Such a decentered world-view allows the acting and knowing subject to adopt different basic attitudes (*Grundeinstellungen*) toward the same world. These differentiated spheres become accessible for cognition and action in different modes: their separation from one another also seems to render fluid the attitudes with which the knowing and acting self can relate to these worlds qua worlds, qua referentially distinct spheres. These basic attitudes are named by Habermas the "objectifying," the "norm-conformative," and the "expressive."[75] Only when these three basic attitudes toward the three worlds become cognitive possibilities are we presented with the full range of the rationalization potential contained in the demise of world religions.

In the second place, in analyzing how this cognitive potential becomes anchored in social life, Weber again restricts the full picture and confines himself to clarifying the elective affinity between the *ethical* orientation resulting from the rationalization of world religions and complexes of purposive-rational action embodied in the economic sphere in particular. But a broader concept of societal rationalization would have to examine the institutionalization of cognitive, normative, and aesthetic ideas in cultural action systems (ThCA 1:234ff.). The differentiation of science, ethics, and aesthetics in modernity is accompanied by their institutionalization in universities, research academies, juridical and legal professions, and an autonomous realm of art production and criticism. Through such institutionalization, modes of appropriating cognitive, social, and subjective values become reflexive, i.e., increasingly subject to discourse validation and argumentation. As argumentative modes of generating beliefs and procedures for testing them are institutionalized, the rationality of such processes is seen to lie increasingly in their *procedural* characteristics rather than in their substantive content. The rationality of belief systems is attributed, first and foremost, to the procedures through which they are acquired and through which they can be revised or refuted.

Habermas' reconstruction of the cultural legacy of modernity in the light of the decentered worldview and the three basic attitudes it permits, and his emphasis on the institutionalization of reflection, lead to a different diagnosis of the tensions in modern culture from that of Weber. Whereas in the increasing differentiation of value spheres and their incompatibility, Weber saw an irresolvable value struggle placing a tremendous psychic burden on the modern individual who nonetheless had to create meaning in a fragmented universe,[76] Habermas stresses that the destruction of the unity of reason does not mean a general loss of rationality. Even if, as regards the substantive content of ideologies and worldviews, the loss of meaning is irreversible, the *unity* of reason can be preserved via those communication processes through which validity claims can be redeemed. The new paradigm of rationality is not *substantive* but *discursive;* it thematizes not the *content* but the *form* of those necessary argumentation procedures in light of which the validity claims of truth, rightness, and truthfulness are to be settled. From the perspective of communicative rationality embodied in processes of argumentation, the loss of meaning in modern culture is not equivalent to a loss of reason.

This last claim must be read in a twofold fashion: first, Habermas claims that *factually* there has been an increase of rationality, a cumulative learning process, in these three spheres—the cognitive-instrumental, the moral-practical, and the aesthetic-expressive ones. But equally he means that *normatively* one ought not to equate loss of meaning with a loss of rational potential in modern culture. Very often, the loss of meaning can be attributed to the cultural impoverishment of the lifeworld in the wake of the emergence of a culture of experts who are in turn incapable of transmitting the achievements of science and art back to the lifeworld.[77]

Habermas' theses concerning the rational potential of the culture of the moderns are extremely strong and controversial: at the present, not only must one contend with an increasing number of rival accounts of cultural modernity—let me mention only those of Foucault, MacIntyre, and Lyotard[78]—but the fact that so many of Habermas' theses are couched in a reconstruction of the history of theories rather than in an actual historical account makes it very difficult for the reader at this stage to accept wholesale his assertions concerning the cumulative increase in rationality in the three spheres he singles out.[79] Equally significant are the conceptual difficulties: they range from questions concerning the philosophical viability of a *procedural* concept of rationality to the meaning of aesthetic-practical "reason" and to the claim that only in these spheres alone could an accumulation of knowledge in modernity occur.[80]

Since I cannot hope to do justice to all these questions, in the remainder of this work I will focus on one aspect of Habermas' concept of communicative reason which is central to the problem of this book, namely, his attempt to develop a communicative ethics as a foundation for critical social theory. By focusing on this issue, I also hope to show that many of the distinctions Habermas draws between the spheres of moral and aesthetical rationality in particular need reexamination and that above all, his program of a strong justification of communicative ethics cannot succeed. Before embarking on this critique, it will be helpful to conclude this discussion by considering Habermas' views concerning the cognitive legacy of the moderns. I will do so by constructing three lines of argument which parallel Weber's reflections on the validity of the standpoint of the moderns. In a much stronger sense than Weber, Habermas wants to claim that the decentered worldview and the reflexive differentiation of value spheres are constitutive of communicative rationality, and that such a structure of rationality and its constituents are quasi-transcendental, irrevocable, and binding upon us.

d. The Quasi-Transcendental Status of Communicative Rationality

It is well known that following *Knowledge and Human Interests*, Habermas distinguished between the two senses of the word "self-reflection" which he conflated in his earlier work: on the one hand, self-reflection means a *critical analysis* of the determinants of concrete life processes of individuals and groups; on the other hand, it refers to the *rational reconstruction* of anonymous rule-systems.[81] The aim of such "reconstructive sciences" is to make individuals aware of the rule competencies which they "always already" practice as an implicit know-how. Reconstructions serve the task of self-reflection in the sense of making individuals aware of what they already know. Reconstructions carry on the task of transcendental philosophy with modified means: just as transcendental philosophy sought to make individuals aware of those necessary presuppositions which operate in all their acts of cognition, reconstructive theories analyze the *deep structures* of cognition and action which are operative in the activities of individuals. However, unlike transcendental philosophy, reconstructive theorems do not assume that such deep structures are ahistorical, non-evolving frameworks. To the contrary, Habermas views such deep structures as patterns of rule competencies which evolve in the history of the individual and of the species. Although individuals are more often than not unaware of the logic and dynamic of such evolution, they are the agents of such evolution, for it is through learning processes that they acquire such rule competencies. In Habermas' account, reconstructive sciences replace transcendental philosophy today, while attempting to accommodate Hegel's critique of Kant. They produce an "empirical phenomenology of mind" tracing the development of ontogenetic and phylogenetic competencies.

The account of modernization as rationalization presented in *The Theory of Communicative Action* relies upon this concept of a reconstructive science. To combine the "internalist" with the "externalist" perspectives in social theory, Habermas utilizes the concepts of a *developmental logic* and *learning processes*. Social change, he maintains, cannot be observed from the standpoint of the observer alone. There are aspects of social evolution which must be viewed as sequences in a developmental logic and which can be reconstructed internally, that is, "insightfully recapitulated from the perspective of the participants."[82] Social development presupposes social learning: at any given stage, it must be possible to identify problems to which social agents respond in meaningful ways; these responses subsequently may be institutionalized. Social innovation occurs through the answers that social agents give to the ever-new problems of their lifeworld.[83] Through institutionalization, the experiences leading to a specific answer set become part of the material and cultural history of society. These previous answers are available to social agents as the legacy of the past; they reproduce their lifeworld by recapitulating these already available answers while creating and seeking new ones. The concept of the reproduction of the lifeworld thus presupposes the related notion of a "learning process" as an internally reconstructable sequence meaningful to participants themselves.

Habermas maintains that if it can be shown that criteria of communicative rationality are the results of learning processes that can be meaningfully reconstructed, then their "quasi-transcendental" status can be redeemed. They would then be shown to be *deep structures* underlying cognitive and interactive human competencies. These competencies are indeed changing and evolving, but their evolution represents an internally compelling sequence. Habermas' reconstruction of the "linguistification of the sacred" and the rationalization of the lifeworld in the course of modernity is intended to present exactly such an account.

Clearly, this is a very weak transcendental claim. Since Kant, the goal of transcendental arguments has been to establish the necessity and uniqueness of certain conceptual presuppositions (e.g., the pure concepts of the understanding) and structural conditions (e.g., the necessary synthetic unity of self-consciousness). Such necessity may be logical in nature, or it may be "quasi-empirical," as for example when we claim that unless we can distinguish between subjective experiences and intersubjectively shared common ones, no human self-consciousness ascribable to a continuing self is possible. While arguments concerning logical necessity can be developed in a straightforward manner, the greatest difficulty faced by transcendental philosophies, and which have led many critics to question their viability altogether, is the claim that there can be such "quasi-empirical" necessity. Quine's critique of the analytic-synthetic distinction is designed precisely to refute the claim that synthetic statements referring to experience but irrefutable by experience are at all meaningful.[84]

A second aspect of transcendental arguments is the claim that such conditions are not only necessary but unique. As R. P. Wolff has observed, this means that transcendental arguments cannot proceed regressively from a conclusion "s" to the conditions under which it is possible, for in a valid argument, there may be any of a number of premises from which "s" could be derived. A transcendental argument would have to establish a first premise "p" from which "s" follows such that "s, if and only if, p."[85]

Reconstructions in the sense suggested by Habermas can by no means meet the stringent requirements of transcendental arguments. First, since such reconstructions of action and speech competencies are developed by synthesizing the conclusions of sciences like genetic epistemology, cognitive psychology, and generative linguistics, they are more empirical than transcendental. As Mary Hesse points out, if we are to take the status of reconstructions as a *science* seriously, then we have to extend to them the same criteria of revisability and fallibilism which we apply to all other sciences.[86] And this greatly reduces the claim to be able to discover a *necessity* which is non-empirical while determining empirical reality. Hesse raises a second objection:

> The . . . difficulty about Habermas's description of reconstructive science is that it seems to presuppose that there is *just one correct explication of linguistic competence, of logic, of human action, and even of theory of science and ethics.* This claim is connected with the assertion that the reconstructive sciences are value-neutral and interest-free. But we have seen that even if the empirical sciences were totally interest-free (which I am shortly going to deny), this would not imply uniqueness of their theoretical frameworks. It is therefore difficult to conceive of such uniqueness in reconstructive sciences. Moreover, its possibility is not borne out by the facts—even logical theory is permeated by ideological preferences. Chomsky's version of structural linguistics has not by any means won universal acceptance, and neither has Piaget's developmental psychology; much less have the various attempts at systematizing "human action" terminology or the theory of ethics.[87]

Thus, if we take seriously the possibility of *competing* frameworks of interpretation and explanation in reconstructive sciences, then the claim to *uniqueness* associated with transcendental arguments will have to be abandoned as well. Reconstructive arguments can fulfill neither the conditions of necessity nor those of uniqueness associated with transcendental argumentations, and still retain their status as empirically fruitfully scientific accounts.

If these objections are essentially correct, as I believe they are, then the line separating "reconstructive" from "hermeneutic-narrative" accounts may be thinner than it first appeared. For, if reconstructive accounts cannot claim necessity for themselves in some strong sense, then what distinguishes them from, and gives them priority over, other modes of narrative accounts? Why is a reconstructive account of the development of modern rationality structures as a cumulative learning process to be preferred to one that views this same process as one of *forgetting*? Is Habermas' account of the progressive development of modern rationality more compelling than the accounts of Nietzsche, Adorno, and Foucault, who view this same process as one of forgetting, repressing, and sublimating?

Within the limits of this work, I cannot hope to address this question adequately. Let me suggest here three possible lines of response Habermas may provide in defense of the cogency of his account of rational reconstructions over and against other deconstructivist accounts.

First, in recent years Habermas himself has recognized that reconstructive arguments are more empirical than transcendental. He writes:

> All attempts at discovering ultimate foundations, in which the intentions of First Philosophy live on, have broken down. In this situation, the way is opening to a new constellation in the relationship of philosophy and the sciences. As can be seen in the case of the history and philosophy of science, formal explication of the conditions of rationality and empirical analysis of the embodiment and historical development of rationality structures mesh in a peculiar way. Theories of modern empirical science . . . make a normative and at the same time universalist claim that is no longer covered by fundamental assumptions of an ontological or transcendental-philosophical nature. This claim can be tested

only against the evidence of counterexamples, and it can hold up
in the end only if reconstructive theory proves itself capable of
distilling internal aspects of the history of science and systematically explaining, in conjunction with empirical analysis, the actual, narratively documented history of science in the context of
social development. (ThCA 1:2–3)

What this passage outlines is a certain methodology of "narrative documentation" that attempts to present developments in
the history of science as "internally motivated" learning sequences. Habermas assumes that certain conceptual processes
can best be accounted for if we view them as learning processes
on the part of the participants themselves.

As a second line of argument, against deconstructionist accounts of cultural modernity, Habermas would maintain that
they confuse *form* and *content*. Rational reconstructions do not
claim that there is progress at the semantic level of the meaning
structures of a given culture, but only that at the formal level the
development of human cognition follows a certain logic. That is,
learning occurs at the level of the mastery of certain formal
operations and distinctions. For example, the decentration of
the worldview in modernity and the formal separation of objective, intersubjective, and subjective spheres is one such formal
achievement which parallels the decentration of the world picture of the human infant. Another such formal sequence is the
transition from conventional to post-conventional modes of
moral reasoning. Whereas at the conventional level the validity
of moral principles is identified with the standpoint of a particular social collectivity—moral validity and social acceptance
are conflated—at the post-conventional level the validity of
moral values and principles is examined independently of the
authority of a particular social group. This step from social particularism to universalism entails enlargening the horizon of
their accountability on the part of the actors, but it does not
imply a necessary normative content. In other words, even at the
post-conventional stage various particularisms and tribalisms
reassert themselves; only now, they must be justified at the normative level required by the formal structures of that particular
stage.[88]

Finally, in defense of rational reconstructions Habermas points out that various lines of empirical social research both in the diachronic and synchronic modes are necessary. At the synchronic level, i.e., at the level of the reconstruction of competencies shared by humans at the same stage of development, one can conduct studies of the general structures of communication and investigate pathological or distorted patterns of communication, just as one can study the application of formal pragmatics to the ontogenesis of communicative competence. The ultimate proof for such reconstructions is how well they articulate the intuitive "know-how" of competent actors into a "know-that." Such studies can be complemented at the diachronic level by examinations of the development of worldviews, normative structures, and the like across history. Habermas maintains that if the developmental sequences which are uncovered in the analysis of the ontogenetic development of the child can with some plausibility be applied to reconstruct the history of the species, then the thesis that a collective learning process takes place in the course of modernity can be strengthened.[89]

These three lines of argument—the first which admits that rational reconstructions are more empirical than transcendental; the second which emphasizes the form/content distinction; and third which points to the empirical fruitfulness of reconstructive studies in diachronic and synchronic modes—suggest that indeed a strong justification of the legacy of cultural modernity is not possible; in fact, even the very concept of a "quasi-transcendental" may be a misnomer. What distinguishes rational reconstructions from both hermeneutical and deconstructivist accounts is not their special philosophical status, but their empirical fruitfulness in generating further research, their viability to serve as models in a number of fields, and their capacity to order and explain complex phenomena into intelligible narratives.

This examination establishes that the battle over the validity and significance of the cultural integrity of the moderns is not resolved, but only that Habermas introduces a number of new criteria into the debate which transcend the traditional modi of philosophical and a priori argumentation. However, this turn to a more empirically oriented approach cannot dispense with the philosophical issues behind this debate, and as I will argue further below, Habermas himself is not altogether consistent in the philosophical hopes he continues to attach to reconstructive argumentations.

e. Reflexivity and Communicative Rationality

It was observed previously that in his comments on the epistemological standpoint of the moderns, Max Weber had singled out the reflexivity of this worldview. I also noted that for Habermas, "reflexivity" was a general characteristic of modern belief systems, institutionalized since the sixteenth and seventeenth centuries in the specialized discourses of science, jurisprudence, and aesthetics.

Any claim concerning the reflexivity of the cultural tradition of the moderns and its bindingness upon us is likely to be subject to an initial misunderstanding. It is quite probable that such a claim will be identified with a theodicy of progress and autonomy. Although not free from such moments, it is at least not Habermas' explicit intention to identify the growth of reflexivity in modernity with moral-practical progress *tout court*. There is a price that one pays for the increased sophistication of belief systems, and this is the ever more subtle exercise of control and domination. So far, Foucault is correct. Adorno and Horkheimer as well saw in Enlightenment morality a more powerful means for justifying the internalization of repression than premodern moral theories in which the inequalities in the distribution of power and in the possibility to attain happiness were accepted as givens. As modern ideologies dispensed with givens and subjected more and more spheres of life to argumentative validation, it became necessary to increase levels of repression precisely to counter the increased demands of the population. Habermas acknowledges the price that the moderns have to pay:

> Despite this progress, the exploitation and oppression *necessarily* practiced in political class societies has to be considered retrogressive in comparison with the less significant social inequalities

permitted by the kinship system. Because of this, class societies are structurally unable to satisfy the need for legitimation that they themselves generate. . . . How is this *dialectic* of progress to be explained? . . . Evolutionarily important innovations mean not only a new level of learning but a new problem situation as well, that is, a new category of burdens that accompany the new social formation. The dialectic of progress can be seen in the fact that with the acquisition of problem-solving abilities, new problem situations come to consciousness. . . . At every stage of development the social-evolutionary learning process itself generates new resources, which mean new dimensions of scarcity and thus new historical needs. (*Communication and the Evolution of Society*, pp. 163–65)

Once we dispense with the connotations of automatic progress and moral improvement associated with any claim about increasing reflexivity in culture, then Habermas' thesis becomes that every new stage of learning brings with it new problems and a new awareness of problems which in turn require new solutions, and among these, new forms of repression. Although Habermas has not provided an analysis of how this "dialectic of Enlightenment" may be at work within the framework of his reconstructive theory, such an undertaking is not in principle *incompatible* with his emphasis upon the growth of reflexivity. For such reflexivity may result in increased repression as well.

Self-questioning, the capacity to justify one's standpont via principled argumentation, the analyses of the hidden or explicit presuppositions of one's standpoint, have constituted the ideals of Western *logos* from its beginnings in Socratic dialogues. It is first with the decentration of the worldview in modernity that activities which were formerly restricted to the culture elites of society—the philosophical few, the Church Fathers, and members of the medieval institutions of learning—entered the consciousness of large masses of the population. Copernicus, Descartes, and Galileo were each in their own way aware of the fact that the modern scientific revolution would institutionalize the distrust of the senses and the attitude of questioning, formerly characteristic of the mind-set of a small philosophical elite.[90] The modern individual had to learn that what one's eyes saw of the movement of the heavens was false; what one's senses told us about the nature of external objects, deceptive; doubt was carried into the very center of one's relationship to the world of appearances. The coming of the age of reason was preceded by the age of doubt.

Clearly, strongly divergent evaluations of this process are possible. For Nietzsche, we have been rolling down an incline toward the abyss ever since Copernicus.[91] For Arendt, Cartesian doubt is at the beginning of a process at the end of which stands our loss of the world, as that public space of appearances which all beings share in common.[92] For Habermas, increased reflexivity and the differentiation of value spheres result in a loss of meaning for the modern individual, but this loss also strengthens those communicative processes through which alone a sense of validity can be regained. Suppose, however, that one were to raise the following objection: whatever one's evaluation of this process, it may be said, the argument concerning the binding nature of reflexivity begs the question. Certainly self-questioning, the justification of one's standpoint through reasoned argumentation, analysis of implicit and explicit presuppositions, and the like have been ideals in Western culture since its inception, but in what sense can they be universalized and applied in judging other cultures?

There are two answers to this objection: first, in confronting other cultures, we have to admit the presence of a hermeneutical circle. We cannot divest ourselves of these criteria and go completely "native." For in order to understand what it would even mean to "go native," we must first engage in a process of translation whereby we, from our perspective, first attempt to make sense of this other culture.[93] In this task, it is inevitable that the characteristics of our own worldviews, decentered and reflexive as they are, will come into play. To understand is to understand in a certain context, and for one whose culture has taken the reflexive turn, this context is no longer eliminable. We cannot divest ourselves of the constituents of our culture at will or by an act of fiat; they are the ones we bring to bear on the analysis of any situation. Furthermore, the very fact that we can ask the question whether reflexivity is a binding criterion implies that we are already in the reflexive circle. Prereflexive systems are not questioned; they are accepted. They do not allow their participants to remain within and without, as ours do. Even those who would like to reject reflexivity reveal that they are products of a culture in which such a posture first becomes meaningful.

The second answer is that *formal criteria of rationality* should not be conflated with the *integrity of forms of life*. To maintain that reflexivity is a criterion of rationality does not imply that we can judge other cultures and other forms of life as "rational" or "irrational" *in toto*. In a recent article, Habermas has observed that we cannot appraise forms of life simply by applying to them standards of procedural rationality, reflexivity, and the like. For "forms of life comprise not only institutions that come under the aspect of justice, but 'language games,' historical configurations of habitual practices, group memberships, cultural patterns of interpretation, forms of socialization, competencies, attitudes, and so forth."[94] All these phenomena as a whole and in their interrelationships cannot be judged from the sole standpoint of their rationality. With respect to the totality of an alien culture, we should still seek a hermeneutical understanding. Certainly such understanding is only possible if we utilize our own standards of historically attained reflexivity, but this standard alone does not provide us with a yardstick by which to judge the entirety of a form of life or of a culture.[95]

Although plausible, this distinction between formal criteria of rationality and the integrity of forms of life suggests a number of problems. First, it is unclear that in fact the concept of communicative action does not commit Habermas to have to disregard this distinction. Communicative action is said by him to necessitate an understanding from the participant's point of view (ThCA 1:115–16). Such understanding is said to require further an understanding of the reasons why agents say and do the things they say and do. To understand their actions and utterances, we must comprehend the reasons given by agents. But according to Habermas, such an understanding of reasons is only possible if the observer enters into a "performative dialogue" with the actor; that is to say, to understand reasons is also to judge them as one would judge them in one's own culture. Clearly, the lines between understanding and judging are not firm. But if so, can one really make the distinction suggested above? It seems that in wanting to draw this distinction, Habermas would have to concede more to the possibility of a *nonevaluative* mode of hermeneutical understanding than his theory of communicative action allows him.

In conclusion, then, it must be said that one can only give one answer to the critic who accuses us of begging the question in positing the bindingness of reflexivity: yes indeed, there is a circularity in our argumentation, but this is not a vicious circularity. It would be a vicious circle only if presuppositionless understanding, an understanding that could divest itself of its own contextuality, were also possible. Since, however, this cannot be the case, it follows that reflexivity is binding for us. To want to divest ourselves of it may be like wanting to jump over our own shadows. Clearly, this is a point of view which Habermas would share with the hermeneuticist.

The passage considered above, where Habermas draws a distinction between formal criteria of rationality and forms of life, suggests nonetheless that he may be searching for a stronger sense of the bindingness of the legacy of modernity than the one I have been attributing to him so far. I believe this to be the case. Habermas continues the above passage with the following observation: "If we do not wish to renounce altogether standards for judging a form of life to be more or less misguided, distorted, unfortunate, or alienated, if it is really necessary the model of sickness and health presents itself."[96] This invocation of a "model of sickness and health" brings with it an issue which goes to the heart of the matter as far as Habermas' reliance upon evolutionary models of "normal" courses of development is concerned.

At an earlier point, the analogy drawn between critical theory and psychoanalysis had given rise to wholly legitimate objections from Gadamer and Giegel that this placed the critical theorist in a privileged epistemic situation which hardly seemed consistent with its emancipatory intentions.[97] In response to this objection, Habermas distinguished between "critique," in which an asymmetrical position of knowledge between the theorist and members of a society obtains, and "discourse," where all are equal to decide upon a common course of action in free and unconstrained debate.[98] This distinction resurfaces in *The Theory of Communicative Action:* "I would like to take account of these special circumstances by always only speaking of 'critique' instead of 'discourse' when arguments are employed in situations in which participants need not *presuppose* that the conditions for speech free of external and internal constraints are fulfilled" (ThCA 1:42). The phrase "the pathologies of the lifeworld" is used in this spirit. It describes a process from the standpoint of "critique," yet it is unclear whether in a discursive situation agents in the lifeworld would concede the use of this term as meaningful in describing their condition. More significant, it is thereby presupposed that the theorist possesses some model of societal "health" or "sickness." In particular, this second claim is implausible; but it is no accident that Habermas makes it. The reasons why can be seen more clearly when we consider his third and last argument in defense of the legacy of the moderns.

f. The Existential Irrevocability of Communicative Reason

Like Weber, Habermas maintains that cultural modernization processes are in some sense "irrevocable." In establishing this point, he often utilizes arguments drawn from cognitive-developmental theories, which maintain that in a "normal" course of development, the individual will make the transition from one stage to another in a sequence which is irreversible.[99] Once having attained stage four, adolescents do not fall back to stage two *unless* functioning as a normal human being is impaired by conditions of severe trauma, breakdown, shock, and the like. Of course, this "unless" covers a number of problems. One would want to know more precisely what these debilitating conditions are or could be.

In a similar vein, at the end of *Legitimation Crisis*, Habermas argued as follows: whether the impact of the monetary-bureaucratic system upon the lifeworld would lead to an increased demand for participation and legitimation would depend upon the presence of meaning- and value-orientations in the culture that could be reactivated such as to generate new motivational patterns for individuals. A crisis of legitimation was likely when expectations were generated which could not be satisfied within available patterns of value or through other compensatory mechanisms. Legitimation crisis presupposed a motivation crisis. Here the argument became extremely hypothetical: Habermas pointed to certain transformations in the culture of late-capitalist societies, like the decline of civic, familial, and vocational privatisms, and maintained that bourgeois and prebourgeois traditions had been replaced by ideologies like scientism, universalistic morality, and post-auratic art that could not prevent or counteract the erosion of such privatisms. The claim that these traditions and their remnants would not be reactivated in such a way as to counteract the erosion of these motivational structures or to channel them in an authoritarian direction was supported by the following argument: "There are no functional equivalents for the spent traditions, for they are precluded by the logic of the development of normative structures" (LC, p. 75). Habermas assumed that the contemporary forms of dominant bourgeois ideologies—scientism, universalistic morality, and post-auratic art—had undergone "irreversible developments, which have followed an internal logic," and which could be reversed only at the cost of regressions (LC, p. 84).

This argument indicates a particular difficulty in the use of evolutionary-developmental models within a critical social theory. When applied to a macro-level, such arguments carry with them the overtones of a speculative philosophy of history. The future projected by the theorist, and which is fundamentally open, is presented as if it were a necessary and "normal" outcome of a course of development. It is only in this light that deviations from the theory can be deemed "regressions." It is presupposed that we already possess the yardstick by means of which to judge the future. But whereas in the case of ontogenesis, concrete life histories of individuals have an end, and every human child that is born recapitulates a given course of development to become an adult, at the level of phylogenesis this is hardly the case. Neither are we at the end of history, nor can we point to a "normal" course of development in light of which we can judge "regressions" and "deviations." The history of the species is so far unique, *sui generis;* we have no established model of development to compare it with.

The words "regression" and "pathology" are meaningful only in one sense: we can imagine that a future course of development *may* fail to embody or realize the *potentials* we see in the present. This means that the present is essentially a horizon open to action. For what is or is not possible can never be determined theoretically alone. Here actuality is prior to potentiality. Just as we become good in the Aristotelian sense only by acting in ways that are good, we discover the potentials of the present only by acting toward the future. Evolutionary theories flatten this horizon of the future by making the future appear like the necessary consequence of the present. To put the objection I am raising to Habermas' reliance on evolutionary theory in a nutshell: if the problem with early critical theory seemed to be that their conception of utopian reason was so esoteric as not to allow embodiment in the present, the difficulty with Habermas' concept is that it seems like such a natural outcome of the present that it is difficult to see what would constitute an emancipatory break with the present if communicative rationality were fulfilled.[100]

To say that the structures of communicative rationality are irrevocable can mean only the following: this legacy contains a potential which we would like to see realized, and for which we are ready to engage ourselves. The theory of cultural modernity is not a philosophy of history but a critical theory with "practical-emancipatory intent." The fulfillment of this legacy is a practical question, not a theoretical one. The question here is: does such a demand for the fulfillment of modern reason *project* the image of a future we would like to make our own? I began this chapter by observing that Habermas' theory marked a shift from utopian to communicative reason in critical theory; I am closing it with the contention that communicative reason can motivate us only if it also contains a *utopian potential.* Before turning to a discussion of this claim, let me briefly summarize the main conclusions of this chapter.

In this chapter I have analyzed the shift in critical theory initiated by Jürgen Habermas. First I traced the development of this shift with respect to Habermas' methodological departures from early critical theory. I subsequently considered his empirical theory of the crisis potentials and tendencies of late-capitalist societies. As a result of conceptual shifts in both areas, Habermas has succeeded in restoring that unique relationship between philosophy and the social sciences that had been characteristic of early critical theory. The second part of this chapter has focused on the more philosophical aspects of Habermas' reinterpretation of modernity as rationalization. I have examined his answer to Weber's query concerning the universal validity and significance of Occidental rationalism. The following chapter will continue this discussion by addressing a more specific aspect of the program of communicative rationality, namely, the attempt to ground the normative foundations of critical theory in a communicative ethic. At this point, if we recall the distinction introduced at the beginning of this chapter between the explanatory-diagnostic and anticipatory-utopian dimensions of critical theory, it would be appropriate to say that the issues examined in this chapter fall under the first aspect of critical theory, whereas the program of communicative ethics belongs more properly to its anticipatory-utopian aspect. As my concluding remarks on the need to recover part of the utopian legacy of early critical theory may suggest, however, I question the extent to which communicative ethics can fulfill the function of serving as anticipatory-utopian critique of the present.

Chapter 8

TOWARD A COMMUNICATIVE ETHICS AND AUTONOMY

The previous chapter has shown that the constituents of communicative rationality like decentration, reflexivity, and the differentiation of value spheres can be said to have "universal significance and validity" only in a weak sense. One cannot claim that they are "quasi-transcendental," only that they are the outcome of contingent learning processes whose internal evolution we can cogently reconstruct: what was once learned for good reasons, cannot be unlearned at will. Furthermore, the "epistemological reflexivity" of modern belief systems gives rise to a hermeneutical circle which we cannot overcome or escape. Finally, these structures are "irreversible" in that the future we would like to see can only be realized by fulfilling their still unexhausted potential.

In this context, Herbert Schnädelbach has correctly pointed out that Habermas' purpose in the *Theory of Communicative Action* is the justification of the "non-relative" (unconditioned—*unbedingt*) standpoint of critique without falling back to fundamentalism or foundationalism.[1] There is a great deal of skepticism in contemporary philosophy that such a program is viable. The decline of the belief in transcendental and other foundationalist programs, "as previously in the nineteenth century . . . has left in its wake a variety of forms of relativism, images of irreducible pluralities of incommensurable language games, forms of life, conceptual frameworks, lifeworlds, cultures, and so on."[2] In view of this contemporary post-transcendental consensus, how plausible is it to seek the normative justification for critical social theory in communicative action and reason?

First, it should be remarked that from the start, the tradition of critical theory has rejected "foundationalism" as well. Adorno's *Negative Dialectics* shows through superb irony the futility of a philosophy seeking to establish its own ultima ratio, and Horkheimer has criticized all modes of ontology, existentialism, and philosophical anthropology to be illusory attempts to provide unchangeable images of nature, humans, and society.[3] For Horkheimer, social philosophy could no longer continue in this a prioristic vein but had to turn to the social sciences in order to substantiate its ancient concepts like reason, freedom, and justice. What was preserved from philosophy was the utopian impulse to unite the claim of reason with that of freedom and dignity.

Second, unlike positivism and analytical philosophy, critical theory neither considers valid knowledge the monopoly of the sciences alone, nor does it seek to analyze the foundations of the sciences exclusively. Critical social theory seeks a *collaboration* between philosophy and the social sciences in particular which goes beyond epistemological critique. It might be worthwhile to dwell on this for a moment, for it is one of the most misunderstood aspects of critical theory in Anglo-American philosophy. The image of the relationship between philosophy and science as presented by Richard Rorty, for example, is exclusively the epistemological one of analyzing the foundation of the sciences.[4] Critical theory, by contrast, proceeds to an *immanent critique* of the sciences. The distinction betwen an epistemological and an immanent critique is the following: whereas in the first mode, only the conceptual foundations of the sciences and their knowledge claims are analyzed, the second approach aids in the development of new scientific theories, conceptualizations, and verification procedures, thus actively collaborating with them. The attempts of the Frankfurt School in the 1930s to synthesize political economy, psychoanalysis, and sociology entailed a genuine critique of the methods as well as the sciences of the period, and led to new modes of analysis and to new empirical results. The Institut für Sozialforschung published throughout the 1930s studies on *Authority and the Family;* these were succeeded by *The Authoritarian Personality* of which Adorno was a coauthor.[5] In Habermas' case as well, after *Knowledge and Human Interests,* an interdisciplinary research program in many ways reminiscent of the early efforts of the institute has come to the fore. As Habermas has summarized in his recent response to Rorty, for the tradition of critical theory, philosophy is not only the "place-holder" (*Platzhalter*) of the sciences, but their genuine collaborator.[6]

Third, if critical theory rejects foundationalism and first philosophies, if it proposes an immanent critique of the sciences as well as a new division of labor between philosophy and the social sciences, it may be asked whether a revised posttranscendental philosophy which does not dissolve into relativism and contextualism is still possible. Such a philosophical analysis is subject to an *indirect validation*. Philosophy cannot establish a priori eternal standards; but it cannot give up the search for criteria of valid knowledge and action altogether. Rather, it seeks indirect confirmation for its results and claims through the available results of the sciences. Philosophy is neither first philosophy nor a "conversation of mankind" (Rorty), but an inquiry which concerns itself with the valid grounds of action and knowledge while still being subject to indirect confirmation. What prevents such a philosophical program from becoming another science is its *self-reflexive* character. Horkheimer has observed that the sciences, whether natural or social, proceed from a naive objectivism (ZfS 1937:254ff.). They take the objects of cognition to be givens. Philosophy breaks with this naive attitude and questions the constitution of the object domain of the sciences. In the tradition of critical theory, such questioning means analyzing both the *context of genesis* and the *context of application* of theories. Self-reflexivity, in the sense emphasized by critical theory, entails critical awareness of the contingent conditions which make one's own standpoint possible (context of genesis), and an awareness of whom and what the knowledge one produces serves in society (context of application). Such self-reflexivity leads us, in Horkheimer's words, to become aware of "the motives of thought" (ZfS 1934:26–27), and is a constituent of individual and collective autonomy.

The development of critical theory after 1941, particularly the equation of modern rationality with instrumental reason, and the unclarity of the alternative juxtaposed to such instrumental reason, meant that the connection between autonomy and self-reflection became extremely tenuous. The transition from utopian to communicative reason, analyzed in the preceding chapter, has consequences in this respect as well. Along with the break from the philosophy of consciousness, the meanings of "reflection" and "self-reflection" change. These no longer refer to the cogitative activities of a Cartesian ego or to the laboring activity of making self but to processes of communication between selves. They designate the activity through which controversial validity claims, as well as rules of argumentation, are disputed, debated, and adjudicated in discourses.

The concept of communicative reason brings with it two major revisions in critical theory: first, the relation between self-reflection and autonomy is reestablished in light of a theory of discourse. It is claimed that the *cognitive* capacity to engage in discursive justification of validity claims also implies a universalist ethical standpoint. Second, autonomy is understood in communicative terms. Autonomy no longer means self-legislation as in Kant, self-actualization as with Hegel and Marx, or mimesis as with Adorno and Horkheimer, but the cognitive competence to adopt a universalist standpoint and the interactive competence to act on such a basis.

The purpose of this chapter is to analyze the project of a communicative ethic, and to develop the communicative concept of autonomy. This discussion concludes the argument of this book. My critique of the models of self-actualization and mimesis presupposed an alternative model of autonomy which had not yet been articulated. In order to clarify this alternative, I will first outline the program of communicative ethics (section 1) and subsequently discuss it in light of two questions: how applicable is Hegel's critique of Kantian morality to the project of a communicative ethics (section 2), and can a communicative concept of autonomy accommodate utopian aspects of the nonrepressive relation to inner and outer nature which Adorno and Horkheimer named "mimesis" (section 3)?

1. The Program of Communicative Ethics

The concepts of a "discourse free from domination" (*herrschaftsfreie Diskurs*) and "unconstrained dialogue" (*zwangslose*

Kommunikation) can be traced back to Habermas' writings in the mid-sixties. In a series of essays in this period, Habermas outlines the contradiction between the *de jure* ideals of democratic culture and the *de facto* imperatives of a scientific-technological civilization.[7] When science and technology come to act not only as productive forces, but the organization of social relations, and the distribution of social wealth is legitimized according to the imperatives of science and technology, two forms of post-bourgeios ideology emerge. The first is technocratism, the second, decisionism. Whereas the technocratic position reduces political choices and normative decisions to merely administrative questions which can be handled by properly trained experts alone, the decisionistic admits that scientific-administrative expertise can never eliminate the burden of moral choice incumbent upon the politician. Both technocratism and decisionism contradict the normative self-understanding of democracies that public decisions are reached by autonomous (*mündig*) citizens in a process of unconstrained exchange of opinion. In this context, the model of an unconstrained dialogue among scientists, politicians, and the public is introduced as being the only one compatible with a democratic self-understanding.[8] The ideal of a communicative ethic is thus intimately tied to the viability and desirability of a *democratic public ethos*. It is important to note this for a number of reasons: particularly after the development of the theory of universal pragmatics, the concepts of "unconstrained dialogue" and "ideal speech situation" were given such formal interpretations that their significance for a critical social theory became increasingly hard to see; also, like theories of consent in the natural right tradition, the theory of communicative ethics is primarily concerned with norms of public-institutional life, or with *institutional justice*. As will be discussed more fully below, this second aspect of the theory is a source of strength as well as weakness.

In the context of Habermas' theory of universal pragmatics, the concepts of an "ideal speech situation" and "unconstrained dialogue" define the formal properties of argumentations named "discourses." According to this theory, anyone engaging in communication, in performing a speech act, raises four validity claims and presupposes that they can be vindicated or justified when challenged.[9] In discourses, the background consensus which we "always already" naively assume has become problematical. This background consensus is constituted by the recognition of four validity claims: the *comprehensibility* of our utterances, the *truth* of their propositional component, the *correctness* or *appropriateness* of their performative aspect, and the *truthfulness* or *authenticity* of the speaking subject. When these background presuppositions of everyday speech are challenged and become problematic, we can engage in argumentations through which we examine these claims in the truth or correctness of which we have "suspended belief."[10]

Strictly speaking, the comprehensibility of utterances is not a validity claim as such. It can, however, become problematical in such a way as to require thematization, as in acts of interpretation, translation, philological or linguistic clarification. Truthfulness as well cannot be thematized in discourses alone. Although argumentations via which we question the authenticity and sincerity of a person's utterances play a great role in establishing whether people mean what they say, it is ultimately the relationship between what is said and what is done which establishes truthfulness.[11] Truth claims and claims to normative validity are more strictly the subject matters of discourse. In discourse we suspend belief in the existence of facts announced by propositions claiming to be true, and in the validity of norms urged by injunctions.

Habermas names discourses through which truth and normative claims are thematized "theoretical" and "practical" ones, respectively. The aim of discourses is to generate a "rationally motivated consensus" on controversial claims. The concept of the "ideal speech situation" is introduced in this context. The "ideal speech situation" specifies the formal properties that discursive argumentations would have to possess if the consensus thus attained were to be distinguished from a mere compromise or an agreement of convenience. The ideal speech situation is a "meta-norm" that applies to theoretical as well as to practical reason. It serves to delineate those aspects of an argumentation process which would lead to a "rationally motivated" as opposed to a false or apparent consensus.

The four conditions of the ideal speech situation are: first, each participant must have an equal chance to initiate and to continue communication; second, each must have an equal chance to make assertions, recommendations, and explanations, and to challenge justifications. Together we can all these the "symmetry condition." Third, all must have equal chances as actors to express their wishes, feelings, and intentions; and fourth, the speakers must act *as if* in contexts of action there is an equal distribution of chances "to order and resist orders, to pormise and to refuse, to be accountable for one's conduct and to demand accountability from others."[12] Let me call the latter two the "reciprocity condition." While the symmetry stipulation of the ideal speech situation refers to *speech acts* alone and to conditions governing their employment, the reciprocity condition refers to existing *action contexts*, and requires a suspension of situations of untruthfulness and duplicity on the one hand, and of inequality and subordination on the other.[13]

By now there is a substantial critical literature on this topic. For some, the ideal speech situation is a dangerous totalitarian utopia that negates all existing institutional relations, and that can only lead to totalitarian politics if actualized.[14] For others, like Raymond Geuss, it is a "transcendental deduction of a series of non-facts."[15] These critics have frequently misunderstood the status of this counterfactual. "The ideal speech situation" describes a set of rules which participants in a discourse would have to follow (the symmetry condition), and a set of relations (the reciprocity condition) which would have to obtain between them, if we were to say of the agreement they reach that it was rationally motivated, dependent on the force of the better argument alone. Indeed, there is nothing particularly counterintuitive about the claim that if parties to an argument reach a consensus under conditions where they do not have equal rights to initiate debate, to question and to make assertions and recommendations, or to challenge justifications, when in short there is an asymmetrical distribution of dialogue roles and of chances to use speech acts, such a consensus is *prima facie* neither genuine nor rational. The presence of power relations between the parties casts doubt on whether they were motivated by the force of the better argument alone. Likewise, if partici-

pants in a discourse have been less than truthful, hiding and
covering relevant information about themselves from their partners, then the consensus they reach cannot be said to be motivated by the force of the better argument alone either. There is
indeed a relation between the idea of a true consensus and that
of a voluntary, sincere agreement between parties, unaffected by
force, coercion, and manipulation. This leads Habermas to
claim that *truth*, interpreted as the attainment of rational consensus, involves the norms of *freedom* (the right to concede to the
force of the better argument alone) and *justice* (the reciprocal
and symmetrical distribution of rights among participants).[16]

Despite this defensible kernel, the concepts of an "ideal speech
situation" and discourse are surrounded by philosophical difficulties. In particular, unresolved questions abound regarding
the consensus theory of truth: is the *meaning* of truth to be defined as rational consensus, or is the attainment of rational consensus a *criterion* of truth?[17] Can truth be identified with a
procedure for attaining it? Like any procedure, if this is misap-
plied or misused, what becomes of the idea of truth? Are the
formal conditions stipulated by the ideal speech situation
sufficient to attain a rationally motivated consensus; that they
are necessary might be conceded but they hardly seem sufficient
for the task at hand. In short, how successful is this attempt
to interpret rational consensus procedurally with no regard
to the content of the reasons and evidence actually used in
argumentations?[18]

Undoubtedly, these questions concerning the consensus theory of truth cast some doubt on Habermas' consensus theory of
normative validity as well, and some of the difficulties encountered in this regard will be discussed in greater detail below (see
section 2). However, what guides both the consensus theory of
truth and the consensus theory of validity is a communicative or
discursive concept of reason. Habermas maintains that it is not
the mind's cogitative relation to an object or to a state of affairs
which defines truth, nor is it some unique, undefinable quality
of actions and affairs, incommunicable to others, that defines
the validity of norms.[19] Both truth claims and normative validity claims are public assertions that can only be tested and contested argumentatively. "I suspect that the justification of the

validity claims contained in the norms of action and of evaluation can be just as discursively tested as the justification of the
validity claims implied in assertions."[20]

The theory of practical discourse develops a cognitivist theory
of ethics, sometimes also referred to as a "cognitive ethics of
language."[21] The main purpose of this theory is to show against
non-cognitivists—especially emotivists and decisionists—that
normative statements, while not being "true" or "false" in the
sense of descriptive ones, do admit "cognitive validitation," in
the sense that there are rational and good reasons for their adoption and rejection. To justify this claim, Habermas attempts to
show that communicative ethics or a cognitivist ethics of language is *grounded* in the "fundamental norms of rational
speech." According to one early formulation: "I do not place my
hopes upon an implicit ethic of logic or grammar, but of speech
[*Rede*]. I proceed from the assumption that the fundamental
norms of action are grounded [*begründet*] in the *form* of the intersubjectivity of possible modes of ordinary language communication [*umgangssprachlicher Verständigung*]."[22] Prior to the non-
foundationalist turn of *The Theory of Communicative Action*,
it was argued that there was a less than contingent, quasi-
transcendental connection between the structures of rational
speech and a communicative ethic.[23] This strong justification
program, which would *ground* a communicative ethic on the
fundamental norms of rational speech, was untenable, and in
his later formulations Habermas has moved away from it. It is
important to see why.

In the first place, there were at least four possible readings
of the ideal speech situation, corresponding to Habermas'
equivocations upon the terms *Rede* (speech), *vernünftige Rede*
(rational speech), *kommunikatives Handeln*,[24] and *verständigung-
orientiertes Handeln* (action oriented toward reaching understanding).[25] Karl-Heinz Ilting has distinguished between these
possible readings of the ideal speech situation in Habermas'
writings of this period: the ideal speech situation as the model
of an ideal communication; the anticipation of the ideal speech
situation as the condition of the possibility of linguistic communication; the anticipation of the ideal speech situation as the
condition of the possibility of discourse; and the ideal speech

situation as a sufficient condition for the attainment of a rationally motivated consensus on controversial validity claims.[26] Given these ambiguities, it was unclear what the claim that conditions of "rational speech" ground the norms of a cognitive ethic of language really meant.

There is, however, another mode of approaching the idea of a communicative ethic, and this is to view it as a proceduralist ethical theory in the Kantian tradition. The program of a communicative ethic has as its starting point the assumption that "a philosophical ethics not restricted to meta-ethical statements is possible today only if we can reconstruct general presuppositions of communication and procedures for justifying norms and values."[27] In fact, the very thrust of the theory of discourse is to show that the idea of truth entails that of rational consensus, but that such rational consensus can only be explicated *procedurally* by defining the strategies and modes of argumentation through which it can be arrived at. Likewise, communicative ethics is a procedural ethics.

But this procedural interpretation as well will not save the strong program of justification which would ground communicative ethics in a universal-pragmatic analysis of rational speech. In order to illustrate the difficulties such proceduralist theories run into, it will be instructive here to compare it briefly with another procedural Kantian theory, namely, John Rawls' theory of justice.[28]

There are two premises shared by Rawls and Habermas. I will call the first the "consensus principle of legitimacy" and define it as follows: the principle of rational consensus provides the only criterion in light of which the legitimacy of norms and of normative institutional arrangements can be justified. More significant, Rawls and Habermas share the meta-theoretical premise that the idea of such rational consensus is to be defined *procedurally*. Rawls maintains that his theory of justice provides us with the only procedure of justification through which valid and binding norms of collective coexistence can be established. Habermas argues that the "ideal speech situation" defines the formal properties of discourses, by engaging in which alone we can attain a rational consensus. The fictive collective choice situation devised by Rawls and the equally fictive "ideal speech situation" devised by Habermas are *normative justification procedures* serving to illustrate the consensus principle of legitimacy.[29]

We can examine the justification offered by Habermas for communicative ethics by drawing an analogy between the ideal speech situation and Rawls' description of the "original position." Rawls specifies three possible modes of justifying the counterfactual thought experiment from which he proceeds: "the thin theory of the good," "reflective equilibrium," and "privileged description."[30] We can likewise distinguish three strands of justification in Habermas' theory. According to one formulation, the ideal speech situation gives a linguistic determination for what we minimally understand by rationality, justice, and freedom. It offers, we may say, a linguistic "thin theory of the good."[31] The *rationality* of the parties can be defined as their capacity and willingness to engage in, comply with, and accept as binding the outcomes of such processes of communication. The ideal speech situation defines *justice* in light of the symmetry and reciprocity conditions as the *equal right* of all participants to an *equal* distribution of the use and initiation of speech acts. *Freedom* means the suspension of all internal and external constraints of action and the right to follow the "force" of the better argument only.

As with Rawls' thin theory of the good, the Habermasian ideal speech situation does not *justify* the normative content of communicative ethics, but serves to *illustrate* it.[32] The symmetry condition already stipulates a prior normative commitment to the *equal right of all* to be considered rational and free beings. In fact, when we examine the reciprocity condition, it becomes clear that Habermas' normative assumptions are stronger than Rawls', for they already define a certain moral conduct, that of truthfulness, and a certain form of life, one in which the complete reciprocity of the parties in power and authority relations is presupposed.[33] The universal-pragmatic interpretations of rationality, justice, and freedom are indeed interpretations, which presuppose the normative validity of communicative rationality, reciprocity, and truthfulness. But what grounds have been given to choose this particular normative interpretation, if it was first the outcome of the ideal speech situation that would establish norms which we would consider binding? The ideal speech situation is a circular construction; it presupposes those very norms whose validity it was supposed to establish.

Habermas could admit this circularity but, like Rawls, argue that the validity of these norms need not be *first* established, for they are *always already* presupposed. Just as the weak description of the original position claimed to make clear to us those "considered judgements duly pruned and adjusted"[34] through an examination called "reflective equilibrium," Habermas argues that the ideal speech situation is anticipated in the structure of all interaction oriented to reaching understanding.[35]

Upon a first reading, this argument is trivially implausible. Non-symmetrical, non-reciprocal, deceitful, and irrational speech and interaction appear to be the rule rather than the exception in human life. If this were not the case, there would be no need for normative philosophy either. All would be as it ought to be. This objection is trivial because universal pragmatics analyzes the conditions for the possibility of speech and interaction in the transcendental sense. Universal pragmatics analyzes the *deep structure* of the possiblity of specifically human modes of speech and communication.

Granted, however, that the deep structure of these rules we "always already" presuppose is not the one that we, as acting and speaking subjects, are immediately aware of, but one which we can understand and accept with the help of adequate means of reconstruction, the problem still remains: even if some *general* norms of symmetry and reciprocity are presupposed by all speech and interaction, these norms do not imply a unique *semantic content*. It does not follow that symmetry and reciprocity ought to be interpreted to mean the right of *all* to symmetrical and reciprocal participation. In order to argue this, we must presuppose a specific concept of *equality*. We must normatively stipulate a content and interpretation in light of which the symmetry and reciprocity rules of the ideal speech situation are given a specific semantic interpretation.[36] Whereas Rawls' procedure of "reflective equilibrium" refers to an already *shared* semantic interpretation of normative contents, Habermas falsely assumes that this semantic content can be univocally deduced from universal pragmatics. But as Albrecht Wellmer points out, universal pragmatics cannot justify the step of abstraction which defines the transition to a universalist ethics, because it presupposes it methodologically.[37] Universal pragmatics proceeds at a level of abstraction from the standpoint of which each and every individual is considered a being capable of consensus. This is a highly counterfactual assumption, which already assumes a moral attitude corresponding to a *universalist ethical* standpoint that disregards all existing natural and social differences as irrelevant in defining the moral core of one's humanity. This means that universal pragmatics reconstructs a system of rules which will be recognized as binding by agents of a certain sort. These have attained, or can attain, a level of moral and practical *Bildung* that corresponds to the level of moral abstraction and universalism from which this theory proceeds.

There is a third justification of the ideal speech situation given by Habermas. It is now admitted that the ability to engage in practical discourse is the result of learning processes dependent on experience,[38] and that communicative ethics offers, we might say, a "privileged description" of post-conventional moral reasoning according to Kohlberg's scheme of moral development. Learning processes are both ontogenetic and phylogenetic. While in the history of the individual, discourses correspond to post-conventional linguistic and interactive competence, in the history of the species, discursive justification procedures first emerge in modernity and are institutionalized by modern law, science, and democratic-parliamentary procedures.[39]

In a recent article on "Rationality and Relativism: Habermas' 'Overcoming' of Hermeneutics," Thomas McCarthy has formulated the difficulties encountered by this line of argumentation very precisely. He points out that in such theories there is a discrepancy between the investigation of the highest stages of cognitive development and that of the lower ones. In the latter case, there is an asymmetry between "the insufficiently decentered thought of the child, traditional culture, or whatever, and the differentiated, reflexive thought of the investigator."[40] This asymmetry breaks down in the investigation of higher stages. With reference to Lawrence Kohlberg's theory of moral development, McCarthy suggests that the higher moral subject is to be placed at the same reflective or discursive level of reasoning as the moral psychologist.

> The subject's thought is now marked by the decentration, differentiation and reflexivity which are the conditions of entrance into the moral theorist's sphere of argumentation. Thus the asymmetry between the pre-reflective and the reflective, between theories-in-action and explications, which underlies the model of reconstruction begins to break down. . . . This discursive symmetry might help to explain why Kohlberg's attempt to get from "is" to "ought" (in part) by establishing the "naturalness" of the higher stages has struck moral philosophers as questionable. He has to adopt and defend a specific position on the very meta-ethical issues they spend their lives debating; the appeal to empirical-psychological considerations brings no dispensation from participation in this debate.[41]

In the context of Habermas' theory of communicative ethics, McCarthy's claim amounts to the following: even if evolutionary-reconstructive arguments play a role in moral theory, they cannot serve to justify a specific kind of theory from among those sharing a post-conventional stage of moral development. Developmental moral theory is *underdetermined* in this respect. Once we reach the stage of a universalist moral orientation in which individuals can generate normative principles of action through formal procedures satisfying criteria of impartiality, universalizability, reversibility, and prescriptivity, we can no longer arbitrate between competing moral theories on the basis of these criteria. Kantian moral theory, as well as the Rawlsian theory of justice, proceeds from such formal criteria but interprets them differently than the theory of communicative ethics. At this point, additional arguments are needed to help arbitrate among universalistic ethical theories.

This examination of Habermas' attempt to ground communicative ethics in the fundamental norms of "rational speech" leads to the following conclusions: according to the first reading, this justification procedure is simply circular. What is said to be binding about the ideal speech situation are certain normative conditions which themselves first need to be argued for. One extracts from the ideal speech situation what one has already put into it. The second interpretation shows that even if certain symmetry and reciprocity conditions may be implicit in all speech and action, it would not thereby follow that the universalist interpretation of these conditions was also implicit. The third analysis reveals that the claim to have articulated in explicit terms the intuitive know-how attained by moral agents in the post-conventional stage hardly helps the case for communicative ethics; the discourse model is not the only ethical theory compatible with this level of competence.

In what follows, I will show that the charge of circularity raised above is to a certain extent met by Habermas' recent attempt to specify exactly the kind of entailment relationship he sees between the structures of communicative action in general, and the minimum normative principles forming the basis of a communicative ethic. Although this modification throws considerable light on the justification strategy for a communicative ethic, it is far from being wholly convincing. For questions concerning the preferred *semantic interpretation* of these minimum normative principles, as well as the *indeterminacy of evolutionary arguments* in establishing the validity of such principles, remain. I will first outline the consequences of Habermas' most recent discussions for the program of a communicative ethic, and then proceed to assess their cogency in the following section.

In a recent paper on "Discourse Ethics: Notes Toward a Justification Program," Habermas has clarified that the relationship between the conditions of argumentative speech and communicative ethics can neither be deductive nor inductive.[42] As suggested by Karl-Otto Apel, this relationship is to be explained via the concept of a "performative contradiction."[43] A performative contradiction does not obtain between two sets of statements but between two types of speech acts. If the propositional content of a speech act contradicts the non-contingent and unavoidable presuppositions on which it itself rests, then the speaker is involved in a performative contradiction. For example, a speaker says: "I question that I exist." This means that the speaker regards it as possible that "I do not exist" (here and now). Yet in order to utter the latter statement, the speaker must necessarily presuppose that "I exist" (here and now).[44]

Apel utilizes this argument, first outlined by Jaako Hintikka in quite a different context, to establish two propositions: first, the skeptic who doubts that it is possible to rationally settle validity claims gets involved in a performative contradiction; for to raise such a claim, she must participate in an argumentation which itself is impossible without the assumption that disputed claims can be rationally settled.[45] Second, Apel thus wants to maintain that the cognitive as well as the moral skeptic must recognize the situation as an "unavoidable" and "uncircumventible" (nicht-hintergehbar) condition of the very possibility of speech acts.[46] Through his analysis of the argumentation situation, Apel arrives at the conclusion that the ideal of a community of communication, in which all beings capable of speech reciprocally recognize one another as discussion partners entitled to equal rights, is an unavoidable supposition. Thus cognitive and moral skeptics who deny that valid normative claims can be established at all, through the very fact that they raise a validity claim to be settled argumentatively, commit themselves to the normative ideal of a community of communication.[47]

In light of this clarification, the relationship between the fundamental norms of argumentative speech and a communicative ethics needs to be reformulated. Habermas claims that not only those who choose to participate in an argumentation situation, but all those capable of speech and action, as competent subjects, dispose of a certain intuitive know-how.[48] The task of universal pragmatics is to render this "know-how" into a "know-that," and to reconstruct the explicit rules governing the implicit knowledge of competent speakers and actors. Such a universal-pragmatic reconstruction of communicative action reveals the four validity claims to be always counterfactually assumed. Such a reconstruction also shows that once these validity claims are no longer taken for granted, consensus can only be established via discourses aimed at the redemption of truth and rightness claims. The question now is whether discourses can proceed under certain argumentative conditions alone, and whether among these conditions, one must also acknowledge the presence of a moral principle, the denial of which would lead the subject to a performative contradiction. Whereas formerly Habermas asked whether the conditions of an ideal speech situation *entailed* the acceptance of certain ethical norms, he is now asking whether all subjects capable of speech and action, in that they act communicatively, do not also dispose of a certain moral know-how which involves recognizing a certain moral principle which they can deny at the risk of a *performative contradiction* only. Whereas the earlier justification strategy sought to establish a *deductive* relation between conditions of argumentative speech and the norms of a communicative ethic, it is now argued that a subject who engages in argumentation presupposes a certain ethical norm which he or she can only deny at the risk of a performative self-contradiction. This reformulation leads to the following clarifications.

First, the concept of an "ideal speech situation" only serves to summarize the rules to be followed in argumentations, if they are to yield a rational consensus. Habermas insists on his original claim that "in argumentative exchange, the structures of a speech situation, especially immunized against repression and inequality, show themselves."[49]

Second, argumentations continue everyday modes of communicative action through other means. What motivates the transition to discourses is the fact that the self-explanatory character of the lifeworld very often fails and requires clarification and mutual interpretation. Discourses are continuous with the questioning, puzzling, explaining, interpreting, negotiating, and clarifying that constitute everyday interactions in the social lifeworld.

Third, the task of universal pragmatics is to reconstruct the presuppositions of communicative action and argumentation. As emphasized previously, such reconstructions continue the task of transcendental philosophy with altered means. The lines separating so-called "a priori" conditions from a posteriori rules of competent behavior get increasingly blurred, for the justification for calling some condition or feature of our action and speech capacities "a priori" is simply that it corresponds to the implicit know-how of competent actors, for which we see no possible alternatives at the present.[50]

Fourth, the discourse theory of ethics is such a "reconstructive science." This program implies a special division of labor between moral theory and moral psychology. Discursive ethics conceives of moral theory as a theory of moral argumentation.[51] In doing so, it finds indirect support from the findings of developmental psychology, which provide rational reconstructions of the pretheoretical knowledge of competent subjects. If it is charged that such a psychological theory itself is informed by a philosophical ethic, and that therefore to regard it as supplying indirect evidence for a philosophical ethic is simply to proceed circularly, Habermas admits that there is a circle here, but maintains that it is not a vicious one.[52] Rather, the interaction between moral philosophy and moral psychology is like a coherence test, each adjusting its results and analysis in light of the other.

Fifth, the basic principle of a discourse ethic is that only those norms can claim validity which meet (or could meet) with the agreement (*Zustimmung*) of all concerned (*Betroffenen*) as participants in a practical discourse (MukH, p. 103).

Sixth, the moral principle which belongs to the presuppositions of argumentation in a discourse ethic is that everyone who participates in a practical discourse must also implicitly and indeed at the cost of getting involved in a performative contradiction recognize that normative validity claims can only be justified if the following is respected: the consequences and side effects which would foreseeably result from the *universal* implementation of a controversial norm, and as they would affect the satisfaction of the interests of each single individual, would be accepted by all without compulsion (*zwangslos*). Habermas names this the principle of universalizability.[53]

Seventh, to complete this account of the program of a communicative ethics, we must identify the object domain of such a theory. The phenomena which need explanation and clarification are the "normative [obligating or binding] validity [*Sollgeltung*] of norms and of validity claims which we raise in relation to norm-related (or regulative) speech acts" (MukH, p. 54). According to Habermas, the familiar positions of philosophical ethics, like naturalism and intuitionism on the one hand, emotivism and decisionism on the other, fail from the outset. These identify normative utterances with propositions like "X is good for man," or with expressive claims such as "I like, approve of, X," or with imperatives such as "Do X" or "Obey God's will who commands X." But a normative utterance of the sort "It is wrong to do X" corresponds to none of these formulations. Its pragmatic meaning is "To do X is wrong." The predicate "wrong" in this statement does not refer to a quality or attribute of X, but means that if you and I were to engage in argumentation, I could with good grounds show you that you and I should refrain from doing X. According to this pragmatic analysis, "You ought not to do X" is equivalent to "There are good reasons not to do X."[54]

These seven points outline the essentials of Habermas' program for communicative ethics subsequent to *The Theory of Communicative Action*. In the following section, I want to examine the difficulties of this program by reformulating Hegel's objection to Kantian ethics in contemporary terms.

2. The Hegelian Objection: A Contemporary Reformulation

In chapter 3 Hegel's critique of Kantian moral theory was summarized around four points: (a) the procedural critique of the universalizability principle, (b) the institutional deficiency of Kantian moral theory, (c) the critique of Kant's moral psychology, and (d) the critique of Kant's theory of action. My formulation of a "Hegelian" objection to communicative ethics will follow the same sequence except that there will be no criticism corresponding to the fourth point. The concept of communicative action was developed to rectify the shortcomings of the Hegelian concept of action as self-actualization. The first reformulated Hegelian objection will concern the status of the universalizability principle; the second, the institutional bases of communicative ethics; and the third, the relation among cognition, motivation, and affect in communicative ethics.

With regard to the first point, my conclusion will be that there is also a dialectic of form and content in the program of a communicative ethics insofar as the principle of universalizability does not result from the formal and minimal premises of the theory alone, but can only be justified with reference to additional assumptions. In examining the institutional bases of communicative ethics, I will indicate what some of these additional assumptions are: communicative ethics vacillates between two models of public life, the first a juridical, legalistic model, and the second a more participatory-democratic model. In conclusion, I will suggest that while communicative ethics does not share the repressive assumptions of Kant's moral psychology, it runs the risk of falling into a certain rationalistic fallacy of the Kantian sort, in that it ignores the contingent, historical, and affective circumstances which made individuals adopt a universalist-ethical standpoint in the first place.

a. The Status of the Universalizability Principle in Communicative Ethics

In its traditional form, the Hegelian objection to the Kantian universalizability procedure—the categorical imperative—consisted of the following: Hegel maintained that one could interpret the categorical imperative either as a procedure for *generating* obligatory moral principles or for *testing* existing ones. If the first alternative were chosen, he argued, the generation of obligatory moral principles could only proceed inconsistently. Such principles could be derived only because certain material assumptions, inconsistent with the alleged formalism of the moral law, had already been introduced into the latter. If one were to choose the second alternative and regard the moral law as a procedure by which to test existing maxims, then it would fail in this task as well. Assuming that the test procedure enjoined by the categorical imperative amounted to the principle of non-contradiction alone, Hegel had no difficulty in showing that any content could be made compatible with the moral law once it was demonstrated to be self-consistent (see chapter 3, section 1).

Much of the nerve of Hegel's critique of Kantian morality rests with his claim that the procedure of universalizability is at best inconsistent, and at worst tautological. Undoubtedly, in assuming that the formula "Act only on that maxim through which you can at the same time will that it should become a universal law" amounted to the principle "Act in such a way that in all your actions your will [*Wille*] does not contradict itself," Hegel was not being a fair critic of Kant. Nonetheless, his arguments did draw attention to the question as to what—according to Kantian moral theory—the moral agent who followed the moral law had to do, what kind of *procedure* he or she had to engage in in deciding to act in one way rather than another.

In an illuminating article evaluating the fairness of this Hegelian criticism, John Silber has drawn attention to the remarkable consistency with which Kant formulates the rational procedure to be employed by judgment in logic, science, aesthetics, and ethics.[55] According to Kant, the general rules to be followed in thinking consistently are: "(1) To think for *oneself;* (2) in communication with men, to imagine [sich denken] oneself in the place of every *other* person; (3) always to think in *agreement with one's self.*"[56] Clearly, the moral law insofar as it is a principle of autonomy fulfills the first criterion. By enjoining the moral agent to think of his or her actions as if he or she were a legislating member of the Kingdom of Ends, it urges consistency of thought and action, thereby fulfilling the third criterion. It may then be suggested that the formula of the End in Itself—to treat others never as means but always also as ends in themselves—corresponds to the second condition, namely, "to imagine oneself in the place of every other person."[57] In the *Critique of Judgement,* Kant defines this as "to think from the standpoint of everyone else."[58]

Most contemporary neo-Kantian ethical theories take their bearings from this formula, and define "universalizability" as a *procedure* that would entail considering the point of view of all. The "moral point of view" is identified with that perspective which would be acceptable for all. Again, most contemporary ethical theories differ from one another in specifying the procedure which best articulates the moral point of view. While John Rawls, for example, maintains that his theory of justice as fairness and the procedural device of a collective bargaining game behind a veil of ignorance best articulate Kant's view of autonomy, Alan Donagan and Alan Gewirth develop the constituents of the moral point of view via a deontological analysis of rational action and agency.[59]

From the standpoint of communicative ethics, the contemporary theories merely repeat the traditional Kantian mistake. Kant thought that, through solitary reflection, a single rational

self could come to define a standpoint which would be acceptable to all qua rational agents. The Kantian moral self was a
pure rational agent, identical to all others in this respect. Having
abstracted from the differences among concrete moral selves,
the Kantian thought experiment in moral theory would proceed
by asking what each could, without self-contradiction, consider
to be a universal law for *all.* In attempting to define the content
of the moral point of view, contemporary moral philosophers
repeat the same mistake: they assume that the solitary moral
thinker can define a relevant moral content for all. In communicative ethics, by contrast, the requirement to articulate the
moral point of view amounts to the formula: only those norms
can claim validity which meet (or could meet) with the consensus of all concerned as participants in a practical discourse.

Thus formulated, communicative ethics cannot be subject to
Hegel's traditional critique of Kant. In fact, one of Hegel's earliest insights, that Spirit has the structure of an "I that is a we,
and a we that is an I," is applied here against Kantian ethics.[60]
Kantian ethics is *monological,* for it proceeds from the standpoint of the rational person, defined in such a way that differences among concrete selves become quite irrelevant. Communicative ethics defends a *dialogical* model of moral reasoning, according to which *real* actors engage in *actual* processes of
deliberation on moral questions. While it is the general intention of this theory to avoid the monologism and deductivism of
traditional Kantian ethics, it remains to be seen whether the
concretization of these intentions does not fall prey to the same
criticism which this theory directs against other neo-Kantian
alternatives. More precisely, my criticism is that the more the
standpoint of a "practical discourse" is articulated in theoretical terms, the less is it possible to distinguish between communicative ethics and other rival accounts of the moral point of
view on procedural grounds alone. According to the theory of
practical discourse as well, a certain procedure is presented to
moral agents as the "privileged description" corresponding to
the moral point of view. This generates a "dialectic of form and
content" in communicative ethics. I want to illustrate this criticism by examining the status of the universalizability criterion
in communicative ethics.

It seems surprising that a discourse or communicative ethic need appeal to the universalizability principle at all. For, as has been correctly observed, "Habermas' discourse model represents a procedural reinterpretation of Kant's categorical imperative: rather than ascribing as valid to all others any maxim that I can will to be a universal law, I must submit my maxim to all others for purposes of discursively testing its claim to universality. The emphasis shifts from what each can will without contradiction to be a general law, to what all can will in agreement to be a universal norm."[61] Discursive argumentation is the new procedure replacing the universalizability test in Kantian ethics. More precisely, universalizability itself is interpreted *discursively*, as what "all can will in agreement to be a universal norm." Why then must Habermas appeal to a universalizability principle, as he does in his early essay on "Theories of Truth" and once more in his recent article "Discourse Ethics: Notes Toward a Justification Program"?

Adapting an analysis given by Toulmin in *The Uses of Argument,* in "Theories of Truth" Habermas presented the following example to explain the procedure of universalizability in practical discourses:[62]

— There is a recommendation "C" which is in need of justification: "You ought to give A fifty dollars by the end of the week."
— Justification "D": A had lent you that money for a period of four weeks.
— Grounding (of the assertion) through a norm of action "W" (a corresponding norm, e.g.): "Loans ought to be refunded within the specified dates."
— Casuistical evidence for the backing of the norm "B" (a series of references to the consequences and side-consequences of the application of the norm for the fulfillment of accepted needs, e.g.): "Loans make possible the flexible use (application) of scarce resources."

The crucial step in analyzing the logic of practical discourses is the relationship of B to W. Habermas writes that "although no deductive relationship exists between the statements that are put forth in the warrant and those in the backing, an argument draws its consensus-producing power from the justification for draws its consensus-producing power from the justification for going from B to W."[63] Whether the norm—"Loans ought to be refunded within specified dates"—is to be consensually accepted depends upon whether the principle that "Loans make possible the flexible use of scarce resources" is agreed upon. The reasoning of the participants then would be: We accept B, and therefore we must respect the institution of loans, and therefore we must accept W. The transition from B to W is attained by means of the principle of "universalizability." "Universalizability acts as a bridging principle, in order to justify the transition from the descriptive references (to the consequences and side-consequences of the application of norms to the satisfaction of generally accepted needs) to the norm itself."[64]

This is a confusing formulation, for it is unclear if we are to test *descriptive* assumptions concerning the consequences of applying norms universally, if we are to test whether a particular *norm* can satisfy generally accepted needs, or if we are to test whether generally accepted *needs* permit a universalizable interpretation. The first alternative is meaningless; since it can only be decided upon by empirical knowledge, it is not the proper subject matter of practical discourse; only the second and third alternatives raise properly normative questions. Habermas has both in view: the criterion of universalizability should provide a specification of *certain kinds of norms*. "The basic premise of universalizability serves the purpose of excluding all norms as not being capable of consensus, whose content and whose field of application are particular."[65] The criterion of universalizability should also serve as a test for allowed need interpretations: "We call appropriate that language of morals, which permits determinate groups and persons, in given circumstances, a truthful interpretation both of their own particular needs, and more importantly of their common needs capable of consensus."[66] Let me dwell on the first point and leave a consideration of need interpretations within communicative ethics to a future section (section 3).

By introducing the principle of universalizability as a condition of *discursive* argumentations—analogous to the principle of induction in theoretical discourses—Habermas is creating a series of problems for his theory: first, since whether or not "the

content and field of application of a norm is or is not particular"
can only be discovered in argumentation, it is unclear what the
universalizability principle *adds* to the argumentation procedure;[67] second, suppose participants in a discourse consensually agree that not the principle of universalizability as
stipulated above, but another meta-principle like "the greatest
happiness of all participating" or "from each according to his
abilities, to each according to his needs" would constitute the
relevant backing B for adopting the norm W. On what grounds
can the theorist of communicative ethics preclude that such a
choice may be made? Can the theory of discourse *define* a priori
which *principles* of normative evaluation should be adopted in
discourses? Would this not contradict the fundamental principle of a discourse ethics that only those norms (and meta-norms)
can claim validity which could meet the consensus of all participants in a practical discourse?

The difficulty faced here, and the reason why the universalizability principle is reintroduced into the theory of discourse in the first place, is an ancient one. All modern consent
theories of legitimacy face a paradox: by making consent the
sole basis of legitimacy or normative validity, such theorists also
run the risk that the consent principle can be *consensually vio-
lated*. Ever since Rousseau's dictum—"On les forcera d'être
libre"—one faces the question of how to meaningfully define the
content of consent such that it would not, for example, include
the right to enslave oneself or to abnegate one's freedom. The
traditional solution to this dilemma has been to distinguish between "empirical" and "rational" consent, or the "will of all" and
the "general will."[68] This distinction brings with it the difficulty
that the wider the gap between "empirical" and "rational" consent, the closer does consent theory move toward other non-
consensual theories of legitimacy which proceed from rationality
or human nature rather than consent as a basic premise.

In the context of the theory of communicative ethics, this traditional difficulty takes the following form: in order to avoid the
undesirable consequence that participants in a discourse may
adopt principles which would contradict the very principles of
discourse itself, it becomes necessary to define theoretically the
rules of discursive argumentation. This attempt in turn gives

rise to the objection that the theorist is proceeding *deductively* and *dogmatically* in maintaining that certain normative principles belong among the rules of argumentation and need not-themselves first be argued for.

In "Discourse Ethics: Notes Toward a Justification Program," Habermas seeks to avoid this charge with the claim that the universalizability principle is derived neither deductively nor dogmatically, but that it belongs among the *pragmatic* presuppositions of argumentative speech, which one can only deny at the risk of a performative self-contradiction. It is maintained that the universalizability principle (U) is not a meta-norm or a substantive norm, but a *rule of argumentation* which belongs to the very logic of practical discourse.

In examining this claim let us first recall how U is defined: "The consequences and side-effects which would foreseeably result from the universal subscription to a disputed norm, and as they would affect the satisfaction of the interests of *each* single individual, could be accepted by all without *constraints*."[69] The argument which leads to the justification of U is in turn summarized as follows: "Everyone who participates in the universal and necessary communicative presuppositions of argumentative speech, and who knows what it means to justify a norm of action, must implicitly assume the validity of a principle of universalizability (either in its above form or in some other equivalent formulation)" (MukH, p. 97). Whether this argument suffices to justify U depends, of course, on the two premises which are defined respectively as "the universal and necessary presuppositions of communicative speech," and the "knowledge of what it means to justify a norm of action." The issue is whether these two premises are sufficiently distinct from U such that one is not simply begging the question or proceeding tautologically in claiming that their acceptance amounts to the confirmation of U; or whether, if these two premises are sufficiently distinct from U, the step leading to U does not entail smuggling in additional assumptions which themselves need justification. Let me examine each premise in turn.

Among the universal and necessary presuppositions of communicative speech, Habermas includes three kinds of rules: *logical-semantic* ones like not contradicting oneself; consistency, i.e., the rule that once a predicate F has been applied to an object A, it also be applied to all other objects that are equivalent to A in all relevant respects. The second kind of rules are *procedural* in nature and regulate modes of interaction that are necessary to successful cooperation in the search for truth, as for example the recognition of the accountability and honesty of all participants. These rules are summarized as those features of *reciprocal recognition* which discourses share with other modes of social interaction oriented to reaching understanding (MukH, p. 98). The third and final category of rules are those *processual* ones that define the essence of communicative speech. Strictly speaking, these are not rules in the sense of being conventional stipulations that can be changed at will, like "Every participant is allowed five minutes to present his or her point of view." They are said to be *pragmatic presuppositions* of argumentative speech, in the sense that they are *unavoidable* and *necessary* assumptions that we all make insofar as we participate in argumentative speech *competently*.[70] The denial of these rules would not only involve us in a performative self-contradiction, but would also indicate that we did not possess the relevant *know-how* to participate in argumentation. Since it is *these* rules that function as the premise of the argument that leads to the justification of U, it will be helpful to spell them out precisely here. Following R. Alexy, Habermas describes them as follows:

3.1 Every agent capable of speech and action can participate in discourses.

3.2 a. Everyone may problematize any assertion.

3.2 b. Everyone may introduce every assertion into a discourse.

3.2 c. Everyone may express his attitudes, wishes, and needs.

3.3 No one may be prevented from enjoying her above-outlined rights in virtue of constraints that may dominate within or without discourses.[71]

Rule 3.1 determines the potential participants in argumentation as the exceptionless inclusion of all subjects, i.e., all humans capable of speech and action. Rule 3.2 guarantees the *symmetrical* distribution among all participants of chances to utilize speech acts, while rule 3.3 restates the *reciprocity* condition among participants that their rights as specified under 3.2 are fully respected.

As I have indicated previously, there is a defensible kernel to these stipulations, insofar as they illuminate our intuition that a consensus among parties reached under conditions of inequality, constraint, domination, deception, and unwillingness to cooperate is *prima facie* neither a genuine consensus nor a rational one. When these conditions prevail, we speak of compromise, giving in, submitting oneself to the opinion of another, blackmail, and the like. But the ethically relevant questions arise at another level. Rule 3.1, which defines every agent that is capable of speech and action as a potential participant in a discourse, already presupposes a strong universalist-egalitarian commitment to consider as irrelevant from a moral standpoint all those natural and cultural characteristics among human groups which distinguish them from one another. This commitment, which I share, cannot be presented as if it were the result of some careful philosophical analysis of conditions of argumentative speech *überhaupt*. The suggestion that *all* speakers of *any* natural language are potential participants in discourses precludes *particularistic* interpretations of rule 3.1 as "those who speak my language and whom I can understand." The exclusion of such a particularistic interpretation is not a consequence of conceptual analysis alone; rather, it reflects the commitments of a moral philosophy as practiced by individuals who are themselves members of a culture that cherishes universalism. Let us recall that for the ancient Greeks the barbarians were those whose language they did not understand, and who, from their point of view, did not speak, but merely babbled.[72] Our assumption that all speakers of any natural language speak and do not merely babble is the product of the moral *Bildung* of the Enlightenment and secularization which destroyed the ontological bases of human inequality. To say that this assumption is a product of such a process is not to say that it is therefore less defensible; my intention is simply to point out that even the so-called "universal" pragmatic presuppositions of human discourse have a cultural-historical content built into them.

A further question concerns not the rules of *inclusion* which are operative in Habermas' interpretation of rules 3.1 to 3.3, but the rules of *exclusion* that are also at work. By the very way in which it defines those excluded, these rules prejudge the content of moral theory. For example, those who cannot speak—children, fools, and animals—have no place in this theory, yet would we really want to deny that our relationship to these beings is an essential aspect of morality in general? This exclusion limits the core of communicative ethics to questions of *justice*, namely to relations between responsible, equal, adult participants. But to make such a limitation of the domain of moral theory is one which must be defended with appropriate normative considerations from the start. This is not an issue that can be settled at the meta-theoretical level of the analysis of universal-pragmatic preconditions of argumentative speech. These objections, therefore, suggest that the first premise—namely the pragmatic rules which govern discourses—leading to the incontrovertibility of U has already been *preinterpreted* in the light of material normative assumptions.

The second premise of the argument, namely "the knowledge of what it means to justify a norm of action," is equally problematical, for depending on how it is interpreted it reads as if it were simply equivalent to some version of U. According to one formulation, with justified norms "we associate the meaning that they regulate societal matters in the common interest of all possibly concerned" (MukH, p. 103). Formulated thus, this principle is not *prima facie* different from U, which states that the consequences and side effects which would result from the implementation of a controversial norm, and as they would affect the satisfaction of the interests of each single individual, would be accepted by all without constraints. The only condition that U adds to the second premise outlined above is that the "common interest" of all concerned means taking into account the satisfaction of the interests of *each single* individual, such that a naive *collectivist* interpretation of the common interest which would violate minority interests is precluded. Again, however, this clarification seems to me to be already implied by the very *idea* of the participation of *all concerned* in discourse, in the following way: if the idea of a communicative ethics suggests that it is not the single insights of an isolated moral philosopher that defines the content of rational consent but the open and free argumentation of all concerned, then why should we assume that in such an argumentation situation members of a minority whose interests are sacrificed to what is seen as the common interest by the majority would accede to this outcome at all? If, however, there are psychological or other cultural factors at work which make individuals prone to accept an ideology of self-sacrifice, or which lead them to believe that another group knows better than they themselves do what is in their own best interest, then it would be desirable to handle such assumptions directly by means of the relevant psychological, sociological, or cultural argumentations. We should not assume that a principle of argumentation alone can settle such substantive disputes by definitional means.

The conclusion that I draw from these reflections on the second premise is that on one interpretation, the argument leading to U becomes tautological, for the conclusion is already contained in the premise; according to a second interpretation, U clarifies how the common interest is to be interpreted in discourses and is thus non-tautological, but this clarification itself in turn entails substantive normative assumptions which would properly belong not among the *rules* of argument but within the *content* of normative argumentation itself.

The Hegelian core of these objections is the following: the presence of a universalizability principle in communicative ethics is either redundant or inconsistent. Either this principle explicates the meaning of rational consent in such a way that nothing new is added to the available explication of the argumentation procedure in practical discourse; or this principle defines the meaning of rational consent in some additional way, but this definition is neither the only one compatible with accepted rules of argumentation, nor can it be said to follow from rules of argumentation without the introduction of additional assumptions not belonging among the specified rules of argument. If, however, it is the case that the universalizability principle is not the only one compatible with discursive rules of argumentation 3.1 through 3.3, nor can it be derived from these rules without the introduction of some additional assumptions, then it follows that the denial of this *particular* formula of universalizability would not involve one in a performative contradiction. Let me be very clear what this critique implies: it does not imply rejecting the basic principle of a discourse ethic that only those norms can claim validity which meet (or could meet) with the consensus of all concerned as participants in a practical discourse. It only rejects that the *specific* version of the universalizability principle U can be derived without *additional* assumptions. The following discussion will seek to clarify what these additional assumptions are.

b. The Institutional Bases of Communicative Ethics

Hegel's second objection to Kantian ethics concerned its institutional deficiency. Distinguishing between morality and ethical life, Hegel maintained that institutions and practices could not be judged in light of their conformity or lack thereof with the moral law alone. They had to be viewed as part of a functionally interdependent totality of social relations and practices. Hegel named this totality "ethical substance." But collective life was not merely a functional network with its intrinsic laws and logic confronting the individual. It also had to be viewed as "ethical life," as a totality of practices that were motivationally meaningful for individuals as well as being cognitively comprehensible to them.

A normative ethics which is embedded in a critical social theory cannot be subject to this Hegelian critique. On the contrary, as the distinction between "system" and "social integration" introduced in the last chapter shows, both the *external* view of social life as an independently functioning mechanism and the *internal* perspective upon it, shared by the actors who live it, constitute aspects of such a critical social theory. Nonetheless, the traditional Hegelian objection has a critical kernel which can be reformulated as a problem concerning the *plurality of norms*. By the *plurality of norms* I mean the following: does Kantian moral theory, or do Kantian moral theories in general, present a procedure for judging all *relevant* norms of human action? Or is it that, as Hegel argues, Kantian moral theory has a privileged object domain, namely, the domain of juridical and quasi-juridical relations, but is blind to all other forms of human relationships—family, friendship, and erotic bonds? Applied to communicative ethics, this question would read: is communicative ethics only relevant for the domain of juridical and quasi-juridical human relations? Does it suffer from the legalistic bias of Kantian moral theory in general?[73]

If, as suggested above, the origins of the concept of a discourse free from domination lie in the search for a democratic public ethos in late-capitalist societies, then it should hardly be surprising that relations of justice would be defined as the privileged object domain of this moral theory. Yet, I want to argue, there is a significant distinction between a legalistic or juridical conception of public life and a democratic-participatory ethos, and the theory of communicative ethics sits between these two stools uncomfortably. This can best be seen if we begin with a clarification of the concept of "interests" in communicative ethics.

In the first place, it might be surprising that a neo-Kantian ethical theory has room for the concept of interests at all. Upon a second look, it becomes clear why this should be so in the case of a communicative ethics. Neither the Kantian psychology of duty nor the doctrine of the two worlds plays a role in communicative ethics. The repressive, puritan legacy of Kantian ethics, as well as its dualism, has been left behind.[74] Furthermore, discursive argumentation is viewed as being continuous with everyday life contexts in which real social actors contend with one another over the validity of norms. The interests that participants in a discourse bring with them to the argumentation situation are ones that they already have as actors in the lifeworld. It can be assumed, then, that in the formula of universalizability examined above, the concept of "interests" is used in a sense that is continuous with such everyday lifeworld definitions and interpretations. Participation in discourses implies no stipulations regarding the ordinary, everyday understanding of interests.

If, however, participants in discourses bring with them their own interpretation of their own interests, then the question immediately suggests itself: given that the satisfaction of the interests of *each* is to be viewed as a legitimate and reasonable criterion in establishing the *universality* of a norm, then is it not the case that universality can only result when a corresponding "compatibility" or even harmony of interests really exists in the lifeworld? Consensual agreement reached in discourses would imply the existence of a harmony of interests in the lifeworld. Now if one were to assume that such a harmony of interests does indeed exist, then it is hard to see why the need for discourses would arise in the first place, since discourses aim to settle validity claims the controversial nature of which implies the presence of conflicting interests in the lifeworld. Yet if no such harmony of interests exists in the lifeworld, then it is questionable whether discourses can create consensus around such conflictual interests without the participants in them coming to change their interpretation of their own interests, and perhaps even the life forms in which they are anchored. If participants in a discourse have conflicting interests, then they could reach consensual agreement either by foregoing some of these interests or by changing the life forms that generate them.

We now have to see the universalizability principle in a new light. This principle is to function as a *maxim-testing* procedure for distinguishing universalizable from non-universalizable interests. Norms are only legitimate when they correspond to the "universalizable" or "general" interest. But as the history of modern political philosophy from Hobbes to Rawls might reveal, this is hardly an unproblematic claim. Let me suggest three ways of interpreting the concept of the "general interest." First, doubting that there can ever be a social condition which reflects *the* general interest in a substantive sense, one may choose to define the general interest *minimally,* as "not taking interest in each other's interests." According to John Rawls' formulation, only the two rules of justice would reflect the "general interest" and define a set of social institutions acceptable to all.[75] These two principles, however, are compatible with the existence of *conflicting* interests, for they merely outline ground rules for processing such conflicts in social life once they arise. The precondition for the acceptance of such general rules is actually "not taking an interest in each other's interests," i.e., limited altruism.

Second, one can interpret the "general interest" *maximally* as describing not merely a set of procedures but an actual social situation in which conflict of interests among individuals disappears. This would imply the reconciliation of the individual and the universal, the private and the public, the empirical and the rational.[76]

Third, one can regard the concept of "general interest" *critically* in order to reveal the partiality and ideological biases of interests claimed to be universal or general. According to this third model, the very concept of a general interest would signify a test procedure. One would reject the *minimalist* interpretation of Rawls, who allows considerable conflict of interests to persist without at the same time falling into the trap laid by Rousseau, of positing the ideal of a wholly conflict-free, harmonious, and self-transparent body politic.

Clearly, since the *Legitimation Crisis*, Habermas intends discourse or communicative ethics to be interpreted in this third way as providing a critical test for uncovering non-generalizable interests rather than for generating a universal one. A closer examination shows, however, that precisely in this work the distinction between the Rousseauian and the critical models is extremely blurred:

> Since all those affected have, in principle, at least the chance to participate in practical deliberation, the "rationality" of the discursively formed will consists in the fact that the reciprocal behavioral expectations raised to normative status afford validity to a *common* interest ascertained *without deception*. The interest is common because the constraint-free consensus permits only what *all* can want; it is free of deception because even the interpretation of needs in which *each individual* must be able to recognize what he wants becomes the object of discursive will-formation.[77]

The latter half of this claim could be interpreted in two ways. Either it means that when individuals stop deceiving themselves and others, and discover what their "true" needs are, they will discover them to be identical with those of others, or at least in harmony with them. Or it could mean that through discourses individuals come to realize a certain truth about their needs and interests and change their previously held beliefs about them. The first model is uncomfortably reminiscent of Rousseau's argument that if only each were to look inside one's heart and listen to its voice, he or she would discover the true "general interest."[78] According to the second interpretation, however, discourses would have to be viewed as *moral-transformative* processes.

This "moral-transformative" moment of practical discourse would serve to distinguish the Habermasian model of the "suppressed generalizable interest" from the position of both Rawls and Rousseau. In fact, I do not see how, without the explicit acknowledgment of this dimension, this model can be distinguished from the others at all. Since those respects in which the discourse model evokes the myth of a self-transparent collectivity in Rousseauian fashion have been mentioned,[79] let me consider the relationship of discourse ethics of the minimalist interpretation of the "general interest."

On more than one occasion, Habermas has explicitly distanced himself from identifying practical discourse with any kind of collective bargaining or negotiating model. "A compromise can be justified as a compromise," he writes, "only if both conditions are met; a balance of power among the parties involved and the non-generalizability of the negotiated interests exist. If even one of these *general* conditions of *compromise formation* is not fulfilled, we are dealing with a pseudo-compromise. In complex societies *pseudo-compromises* are an important form of legitimation."[80]

In the light of this argument, the Rawlsian theory of justice appears as a normative model of a pseudo-compromise on the general interest, for it fails to meet the second condition. In virtue of existing under a "veil of ignorance," Rawlsian agents in the original position fulfill the first condition of having a balance of power between them. Yet the second condition, namely, that of the "non-generalizability of the negotiated interest," is not demonstrated by Rawls, but simply taken for granted. Interests and their interpretations are not subject matters of the collective-choice game at all. In Rawls' theorem, individuals do not debate the content of their interests, but bargain about the distribution of a package of primary goods which all are assumed to want whatever else they want. Habermas points out that this assumption of Rawls' already preempts a certain interpretation of interests. Rawls' definition of "primary goods" is not a neutral or even minimal definition, but one reflecting the biases of a way of life that is based on the private happiness of consumers. The "pursuit of happiness" might one day mean something different: "not accumulating material objects of which one disposes privately, but bringing about social relations in which mutuality predominates and satisfaction does not mean the triumph of one over the repressed needs of the other."[81] Habermas proposes a dialogical instead of a monological model of need constitution, and prefers a system of justice in which individuals are not allowed to pursue their "thin" conception of the good at the expense of repressing the needs of others.

Such a critique of the Rawlsian position is not possible, I want to argue, unless discourses are viewed as moral-transformatory processes. If Habermas assumes that in discourses individuals preserve the same need and interest interpretations as they had in ordinary, everyday contexts, then a consensual acceptance of norms reflecting the general interests of each can hardly follow. For this to be the case, either one must assume that a pre-established harmony of interests exists—clearly an unacceptable premise for a critical social theory—or one must interpret this process minimalistically as aiming at the establishment of the lowest common interest, while leaving substantive conflict of interest untouched. This could consist in the formation of a legal system, a constitution embodying the two principles of justice and the like. The content of a universalist ethical position would then be exhausted by a legalistic or juridical construction. But if neither of these alternatives is acceptable, then we must assume that discourses are processes through which *new* needs and interests, such as can lead to a consensus among the participants, emerge.

We can now return to the critique of the discourse model raised at the beginning of this section. I suggested that this model vacillated between the legalistic and participatory-democratic versions. It should be clear that the discourse model would fall into legalism if its moral-transformatory aspect, entailing not a compromise on interests but the real transformation of certain interests, were underplayed, and the theory were presented as a more refined version of a universalizability formula in neo-Kantian ethics. Particularly when communicative ethics is defended in developmental-logical terms, the fact that it is not one more thought experiment in universalizability but an ethics of practical transformation through participation tends to drop from sight. It is for lack of an understanding of this point that some commentators like Raymond Geuss ask in bewilderment *who* the participants in practical discourse are: whether "all" refers to all human beings or all beings capable of speech or "all concerned."[82] In principle, of course, all beings capable of speech are entitled to participate in discourses, but particular discourses take place among those concerned, affected by, and interested in the implementation and establishment of particular norms. Discourse ethics does not simulate a thought experiment for all beings capable of speech, and establish what norms they ought to accept as binding. It requires that controversies over the validity of contested norms be settled through an argumentative process in which the *consensus of all concerned* decides upon the legitimacy of the controversial norm. Participation precedes universalizability. The old adage "no taxation without representation" is now reformulated as "no universalizability without participation."

If this line of analysis, which emphasizes the participatory aspects of a discourse ethic, is appropriate, it implies that Habermas' critique of Rousseau is unjustified on one point. He criticizes Rousseau for confusing a level of normative justification with a concrete institutional proposal: "He mixed the introduction of a new principle of legitimation with proposals for institutionalizing a just rule. . . . This has confused the discussion of democracy right up to the present day. . . . If one calls democracies precisely those political orders that satisfy the *procedural* type of legitimacy, then questions of democratization can be treated as what they are: as organizational questions."[83] But the analysis of this section has attempted to show that this distinction between questions of justification and questions of organization cannot be a hard one. Unless discourse ethics is interpreted as a participatory democratic process on the part of all those affected, concerned, or influenced by the adoption of a contested norm, it can only be viewed as one more universalizability theorem in the tradition of neo-Kantian ethics operating with the myth of a general interest transparent to all rational minds.

The concept of "moral transformation," introduced in this section, suggests that the relationships between "discourse" and "action" is complex. On the one hand, discourses involve a certain "bracketing" of the constraints of action; they represent a momentary pause of deliberation amid the intensity of engaged conflict and disagreement. On the other hand, they themselves reach back upon contexts of action in ways that deserve closer scrutiny. As a final step, I want to examine this relationship between discourse and action with respect to both the beginnings and the end of discourses.

c. Cognition, Motivation, and Affect in Communicative Ethics

In his original critique of Kantian moral psychology, Hegel attacked the severity of the dualism between the rational and the emotive which this theory supposed. Maintaining that there was no conflict between *Sittlichkeit* and *Sinnlichkeit*, Hegel emphasized the transformative and educative role of reason in shaping and transforming human desire. The relationship of reason to desire is not one of mastery (*Herrschaft*), but one of formation and education (*Bildung*). The individual's desire for happiness and recognition is not incompatible with moral autonomy; in fact, moral autonomy requires the formulation of a coherent conception of the good life on the part of the individual and the search for its realization. Adorno's and Horkheimer's psychoanalytically inspired critique of Kantian morality takes its bearings from this Hegelian argument. They seek to disclose the repressive content of a morality which defines nature, inner as well as outer, as the "other" of reason, and as subject to reason's domination. The Kantian concept of autonomy glorifies the self-sameness of an abstract ego whose primary fear, Adorno maintained, is of the other. But the utopian promise of reason requires that we conceptualize a form of non-dominating, non-threatened, and non-threatening relation to otherness.

Before addressing the extent to which the communicative concept of autonomy stands in or departs from the tradition of utopian reconciliation between reason and nature, I would like to consider the relationship between cognition, motivation, and affect in communicative ethics.

Communicative ethics presupposes neither a Kantian law of

duty nor a Kantian moral psychology which radically juxtaposes reason to emotion. It shares with Kantian moral theory the emphasis on the role of reason in ethics, and the necessity of viewing rationality as universally binding. A contemporary reformulation of the Hegelian objection to Kantian moral psychology as applied to communicative ethics would have to take a different form. I suggest the following: does the cognitivist bias of communicative ethics also lead to the *rationalistic fallacy*, namely, to a view of reason as a self-generating faculty, determining both the conditions of its own genesis and application? Such an ideal of the total self-determination of reason is essential to the idealist concept of "reflection." Critical theory, by contrast, began with the insight that the total self-reflection of reason amounts to the impossible demand to transcend the human situatedness of reason, but the requirement that reason engage in self-reflection was also justified by critical theorists, insofar as they argued that reason which is incapable of becoming aware of its own contingent origins and applications in society would turn into an instrument of domination. The rationalistic fallacy arises when the continuing critical self-reflection upon the conditions of the possibility of reason, conditions which reason never wholly determines, is minimized and reason is viewed as self-generative.

Let me concretize these considerations by turning to the question of the beginnings of discourse. On a number of occasions Habermas has criticized both Karl-Otto Apel and the normative-logic school of Paul Lorenzen for leaving a "decisionistic residue" in their theories with regard to the beginnings of discourse.[84] According to Lorenzen (and Schwemmer), once individuals have committed themselves to the minimum rules of logic, they will also have to recognize that this commitment has a normative dimension.[85] The canons of logic are indeed normative, and require us to adopt the transsubjective standpoint. Karl-Otto Apel, by contrast, does not consider the normative dimension of theoretical reason to be primarily contained in the commitment to logic; he claims that anyone engaged in *reflection* and *questioning*, in raising a knowledge claim, will come upon the normativity of the ideal community of communication.[86] On Habermas' view, both positions give far too restricted an account of the relationship between action and practical discourse. The

Lorenzen school is wrong in restricting normativity to logic alone and in overlooking the normative bases of speech acts. With his acknowledgment that only one who *chooses* to participate in argumentation stands under the normative strictures of the a priori community of communication, Apel as well leaves a decisionist remainder. Against anyone who *chooses* not to participate in argumentation, Apel has no defense. Habermas comments:

> Anyone who does not participate, or is not ready to participate in argumentation stands nevertheless "already" in contexts of *communicative action*. In doing so, he has already naively recognized the validity claims—however counterfactually raised—that are contained in speech acts and which can be redeemed only discursively. Otherwise he would have to detach himself from the communicatively established language game of everyday practice.[87]

In "Discourse Ethics: Notes Toward a Justification Program," Habermas utilizes this argument in the context of the refutation of skepticism. The moral skeptic can indeed refuse argumentation; but "through denial of argumentation he cannot indirectly deny that he shares a sociocultural form of life, that he has been raised in contexts of communicative action, and that he reproduces his life in them. In a word, he can deny morality but not the ethical content of lived relations in which he abides, so to speak, day by day. Otherwise he must take flight in suicide or in a deep psychosis."[88] Skepticism is the refusal to share a common way of life.

As powerful as it is, this argument does not dispense with the "decisionist" problematic. Actually, I consider it unfortunate that Habermas has chosen to apply this particular concept to the issue at hand, for the term "decisionism" makes it appear as if the question of the beginnings of discourse concern the *subjective volition* of the individual to argue or not to argue. Once framed in these terms, of course, Habermas can show that *some* form of argumentative speech, if only our capacity to take an affirmative or negative stance in the lifeworld and to justify this with reasons, is inherent in the structure of everyday linguistic practice. In this sense, there can be no speech without the beginning of argument, without the capacity to say "Yes, I agree" or "No, I disagree." This strikes me as being obviously true, and a genuine transhistorical aspect of speech and language in use. It is hard to see what it would mean to be the speaker of any language if one could not also say "yes" or "no" to certain injunctions and give reasons for this choice, whatever the ultimate nature of those reasons may be, appeal to nature, gods, Allah, or fate. In this sense, even the radical skeptic cannot avoid participating in the normative presuppositions of such linguistic practices.

Discourses, however, are very specialized modes of argumentation. They derive their particular normative force from the fact that individuals are willing to settle a controversial and conflictual matter without recourse to force, violence, false compromise, or silent acquiescence. No matter how intrinsic argument may be to speech, certainly neither the *ability* nor the *willingness* to engage in discourses is always, everywhere, and for each individual at hand. The ability and the motivation for reason have their genesis in conditions which reason does not control, but out of which it itself emerges. The term "decisionism" suggests a cursory dismissal of this problem.

Habermas admits that the commitment to consider all individuals as potential participants in discourse presupposes a universalistic commitment to the equality, autonomy, and rationality of individuals. "Neither the willingness nor the ability to consider moral questions from the hypothetical and disinterested perspective of a participant in practical discourse falls from heaven; they result from *interests* that are formed only under certain social conditions, as well as from *learning processes* and *experiences* that are open to social groups only in certain situations."[89] The *interest* in rational discourse is itself one which *precedes* rational discourse, and it is *embedded* in the contingency of individual life histories and in collective patterns of memory, learning, and experience. This interest can be enabled or frustrated in the life of the individual; just as available patterns of political culture and traditions in society may encourage or hinder the development of discursive rationality.

In his provocative presentation of the Gadamer-Habermas debate, Jack Mendelson astutely observes that

the historical potential of the ideal speech situation for becoming the actual organizing principle of a society can only come to frui-

tion in a society which comes close to articulating it on the level of
more historically specific and conscious traditions, for instance
the Western democracies of the twentieth century. While in a sense
the ideal of rational consensus may be immanent in language *per
se* and not simply an external standard, in most societies it is
bound to remain unarticulated in the actual culture. It becomes
politically relevant as an ideal to be consciously striven for only in
societies which have begun to approach it on the level of their own
cultural traditions.[90]

In what way does this constitute an objection to the program
of a communicative ethic, or show it to have fallen into a "rationalistic fallacy"? Is it not the purpose of *The Theory of Communicative Action* precisely to make visible those processes of
rationalization of the lifeworld which constitute the tradition of
the moderns *for us*, and which first make the ideal of discourse
possible? Undoubtedly, this is the case. Yet, as Mendelson also
remarks, it might be questioned whether the *specificity* of the
cultural, political, and institutional configurations which would
enable the ideal of discourse embodiment can be captured via a
general theory of rationalization which radically distinguishes
between the rational reconstruction of logics of development
and the narrative unfolding of historical traditions.[91] A rational
reconstruction of the tradition of the moderns in general does
not capture the *concrete* traditions of modern societies which
come to embody the discursive ideal; for such an explanation
fails to differentiate between the political and public culture of
different modern societies.[92] It may well be that to investigate
the conditions of the possibility of discourses becoming embedded in societal ways of life, a different kind of sociological and
cultural investigation from the one hitherto proposed by Habermas will be necessary. Nevertheless, what I have termed the
"rationalistic fallacy" in communicative ethics cannot be dealt
with primarily at this level.

Communicative ethics demands from its participants a *willingness* and an *ability* to consider normative questions from a
universalist standpoint and to regard every being as an equal
regardless of the actual constellation of relations in real life.
Even if we admit that such willingness and such ability emerge
out of contingent circumstances, there is a dilemma here. The
necessity of discursive argumentation arises when, through con-

flict and crises, social and political agents challenge an established background consensus. Yet the very step of "abstraction" that leads such agents to engage in discourses, namely, the *virtualization* of the constraints of action, can only take place when such agents are willing to *suspend* the motivating force and content of these real conflict situations. Discourses arise when the intersubjectivity of ethical life is *endangered;* but the very project of discursive argumentation presupposes the ongoing validity of a *reconciled* intersubjectivity. For those who feel that the reconciliation in social life has been achieved at their expense, it might be morally justified to refuse participating. This does not imply resorting to violence or to force, but simply the refusal to engage in dialogue *before* the realization has been reached that the mutuality of shared existence is indeed endangered by the existing constellation of power. Too quick a willingness to compromise and to be "reasonable" can also endanger true universalism. There are some situations when the nature of the conflict between the parties is such that there can be no dialogue, for the preconditions of dialogue— namely, the mutual recognition of each other as discursive partners—simply do not obtain.[93] Structural inequalities between the parties, such as pertain to wealth, power, or status may be such that reciprocal recognition does not exist; or the emotional burden of the conflict between the parties may be so overwhelming that the equilibrated distance necessary for ongoing discourse does not result. Social conflicts, but also familial and erotic ones, may resist being cast into the discourse model of conflict resolution.[94]

Why is it necessary for the theory of communicative ethics to address such questions, for these seem to concern the conditions of the *application* of the discursive ideal to real life situations? They are external to the internal construction and *validity* of the normative claims of the theory. Habermas himself has named such considerations problems of "mediating" an abstract, universalistic morality (*Moralität*) with concrete forms of ethical life (*Sittlichkeit*).[95] Indeed, some of the concerns I voiced above about the appropriateness of the discourse model for conflict resolution in all instances, the right time to engage in discursive argumentation, and the like can be named questions of *prudence*

—of correct, appropriate, fit moral judgment—and in some cases, of *strategic-political* cleverness—at times it might be more correct to strike, to break off negotiations, to leave the room, or to demonstrate than to go on bargaining and negotiating. Both moral *sagacity* and strategic-politic *savvy* would be involved in the *application* of communicative ethics to life contexts. And about them this theory has little to say. But this admission simply means that communicative ethics is contingent on both ends: the *willingness* and *capacity* of individuals and the culture at large to adopt such an ethical standpoint in the first place, as well as the moral sagacity and political insight necessary to concretize the principles of such ethics in action or policy, are external to the theory. Committing the rationalist fallacy would involve disregarding this contingency surrounding the beginnings and end of discourses, and to assume that the communicative-ethical ideal is not subject to contingencies of life contexts.

In recent years such questions concerning the application of the principles of a universalistic-ethical theory have given rise to a lively debate under the heading of "contextualization." Kohlberg and Habermas have had to admit that the hypothetical moral capacity tested by cognitive-developmental theories does not translate into a corresponding capacity to form the right, correct, appropriate judgment in *real* life contexts.[96] Nonetheless, they insist that the *moral justification* of principles must be distinguished from their *contextualization*—their appropriate and skillful embodiment in right actions as well as the exercise of perspicacious judgment.

This distinction between *justification* and *contextualization* shows once again the limits of a rationalistic interpretation of communicative ethics and creates a number of thorny questions both for the methodology of moral-developmental psychology and, philosophically, for a universalist-ethical theory. With regard to the first: if the hypothetical resolution of moral dilemmas in test situations does not translate into a corresponding ability to *judge* correctly in real life situations, then exactly what is this kind of theory a theory of? What kind of an ability is being judged or evaluated? Second, if indeed there is a gap between the resolution of hypothetical moral dilemmas and responses in real life situations, then what is this gap a function of—is it a function of strength of character, of moral personality as opposed to moral cognition? Surely the history of moral theory, as well as our own experiences, provides us with abundant examples of discrepancies between claims and action, acknowledgment of principles and the capacity to act on them, of such magnitude that one might wonder with Aristotle whether the real nature of moral virtue does not consist "in a state of character," a constant disposition to act in certain ways rather than in others. Equally, does not a similar consideration of discrepancies between word and deed, between ideals and actual behavior, lead to the psychoanalytic insight that certain, systematic patterns of discrepancy should force us to inquire into mechanisms of repression, sublimation, and displacement in the behavior of the individual?

As to the philosophical lines of objection, it might be wondered whether the phenomenon of moral judgment can be explained simply in terms of the *application* of an already given principle to a certain context. Here we have a model of moral judgment which assumes that in the act of judging, what we do is subsume a particular case under a general rule. We judge this particular X to be an instance of the rule Y. Presumably, communicative ethics is a procedure which enables us to establish the normative rightness or correctness of the rule Y. Yet this is a very poor model of moral judgment, for moral judgment concerns precisely that mental activity which allows us to *identify* X *as* an instance of Y. How do we know in any given moral situation that what is required of us is to act on the rules of friendship and generosity rather than of contractual justice? How do we know *this* situation to be one of friendship rather than one of justice? Why call a situation a breach of loyalty rather than a thoughtless slip? In such cases, description already seems to entail evaluation. To say that a situation is of such and such a kind already seems to invoke a very complex process in which just as much is revealed about the character of the person judging as it is about the situation judged. Stanley Cavell has very well observed that

apparently, what the "case" in question is *forms part of the content of the moral argument itself.* Actions, unlike envelopes and goldfinches, do not come named for assessment, nor, like apples, ripe for grading. The most serious sense, to my mind, in which Kant's moral theory is "formalistic" comes not from his having said that actions motivated only in *certain* ways are *moral* actions, but in his having found too little difficulty in saying *what* "the" maxim of an action is in terms of which his test of its morality, the Categorical Imperative, is to be applied.[97]

These brief considerations indicate that the problem of moral judgment cannot be resolved by distinguishing between justification and application alone. Moral judgment is a complex phenomenon and it is important to know what, if any, light a theory of communicative ethics can throw on the matter.[98]

Closely related to the issue of the contextualization of discursive principles in real life situations is the question of the motivating power of the normative contents of discourses in real action contexts. How do the insights gained in counterfactual argumentation situations translate into action-governing *motives* and principles in real life contexts? Or conversely, why do they fail to do so? One faces not only the question as to what the transition from action to discourse means; the ability of discourses to generate motives of action is an issue as well. What Habermas names the "motivating power of rational argument" (*die motivierende Kraft rationaler Argumentation*)[99] returns us once more to Hegel's critique of Kantian moral psychology. As is well known, Kant, unable to solve the question of how pure reason could be the motive of action, had to postulate a *Faktum der Vernunft* to explain how a finite human being could be motivated to act out of a sense of duty to the moral law alone. For Hegel, by contrast, reason becomes a fact only if it shapes and transforms desire, without condemning it to silence. The desirability of reason entails the rationality of desire. Reason that refuses to heed inner nature and the individual's demand for happiness and fulfillment can lose its motivating power. Perhaps then the motivating power of reason can only be established if not only justice but happiness too is promised? Perhaps, to become embedded in action contexts, communicative ethics has to appeal to this utopian impulse for happiness as well. In this sense, "communicative ethics does indeed have a utopian content, but it does not *sketch* out a utopia."[100] Before proceeding to examine this utopian content, I would like to clarify the general intention behind my critique of Habermas' concept of communicative rationality and ethics.

In chapter 7 it was concluded that the constituents of communicative rationality—like decentration, the differentiation of value spheres, and the growth of reflexivity—could not be justified in a strong sense as being universally binding. After having formulated a *weak justification* of communicative rationality, in this chapter I turned to the program of a communicative ethic. Here too my goal has been to show that a *strong* justification strategy such as would lead from the analysis of the universal-pragmatic conditions of argument to a communicative ethic is untenable. Instead, we have to concede two things: first, that some minimal norms like reciprocity and symmetry among participants belong among the rules of argumentation which we have no good reasons to want to deny. We cannot deny these conditions and continue to assert that our argumentation procedure was a fair, just, or rational one. Second, however, these general norms of reciprocity and symmetry, and any additional ones which belong among the rules of fair and rational argumentation, do not imply or entail a specific version of the universalizability principle. There may be many and very good reasons, both of an empirical and normative nature, for adopting this principle; but as I tried to show in this chapter, the specific version given to it by Habermas simply does not follow from universal-pragmatic rules of argumentation.

Thus one faces a dilemma. On the one hand, the minimum norms of argument or rational speech are not strong or contentful enough to lead to an interesting formulation of communicative ethics. Any of a number of universalistic ethical theories are compatible with these rules of argumentation. On the other hand, if one does formulate a strong version of communicative ethics, this can only be attained in the light of strong assumptions which themselves do not follow from the minimum rules of argumentation, but which presuppose assumptions of a sociological and pyschological nature. In other words, if one keeps to a minimalist formulation of communicative ethics, one is at a loss to distinguish its intentions from those of other theories in the universalist mode; for, in order to distinguish between the

Rawlsian theory of justice and Kantian ethics on the one hand and communicative ethics on the other, it is necessary to give a strong and non-minimal account of this theory, and the non-minimal account will entail assumptions that are stronger than may be acceptable to a moral skeptic.

The two horns of the dilemma I have been articulating can be named more precisely the Scylla of naturalism and the Charybdis of decisionism. On the one hand, the ideals of a communicative ethic appear as if they were "always already presupposed," whether in virtue of being the minimum and incontrovertible conditions of communicative action or in virtue of being the acquired competencies of normally developing subjects. On the other hand, if one rejects this naturalization of one's ethical commitments and their presentation as if they were facts in the world, one faces the objection that these commitments are products of a mere decision, of an act of choice, and that this act of choice cannot be backed with reasons.

The only way that I can see out of this dilemma is to deny that avoiding its first horn—naturalism—implies decisionism. Since I will consider problems of evolutionary naturalism in Habermas' theory more fully in the next section, let me concentrate here on decisionism. Decisionism, whether it be that of Kierkegaard, Sartre, or Weber, operates with a twofold assumption: first, a strong, traditional concept of reason, which is viewed as capable of providing ultimate grounds, is presupposed. Let us remember that both Kierkegaard and Sartre take Hegelian reason, which claims to be able to show the rationality of the actual and the complete mediation of the universal and the particular, as paradigmatic; whereas Weberian decisionism can only be comprehended in the context of Weber's diagnosis of the destruction of integrative worldviews and the ensuing differentiation of incompatible value spheres. For none of these thinkers, a non-foundationalist, fallibilist, and communicative concept of reason is a possibility. Therefore, they frame the problem as being one of ultimate justification or of sheer choice. The possibility that ultimate justification can be replaced by processes of communicative argumentation and discourse which produce a consensus that is always subject to revision is not entertained.

Second, ethical decisionism asks ethical theory to eliminate the burden of choice of a particular individual. No modern ethical theory can meet this challenge without falling into dogmatism. This is precluded above all for a critical social theory through its insistence on the value of the autonomous personality. To assume that the theorist can advise concrete individuals how to lead their lives is to assume in the first place that the theorist possesses an *authority* which has not been granted her, and in the second place that theory bestows some unique ethical *insight*. In other words, if the demands of decisionism were fulfilled, one might end up with an ethics of authority or of wisdom. Critical theory, precisely because it assumes that the moral individual is as autonomous as the theorist, that theoretical enlightenment bestows no *prima facie* moral and political authority, and that moral insight can be shared by all, *cannot* in principle answer the demand of decisionism that it eliminate the burden of choice of the individual. To think otherwise would be "bad faith." Thus, a weak justification of communicative ethics, based on a discursive and fallibilistic conception of reason, would not need to fall into decisionism; for it is shown that what decisionism asks of normative theorizing, as well as the search for "ultimate" grounds, is itself unreasonable.

3. Communicative Autonomy and Utopia

In his retrospective on Walter Benjamin, "On the Actuality of Walter Benjamin: Consciousness-Raising or Rescuing Critique," Habermas discusses an issue which for many has seemed to point to a lacuna in his own understanding of moral progress and emancipation:

> In the tradition that reaches back to Marx, Benjamin was one of the first to emphasize a *further* moment in the concepts of exploitation and progress: besides hunger and oppression, failure; besides prosperity and liberty, happiness. Benjamin regarded the experience of happiness he named secular illumination as bound up with the rescuing of tradition. The claim to happiness can be made good only if the sources of that semantic potential we need for interpreting the world in the light of our needs are not exhausted.[101]

In the semantic heritage of a cultural tradition are contained those images and anticipations of a fulfilled life history and of a collective life form in which justice does not exclude solidarity, and freedom is not realized at the expense of happiness. Certainly, Habermas continues, it is not possible to achieve freedom and to realize justice without unleashing (*entbinden*) the hidden potentials of culture. In that sense, the semantic unleashing of culture and the social overcoming of institutional repression are mutually supportive. Yet the suspicion remains whether "an emancipation without happiness and lacking in fulfillment might not be just as possible as relative prosperity without the elimination of repression."[102]

As Joel Whitebook has observed, written a year before the *Legitimation Crisis* (1973) and four years before *The Reconstruction of Historical Materialism* (1976), this essay contained a programmatic anticipation of how Habermas proposed to argue not only against the tradition of counter-Enlightenment (Nietzsche, Spengler, Jünger, and Heidegger) but against the messianic utopian strand of critical theory as well—Bloch and Benjamin in particular.[103] But these subsequent works have not dissipated the force of the suspicion which has been voiced. Increasingly in recent years, Habermas has had to point to the *limits* of a theory of practical discourse which focuses on freedom while excluding the good life; which concerns the validity of normative sentences (*Sollsätze*) while ignoring the question of the integrity of values (*Werte*); which, in short, concerns institutional justice but cannot say much about those qualities of individual life histories and collective life forms which make them fulfilling or unfulfilling.[104] This questioning is neither a coincidence nor of mere philological interest. It reveals the intimate relation between the poles of *norm* and *utopia*, justice and the good life, between which the discourse of a critical social theory unfolds.

Since Marx's early critique of civil society, the project of emancipation was viewed both as the fulfillment and transfiguration of the existing order. In developing an immanent critique of capitalism, critical Marxism held this social order to its own promises, and required that social rationality, abundance, the betterment of human life, and an end to exploitation and misery be realized for all, and not only for some. This demand did not call into question the Enlightenment project of combining human freedom and happiness with the scientific-technologically based progress of productive forces. The course of European history after the beginning of the twentieth century left little hope that the Enlightenment could fulfill its own *promêsse du bonheur*. Critical theory lamented the dialectic of an Enlightenment condemned to leave its own promises unfulfilled. The project of emancipation was increasingly viewed not as the fulfillment, but as the transfiguration of the Enlightenment legacy. The aporias into which this increasingly esoteric conception of emancipation forced the critical theory of Horkheimer, Adorno, and Marcuse have been analyzed. More and more, emancipation ceased to be a public project and became a private experience of liberation achieved in the nondominating relation with nature, and in moments of revolutionary eros.

Habermas has attempted to reestablish the link between Enlightenment and emancipation, and to bring the project of emancipation into the light of the public by going back to the Enlightenment legacy of practical reason. His project requires the fulfillment of the universalistic promise of bourgeois consent theories which, since the seventeenth century, have always limited such universalism on the basis of sex, class, race, and status considerations. But even when we concede that the realization of bourgeois universalism is a necessary condition for emancipation, it seems hardly sufficient. "Can we preclude," asks Habermas, "the possibility of a meaningless emancipation? In complex societies, emancipation means the participatory transformation of administrative decision structures."[105] If this were all that was meant by "emancipation," if indeed the goal of critique exhausted itself in the "joyless reformism" of a welfare-statist or social-democratic compromise, then indeed critical theory would have established the link between Enlightenment and emancipation by forsaking far too much of its utopian tradition. Let me ask, therefore, if the goal of realizing bourgeois universalism, of making good the unfulfilled promise of justice and freedom, must exhaust itself in a "joyless reformism," or whether, speaking with Benjamin, one cannot see a *Jetztzeit*, a moment of transfiguration, in this very process? I want to suggest that the seventh stage of moral development postulated by

Habermas as a corrective and extension of the Kohlbergian scheme, that is, the stage of "universalizable need interpretations," has an unmistakable utopian content to it, and that it points to a transfigurative vision of bourgeois universalism.

With these considerations I initiate a critique of those aspects of Habermas' thought which remain caught in the standpoint of the philosophy of the subject. Let me first recall what I mean by the philosophy of the subject. This position has been characterized by its adherence to four premises: first, the assumption is made that there is a unitary model of human activity named "objectification" or "externalization"; second, it is likewise assumed that there is a transsubjective subject in history; third, it is claimed that history is the story of this subject; and fourth, emancipation requires that we in the present rediscover our identity qua constituted subjects of the past.

Clearly, Habermas categorically rejects the first two premises. In fact, it is in light of his crucial distinction between labor and interaction, and his development of the structures of intersubjectivity via the concept of communicative action, that one can delineate the assumptions of the philosophy of the subject at all.[106] Also, one of Habermas' main reasons for distinguishing between critique and reconstruction is to reject the conflation he sees to be endemic to Horkheimer's concept of the subject of critical theory. On the one hand, this was assumed to be the empirical human species who created the objective world through its own praxis; on the other hand, it was assumed that humanity in the present would become the subject of history in the normative sense by reappropriating the legacy of this past subject. Habermas pointed out that this equation conflated the achievements of the anonymous subject—the species—with the experience of a historically constituted, specific human group.[107] In what sense, then, can it be maintained that Habermas as well remains within the discourse of the philosophy of the subject?

Habermas reverts to the discourse of the philosophy of the subject at those points in his theory when the reconstruction of the species competencies of an anonymous subject—humanity as such—does not remain merely an empirically fruitful research hypothesis, but assumes the role of a *philosophical narra-*

tive of the formative history of the subject of history.[108] Much like Hegel's *Phenomenology of Spirit*, reconstructions then begin to speak in the name of a fictional collective "we" from whose standpoint the story of history is told. This fictive subject appears both as the subject of the past and of the future; it is empirical and normative at once. In Habermas' account too the empirical subject(s), as whose learning process the cultural evolution of modernity takes place, shifts its status, and this process becomes a representative tale in which "we," the subjects of the present, are to discover ourselves.[109]

What is objectionable in this procedure is twofold. First, who is the "we" in the present such that reconstructions present a process of development with which all can identify? Why is it assumed that one is already facing a collective singularity—mankind as such?[110] This shift to the language of an anonymous species-subject preempts the experience of moral and political activity as a consequence of which alone a genuine "we" can emerge. A collectivity is not constituted theoretically but is formed out of the moral and political struggles of fighting actors. In the second place, this shift to the language of a hypostatized subject has as a further consequence that the historical process is *neutralized*. History begins to appear as the semantic gloss on a structural process which proceeds with necessity and invariably from one sequence to the next.

I already pointed out in the preceding chapter that we cannot naturalize the history of the species, for we have no models of development to compare it with. I also pointed out that from within the post-conventional stage of moral development, one could no longer arbitrate between competing universalistic theories and positions with recourse to evolutionary argumentations. At this point, a certain anticipatory utopia, a projection of the future as it could be, becomes necessary. Since the lines of development leading from present to future are fundamentally underdetermined, the theorist can no longer speak the language of evolution and necessity, but must conceive of him or herself as a participant in the formation of the future. By focusing on the seventh stage of moral development, which in Habermas' construction concerns universalizable need interpretations, I shall attempt to render visible this utopian moment.

As early as the essay on "Theories of Truth," we encounter the claim that the appropriate language of morals "permits determinate groups and persons, in given circumstances, a truthful interpretation both of their own particular needs, and more importantly, of their common needs capable of consensus."[111] From the standpoint of universalistic ethical theories, whether it be Kant's or some contemporary version of it, like Rawls', Gerwirth's, or Baier's, such a requirement would transgress the *limits* of practical discourse. In Kant's case this would be so, simply because the requisite universality of morality could only be established by abstracting away from, indeed by repressing, those very needs, desires, and inclinations which tempt moral agents away from duty. The disregard in contemporary deontological theory for "inner nature" is more complicated, but ultimately, it seems to me, it is based on the classical liberal doctrine that as long as the *public* actions of individuals do not interfere with each other, what they need and desire is their *business*. To want to draw this aspect of a person's life into public-moral discourse would interfere with their autonomy, i.e., with their right to define the good life as they please as long as this does not impinge on others' rights to do the same.[112]

Against this assumption of Kantian moral theories, Habermas draws upon an insight of Hegel's that has both empirical and normative force: this is the insight that the relation between self and other, I and thou, is *constitutive* of the structure of human self-consciousness. Empirically, this leads to a conception of the human personality as developing only in *interaction* with other selves. For various schools of social research, like psychoanalysis, symbolic interactionism, and ego psychology, this is no longer a speculative insight but an empirical hypothesis guiding their theories of human socialization and identity formation.[113] Normatively, this conception of identity implies a model of autonomy according to which the relation between self and other is not external to the ego's striving for autonomy.

In requiring that need interpretations become the subject matter of practical discourses, Habermas is underscoring both points. From the standpoint of socialization theory, individual nature, while being "private," is not immutable; individual need interpretations and motives carry with them the marks of societal processes by participating in which alone an individual learns to become an "I." The grammatical logic of the word "I" reveals the unique structure of ego identity: every subject who uses this concept in relation to himself or herself also learns that all other subjects are likewise "I's." In this respect the ego becomes an I only in a community of other selves who are also I's. Yet every act of self-reference expresses, at the same time, the uniqueness and difference of this I from all others. Discourses about needs and motives unfold in this space created by commonality and uniqueness, general societal processes, and the contingency of individual life histories.

From the standpoint of a normative ego-ideal, the requirement that a "truthful" interpretation of needs also be part of discursive argumentation means that ego autonomy cannot and should not be achieved at the expense of internal *repression*. "Internal nature is thereby moved in a utopian perspective; that is, at this stage internal nature may no longer be merely examined within an interpretive framework fixed by the cultural tradition in a nature-like way. . . . Inner nature is rendered communicatively fluid and transparent to the extent that needs can, through aesthetic forms of expression, be kept articulable or be released from their paleosymbolic prelinguisticality."[114] Ego autonomy is characterized by a twofold capacity: first, the individual's *reflexive* ability to question the interpretive framework fixed by the cultural tradition—to loosen, if you wish, those sedimented and frozen images of the good and happiness in the light of which we formulate needs and motives; second, such reflexive questioning is accompanied by an ability to *articulate* one's needs linguistically, by an ability to communicate with others about them. Whereas the first aspect requires us to assume a reflexive distance toward the content of our tradition, the second emphasizes our ability to become articulate about our own affective and emotional constitution.[115] In both instances, reflection is to be understood not as an abstracting away from a given content, but as an ability to communicate and to engage in dialogue. The linguistic access to inner nature is both a distancing and a coming closer. In that we can name what drives and motivates us, we are closer to freeing ourselves of its power over us; and in the very process of being able to say what we mean, we come one step closer to the harmony or friendship of the soul with itself.

If the highest stage of a universalistic ethical orientation is this open, reflexive communication about our needs and the cultural traditions in light of which they are interpreted, then a number of oppositions on which communicative ethics seemed to rest begin to lose their force: questions of justice merge with questions of the good life; practical-moral discourses flow into aesthetic-expressive ones; autonomy is not only *self-determination* in accordance with just norms but the capacity to assume the standpoint of the *concrete other* as well.

Ancient and modern practical philosophies are usually distinguished from one another on the grounds that whereas the first are oriented toward questions of the good life, the second concern justice. As Aristotle expressed it, the task of the *polis* is not the assurance of mere life but the attainment of the good life. Beginning with Hobbes, modern political philosophy maintains that in a mechanical, non-teleological universe, the "good for men" could no longer be defined unequivocally and with certainty. The ends and goals of nature are hidden from our intellect. The task of practical philosophy, therefore, is not to define the good life, but to discover those rules of justice which guarentee the coexistence of self-interested individuals, each of whom defines the good as what is pleasant for him or her.

In Kant's distinction between autonomy and heteronomy, between maxims of the will based on the pure *form* of an imperative and those maxims of the will which aim at attaining a given good, this Hobbesian legacy is maintained. As Kant explicates it in the *Critique of Practical Reason*, the "paradox in the method of a critique of practical reason is that the concepts of good and evil are not determined prior to the moral law . . . rather . . . are defined according to it and through it."[116] This determination of the good on the basis of a formal moral law indicates that the Hobbesian argument against Aristotelian practical philosophy, the unknowability of the material good, has been accepted. The "natural good" is either a metaphysical category of perfection, from which no determinate principles of obligation can follow, or it is an anthropological category of happiness. On the basis of this category as well, one can generate no binding principles of obligation for all rational agents. Although all finite agents desire their own well-being, each defines this well-being in a different way. Kant accepts as a basic premise that happiness is not activity in accordance with virtue. At the most, such virtuous activity makes us worthy of happiness.

The suggestion made above that in the final analysis, in communicative ethics as well, questions of justice merge with questions of the good life needs to be placed in this context. This suggestion is not a plea for the revival of an Aristotelian ethics of the "good life." Any ethical theory today which would claim that one and only one form of life is compatible with virtue, reason, or morality, and which would venture a material definition of this mode of life, would fall into dogmatism. In ethics as well, the Copernican Revolution, though much lamented today, is irreversible and its consequences cannot be unlearned.[117] Any attempt to skirt this reflexive turn in moral theory and to establish the *object* of moral obligation prior to an analysis of the basis of *valid obligation* is incompatible with moral autonomy. Communicative ethics proceeds from this Kantian insight that the validity of specific norms is to be established in light of a procedure which first defines the grounds of all normative validity, and this is the rational consensus of all concerned.

If one is not pleading for a revival of a neo-Aristotelian ethics of the good, what then is the force of the suggestion that questions of justice merge with questions of the "good life"? If, as is the case with communicative ethics, institutional justice is seen to rest on a certain understanding of human needs and wants; if, furthermore, it is maintained that the definition of such needs and wants is shaped by the cultural tradition and by socialization processes; then a *critique* of culture and socialization may be the only way today that a philosophical theory can regain access to those contents which define the good life, without falling into dogmatism. This would mean recognizing that practical discourses are embedded in cultural traditions which influence the subject matter of discourses via need interpretations and evaluative orientations. Furthermore, since the participants in discourses are individuals who bring with them their own life histories, socialization processes sedimented in such life histories also shape the content of discourses. Culture and personality patterns enter into those practical discourses which explicitly seem only concerned with institutional justice.

The requirement that needs and their interpretations become the focus of discursive argumentation has the consequence that those traditions and practices, the semantic content of which defines the good life and happiness, are thematized. In practical discourses, a certain conception of justice is revealed to rest on a certain understanding of our needs, the cultural traditions which justify them, and the socialization patterns which shape them. If the subject matter of discourses is not artificially restricted, if the process of self-reflection reaches these presuppositions, then issues of justice and the good life flow into one another.

It should be emphasized how *different* this outcome is from that usually associated with universalistic ethical theories. As the definition of stage six in Kohlberg's moral theory reveals, the highest stage of moral orientation is the *public* discourse of rights and entitlements. Neither the needs which drive the actions through which rights are exercised, nor the concept of entitlement which the *ethos* of a right-bearing and invariably adult male implies, is called into question in such a moral theory.[118] Thus, the insistence that "universalizable need interpretations" move into the center of moral discourse is not simply a further *evolution* of such a perspective; it entails a *utopian break* with it, or what I have named its "transfiguration." "Inner nature is moved into a utopian perspective," in the sense that its contents, our needs and affects, become communicatively accessible; in psychoanalytic terms, the threshold of repression is lowered. The utopia of a society in which association (*Vergesellschaftung*) is attained without domination—justice—and socialization without superfluous repression—happiness—moves to the fore.

In many ways this is a belated vindication of one of the central insights of early critical theory, that an emancipated society and a fulfilled individuality imply one another and that the project of the future begins also by revolutionizing our needs and wants. Marcuse's critical theory, which paid the most attention to this problem, also seemed to lead the issue to a dead end. On the one hand, in order to anchor the possibility of revolt in some domain that could escape the ravages of the administered world, Marcuse had to turn to the resistant and immutable core of human instincts; on the other hand, faced with the utter malleability of conscious needs and the formation of false ones, he had to draw a distinction between true and false needs.[119] As is well known, this attempted distinction between true and false needs led to positing the "educational dictator," one who would have to teach people to be free and to want the right thing. Undoubtedly, it is partly the authoritarianism of such a project which has led Habermas to emphasize the merits and significance of bourgeois democratic-liberal traditions.[120] But refusing the unacceptable political implications of the Marcusean distinction between true and false needs should not lead to the opposite view that a consideration of needs has no place in critical theory at all, for these are to be viewed merely as the private concern of individuals. The latter is patently untrue. It is an assumption that goes back to the "state of nature" myth in early bourgeois theories. As Hobbes admits with marvelous clarity, in such theories men are considered "as if but even now sprung out of the earth, and suddenly, like mushrooms, come to full maturity, without all kind of engagement to one another."[121] The *genesis* of the moral subject is shrouded in some mystery; individuals are adults before they are children; they reason before they feel and desire. Once this bias of such theories is replaced by a genetic-developmental perspective, one has to admit that every need and desire reveals the traces of a unique life history, but also the traces of shared values of the culture into which we are born and the socializing institutions that have shaped us.

Taking their orientation from early psychoanalytic theory, early critical theorists emphasized the extent to which human needs and inner nature were shaped by forces and processes which eluded the individual's conscious control. This emphasis on psychoanalytic theory, to the exclusion of some other perspectives on socialization, meant that the line between early, unconscious childhood memories and conscious developments focusing on role-model formation at much later stages of a child's life was largely blurred. In effect, Marcuse could not draw the distinction between true and false needs except by appeal to a divine legislator operating with intuitive reason, for he proceeded from a prelinguistic theory of socialization and need formation. Had it been possible to establish a distinction between instincts (*Triebe*) and needs (*Bedürfnisse*), between primary urges that have to be satisfied or cathected to maintain the life of a human animal, and patterns of motives which also impel us to act in certain ways, but which are fundamentally linguistic and social in character, then the distinction between true and false needs could have been drawn along different lines. False needs would then be viewed as those aspects of inner nature which resist verbalization and articulation, leading instead to distorted communication and action.

In the communicative ethics model, therefore, the emphasis is not on a pregiven human essence to which we succeed or fail in corresponding, but on the dynamic and logic of those blockages—on those silences, evasions, and displacements which point to the presence of an unmastered force in the life of an individual. The psychoanalytic notion of fate is interpreted as the silent force of those experiences that shape the spoken word. The communicative concept of autonomy implies that what resists articulation, even to oneself, originates in the dark recesses of the psyche and has not lost its "paleosymbolic linguisticality." Epistemically, we cannot say that *all* needs that permit linguistic articulation are true, but only that those which do *not* permit linguistic articulation cannot be true. It is ultimately the *process* of discourse, what I have named the moral-transformative experience, that establishes the truth and falsehood of our needs. But even then, we must admit that a genuinely fluid and unrepressed relation to inner nature consists in the capacity for constant critical reevaluation and reconsideration of our most cherished needs.

Discourses in which our needs and the cultural traditions shaping them are thematized, the semantic content of those interpretations defining happiness and the good life, are brought to life, and what is fitting, pleasing, and fulfilling are debated, are named by Habermas "aesthetic-expressive" ones.[122] It is maintained that modernity institutionalizes not only the discursive evaluation of moral and political questions, but those of aesthetic and expressive subjectivity as well. Whereas practical discourses are oriented toward what is public and universalizable, aesthetic-expressive discourse is oriented toward what is semi-public, non-universalizable, and culturally specific. Expressive discourses cannot be abstracted from the hermeneutical and contingent horizon of shared interpretations and life forms.

This distinction between normative and aesthetic-expressive discourse does not do justice, however, to the significance of needs and their interpretations in the moral realm. In fact, by confining such debate concerning need interpretations to the expressive mode alone, Habermas is making an effort to preserve the purity of the normative realm, which he had earlier defined as concerning the binding force of "normative ought sentences" (*Sollsätze;* see section 2). But the very fact that need interpretations also become thematized in moral discourses once more indicates that Habermas' construction of the model of communicative ethics is ambiguous. On the one hand, it shares with deontological theories like Rawls' the desire to separate the public discourse of justice from the more private discourse of needs; on the other hand, inasmuch as it is critical of theories of justice which do not extend to a critique of consumerist and possessive-individualist modes of life, it has to revert to the critique of needs, false socialization, and the like. Earlier I maintained that the discourse theory vacillated between a legalistic-juridical and a more participatory concept of public life (section 2). Now we can say that two different versions of community seem equally implied by this model: the one a community of rights and entitlements, the other a community of needs and solidarity.

I want to suggest that Habermas does not thematize adequately the community of needs and solidarity for, following George Herbert Mead, he assumes the standpoint of the "generalized other," of rights and entitlements, to represent the moral point of view par excellence. Mead formulates the ideal of a community of communication as follows:

> In logical terms there is established a universe of discourse which transcends the specific order within which the members of the community, in a specific conflict, place themselves outside of the community order as it exists, and agree upon changed habits of action and a restatement of values. Rational procedure, therefore,

sets up an order within which thought operates; that abstracts in varying degrees from the actual structure of society. . . . It is a social order that includes any rational being who is or may be in any way implicated in the situation with which thought deals. . . . It is evident that a man cannot act as a rational member of society, except as he constitutes himself a member of this wider common-wealth of rational beings.[123]

In this sociological reformulation of the Kantian Kingdom of Ends on Mead's part, Habermas sees two utopian projections: he names the first the perspective of *self-determination*, that is, of autonomous action oriented toward universalistic principles; the second perspective corresponds to that of *self-actualization*, the capacity to unfold one's individuality in its uniqueness (ThdkH 2:148). "The ideal community of communication corresponds to an *ego identity* which allows self-actualization to unfold on the basis of autonomous action" (ThdkH 2:150). But whereas the perspective of autonomous action corresponds to the standpoint of the "generalized other," what, following Carol Gilligan, I would like to call the standpoint of the "concrete other" cannot be accommodated within the rather ego-centered notion of self-actualization.

The standpoint of the "generalized other" requires us to view each and every individual as a rational being entitled to the same rights and duties we would want to ascribe to ourselves. In assuming this perspective, we abstract from the individuality and concrete identity of the other. We assume that the other, like ourselves, is a being who has concrete needs, desires, and affects, but that what constitutes his or her moral dignity is not what differentiates us from each other, but rather what we, as speaking and acting rational agents, have in common. Our relation to the other is governed by the norm of *formal reciprocity:* each is entitled to expect and to assume from us what we can expect and assume from him or her. The norms of our interactions are primarily public and institutional ones. If I have a right to "x," then you have the duty not to hinder me from enjoying "x," and conversely. In treating you in accordance with these norms, I confirm in your person the rights of humanity, and I have a legitimate claim to expect that you will do the same in relation to me. The moral categories that accompany such inter-actions are those of right, obligation, and entitlement; the corresponding moral feelings are those of respect, duty, worthiness, and dignity, and the vision of community is one of rights and entitlements.

The standpoint of the "concrete other," by contrast, requires us to view each and every rational being as an individual with a concrete history, identity, and affective-emotional constitution. In assuming this standpoint, we abstract from what constitutes our commonality and seek to understand the distinctiveness of the other. We seek to comprehend the needs of the other, their motivations, what they search for, and what they desire. Our relation to the other is governed by the norm of *complementary reciprocity:* each is entitled to expect and to assume from the other forms of behavior through which the other feels recognized and confirmed as a concrete, individual being with specific needs, talents, and capacities. Our differences in this case complement rather than exclude one another. The norms of our interaction are usually private, non-institutional ones. They are the norms of solidarity, friendship, love, and care. Such relations require in various ways that I do, and that you expect me to do in the face of your needs, more than would be required of me as a right-bearing person. In treating you in accordance with the norms of solidarity, friendship, love, and care, I confirm not only your *humanity* but your human *individuality.* The moral categories that accompany such interactions are those of responsibility, bonding, and sharing. The corresponding moral feelings are those of love, care, sympathy, and solidarity, and the vision of community is one of needs and solidarity.

These moral ideals and the corresponding moral emotions have been separated radically from each other in moral and political thought since Hobbes. The institutional distinction between the public and the private; between the public sphere of justice, the civic sphere of friendship, and the private sphere of intimacy, has also resulted in the incompatibility of an ethical vision of principles and an ethical vision of care and solidarity. The ideal of moral and political autonomy has been consistently restricted to the standpoint of the "generalized other," while the standpoint of the "concrete other" has been silenced, I want to suggest, even suppressed by this tradition.[124] As is evidenced by Kantian moral theory, a public ethics of principles entails a repressive attitude toward "inner nature." Our needs and affective nature are excluded from the realm of moral theory. This results in a corresponding inability to treat human needs, desires, and emotions in any other way than by abstracting away from them and by condemning them to silence. The universalistic ethics of justice was attained at the cost of robbing inner nature of its voice. Institutional justice is thus seen as representing a higher stage of moral development than interpersonal responsibility, care, love, and solidarity; the respect for rights and duties is regarded as prior to care and concern about another's needs; moral cognition precedes moral affect; the mind, we may summarize, is the sovereign of the body, and reason, the judge of inner nature.

By allowing need interpretations to move to the center of moral discourse and by insisting that "inner nature be placed in a utopian perspective," Habermas comes close to subverting this bias of traditional normative philosophy; but his insistence that the standpoint of the "generalized other" alone represents the moral point of view prevents this move. It is also inadequate to claim that aesthetic-expressive discourse can accommodate the perspective ot the "concrete other," for relations of solidarity, friendship, and love are not aesthetic but profoundly moral ones. The recognition of the *human* dignity of the generalized other is just as essential as the acknowledgment of the *specificity* of the concrete other. Whereas the perspective of the generalized other promises justice, it is in the relation to the concrete other that those ephemeral moments of happiness and solidarity are recovered.

A communicative concept of autonomy attains utopian and motivating force insofar as it promises neither a merger nor a fusion, but the necessary complementarity of these two perspectives.[125] The ideal community of communication corresponds to an ego identity which allows the unfolding of the relation to the *concrete other* on the basis of *autonomous* action. Only then can we say that justice without solidarity is blind and freedom that is incompatible with happiness, empty.

As this discussion may indicate, while endorsing the necessity of the paradigm shift from the work model of activity to communicative interaction, I am less convinced by the abandonment of utopian-anticipatory moments of critique in Habermas' work.

When communicative ethics, and the perspective of moral autonomy and community it entails, are presented as if they were the logical and inevitable outcome of a normal sequence of development, only carrying to its conclusion what is implicit in the process itself, one reverts back to the philosophy of the subject. Evolutionary argumentations cease to be fruitful research hypotheses and assume instead the role of a philosophical narrative of the formative history of the species. The theorist begins to speak in the name of a fictional collective "we" that not only is the constituted subject of the past, but the constitutive subject of the future as well. By focusing on the internal ambiguities and tensions of the program of a communicative ethic, this chapter has attempted to reconstruct it from within. I have sought to emphasize those moments of transfigurative experience which implied a break with bourgeois universalistic theories. Communicative ethics vacillates between a legalistic-juridical conception of public life on the one hand and a democratic-participatory conception on the other. Likewise, the communicative conception of autonomy can be read as corresponding to the "generalized other" and to a community of rights and entitlements, while the emphasis on inner nature and need interpretations in moral discourse moves the vision of communicative autonomy closer to the standpoint of the "concrete other" and to a community of needs and solidarity. Whereas the first of these pairs of concepts—the legal-juridical concept of public life, community of rights and entitlements—corresponds to the project of fulfilling the legacy of bourgeois revolutions and of the liberal-democratic tradition, the second set of concepts—democratic-participatory vision of public life, community of needs and solidarity—corresponds to the project of transfiguring this tradition. This means creating qualitatively new self- and other-relations that lie beyond the logic of capital, and of administrative-bureaucratic and technical rationality.

4. Concluding Reflections: Beyond the Philosophy of the Subject

No idea has been as central to the tradition of critical social theory as the belief that the exercise of human reason is essential to the attainment of moral autonomy and fulfillment, public justice and progress. This ideal, which critical theory shared with the great thinkers of the bourgeois Enlightenment from Hobbes to Kant, was never really repudiated. The critical theorists took a new approach. Integrating Hegel's and Marx's insights that the autonomous subject was not an isolated Cartesian ego, but a historically and socially *situated*, concrete, and embodied self, in the early phases of their formulations, they extended this Enlightenment ideal into a general critique of the material and social conditions which hindered its realization. In this task, they were inspired by Hegel's critique of Kant, which showed the necessity of developing a critique of pure reason into a phenomenology of human spirit—the story of reason's historical and cultural becoming. Reason was thus given a historical, developmental core.

Marx's critique of Hegel initiated the turn from the *reflective* to the *productive* subject. The essential constituents of our humanity and rationality no longer defined us as an *animal rationale* but as an *animal laborans*. The act which raised us out of nature was not reflection but production. As Horkhemier saw in his 1937 essay, "Traditional and Critical Theory," this shift from reflection to production, understood now as material-constitutive praxis, entailed recognizing the differences between mind and nature. Nature was not an emanation of Spirit, as Hegel would have it; "nature" signified the totality of those objective conditions, shaped, and altered by the activity of human subjects. Nevertheless, neither the Kantian emphasis on the difference between mind and nature nor the active vision of the epistemic subject, was sufficient to eliminate the presuppositions of the philosophy of the subject. The model of Hegel's *Phenomenology*, the concept of a collective singular subject, creating the historical-objective world through its activity, dominated. Whereas Hegel posited a reconciliation that would result from reflection upon the conditions of our becoming, Marx and, following him, the critical theorists envisaged the "reappropriation" by concrete individuals of the objectivity which was a product of their own work. Already in the 1937 essay, however, there was uncertainty regarding the putative subject of this historical process: increasingly, critical theorists spoke not of the proletariat but of all those individuals with a critical sense as the agents of historical change.

After the triumph of National Socialism, the destruction of European Jewry, and the horrors of Stalinism, this uncertainty regarding the subject of history was transformed into despair. In this context the ideals of the Enlightenment, which linked reflection to autonomy, reason with justice and progress, came to sound increasingly hollow. Yet the self-consciously aporetic nature of the *Dialectic of Enlightenment*, and Adorno's relentless deconstruction of these ideas, showed that critical theory, aware of its own situatedness in history and society, had reached an impasse. This impasse indicated that the shift from the *reflective* subject of idealism to the *productive* subject of Marxism offered no real alternatives. For one could no longer agree with Marx that the history of man's emancipation from nature via the development of productive forces also contained the seeds for the reversal of the natural history of mankind. Quite to the contrary: the development of productive forces and technical rationality were seen as the natural outcome of the ambivalences of bourgeois Enlightenment. Enlightenment thinkers, on the one hand, proclaimed the autonomy of the self. On the other hand, they either, like Hobbes, claimed that reason was a mere instrument for achieving whatever ends the subject set for itself, or, like Kant, gave reason a legislative core, but concluded by dividing the world into one of earthly selfishness and an otherwordly Kingdom of Ends. The two legacies of Enlightenment, technical and practical reason, were incompatible, argued critical theorists. In fact, they even suggested that no content could be redeemed from the Enlightenment legacy of reason that was not confined to instrumentality.

The paradigm shift from the production or work model of action to communicative interaction is a response to this impasse. This paradigm shift has brought with it irreversible gains: first, the concept of truth, which critical theory shares with the philosophical tradition in general, has been replaced by a discursive, communicative model of argumentation among a community of investigators. Second, the model of reflection has been revised: it no longer means cogitation, as in Descartes, or the creative imagination of the human architect, as in Marx, but the discursive ability to enter into processes of argumentation and to entertain the standpoint of others. Third, autonomy is no longer conceived of as self-legislation (Kant), self-actualization (Hegel and Marx), or reconciliation with otherness (Adorno and Horkheimer). It is viewed instead as the capacity to adopt a universalist standpoint and to act on this basis. Finally, normative legitimacy means the generation of norms under conditions of communicatively achieved, and rationally motivated, arguments.

At the same time that it brings these irreversible gains, the paradigm shift in critical theory runs the risk of certain losses. The attempt to avoid the historicism of Hegel and Marx has led to certain modes of argumentation that are considered sometimes "transcendental," sometimes "quasi-transcendental," sometimes "reconstructive." The project of Hegel's *Phenomenology* has also returned in the form of a "reconstruction" of the empirical history of the competencies of the species. Both strands of argumentation involve stronger claims than can be justified. Both obscure some of the essential insights that the paradigm shift to communicative reason and action bring with them, namely, the emphasis on human *plurality;* the *narrative* and *interpretive* structure of action; the utopian hopes of a communicative access to need interpretations, and the vision of a community of *justice* that fosters a community of *solidarity.*

Throughout this study my goal has been to point to essential tensions in the project of critical social theory. I have attempted to distinguish aspects of this project which rest on questionable philosophical and sociological assumptions from those of its insights which still have illuminating power. I have juxtaposed the concepts of plurality and the interpretive indeterminacy of action to the collective singular subject and to the work model of action. I shall not recapitulate these arguments here. Only, I would like to emphasize again the relation between such concepts of the subject and action, and various visions of ethical and political life.

The discourse of the philosophy of the subject, which nineteenth-century Marxism and twentieth-century critical theory share, is unacceptable today for two major reasons. In the first place, insofar as this discourse focused on work as the primary activity in the constitution of self and society, it is deficient in an explanatory sense. Attempts have been made to expand the concept of work to mean social production and not merely instrumental action. Others have admitted that production relations could not be easily distinguished from relations of production, but insisted that they remained "determinant in the last instance." Most contemporary Marxist social theorists, however, have reached a similar conclusion: the fundamental categories of Marxian social theory are very much colored by the experience of nineteenth-century capitalism.[126] They cannot be utilized to explain the crises phenomena of our societies without fundamental revision.

The social theory of the Frankfurt School, despite the weaknesses it shares with classical Marxism, remains exemplary in one respect, namely, in its attempt to reformulate Marxian theory in view of the changed relations between politics, economics, and culture in our societies. Even in their aporetic formulations, critical theorists shared the view that the nature of social and political conflict in our societies, their manifestations and consequences, could not be explained in light of the wage-labor-capital conflict alone.

The second reason why the discourse of the philosophy of the subject has become unacceptable is normative. In classical Marxism, the emphasis on the economy went hand in hand with a political commitment that privileged class, especially the working class, as being representative of humanity. This view is to be rejected not only because it cannot explain the nature and causes of conflicts faced by late-capitalists societies, but for an additional reason as well. It leads to the politics of collective singularity. By this I mean a mode of politics where one group or organization acts in the name of the whole. As previously emphasized, this conception of politics, and its authoritarian implications, are not the only ones that can be drawn from classical Marxism. They have, however, played a dominant role in it.

My attempts to emphasize aspects of Marx's thinking that concern "sensuous finitude" and "lived crisis," or features of Adorno's theory of non-identity, aimed at revising the philosophical foundations of this tradition to make it more compatible with a radical, participatory, and pluralist conception of politics. The neglect of such a theory of democracy and politics is one of the chief blind spots of the critical theory of the Frankfort School. With the exception of Franz Neumann and Otto Kirchheimer, who were political sociologists, other members of the Frankfurt School by and large retained the orthodox Marxist distrust toward questions of legitimacy and the normative dimension of political institutions. Again, it is one of the irreversible gains of the paradigm shift to communicative rationality and action to have refocused attention on this neglected dimension. The idea of a communicative ethic is intimately linked to the vision of a democratic public ethos in late-capitalist societies. To articulate the full implications of this position for a macro-theory of democratic institutions, it is important that the concept of "generalizable interests" be differentiated adequately from its Rawlsian and Rousseauian counterparts. In this task, it is also essential that the moments of norm and utopia, of a community of rights and entitlements and one of solidarity and empowerment, be brought together such as to reveal their essential tension as well as their mutual compatibility. Only then can we find an alternative beyond the "possessive individualist" or "disinterested rational agents" of classical and contemporary liberalism, while avoiding the unjustifiable neglect of democratic institutions in orthodox Marxism.

I see the concepts of human plurality and that of the narrative and interpretive structure of action as essential to such a project. By "plurality" I do not mean that we are distinct bodies in space and time, but that our embodied identity and the narrative history that constitutes our selfhood give us each a perspective on the world, which can only be revealed in a community of interaction with others. Such community and commonality arise and develop between us not, as Marx thought, because we are thrust into objectively similar life-conditions. A common, shared perspective is one that we create insofar as in acting with others we discover our difference and identity, our distinctiveness from, and unity with, others. The emergence of such unity-in-difference comes through a process of self-transformation and collective action. It cannot be preempted either by a discourse that defines the identity of struggling subjects for them or by methods of organizing which eliminate normative processes of consensus formation and self-transformation.

Through such processes we learn to exercise moral and political judgment. We develop the ability to see the world as it appears from perspectives different than ours. Such judgment is not merely applying a given rule to a given content. In the first place it means learning to recognize a content and identifying it properly. This can only be achieved insofar as we respect the dignity of the generalized other, who is our equal, by combining it with our awareness of his or her concrete otherness. What we call content and context in human affairs is constituted by the perspectives of those engaged in it. Human situations are perspectival, and to appreciate such perspectives involves empathy, imagination, and solidarity.

Differences in perspective result from the different narrative histories in which selves are embedded. At any point in time, we are one whose identity is constituted by a tale. This tale is never complete: the past is always reformulated and renarrated in the light of the present and in anticipation of a future. Yet this tale is not one of which we alone are the authors. Others not only play a role in our tale but often tell our stories for us and make us aware of their real meaning. The self's identity is revealed only in such a community of interaction; who we are is how we reveal ourselves to others and to ourselves in such processes. The interpretive indeterminacy of action arises from the interpretive indeterminacy of a life-history.

Nevertheless, such a phenomenological perspective must be complemented through an analysis of those *social constraints* under which action takes place and self-identities are constituted. A critical social theory cannot remain satisfied with an ahistorical analysis of the constitution of our lifeworld through the agents' perspectives. It is also necessary to place this lifeworld within a larger picture of the social whole, its limits and possibilities. Such social constraints are not formed by tales but by the logic of those unintended consequences that escape the lifeworld perspective of social agents. In this sense, the perspectives of systemic and lived crises, of the structural contradictions of the whole and the felt experience of individuals, is fundamental. The task ahead is to think their unity, not to emphasize one at the expense of the other.

Following this principle of mediating the perspective of social actors with that of the social theorist, the experience of lived crisis with the knowledge of the systemic problems of society, I have stressed the central tension between the vision of a community of rights and entitlements and that of a community of needs and solidarity. These are not abstract moral imperatives but concrete options of action and interaction in our societies. One of the central problems of late-capitalist societies lies in their viewing public life from a legalistic-juridical perspective alone, while the vision of a community of needs and solidarity is ignored and rendered irrelevant.[127] As explained in chapter 7, a fundamental dynamic of such societies is the ever-rapid expansion of systems of economic and administrative action into the lifeworld. But such expansion can be accomplished only by subjecting life contexts to monetarized, bureaucratic, and juridical norms of action. This in turn means that the extension of the logic of rights and entitlements is endemic to such social structures. Welfare-state or social-democratic reformisms always increase those spheres of life subjected to public regulation, administration, and policy decisions.

Such developments of extended normatization and juridification are ambivalent: on the one hand, the juridification of everyday life contexts can redress inequalities and injustices endemic to them; on the other hand, it may impoverish the lifeworld further, by limiting rather than enhancing the possibilities for autonomous action of individuals. The ideal of a communicative ethic needs to be seen against this background. Communicative ethics advocates a participatory rather than bureaucratic model of collective decision-making, and encourages increased public debate on decisions that are usually reached at the expense of those on whose behalf they are carried out. Thus the juridification of everyday life can result in an increased demand for participation and self-government, just as it can foster an attitude of dependence, passivity, and clientilism. The ideals of a community of rights and entitlements and those of needs and solidarity are articulated with these trends in mind. They formulate visions of human togetherness, out of whose interaction new modes may emerge in the future.

If, however, these normative ideals are offered as genuine options in the present one correction is necessary. It is more correct to speak of a "polity" of rights and entitlements and an "association" of needs and solidarity. By a "polity" I understand a democratic, pluralistic unity, composed of many communities, but held together by a common legal, administrative and political organization. Polities may be nation-states, multi-national states, or a federation of distinct national and ethnic groups. An association of needs and solidarity, by contrast, is a community in action, formed by a set of shared values and ideals, which uphold the concreteness of the other on the basis of acknowledging his or her human dignity and equality. The perspective of the generalized other urges us to respect the equality, dignity and rationality of all humans qua humans, while the perspective of the concrete other enjoins us to respect differences, individual life-histories and concrete needs. Such communities, in my view, are not pregiven; they are formed out of the action of the oppressed, the exploited, and the humiliated, and must be committed to universalist, egalitarian, and consensual ideals. Traditional ethnic, racial, and religious communities are neither necessarily nor primarily such communities of needs and solidarity. They become so only insofar as they uphold the ideal of action in a universalist, egalitarian, consensual framework.

The demise of the philosophy of the subject changes the meaning of utopia in our societies. Marx proceeded from the model of a demiurge-like humanity externalizing itself through its own activity in history and yet facing its own externalized capacities as "capital," as the sum total of those alien forces that oppress individuals. Emancipation signified that this alienated potential would be reappropriated by individuals themselves. Here Marx committed a distributive fallacy. He assumed that since humanity as an empirical subject was *one*, humanity qua normative subject could be represented by *one* particular group. This distributive fallacy, along with the primacy of the work model of activity, led away from the politics of intersubjectivity to the politics of collective singularity. For critical theorists like

Adorno, Horkheimer, and Marcuse, in the aftermath of World War II the vacuum left by the disappearance of hopes in the revolutionary working class was filled by absolute spirit—art, religion, and philosophy—or by subjective spirit—the rebelling psyche. It was assumed that objective spirit was hopelessly rationalized and contained no emancipatory potential.

The moment of communicative utopia rests on assumptions different from both. It is no longer assumed that there is a privileged standpoint in the social structure which bestows upon its occupiers a special vision of the social totality. Nor is it presupposed that the utopian sources of objective spirit have dried up. The community of needs and solidarity is created in the interstices of society by those new social movements, which on the one hand fight to extend the universalist promise of objective spirit—justice and entitlements—and on the other seek to combine the logic of justice with that of friendship. These new social movements do not share the hubris of the nineteenth century that one particularity can represent universality as such. They are aware of "difference" and regard this as a positive moment. Beyond the philosophy of the subject lies a politics of empowerment that extends both rights and entitlements while creating friendship and solidarity.

The traditional politics of the subject assumes that there is one group of humans whose strategic position uniquely entitles them to represent the plurality. The philosophy of the subject always searches for a particular group—be it the proletariat, women, the avant-garde, Third World revolutionaries, or the Party—whose particularity represents universality as such. The politics of empowerment, by contrast, proceeds from the assumption that there is no single spot in the social structure that privileges those who occupy it with a vision of the social totality. This is so not only because late-capitalist societies and their grievances generate a *pluralization* of social victims, their objectives, and their modes of struggle, but also so because the experience of difference that cannot be co-opted in imposed identity is liberatory. Genuine collectivities are formed out of struggle, not out of the logic of substitution that preempts the experience of one social group with categories derived from the language of another. In late-capitalist societies, emancipation does not mean alone "the democratization of administrative decision-making processes," but the formation of communities of need and solidarity in the interstices of our societies. Such utopia is no longer utopian, for it is not a mere beyond. It is the negation of the existent in the name of a future that bursts open the possibilities of the present. Such utopia is not antagonistic to norm; it complements it. In the words of Ernst Bloch:

> The question of the legacy of classical natural right is in its own way just as urgent as the question of the legacy of social utopias had been. Social utopias and natural right had a mutually supporting task in the same human space; marching separately, unfortunately without fighting jointly. . . . Social utopia concerned human happiness; natural right, human dignity. Social utopias painted images of human relations in which the *weary* and the *downtrodden* no longer had a place; natural right constructed relations in which there were no *humiliated, demeaned* ones.[128]

NOTES

Introduction: The Critical Theory of Society: Between Practical Philosophy and Social Science

1. The transformation of the Aristotelian concept of practical philosophy into the doctrine of ethics (neo-Kantianism), the doctrine of material values (Max Scheler), and various philosophies of praxis (Marxism and existentialism) is analyzed by Manfred Riedel and Helmut Fahrenbach; see Manfred Riedel, Vorwort, and H. Fahrenbach, "Ein programmatischer Aufriss der Problemlage und systematischen Ansatzmöglichkeiten praktischen Philosophie," in M. Riedel, ed., *Rehabilitierung der praktischen Philosophie*, 1:15–17. For general accounts of the history of the concept of praxis, see R. Bernstein, *Praxis and Action*, and N. Lobkowitz, *Theory and Practice*.

2. Emile Durkheim, "Montesquieu's Contribution to the Rise of Social Science," p. 4. First printed in Latin at Bordeaux in 1892, this text reappeared in translation in *Revue d'histoire politique constitutionelle*, by F. Alengry (July–September 1937). Durkheim's subsequent development considerably modified the position presented in his dissertation. In particular, the *Division of Labor* (1893) meant a radical reinterpretation of the original criteria of social facts. As Talcott Parsons observes, "The concept of social facts was developed, then, through three phases: first, exteriority or the giveness of empirical existence, as in the case of the physical environment; second, constraint, or the effect of a normative rule to which sanctions are attached; and now, third, what Durkheim called the 'moral authority' of internalized values and norms, which 'constrain' the individual by arousing guilt in his own conscience if he does not conform." Talcott Parsons, "The Life and Work of Emile Durkheim," vol. 4 of *International Encyclopedia of the Social Sciences*, reprinted in Emile Durkheim, *Sociology and Philosophy* (New York: Free Press, 1974) p. liv. In *The Elementary Forms of the Religious Life* (1912), Durkheim also modified the sharp contrast between doxa and episteme, opinion and social science, with which he operates in this particular essay, by explaining the social constitution of intellectual categories in general; see Introduction, "The Subject of Our Study: Religious Sociology and the Theory of Knowledge," in *The Elementary Forms of the Religious Life*, 6th ed. (New York: Free Press, 1965), pp. 13–33.

3. Durkheim, "Montesquieu's Contribution to the Rise of Social Science," p. 41.

4. *Ibid.*

5. *Ibid.*, p. 3.

6. *Ibid.*, pp. 4–5.

7. *Ibid.*, pp. 6ff.

8. The institute's key figures were Max Horkheimer, Theodor Adorno, Erich Fromm, Herbert Marcuse, Franz Neumann, Otto Kirchheimer, Leo Löwenthal, and, less centrally, Henryk Grossmann and Arkadij Gurland, while Walter Benjamin belonged to the "outer circle." In this book I concentrate primarily on the work of the philosophers among them— namely, Horkheimer, Adorno, and Marcuse, while using the term "Frankfurt School" more broadly to refer to positions that were also shared by Löwenthal and Pollock; see David Held, *Introduction to Critical Theory*, pp. 14–15. All references in the following to articles that have appeared in the Institute's journal, *Zeitschrift für Sozialforschung*, are given in the text, abbreviated as ZfS. The first number following the date gives page references in this edition; when available, the page references of corresponding English translations follow. I have modified these translations as I saw fit. Here, M. Horkheimer, "Traditional and Critical Theory," pp. 188–214.

9. Aristotle, *Nicomachean Ethics*, book X, ch. 7, 1177a13ff.; *Politics*, book I, ch. 2, 1253aff.; in *The Basic Works of Aristotle*.

10. Thomas Hobbes, *Leviathan*, pp. 225ff.

11. Albert Hirshman, *The Passions and the Interests*.

12. J. Habermas, "Historical Materialism and the Development of Normative Structures," in *Communication and the Evolution of Society*, p. 96.

13. G. W. F. Hegel, *Phänomenologie des Geistes*. The Hoffmeister edition of the *Phenomenology* is referred to in the text as PhG. The number following this gives page references for this edition; when followed by a second number, this indicates page references for Miller's translation.

14. G. W. F. Hegel, "Über die wissenschaftlichen Behandlungsarten des Naturrechts," the first number following the abbreviation NR, gives page references for the German edition, the second for the English. Although I have consulted Knox's translation, I have not uniformly relied upon it.

15. Alasdair MacIntyre, *After Virtue;* Richard Rorty, *Philosophy and the Mirror of Nature;* J.-F. Lyotard, *The Post-Modern Condition*.

16. Since I will deal more extensively with the relationship between Rawls' position and the program of a communicative ethics (chapter 8, section 2), let me briefly suggest here where the disagreements with Gewirth's project would lie. Although the mode of analysis defined by Gewirth as "the dialectically necessary method" bears some affinities to the emphasis in communicative ethics on "the performative standpoint of the agent," there are fundamental differences. First, Gewirth pro-

ceeds from a strictly monological or self-centered (although not egotistical) point of view in constructing his dialectically necessary method, while communicative ethics proceeds from the standpoint of dialogue and constructs the standpoint of agents as members of a linguistic and social community. Second, Gewirth dissolves all "interaction" into "transactions" among selves, on the grounds that interaction represents an "organicist" perspective, according to which all agents are mutual recipients and agents to one another. He writes, "There still remain, however, more or less stable interrelations where one or more persons is agent and another person or group is recipient" (see *Reason and Morality*, p. 130).

From the standpoint of a communicative ethics, this dissolution of interaction into transactions is completely unacceptable, for it puts the cart before the horse. It ignores that individuals become beings capable of transactions by first learning to interact according to rules of mutuality and reciprocity. Also, this concept of transaction is extremely limited as a concept of social action, as is evidenced by Gewirth's paradigmatic examples: "As examples of such interactions, consider the cases where, on the one hand, X, after careful planning, hits Y over the head with a club in order to rob Y of his money, and where, on the other hand, X asks Y to lend him some money, and Y then decides either to lend or not to lend it" (*ibid.*). While the second example would fall under the category of "strategic action," as explained later (see chapter 4, section 4), the first example is simply an instance of the breakdown of social interaction altogether. This integration of social-theoretical with philosophical concerns in the project of critical social theory just illustrates the point made in the text about the differences between this project and other forms of neo-Kantianism.

17. For a more extensive analysis of Lyotard's position, as well as of the dispute among Habermas, Lyotard, and Rorty, see my "Epistemologies of Post-Modernism," *New German Critique* (Fall 1984), no. 33, pp. 103–127.

18. For Horkheimer's critique of epistemological foundationalism as a version of the myth of the "given," see "Traditional and Critical Theory," ZfS 1937:253ff./191ff.; also, "Zum Rationalismusstreit in der gegenwärtigen Philosophie," ZfS 1934:33ff.

19. See Adorno, *Zur Metakritik der Erkenntnistheorie*.

1. The Origins of Immanent Critique

1. R. Koselleck, *Kritik und Krise*, pp. 196–97, *n.* 155. Cf. J. Habermas, "Between Philosophy and Science: Marxism as Critique," in *Theory and Practice*, pp. 195–253.

2. Koselleck, *Kritik und Krise*, p. 198.

3. *Ibid.*, p. 86.

4. *Ibid.*, p. 101.

5. I. Kant, *Kritik der reinen Vernunft*, p. 13 (A xi, xii); English trans., Norman Kemp Smith, p. 9. I have amended Smith's translation slightly.

6. G. W. F. Hegel, "Differenz des Fichteschen und Schellingschen Systems der Philosophie."

7. G. W. F. Hegel, "Glauben und Wissen."

8. Hegel, "Differenzschrift," p. 20, my translation; emphasis in the text. See also H. Marcuse, *Hegels Ontologie und die Theorie des Geschichtlichkeit*, pp. 9–23, for an analysis of the problem of *Entzweiung* in Hegel's thought.

9. Thomas Hobbes, *Leviathan*, p. 186.

10. *Ibid.*, ch. 20; J. Locke, *First and Second Treatises of Civil Government*, ch. 8.

11. Hobbes, *Leviathan*, p. 186.

12. Locke, *Second Treatise of Civil Government*, pp. 144ff.

13. Hegel's critique of Kant in the "Naturrecht" essay is abrupt, undifferentiated, and at times sophistical. Three charges are raised against Kant. First, since pure *unity* constitutes the essence of practical reason, one can hardly speak of a "system of the ethical," for out of such pure unity no *plurality* of laws can be deduced (NR 459/75). Second, the moral law of freedom can only *test* maxims, it can *generate* none of its own (NR 460/75). Third, the universalizability procedure of the moral law amounts to the principle of contradiction. For a more detailed examination of Hegel's critique of Kant's moral philosophy, see chapter 3, section 1.

14. Hegel's critique of Fichte does not focus on the emptiness of the principle of universalizability, but on the fact that the separation between morality and legality nullifies the moral foundations of ethical life. The sphere of legality is deduced by Fichte from the contradiction between universal pure self-consciousnesses and individual self-consciousness; see J. G. Fichte, *The Science of Right*. Legality is the sphere in which finite self-consciousness that causally act upon one another coexist, and in this sphere their relations must be made to conform to the universal law of freedom. The legal sphere is based upon the contradiction that the I, as finite self-consciousness, can act in such a way as to violate the principle of rational self-consciousness. Therefore, in the legal sphere my will is *constrained* to conform to the principle of the coexistence of the will of each, under a universal law of freedom. But since as a finite self-consciousness I am a rational and free being, infinite self-consciousness as well, this constraint must not violate my freedom and rationality. On the one hand, the sphere of legality presupposes that there is a constraining power, but on the other hand, this constraining power must not be arbitrary, but must conform to the principle of freedom. So there must be limits to the latter in conformity with the law of freedom. The same can be said of the second instance: it must likewise be constrained, and so on *ad infinitum*. "Now the question is how this supreme will, by compulsion and supervision can be made to

conform to the concept of the universal will and how the system can remain immanent and transcendental" (NR 472/85–86).

15. See I. Kant, "Allgemeines Prinzip des Rechts," *Die Metaphysik der Sitten*, pp. 387ff. (A 33; B 33, 34); English trans., pp. 33ff.

16. G. Lukacs, *Der junge Hegel*, pp. 52ff; F. Rosenzweig, *Hegel und der Staat*, 2:30ff.

17. R. P. Horstmann, "Über die Rolle der bürgerlichen Gesellschaft in Hegels politischen Philosophie," pp. 276ff.

18. For general accounts of Hegel's concept of civil society in addition to the source mentioned in note 17, see Joachim Ritter, *Hegel and the French Revolution;* M. Riedel, "Hegels Begriff der 'bürgerlichen Gesellschaft'"; James Schmidt, "A Paideia for the 'Bürger als Bourgeois,'" *History of Political Thought*, pp. 469–93; Z. A. Pelczynski, ed., *Hegel's Political Thought*, Introduction.

19. Cf. Hegel's concluding remarks to the *Natural Law* essay: "The Absolute Idea is in itself absolute intuition . . . and is precisely . . . Absolute Spirit and fulfilled ethical life, which as presented above, guards itself against getting mixed up with the negative . . . through the fact that it consciously allows the negative violence and dominion through the sacrifice of a small part of itself, it keeps its life purified from it (the negative)" (NR, p. 530).

20. It is the great merit of K. H. Ilting's and Manfred Riedel's analyses to have shown against earlier interpretations of this essay by Rosenkranz, Th. Haering, and Glockner that the metaphysical foundations of Hegel's argument are based upon an incoherent conflation of Aristotelian and Spinozist conceptions of nature. [See K. H. Ilting, "Hegels Auseinandersetzung mit der Aristotelischen Politik"; M. Riedel, "Hegels Kritik des Naturrechts"; K. Rosenkranz, *Hegels Leben* (Berlin, 1844), pp. 173ff.; H. Glockner, *Hegel* (Stuttgart: Fromann, 1958), pp. 302ff.; Th. Haering, *Hegel: Sein Wollen und sein Werk*, 2:389, 404ff.]

21. K. Marx and F. Engels, *Die Heilige Familie oder Kritik der kritischen Kritik*, pp. 82ff.; D. Howard, "On the Transformation of Marx's Critique into Dialectic," *Dialectical Anthropology*, pp. 75ff.; Jean Cohen, *Class and Civil Society*, pp. 23–53.

22. K. Marx and F. Engels, *MEW* 1:344, my emphasis.

23. See the little-known but very insightful discussion by K. Bekker, *Marx' philosophische Entwicklung*, pp. 27–37; D. Henrich, "Karl Marx als Schüler Hegels," pp. 196ff.

24. Cf. the following statement from Hegel's *Logic:* "And now this unity in which existence or immediacy, and the in-itself, the ground or the reflected are simply moments, is *actuality*" (*Wissenschaft der Logik*, 2:170; English trans., p. 542). Particularly in the *Critique of Hegel's Philosophy of Right*, Marx maintains that Hegel has failed to practice this principle consistently. He points out that there are moments posited by the concept which appear as actuality, but which are in fact simply immediacy. Another way of expressing this objection is that instead of

demonstrating the unity of existence and the concept as actuality, Hegel merely rationalizes the existent (MEW 1:206); and K. Marx, *Critique of Hegel's Philosophy of Right*, p. 8.

25. "If on the other hand the Idea passes for 'only an Idea,' for something represented in opinion, philosophy rejects such a view and shows that nothing is actual except the Idea. Once that is granted, the great thing is to apprehend in the show of the temporal and the transient the substance which is immanent and the eternal which is present." G. W. F. Hegel, *Hegel's Philosophy of Right*, p. 10.

26. L. Feuerbach, *The Essence of Christianity*, pp. 32–43.

27. In this discussion I will not address the cogency of Bauer's and Marx's understanding of Judaism. That their characterization of Judaism as a culture and religion has little to do with its actuality has been argued by J. Carlebach in *Karl Marx and the Radical Critique of Judaism*, pp. 125–87.

28. K. Marx and F. Engels, *The German Ideology*, p. 39.

29. H. F. Fulda, "These zur Dialektik als Darstellungsmethode im 'Kapital' von Marx" *Hegel Jahrbuch* (1974), pp. 204–10; Michael Theunissen, *Sein und Schein*, pp. 13ff.

30. J. J. Rousseau, *Emile, ou de l'éducation*, p. 9. In "On the Jewish Question," Marx conflates the Rousseauian concept of the "general will" with the Feuerbachian notion of "species essence" (in *Karl Marx: Early Writings*, pp. 211–43). Both concepts are based on the assumption that a unity of individual and universal interests is possible; the mediations through which such a unity can be attained are not explicated. See E. M. Lange's insightful discussion of the problem of lack of mediations in Marx's thought in *Das Prinzip Arbeit*, pp. 73–96.

2. The Origins of Defetishizing Critique

1. General accounts of Hegel's development in this period are given by G. A. Kelly, *Hegel's Retreat from Eleusis;* and Raymond Plant, *Hegel*. James Schmidt gives a very incisive overview of recent literature on Hegel's development in "Recent Hegel Literature," Part I, *Telos*, no. 46, pp. 113–48; Part II, *Telos*, no. 48, pp. 114–41.

2. See J. Habermas, "Labor and Interaction: Remarks on Hegel's Jena *Philosophy of Mind*," in *Theory and Practice*, pp. 142–70; M. Riedel, "Objektiver Geist und praktische Philosophie."

3. I. Kant, *Kritik der reinen Vernunft*, p. 12 (A x); *Critique of Pure Reason*, p. 8.

4. Kant, *Critique of Pure Reason*, p. 9 (A xii).

5. See O. Pöggeler, "Qu 'est-ce que la phénoménologie de l'esprit?"; H. F. Fulda and D. Henrich, eds., *Materialien zu Hegels "Phänomenologie des Geistes"*; Jean-Pierre Labarrière, *Structures et mouvement dialectique dans la phénoménologie de l'esprit de Hegel;* Merold Westphal, *History and Truth in Hegel's Phenomenology;* K. L. Dove, "Hegel's Phenomenological Method."

6. See H. F. Fulda, "Zur Logik der Phänomenologie," *Materialien zu Hegels "Phänomenologie des Geistes,"* pp. 391ff.

7. H. Schnädelbach, "Zum Verhältnis von Logik und Gesellschafts-theorie bei Hegel," pp. 65ff.

8. G. W. F. Hegel, *Die Vernunft in der Geschichte,* p. 67.

9. My attempt to render Hegel's account of this process in Weberian terms is based upon Weber's claim that the development of world re-ligions presents a process through which the divine is purified of "naturalistic" and immediate elements. Hegel anticipates many ele-ments of Weber's account of the rationalization of world religions. See M. Weber, *The Religion of China,* pp. 226ff; "Science as a Vocation," p. 155.

10. This claim seems to be contradicted by the varieties of the experi-ence of consciousness discussed by Hegel, such as desire, recognition, moral and religious action and their dilemmas, art, etc. I distinguish between the status of the category of externalization (*Entäusserung*) modeled on wealth-creating labor at the *meta-level* of Hegel's phe-nomenological argument and its status as a concrete *form* of the activity of consciousness. My critique concerns the *meta-status* of this category which is used by Hegel to characterize the activity of Spirit as such. See T. W. Adorno, *Negative Dialektik,* pp. 297ff.; J. Habermas, "Labor and Interaction," pp. 142ff.; G. Lukacs, *The Young Hegel,* pp. 537–69.

11. Karl Marx, *Capital,* 1:177. All future references in the text are to this volume and edition unless otherwise specified.

12. Aristotle, *Ethics,* 1140aff., and *Metaphysics,* 1032a13ff., in *The Basic Works of Aristotle;* see also Carol Gould, *Marx's Social Ontology.*

13. Living labor can perform this function only insofar as it is also concrete labor, transforming the posits of the past into useful objects in the present. The distinction between "abstract" and "concrete" labor is thus a distinction in thought—one required by a certain social struc-ture—but not one in actuality. See the following note.

14. The gist of Marx's analysis of the concept of labor in *Capital* is that only in capitalist society is labor stripped of all its symbolic-normative properties and reduced to a purely physiological-naturalist expression of human force. Capitalism reduces laboring activity to its bare ele-ments. This is also the sense of Marx's famous statement that "human anatomy contains a key to the anatomy of the ape" (*Grundrisse,* p. 105). "Indifference towards a specific kind of labor," writes Marx, "presup-poses a very developed totality of real kinds of labor, of which no single one is predominant. . . . Indifference towards specific labor corresponds to a form of society in which individuals can with ease transfer from one labor to another" (*Grundrisse,* p. 104). Whether Marx means this in a solely evolutionary sense, or whether he is also critical of this evolution and the reduction of labor in capitalist society to its pure form is debat-able. C. Castoriadis chooses to ignore the critical dimension of Marx's comments and concentrates on their naturalistic evolutionism alone;

see "From Marx to Aristotle, from Aristotle to Us," *Social Research,* no. 44, pp. 3–24.

15. The emergence of the new object of consciousness as a consequence of anterior experience is a structural feature of the PhG which entails non-phenomenological assumptions concerning the procedure which Hegel describes as "reflection-into-self." Every subsequent object of consciousness is a "return to the ground" and a "reflection-into-self" of the previous object. Both Fulda ("Zur Logik der Phänomenologie") and Labarrière (*Structures et mouvement*) stress this aspect of Hegel's procedure when analyzing the question whether Hegel's argument is purely phenomenological.

16. This claim requires elucidation; in particular, I would like to clarify why for Hegel *Erinnerung* is a process of *Wiederaneignung* (reappropriation). Throughout the *Phenomenology* Hegel plays on the double meaning of the word "Erinnerung"—remembrance and interiorization. When the word is divided into its prefix and root, we have "Er/innerung," namely, a compounded, intensified activity of interiorization. *Erinnerung* is taking back into oneself what is externalized; it is interiorizing, reabsorbing what has become external to the self. (The English words "re/membrance" or "re/collection" also echo an aspect of this meaning. Re/membering is putting back together the members of the elements of a process.)

For Hegel, remembrance is the return-to-self from the becoming of Spirit in time (PhG, p. 563). History is Spirit which exists in time, "time is the fate and the necessity of Spirit, which is not completed in itself" (PhG, p. 558). Memory overcomes this externality and necessity through the insight that history is the becoming of Spirit. This insight brings with it reconciliation in the face of necessity, i.e., it means knowing that Spirit is by-itself-in-its-otherness. The model of externalization, return-to-self, and reappropriation characterizes for Hegel the relation of history and memory. History can be *remembered*—its members can be put back together—because it is the work, the self-realization of Spirit, that has let itself go into time and has assumed a form external to itself.

Thus, for Hegel memory is not interpretation, a "recalling" of the past in the present. By re/calling the past, we make it present to ourselves. We name the forgotten and thus we beckon it to appear for us. We raise the past out of its anonymity and recognize it once more. Re/calling is naming, renaming, interpreting, and reinterpreting, an activity in which we often fail to remember because we have forgotten to name and about which we disagree because we do not interpret it alike. For Hegel, by contrast, memory is reappropriating, making one's own, remembering that what was, once was made or constituted by the activity of Spirit. There is no room in this process for disagreement, for conflict of interpretations, or for renaming. As I will show in the following chapter, this interpretation of memory as reappropriation goes very well together with Hegel's denial of the "interpretive indeterminacy of action."

17. The attack on the concept of the "subject" in contemporary philosophy has different sources. The first tradition originates with French structuralism's critique of hypostatized intentions in social explanation and its turn to the logic of form as opposed to the intentions of content. Althusser (*Reading Capital*, pp. 119–45) and P. Bourdieu and J. C. Passeron ("Sociology and Philosophy in France Since 1945", *Social Research*, pp. 162–212) provide general accounts of the consequences of this move for Marxism, and sociology and philosophy, respectively. The extension of this line of argument into psychoanalytic theory can be found in Lacan's "The Subversion of the Subject." The second line of interpretation can be traced back to Heidegger's critique of the *hypokeimenon* and the ontology of presence qua substance in modern Cartesian philosophy; see Martin Heidegger, *What Is a Thing?* pp. 24ff., and *Being and Time;* Rainer Schürmann, "Anti-Humanism," *Man and World*, vol. 12, no. 2.

18. Karl Marx, *Texte zur Methode und Praxis, II, Pariser Manuskripte, 1844*, p. 119. There are currently two translations of his text available in English, one by Dirk J. Struik, *The Economic and Philosophic Manuscripts of 1844*, and one by R. Livingstone and G. Benton, *Economic and Philosophical Manuscripts*, in *Karl Marx: Early Writings*. I have found neither translation adequate.

19. Even when one fundamentally disagrees with it—as I do throughout this entire manuscript—one must acknowledge Lukacs' influence on this way of interpreting the relation between Hegel and Marx; see Georg Lukacs, *History and Class Consciousness*, pp. 110ff. Arato and Breines state clearly the difficulties in this model of subjectivity which I criticize in the text: "In both cases the analysis is debilitated by an egological ('I,' 'we,' 'theory of totality') model of subjectivity (excluding interaction, intersubjectivity in work, everyday life, institutional existence) that flows from both the uncompromising totalization of the logic of reification to all social spheres and from the complementary conceptual myths inherited from classical German philosophy" (Andrew Arato and Paul Breines, *The Young Lukács*, p. 136).

20. J. J. Rousseau, *Discours sur l'inégalité parmi les hommes*.

21. See E. M. Lange for an insightful critique of the social reductionism behind this equation, in *Das Prinzip Arbeit*, pp. 86ff.

22. A lucid analysis of the tension between these two points of view is given by G. Markus, "Practical-Social Rationality in Marx: A Dialectical Critique," Part I, *Dialectical Anthropology*, pp. 255–88.

23. In an earlier piece, Agnes Heller developed an argument which showed the fundamental ambivalence in Marx's project of emancipation in the *1844 Manuscripts* ("Towards a Marxist Theory of Value," *Kinesis*). Heller claims that "Marx did not *work out* a universal concept of value although he had a fundamental value concept (abundance) and basic value axioms" (p. 22). Abundance means the many-sided unfolding of the essential powers of the species. This category can be interpreted in a literal sense as increased wealth, productive capacity, intensification of

scientific and technological achievement, and the like. It can, however, also be interpreted qualitatively as the emergence of *new* needs, modes of interaction, forms of subjectivity, and relation to others. In "Towards a Marxist Theory of Value," Heller does not draw this distinction between the two projects of emancipation. Heller's *The Theory of Need in Marx* by contrast develops most extensively the view I describe here as "sensuous finitude."

24. This point has been most forcefully argued by Jürgen Habermas, in *Knowledge and Human Interests*, pp. 25–43; see also Albrecht Wellmer, *Critical Theory of Society*, pp. 67–121. The endless critiques of Habermas' interpretation of Marx for wanting to bifurcate the original concept of "praxis" into labor and interaction in general have missed the purpose behind this criticism. Habermas did not deny that the Marxian concept of praxis entailed both; he simply pointed out that if historical materialism were also a theory of the development and evolution of social formations, one had to provide an account of such processes as language acquisition, socialization and identity formation, acculturation and symbolic reproduction of tradition. If the concept of praxis allows us to explain the developmental dynamics of these processes, and how they are acquired by societal subjects, then it can continue to be used. But it is hard to see how any careful reader of Marxian texts fails to see that Marx truly developed the logic, structure, and dynamism of one mode of activity alone, namely, that of objectification and more narrowly of production. See chapter 4 for a further discussion of this problem; for Habermas' recent analysis of the labor/interaction distinction, see "A Reply to My Critics" in Thompson and Held, eds., *Habermas: Critical Debates*, pp. 225ff. Cf. Axel Honneth, "Arbeit und instrumentales Handeln."

25. See J. Habermas, "Historical Materialism and the Development of Normative Structures" and "Towards a Reconstruction of Historical Materialism" in *Communication and the Evolution of Society*, pp. 95–178.

26. H. G. Gadamer gives an extremely subtle account of the dialectics of interaction and understanding in *Truth and Method*, pp. 321–25.

27. This passage is from Marx's brief commentary on James Mill in the *Notebooks* appended to the *Pariser Manuskripte*, pp. 180ff.

28. A general account of the prevalence of this model of activity in the thought of the German idealists is given by Charles Taylor, *Hegel*, pp. 3ff. In the next two chapters I will develop this model of "expressive" activity further.

29. General accounts of Marx's concept of praxis are given by R. J. Bernstein, *Praxis and Action;* and Shlomo Avineri, *The Social and Political Thought of Karl Marx*, pp. 65–150; L. Kolakowski's "Karl Marx and the Classical Definition of Truth" remains one of the most masterful accounts. My analysis is much indebted to Hannah Arendt, *The Human Condition*.

3. Integrating Crisis: Autonomy and Ethical Life

1. For Hegel's early critique of Kant, see "The Spirit of Christianity and Its Fate" and "Love" in *Early Theological Writings;* and Ingtraud Görland, *Die Kantkritik des jungen Hegel.* Cf. Hegel, *Phenomenology of Spirit,* cp. 6, section C, "Spirit That is Certain of Itself. Morality"; *Hegel's Philosophy of Right,* #40 Addition, pp. 39ff.; *Wissenschaft der Logik,* vol. 1, "Die Schranke und das Sollen: Anmerkung," pp. 119ff. (English trans., pp. 133ff.).

2. In *The Metaphysical Elements of Justice* under "private right," Kant includes "personal rights of a thinglike nature" (*auf dingliche Art persönliche Rechte*). These can be of three sorts: the man acquires (*erwirbt*) a wife and has rights over her; the married pair acquires children and has rights over them; the family as a unit acquires servants and has rights over them. Such rights are not rights *against* a person nor are they property rights over a disposable object, but are like rights of possession (*Die Metaphysik der Sitten,* pp. 106ff.; *The Metaphysical Elements of Justice,* pp. 54–55). Hegel criticizes Kant for extending the traditional confusion at the root of Roman law which divides rights into *jus ad personam* and *jus ad rem* even further by introducing the category of *jura realiter personalia.* Kant has also intermixed "rights which presuppose substantial ties, e.g., those of family and political life, and rights which only concern abstract personality as such" (PhR, #40A, p. 39). Hegel argues against the traditional rights of the male head of household over his wife, children, and servants. The privilege of patriarchy is no longer justified legally by Hegel but anthropologically and psychologically on the basis of the constitutional differences between the sexes and the so-called "superiority" of the male; see PhR, #165, #166, and Addition. Hegel's "advance" is thus to have shifted the justification of patriarchy from a late feudal to its bourgeois form.

3. For two recent and provocative treatments of this theme, see Andreas Wildt, *Autonomie und Anerkennung;* Paul Stern, *Practical Philosophy and the Concept of Freedom.*

4. John E. Silber, "Procedural Formalism in Kant's Ethics," *Review of Metaphysics,* pp. 197–236; J. L. Mackie, *Ethics: Inventing Right and Wrong.*

5. Immanuel Kant, *Groundwork of the Metaphysics of Morals,* pp. 89ff.

6. Hegel's interpretation of Kant's formula of universalizability is notoriously ungenerous. Interpreters like Paton move away from this analysis of the principle of universalizability as a principle of non-contradiction to give it a more *teleological* reading. For Paton, the question is not whether the maxim of my will would *contradict* itself if I were to act in a certain way, but whether I can consistently, qua rational being, *will* that such a universe as that implied by my action, if my action were to become a universal law, should come into existence. See H. J. Paton, *The Categorical Imperative,* pp. 149ff. and 157–64.

7. John Rawls, *A Theory of Justice*, pp. 17ff.

8. Silber, "Procedural Formalism in Kant's Ethics," pp. 201ff.

9. J. Habermas, "Moral Development and Ego Identity," in *Communication and the Evolution of Society*, pp. 69ff.

10. Manfred Riedel, "Objektiver Geist und praktische Philosophie," pp. 32ff.

11. PhR, #146: "The ethical substance and its laws and powers are on the one hand, an object over and against the subject, and from this point of view they 'are' in the highest sense of self-subsistent beings." In the *Logic*, substance is defined as "the totality of the whole" which embraces accidentality within it (*Wissenschaft der Logik*, 1:186; *Hegel's Science of Logic*, p. 556). The accidents of substance all belong to it and are held together by it in virtue of its "power" (*Macht*) as a totality (German, p. 187; English, p. 557). Substance is objective and active. Ethical substance is substance only in the first sense as an objective totality. For the accidents of ethical substance, the individuals, are held together not merely by "power" but primarily by insight, will, conviction, and custom. Ethical substance has "power" only when it is "ethical life," only when individuals in their actions consciously and intentionally abide by the objective order. Nonetheless, the use of the category of "substance" to designate the totality of ethical institutions shows the limits of Hegel's analysis and his premodernist bias. Individuals are not mere appendages of ethical institutions, but ethical institutions can continue to function only insofar as individuals act in such ways as to keep them alive.

12. "Ethical life is the Idea of freedom in that on the one hand it is the good become alive . . . while on the other hand self-consciousness has in the ethical realm its absolute foundation and the end which actuates its effort" (PhR, #142, p. 105).

13. Andreas Wildt in particular emphasizes Hegel's concept of friendship; see *Autonomie und Anerkennung*, part III.

14. Bradley, "My Station and Its Duties"; W. H. Walsh, *Hegelian Ethics*, pp. 69–77.

15. Kant, *Kritik der praktischen Vernunft*, p. 128; English trans., p. 133: "All material principles are, as such, of one and the same kind and belong under the general principle of self-love or one's own happiness [*Glückseligkeit*]."

16. Kant, "Ideen zu einer allgemeinen Geschichte in weltbürgerlicher Absicht," p. 41; English trans., pp. 17–18.

17. "Theoretical and practical mind reciprocally integrate themselves. . . . Both modes of mind are forms of Reason: for both in theoretical and practical mind what is produced . . . is that which constitutes Reason, a unity of subjectivity and objectivity." Hegel, *Hegel's Philosophy of Mind*, #443A, pp. 185ff.; see also #443.

18. See Hegel's *Wissenschaft der Logik*, 2:15ff.; *Hegel's Science of Logic*, pp. 401ff.

19. See G. H. Mead's illuminating discussion of Kant in "Fragments on Ethics," *Mind, Self, and Society*, pp. 379ff.

20. C. Taylor, *Hegel*, pp. 15ff.

21. Both action (*Handeln*) and doing (*Tun*) have a broader meaning than mentioned above. In the broader sense "action" refers to the completed performance, to intention and its execution, while "doing" refers both to the process and to the end result, or to that which is done (PhG, p. 292). For the purposes of this discussion, I am not exploring the differences between these two concepts of action. The specifics of Hegel's action theory have not awakened much interest in the secondary literature; an exception is H. Derbolav, "Hegels Theorie der Handlung."

22. It should be emphasized that by "work" in this context is not meant production or the product. Hegel clearly includes under his concept of work the traditional Aristotelian distinction between *praxis* and *poiesis*. The very categories of *Entäusserung* and *Wiederaneignung* developed in the *Phenomenology* refer both to speech and action and to making. My point is that this conflation between acting and making only makes sense from the transsubjective standpoint, i.e., from the standpoint of a collective singular subject that contemplates itself in its own history as if the latter were its own "work." From the intersubjective standpoint, the distinction between acting and making cannot be ignored, for it is only at the level of relations to others that action can be conceptualized at all. The transsubjective subject has no *Gegenspieler*, no partner in action; it can only shape a world after its own image. See Manfred Riedel, *Theorie und Praxis im Denken Hegels*, pp. 46–73 and 179–204, for his relation to Aristotle on this point.

23. I follow Hannah Arendt here: "The disclosure of the 'who' through speech, and the setting of a new beginning through action, always fall into an already existing web where their immediate consequences can be felt. . . . It is because of this already existing web of human relationships, with its innumerable, conflicting wills and intentions, that action almost never achieves its purpose; but it is also because of this medium in which action alone is real, that it 'produces' stories with or without intention as naturally as fabrication produces things. . . . Although everybody started life by inserting himself into the human world through action and speech, nobody is the author or producer of his own life story" (*The Human Condition*, p. 184).

24. "At the same time, however, the action, as the aim posited in the external world, has become the prey of external forces which attach to it something totally different from what it is explicitly and drive it into alien and distant consequences" (PhR #118 and Addition).

25. On the relationship of action, interpretation, and narrative, see Charles Taylor, "Interpretation and the Sciences of Man" pp. 3–51; Alasdair MacIntyre, *After Virtue*, pp. 190–203; Paul Ricoeur, *Hermeneutics and the Social Sciences*.

26. The concept (*der Begriff*) and absolute Spirit both have the logical

structure of individuality, i.e., of a single existent incorporating universality. This structure of individuality cannot be reconciled with the intersubjectivity inherent in the domain of objective Spirit. The transition from action to work is required by the logical structure of the concept. This may in part explain why art, and particularly plastic art, which shapes the given material into an individual shape or form, is the first stage of absolute Spirit; see PhG, p. 556.

27. The distinction between intersubjectivity and transsubjectivity drawn so far does not address problems of methodology and concept formation in the social sciences. I want to stress that a number of social-methodological perspectives may be compatible with both; for example, the standpoint of intersubjectivity may be captured by a phenomenological social analysis à la Schutz, by an ethnomethodological one as advocated by Garfinkel or Cicourel, or by a reconstructive science as defended by Habermas. Equally, transsubjectivity may correspond to structuralism of the Althusserian sort, to functionalism à la Parsons, or systems analysis of the type proposed by Luhmann. For the purposes of my argument it is not necessary to elaborate upon or debate the methodological strengths and weaknesses of these various positions. As will become clear in the following chapter, the significance of the distinction between intersubjectivity and transsubjectivity is to lead to the dual concept of crisis as lived and systemic crisis and to argue that a critical social theory must incorporate both perspectives and show their mediation; see chapter 4 and also chapter 7, section 1. Richard Bernstein gives a helpful, general discussion of issues in the social sciences in *The Restructuring of Social and Political Theory*.

28. "Dies, dass ein Dasein überhaupt *Dasein des freien Willens ist*, ist das *Recht*—es ist somit überhaupt, die Freiheit als Idee." Hegel, *Grundlinien der Philosophie des Rechts*, p. 80; emphasis in the text.

29. "When reflection is brought to bear on impulses, they are imaged, estimated, compared with one another, with their means of satisfaction and their consequences, etc., and with a sum of satisfaction (i.e., with happiness). In this way reflection invests this material with abstract universality and in this external manner purifies it from its crudity and barbarity. This growth of the universality of thought is the absolute value in education" (PhR, #20, p. 29; see also #24 and #25).

30. Hegel, *Hegel's Philosophy of Mind*, #430–35.

31. I am much indebted to Michael Theunissen's analysis in "Die verdrängte Intersubjektivität in Hegels *Philosophie des Rechts*."

32. "Illusory being [*der Schein*] is essence itself in the determinateness of being" (Hegel, *Hegel's Science of Logic*, p. 398).

33. See Talcott Parsons on the sociological concept of action in its relation to the dialectic of unintended consequences, in *The Structure of Social Action*, 1:87ff.

34. "The most remarkable thing here [in political economy] is the mutual interlocking of particulars, which is what one would least ex-

pect because at first everything seems to be given over to the arbitrariness of the individual and it has a parallelism in the solar system which displays to the eye only in irregular movements though its laws may nonetheless be ascertained" (PhR, note to #189, p. 268).

35. See my "The Logic of Civil Society," *Philosophy and Social Criticism*, pp. 149–67.

36. "It is only because of this identity between its implicit and its posited character that positive law has obligatory force in virtue of its rightness. In being posited in positive law, the right acquires determinate existence" (PhR, #212, p. 136; see also #211 and #213). I elaborate the convergence between Hegel's concept of right and the structures of formal rationality further in "Obligation, Contract, and Exchange."

4. Critique as Crisis Theory: Autonomy and Capitalism

1. In recent years a number of thinkers from Jean Baudrillard (*The Mirror of Production*) to Leszek Kolakowski (*Main Currents of Marxism*) have undertaken an examination of the philosophical foundations of Marxism in light of the politics and ideology of "productivism." Whereas Baudrillard emphasizes the unsalutary consequences this productivist ideology has for a world in which societies in different developmental stages have to coexist (pp. 22–25), Kolakowski emphasizes that the "self-deification of mankind" inherent to the Marxian project leads to authoritarianism when not Stalinism (3:530). In his review of Kolakowski, Marx Wartofsky introduces a word of caution to such rereadings of Marx. Kolakowski's thesis is normative; he claims that: "Stalinism is one legitimate interpretation of the Marxism of Marx's own works, of the sources themselves. . . . In order to do this, Kolakowski has to argue that there are in Marx's own formulations those very sources of totalitarianism, of the subordination of moral choice to so-called historical necessity, of the working class to the party, or of individuality to the collective, or of responsibility for one's action to utter automatism, or of socialist legality to terror. . . . Kolakowski has to show that the sources of Stalinism in Marx (and Engels) are not fortuitous . . . but instead are systematic and central, if indeed 'Stalinism' is to be shown as a 'legitimate' possible interpretation 'equally entitled to invoke the name of Marx' . . . along with other possible interpretations" (Marx Wartofsky, "The Unhappy Consciousness," *Praxis International*, p. 289).

Wartofsky, in my opinion, succeeds in showing that the equal legitimacy of a Stalinist reading of Marx is hardly tenable in view of Marx's own philosophical positions. Stalinism can be made consistent with Marxism only at the cost of rendering classical Marxism unrecognizable. I find this position plausible not only because it does philosophical justice to Marx, but also because no theory—not even Marxism—can be made responsible for all that historical actors do in its name. There is no *deductive* logic that leads from Marx to Lenin and to Stalinism, as a reign of terror, White Russian chauvinism, and brutality. One has to see also the contingencies, the unexpected turns of events that history holds in store.

Let me therefore clarify the spirit behind the opening paragraphs of this chapter. I am concerned not with proving that "the distortions of the ideal of socialism" imply Stalinism; only—and here is where I part from Wartofsky—that there are some ambiguities in Marx's thought that are so fundamental to his project of emancipation that we cannot dismiss how they could have been used to justify certain positions which a careful philosophical reading cannot impute to Marxism. One of these ambivalences, as I will try to show in this chapter, is that surrounding the concept of "reappropriation" and the politics and interactional patterns it leads us to envisage. The politics of reappropriation, the work model of activity, and the philosophy of the subject do not *deductively* lead to authoritarian politics but they *permit* a mode of thinking about politics which is authoritarian. I do believe that there are other aspects of Marx's thought which are incompatible with such authoritarianism, but they need spelling out more clearly.

2. More precisely, wages are the cash remuneration of the exchange value of labor power, while the use of labor power is concrete laboring activity measured in terms of labor hours. The generation of surplus value is a consequence of the distinction between the value created by concrete laboring activity on the one hand and the exchange value of labor power on the other. Marx, *Capital*, 1:177ff.; *Grundrisse*, pp. 307 and 460ff.

3. Marx, *Capital*, vol. 1, ch. 24, "Conversion of Surplus Value Into Capital"; *Grundrisse*, pp. 304–18.

4. Marx, *Capital*, 1:176.

5. *Ibid.*, p. 72.

6. There is a certain hastiness in this conclusion which relates the awareness of crisis to political praxis in an immediate way. Crisis phenomena may not result in collective struggle at all; withdrawal, compensation by other means, indifference, and cyncicism are also likely mechanisms by which one can deal with the crisis. See chapter 7 for a discussion of the crisis and protest potentials of late-capitalist societies.

7. Marx, *Grundrisse*, p. 83.

8. *Ibid.*

9. See M. Godelier, "Fetishism, Religion and Marx's General Theories Concerning Ideology"; J. Habermas, "Historical Materialism and the Development of Normative Structures," in *Communication and the Evolution of Society*, pp. 95–130; Marshall Sahlins, *Culture and Practical Reason*.

10. Marx, *Grundrisse*, p. 487.

11. *Ibid.*, p. 488; see also Karl Polanyi and C. M. Arensberg, eds., *Trade and Market in Early Empires*.

12. These passages from the *Grundrisse* also reveal the limits of Marx's analysis of the emergence of capitalism and modernity. Marx views both the development of normative structures—morality, law, and politics—and the development of the material means of production as analogous processes in which the given or the "posit" is reposited, or transformed. We know since Max Weber that the processes of *cultural rationalism* leading to the emergence of the free, autonomous individual as an ideal, and processes of *societal rationalization*—the development of law, economy, and the market—must not be collapsed into one, for they follow different patterns and logics. See further W. Schluchter, "Die Paradoxie der Rationalisierung"; J. Habermas, *The Theory of Communicative Action*, 1:143–273.

13. Marx, *Grundrisse*, p. 488.

14. Marshall Berman, *All That Is Solid Melts Into Air*, p. 98.

15. To explain why these inversions arise, Marx himself resorts to an abstraction. Fetishism characterizes a state of consciousness appropriate to the perspective of social agents who are independent commodity owners and producers and who come together in the marketplace to exchange their products. Marx writes: "Since the producers do not come into social contact with each other until they exchange their products, the specific social character of the producer's labor does not show itself except in the act of exchange" (*Capital*, p. 73). Here Marx proceeds from the counterfactual assumption that commodity owners are themselves independent producers and that the production as well as the exchange of commodities is carried out by the same individuals. From the standpoint of a developed capitalist economy, this assumption is clearly false. The capitalist mode of production is characterized by the fact that large masses of immediate producers—the laborers—do not own their products, but only the value of their labor power which they receive in the form of wages. Workers are not independent producers in the marketplace, and once wage labor is institutionalized the production and exchange of commodities is not carried out by the same person. Why then does Marx resort to this abstraction?

This abstraction corresponds to the social perspective implicit in exchange relations. The latter are considered by classical political economy as contractually regulated, free transactions taking place among juridically equal property owners. This *abstraction* which views individuals as commodity owners is constitutive of capitalist society, for the market indeed institutionalizes a sphere in which juridically free owners exchange their products with one another. In the marketplace the sale and purchase of commodities is governed by the laws of supply and demand, and this movement among commodities appears to their owners not as something determined by them and by their labor; rather, all must submit to the laws of the market. If one proceeds from the perspective of the free marketplace and observes the surface phenomenon of capitalist civil society—the exchange of commodities among independent property owners—the abstraction described by Marx as fetishism is constitutive of this domain.

16. The argument reconstructed in this section corresponds most closely to an interpretation developed by E. M. Lange in "Wertformanalyse, Geldkritik und die Konstruktion des Fetischismus bei Marx," *Neue Hefte für Philosophie*, pp. 224 and 33ff. Lange sees behind Marx's critique of fetishism a "sanction against mediation" (*Mediatisierungsverbot*) which is inspired by Rousseau's model of immediate relations between individuals and the community.

17. Under the heading of "systems rationality," N. Luhmann has made this functionalist perspective the cornerstone of his objection to normative political philosophy; see Luhmann, "Moderne Systemstheorie als Form gesamtgesellschaftlicher Analyse," Habermas and Luhmann, *Theorie der Gesellschaft oder Sozialtechnologie*, pp. 9ff.

18. Hegel, *Hegel's Philosophy of Right*, #199.

19. Marx, *Grundrisse*, p. 157.

20. *Ibid.*

21. *Ibid.*, p. 162.

22. For the formulation of this point I am much indebted to Moishe Postone's "Labor, Time and Necessity", *Social Research*, pp. 739–89. Postone names a theory of socialism which reconstructs distribution relations while leaving production relations under the domination of the law of value "traditional Marxism" (p. 739).

23. Marx, *Grundrisse*, p. 157.

24. *Ibid.*, p. 706.

25. *Ibid.*, p. 708, emphasis in the text.

26. *Ibid.*, p. 712.

27. This interpretation is developed by G. Markus in his "Four Forms of Critical Theory"; *Thesis Eleven*, pp. 90ff.; cf. my comments on this essay, "The Hermeneutics of Critique," *Thesis Eleven*, pp. 189–98.

28. Marx, *Grundrisse*, p. 708; see also Postone, "Labor, Time and Necessity."

29. F. Tönnies, *Community and Society (Gemeinschaft und Gesellschaft)*, Charles P. Loomis, trans. and ed. (East Lansing: University of Michigan Press, 1957).

30. Marx, *Grundrisse*, p. 488.

31. H. Arendt, "Tradition and the Modern Age," p. 20.

32. In an illuminating criticism of an earlier version of this chapter which was delivered at the Boston Philosophy of Science Colloquium (January 18, 1983), Joshua Cohen has maintained that the historical chapters "are illustrations of the laws of motion of capitalism; that is, tendencies of development that express the specific structure of capitalist property relations. They are not on the whole about struggles, not about periods of crisis, and certainly not about struggles during periods of crisis. Like it or not, Marx's history—in chapters 15, 25, and 26–31—is history from above, not a kind of subtext of social history proceeding

beneath the surface text of the development of capital" (written communication to the author).

In response to this important criticism, I would argue as follows: there is no question that the historical material in these chapters illustrates the impact of the development of capitalist property relations upon the working class. The significant question is, from whose perspective? I would still maintain that in these chapters, it is the laborer's voice—his or her lived experiences—along with that of his or her social antagonists (factory inspector; capitalist; legislator) that are heard and narrated. I am using the term "lived crisis" in the text broadly to refer to feelings of misery, oppression, and exploitation as well as to actual struggle.

Let me illustrate. Chapter 15 begins with a general discussion of machinery and modern industry; section 3 then shifts to consider "the general effects of this revolution on the laborer himself" (*Capital*, p. 394), while section 5 narrates "the strife between workman and machine" (pp. 427ff.). Similarly, chapter 25 considers "the influence of the growth of capital on the lot of the laboring class." The abstract discussion at the beginning of this chapter gives way to an analysis of the formation of the industrial reserve army, and subsequently to the organizing attempts of early working class institutions (p. 640). These passages can be multiplied with reference to chapters 26–31. My point is simply that even when considering the general development of the laws of capitalism, Marx refocuses again and again on the experience of laborers as concrete, living individuals.

33. Some of the earlier contributions to this debate concerning the meaning and significance of the historical materialist "science" of *Capital* are Georg Lukács' "The Marxism of Rosa Luxemburg" (1921), in *History and Class Consciousness*, pp. 27–46; and Karl Korsch's "Marxism and Philosophy" (1923). During this period the debate revolved around the question of economic determinism versus the subjective/revolutionary factor in history. Lukács, Luxemburg, and Korsch were one in their critique of the economic determinism of the Second International and in their emphasis on the compatibility of revolutionary praxis with the "science" of historical materialism developed by Marx. In recent years an updated version of this debate occurred between Althusser and Balibar (see *Reading Capital*) and their English followers like Barry Hindess and Paul Q. Hirst, *Pre-Capitalist Modes of Production* (London: Routledge & Kegan Paul, 1975) on the one hand, and E. P. Thompson, *The Poverty of Theory*, on the other.

34. I am much indebted to Georg Lohmann's insightful analysis "Gesellschaftskritik und normativer Massstab," pp. 270ff.

35. See David Lockwood, "Social Integration and System Integration." In this essay Lockwood gives a more positive account of Marx's achievement in this regard than I have suggested is warranted. He writes: "Yet it is precisely Marx who clearly differentiates social and

system integration. The propensity to class antagonism (social integration aspect) is generally a function of the character of production relationships (e.g., possibilities of intra-class identification and communication). But the dynamics of class antagonism are clearly related to the progressively growing 'contradiction' of the economic system. One might also say that the 'conflict' which in Marxian theory is decisive for change is not the *power* conflict arising from relationships in the productive system, but the *system* conflict arising from 'contradiction' between 'property institutions' and 'forces of production'" (p. 250).

This is a curious passage, for after having suggested that a distinction needs to be made between social and system integration, Lockwood reverts precisely to an orthodox mode of Marxist theorizing and relates the "dynamics of class antagonism" to the progressively growing "contradiction" of the economic system. I rather thought that the main reason for distinguishing between social and system integration was to enable one to see that system problems at the economic and administrative levels do not immediately translate into social power struggles and class antagonisms. Lockwood on the one hand acknowledges this; on the other hand, he denies it.

N. Mouzelis' remarks on Lockwood, "Social and System Integration," are illuminating in this regard. Mouzelis succeeds in stating the dichotomy between social and system integration more clearly by defining social integration in terms of the actions of collective groups or quasi-groups, and shows that the link between system and social integration in fact hinges on a successful mediation of action-theoretic and system-theoretic approaches (pp. 396 and 402ff.). Again, it seems to me that Mouzelis as well overrates the extent to which Marx himself has managed to mediate these perspectives; see his statement "Marx linked systematically institutional incompatibilities with collective actors, with their strategies for maintaining and changing the *status quo*" (p. 402). In chapter 7 I will indicate how this distinction can be drawn and made fruitful for the two concepts of crisis.

36. Claus Offe, "'Unregierbarkeit,'" p. 313.

37. I return to this problem in chapter 7, section 1, in the context of considering Habermas' methodological contributions to critical social theory.

38. See W. Schäfer's excellent reconstruction and demystification of Marx's relationship to the early worker's movement, in "Collective Thinking from Below." *Dialectical Anthropology*, pp. 193–214.

39. Karl Marx and Frederick Engels, *The German Ideology*, pp. 75ff. These passages in *The German Ideology* also show that Marx and Engels are critical of the subsumption of individuals under the category of "class" but have faith in the power of double negation. They write: "This subsuming of individuals under definite classes cannot be abolished until a class has taken shape, which has no longer any particular class

interest to assert against the ruling class" (p. 76). The negation of class subsumption will occur through the formation of class by the negative class.

40. See Jean Cohen, "The Subversion of Emancipation," *Social Research*, pp. 789–844.

41. Karl Marx, "Zur Kritik der Hegelschen Rechtsphilosophie, Einleitung," p. 390; English trans., p. 142. I have amended the English translation.

42. See Immanuel Kant, "Anthropologie in pragmatischer Hinsicht," pp. 399–400, for the dual concept of humanity analyzed here.

43. Jean Cohen, *Class and Civil Society*, p. 78.

44. "A spider conducts operations that resemble those of a weaver, and a bee puts to shame many an architect in the construction of her cells. But what distinguishes the worst architect from the best of bees is this, that the architect raises his structure in imagination before he erects it in reality" (*Capital*, 1:178).

45. I should emphasize that Hegel as well as Marx at times stresses the role of language. In fact, in Hegel's case, one of the more puzzling aspects of his thought is that after giving an extensive place to name giving in the formation of individual self-consciousness in the *Jenaer Realphilosophie* (pp. 182ff.), he lets language drop out of his systematic reflections on the formation of individual and collective consciousness. In Marx's case the issue is even more complicated; see the following note.

46. Since there are so many passages in Marx's works where language seems to be a model of social relations as such, or to indicate the social bond that brings individuals together, these remarks should not be taken to mean that Marx had a private theory of language as name giving or sign assigning, etc., which were popular in the eighteenth century (e.g., "Production by an isolated individual outside society . . . is as much of an absurdity as is the development of language without individuals living *together* and talking to each other" [*Grundrisse*, p. 84]). The claim that classical Marxist social theory ignores socialization through linguistic interaction must be understood in the more general context of my thesis that the dimension named above "social integration," the relation of collective actors to the cultural, symbolic, and normative legacy of their societies, is—when not missing—not developed by Marx. Although I cannot prove this point here, I rather suspect that the model of language to be found in Marx's works is, to use Ferdinand deSaussure's distinction, more likely of "langue" (language) than of "parole" (speech).

47. Arendt, *The Human Condition*, pp. 181ff.

48. J. Habermas, *Theorie des kommunikativen Handelns*,1:384ff.; English trans., 1:285ff.

49. Communicative action is "meta-action" in the sense that language and communication serve as media for all other forms of action as

well—be they instrumental, strategic, or expressive. In this sense, communicative action is both a pure action type "oriented to reaching understanding" and meta-action implicated in all other action types that also rely on language. Also, when action coordination breaks down and the activities of social agents can no longer be meaningfully oriented to one another, communication is the only means whereby social activity can continue, if one is not to resort to force, coercion, or violence. See chapter 7 for a further elucidation of this concept.

50. This distinction between "instrumental" and "communicative" should not be taken to mean that technology and technological relations have no social content. Technology is a complex social institution, not an action type, like mending a bicycle or a dishwater. In this sense, whereas we can speak of the latter as "instrumental" action types, it makes no sense to reduce the institution of technology, whether it be in the factory, in the offices, or in the military, to a purely instrumental action. Power relations codefine the content of technology as a social institution. See here the old but still very instructive essay by Herbert Marcuse, "Some Social Implications of Modern Technology."

51. Arendt, *The Human Condition*, pp. 175ff.

52. Aristotle, *Politics*, book I, ch. 2, 1253a28–30, p. 1130, in *The Basic Works of Aristotle*.

53. Two examples of masterful analysis in this regard are Karl Marx, *The Eighteenth Brumaire of Louis Bonaparte* and *The Civil War in France*.

5. The Critique of Instrumental Reason

1. Max Horkheimer, Foreword, in Martin Jay, *The Dialectical Imagination*, p. xii.

2. *Ibid.*

3. ZfS 1937:637; my translation. Marcuse's section in the jointly coauthored "Philosophie und kritische Theorie" is not included in the standard English translation of Max Horkheimer, "Traditional and Critical Theory."

4. Jay, *The Dialectical Imagination;* David Held, *Introduction to Critical Theory;* and Andrew Arato and Eike Gebhardt, eds., *The Essential Frankfurt School Reader.* Held and Arato and Gebhart provide helpful bibliographies of works by and on the Frankfurt School. In recent years a number of studies have appeared which, more often than not, are motivated by political impulses to discredit the influence the Frankfurt School has enjoyed in this country. Among them Zoltan Tar, *The Frankfurt School;* George Freedman, *The Political Philosophy of the Frankfurt School;* and Perry Anderson, *Considerations on Western Marxism*, stand out for their misunderstandings. Douglas Kellner and Rick Roderick give a helpful overview of this new literature in their review essay "Recent Literature on Critical Theory," *New German Critique*, pp. 141-71. For recent German literature, see the following note.

5. Helmut Dubiel, *Wissenschaftsorganization und politische Er-*

fahrung; Alfons Söllner, *Geschichte und Herrschaft;* Wolfgang Bonss, *Die Einübung des Tatsachenblicks.*

6. ZfS 1935:345; Max Horkheimer, "Zum Problem der Wahrheit," trans. as "The Problem of Truth" in Arato and Gebhardt, *The Essential Frankfurt School Reader,* p. 429. "Die Wahrheit ist ein Moment der richtigen Praxis" is rendered in this translation as "Truth is an impetus [?] to correct praxis."

7. Horkheimer's main philosophical effort in this period is to defend this materialist thesis of the "conditioned" character of thought against the relativism of the sociology of knowledge on the one hand and the ahistorical absolutism of "philosophies of essence" on the other ("Zur Rationalismusstreit in der gegenwärtigen Philosophie," ZfS 1934:40). Vis-à-vis the sociology of knowledge, Horkheimer argues that the "conditioned" and "situation-bound" character of thought need not lead to relativism, for there is an objective logic of the historical process which constitutes the independent moment of truth. This logic manifests itself in social praxis, and truth is to be defined as a moment of correct praxis (*ibid.*). Vis-à-vis the absolutism of ahistorical philosophies of essence—among which are included philosophical anthropolgy, philosophies of life and existence, and particularly the existential ontology of Martin Heidegger—Horkheimer defends the thesis that there can be neither a complete picture of reality nor one of an atemporal, eternal subject (ZfS 1934:25). The subject-object relation is an evolving one, defined by the degree of mankind's control and knowledge of itself and of nature.

8. This is the one point that is underestimated in Dubiel's otherwise cogent and clear account of the development of the Frankfurt School. The epistemological critique of traditional theory, as developed by Horkheimer's 1937 essay, indeed presupposes a "rephilosophizing" of the program of critique. But this rephilosophizing is not a regression as Dubiel suggests. Quite to the contrary, only an epistemology carried out as social theory can provide the program of interdisciplinary materialist research with the reflexive legitimation that no specialized science can lend to it (see Dubiel, *Wissenschaftsorganization und politische Erfahrung,* pp. 113–14). The early program of interdisciplinary materialist research was naive in this epistemological sense. For when a materialist theory of social life process explains the conditions of its own genesis as an aspect of the very process it investigates, it introduces the epistemological problem of genesis and validity, or in modern terms, of "context of discovery" and "context of justification." This problem cannot be resolved by the methods of the specialized sciences, but presupposes a meta-theory of the development and justification of human knowledge, and this remains a philosophical task.

9. On the distinction between "internalist" and "externalist" critiques of science, see Wolf Schäfer, "Finalization in Perspective," *Social Science Information,* pp. 915-43.

10. See W. Bonss and Norbert Schindler, "Kritische Theorie als interdisziplinärer Materialismus" (an English translation will appear in S. Benhabib and W. Bonss, eds, *Max Horkheimer: A Retrospective*, in preparation); W. Bonss, "Kritische Theorie und empirische Sozialforschung," pp. 7ff.

11. ZfS 1937:262/207. For a masterful critique of the conflation of these two concepts of praxis by Horkheimer, and its sociological implications, see Axel Honneth, "Horkheimers ursprüngliche Idee," pp. 2ff.

12. G. Marramao, "Zum Verhältnis von politischer Ökonomie und kritischer Theorie," *Ästhetik und Kommunikation: Beiträge zur politischen Erziehung* 4(11):79–93; A. Arato, "Political Sociology and Critique of Politics," in Arato and Gebhardt, eds., *The Essential Frankfurt School Reader*, pp. 3–25.

13. Moishe Postone and Barbara Brick, "Kritische Theorie und die Grenzen des traditionellen Marxismus"; a shorter version of this article appeared as "Critical Pessimism and the Limits of Traditional Marxism," *Theory and Society* (1982), no. 11, pp. 617–58.

14. In his controversial essay "Die Juden und Europa," Horkheimer analyzes the decline of economic liberalism in Europe and examines the role of anti-Semitism in allowing segments of the population to express their frustration against the system of free enterprise by identifying the Jews to be the representatives of this sphere (ZfS 1939/40:115–37). The essay indicates a certain blindness in Horkheimer's conception of the transition from liberalism to fascism. He fails to distinguish between the system of free market and free enterprise, and political principles like representative government, the separation of powers, constitutionality, rule of law, etc.

This denigration of the role of political liberalism is one of the respects in which the Frankfurt School continues the tradition of orthodox Marxism and conflates, or rather reduces, political to economic structures. In this respect, Franz Neumann's work is an exception. Neumann's analysis of the inner contradictions and ambivalences of political liberalism, particularly his exposition of the contradictions between the "rule of law" and "sovereignty," remains one of the finest treatments of the history of liberal political thought; see F. Neumann, *Die Herrschaft des Gesetzes*, first submitted as a doctoral dissertation to the London School of Economics and supervised by Harold Laski under the title "The Governance of the Rule of Law" (1936). See also the collection of essays by Neumann, *Wirtschaft, Staat und Demokratie* (Frankfurt: Suhrkamp, 1977).

15. In addition to works mentioned in the preceding note, see Neumann, *Behemoth* and *Democratic and Authoritarian State*.

16. After the emigration, Otto Kirchheimer was professor of political science at Columbia University until 1965. His most important publications are *Punishment and Social Structure*, with G. Rushe (New York: Columbia University Press, 1939); *Political Justice; Politik und Verfassung; Funktionen des Staates und der Verfassung*.

17. I am referring to the analyses in Adorno and Horkheimer, *Dialektik der Aufklärung* (1947); 1980 edition used here; the English translation by John Cumming, *Dialectic of Enlightenment*, is unreliable and I will not refer to it in the text; and M. Horkheimer, *The Eclipse of Reason* (1947); trans. into German by A. Schmidt as *Kritik der Instrumentellen Vernunft* (abbreviated in the text as KiV). Also included in this general discussion are Horkheimer's essays "Die Juden und Europa" (1939); "Autoritärer Staat" (1940), English translation in Arato and Gebhardt, eds., *The Essential Frankfurt School Reader*, pp. 95–118, and reprinted in H. Dubiel and A. Söllner, eds., *Wirtschaft, Recht und Staat im Nationalsozialismus* (Frankfurt: EVA, 1981); "The End of Reason," ZfS: 1941:366–88 (also included in Arato and Gebhardt, eds., *The Essential Frankfurt School Reader*, pp. 26–49). I include Marcuse's essay "Some Social Implications of Modern Technology" (ZfS 1941:414-39) in this general discussion as well.

18. While Neumann, Gurland, and Kirchheimer defended the continuity of the political and economic order of National Socialism with monopoly capitalism, Pollock, along with Adorno and Horkheimer, defended the newness of the social order created by National Socialism. In his essay "Some Social Implications of Modern Technology," Marcuse on the one hand agrees with Neumann's and Gurland's continuity thesis, but on the other introduces a new concept of "technical" or "technological" rationality to characterize the new form of domination emerging under National Socialism; see pp. 416ff.

19. "Societal rationalization" processes can be analyzed at two levels: on the one hand, *institutionally* they initiate a process of differentiation, as a consequence of which the economy and the polity are separated and relegated to independent spheres: market and production on the one hand, the state with its administrative and judiciary bureaucracy on the other (see Max Weber, *Economy and Society*, 1:375ff.). At the level of *social* action orientations, Weber analyzes "societal rationalization" via the transition in the economy, state administration, and the law from substantive to formal rationality (see *Economy and Society*, 1:85, 107, 178–80, and 217–26; 2:666ff. and 875–89). It is this aspect of Weber's analysis which Adorno, Horkheimer, and Marcuse integrate with their diagnosis of state capitalism in the 1940s. The interdependence of capitalism and bureaucratically administered political domination, oddly enough, provides them with a model to analyze fascism and, after 1945, post-war industrial mass democracies.

By "cultural rationalization" Weber means in the first place the *systematization* of various worldviews ("The Social Psychology of World Religions," p. 293). He describes this process as originating with the demand that "the world order in its totality is, could and should somehow be a meaningful 'cosmos'" (*ibid.*, p. 281). Such efforts at systematization are present in all world religions, at times resulting in monotheism, at times in mystical dualism, and at others in mysticism. Second, common to all such efforts at systematization over the centuries is a *decline in the role of magic (Entzauberung)* (*ibid.*, pp. 290ff.). Weber appears to have analyzed such processes of cultural rationalization in light of a major distinction, namely, the distinction between those worldviews leading to an ethics of world abnegation and those leading to world affirmation. See Weber, "Religious Rejections of the World and Their Directions," in *From Max Weber*, H. H. Gerth and C. W. Mills, eds. and trans., pp. 233ff.; originally "Zwischenbetrachtung" to *Gesammelte Aufsätze zur Religionssoziologie* (1920); W. Schluchter, "Die Paradoxie der Rationalisierung," pp. 19ff.

20. See appendix to chapter 5, "Lukács, Weber, and the Frankfurt School."

21. See most recently J. Habermas, "The Entwinement of Myth and Enlightenment," *New German Critique*, pp. 13ff.

22. F. Grenz, *Adornos Philosophie in Grundbegriffe*, p. 275, note 26, as cited by J. Schmucker, *Adorno—Logik des Zerfalls*, p. 17.

23. Martin Jay, "Positive und negative Totalität," pp. 67–87.

24. Theodor W. Adorno, *Minima Moralia*, p. 50; Herbert Marcuse, *One-Dimensional Man*.

25. See W. Bonss, "Psychoanalyse als Wissenschaft und Kritik," pp. 367ff.

26. J. Benjamin, "The End of Internalization," *Telos*, pp. 50ff.

27. The critique of identity logic underlying Western reason had been a concern of Adorno's since his 1931 lecture on the "Actuality of Philosophy." Whatever differences may exist between Adorno and Horkheimer in this regard, the search for a non-discursive, non-identitary logic, be it in an esoteric philosophy of language, in symbol, or in the collective unconscious of the species, characterizes both the *Dialectic of Enlightenment* and *The Eclipse of Reason*.

28. Thomas Baumeister and Jens Kulenkampff, "Geschichtsphilosophie und philosophische Ästhetik." *Neue Hefte für Philosophie*, pp. 74ff.

29. Adorno and Horkheimer, DA, p. 117. *The Eclipse of Reason*, which traces the inevitable destruction of the "objective reason" embodied in premodern metaphysical and cosmological conceptions of the world, by the "subjective," utilitarian, and skeptical reason of the moderns, does not reach a different conclusion from this redemptive appeal to the utopian moment of the non-identical. Horkheimer does not assert that the differentiation of reason into irreconciliable value spheres in modernity can be overcome by a philosophy of "Substantive Reason" (KiV, p. 63; *Eclipse of Reason*, pp. 58ff.). Philosophy cannot totalize; it cannot reunite the value of the autonomous personality with a unified concept of the world and society. It also shares the intentions of the art work to express the right of the other, of the non-identical, to be. It can accomplish this task insofar as it rejects the burden of the concept, and returns to the forgotten and repressed meanings and associations of the word (KiV, p. 158; *Eclipse of Reason*, p. 167). Philosophy gives "the mute wit-

nesses of language" their voice back (KiV, p. 155; *Eclipse of Reason*, p. 165).

30. Baumeister and Kulenkampff, "Geschichtsphilosophie und philosophische Ästhetik," p. 80; my translation.

31. In this context, Habermas has distinguished between the "traditional critique of ideology" and "totalizing critique" as practiced by Adorno and Horkheimer. "The critique of ideology wants to demonstrate that the validity of a theory under investigation has not freed itself from the context of its genesis. It wants to demonstrate that hidden behind the back of this theory is an inadmissible *tension of power and validity* and that it is moreover to this tension that it owes its recognition" ("The Entwinement of Myth and Enlightenment," p. 20). Totalizing critique, by contrast, assumes that reason, "once instrumentalized, has become assimilated to power and has thereby given up its critical power" (*ibid.*). It is forced to renounce "the totalitarian development of the Enlightenment with its own means—a performative contradiction of which Adorno was well aware" (*ibid.*).

32. T. W. Adorno, "Sociology and Empirical Research," in *The Positivist Dispute in German Sociology*, Glyn Adey and David Frisby, trans. (London: Heineman, 1969), p. 69.

33. Hegel, *Wissenschaft der Logik*, 2:11–12, 101–2; *Hegel's Science of Logic*, pp. 396–97, 479–80.

34. Hegel, *Wissenschaft der Logik*, 2:180–84; *Science of Logic*, pp. 550–53.

35. Hegel, PhG, p. 28; *Hegel's Phenomenology of Spirit*, p. 18.

36. T. W. Adorno, *Negative Dialektik*, esp. pp. 32–42.

37. *Ibid.*, pp. 295–354.

38. Adorno, "On the Logic of the Social Sciences," in *The Positivist Dispute in German Sociology*, p. 107.

39. Adorno, "Kultur und Verwaltung," in *Soziologische Schriften*, 1:131.

40. "Culture today stamps everything with likeness" (Adorno and Horkheimer, DA, p. 108).

41. "Society perpetrates menacing nature in the form of the ever-lasting organizational compulsion, which reproduces itself in individuals as persistent self-preservation, and thereby strikes back at nature as the social domination over nature" (*ibid.*, p. 162).

42. Pollock, "State Capitalism: Its Possibilities and Limitations," ZfS 1941:217–21.

43. Marcuse, *Eros and Civilization*, p. 84. Since this volume is in fact the third of Marcuse's *Gesammelte Schriften*, I have used it as the main text for the following discussion.

44. "Eros which thrusts itself upon consciousness is moved by memory; with memory, it turns against the order of deprivation; it uses memory in its effort to overcome time in a world that is dominated by time" (TuG, p. 198).

45. Claus Offe, "Technik und Eindimensionalität," p. 87.

46. Rüdiger Bubner, "Was ist kritische Theorie?" p. 179.

47. Adorno, *Negative Dialektik*, p. 15.

48. Adorno, "Spätkapitalismus oder Industriegesellschaft," in *Soziologische Schriften*, 1:369.

49. Adorno, "Anmerkungen zum sozialen Konflikt heute," in *Soziologische Schriften*, 1:193.

50. Stephen Kahlberg, "Max Weber's Types of Rationality: Cornerstone for the Analysis of Rationalization Processes in History," *American Journal of Sociology* (1980), 85(5): 1158.

51. Lukas, *History and Class Consciousness*, p. 83.

52. Herbert Marcuse, "Industrialization and Capitalism in the Work of Max Weber," *Negations* (Boston: Beacon Press, 1969), pp. 240ff.

53. Max Weber, Introduction, *The Protestant Ethic and the Spirit of Capitalism*, p. 21.

54. Maurice Merleau-Ponty, *Les adventures de la dialectique* (Paris: Gallimard, 1955), p. 29; English trans., *Adventures of the Dialectic* (Evanston, Ill.: Northwestern University Press, 1973); emphasis in the original.

6. Autonomy as Mimetic Reconciliation

1. For this distinction, see Paul Ricoeur, *Freud and Philosophy*.

2. Friedrich Nietzsche, *The Genealogy of Morals*, Preface, in *The Birth of Tragedy and the Genealogy of Morals*, p. 149.

3. English translation by John Torpey as "Materialism and Morality", *Telos* (Fall 1986), No. 69, pp. 85–119.

4. See the collection of essays edited by Hans Ebeling, *Subjektivität und Selbsterhaltung*, and the study by Hans Blumenberg in this collection, "Selbsterhaltung und Beharrung: Zur Konstitution der neuzeitlichen Rationalität," pp. 144–207.

5. R. Spaemann, "Bürgerliche Ethik und nichtteleologische Ontologie," *Subjektivität und Selbst-Erhaltung*, pp. 76–97.

6. For an analysis of the transition from ancient to modern political theory in Hobbes' thought, see Leo Strauss, *The Political Philosophy of Thomas Hobbes*.

7. Thomas Hobbes, *Leviathan*, p. 190.

8. *Ibid.*, pp. 189–90.

9. *Ibid.*, p. 189. For an extremely interesting account of the development of the concept of "jus" in early modern thought, see R. Tuck, *Natural Right Theories* (Cambridge: Cambridge University Press, 1979), esp. pp. 119–43.

10. Max Horkheimer, "Zum Begriff der Vernunft," p. 49.

11. E. Tugendhat formulates this critique of the Kantian moral law in "Zur Entwicklung von moralischen Begründungsstrukturen in modernen Recht," in *Archiv für Rechtsund Sozialphilosophie*, pp. 1ff.

12. I. Kant, *Grundlegung der Metaphysik der Sitten*, p. 51; English trans., p. 89.

13. E. Tugendhat, "Zur Entwicklung von moralischen Begründungsstrukturen im modernen Recht," p. 5.

14. See Kurt Baier, *The Moral Point of View*, pp. 110–38; and R. Wimmer, *Universalisierung in der Ethik*, for a general discussion of Anglo-American and German universalist-ethical theories.

15. For a parallel analysis of the sociology of moral feelings, see Agnes Heller, *A Theory of Feelings*, and my review in *Telos* (Summer 1980), no. 40, pp. 211–21.

16. Herbert Marcuse, *Eros and Civilization*, English ed., pp. 32ff.

17. John Rawls, *A Theory of Justice*, pp. 265ff.

18. A recent critique of the Marxian theory of justice is developed by A. Buchanan, *Marx and Justice*.

19. See Claus Offe, "Spätkapitalismus—Versuch einer Begriffsbestimmung," in *Strukturprobleme des kapitalistischen Staates*, pp. 17ff.

20. For the concept of the "solidarity of the living," see Peter Singer, *Animal Liberation: A New Ethics for Our Treatment of Animals* (New York: Avon Books, 1975), pp. 192–223.

21. "But the transition from objective to subjective reason was not an accident, and the process of development of ideas cannot arbitrarily at any given moment be reversed. If subjective reason in the form of Enlightenment has dissolved the philosophical basis of beliefs that have been an essential part of Western culture, it has been able to do so because this basis proved too weak. Their revival, therefore, is completely artificial: it serves the purpose of filling a gap" (Max Horkheimer, *The Eclipse of Reason*, p. 62).

22. Horkheimer, "Zum Begriff der Vernunft," p. 56.

23. Adorno, *Negative Dialektik*, p. 268, my translation.

24. *Ibid.*

25. *Ibid.*

26. *Ibid.*

27. *Ibid.* Russell Jacoby discusses the controversy over revisionism in psychoanalysis in *Social Amnesia*, pp. 73–101.

28. See Adorno, *Negative Dialektik*, p. 269.

29. *Ibid.*

30. *Ibid.*, pp. 270ff.; Adorno, "Sociology and Psychology" (1955) and "Die Revidierte Psychoanalyse."

31. This critique of the "subject" is one more respect in which Adorno anticipates philosophies of post-modernity; see note 17, chapter 2.

32. Adorno, *Negative Dialektik*, p. 277.

33. *Ibid.*, p. 273; Herbert Marcuse, "Das Veralten der Psychoanalyse."

34. Adorno, *Negative Dialektik*, p. 285.

35. J. Benjamin, "Die Antinomien des patriarchalischen Denkens," pp. 426–27.

36. The claim that the changing role of the father in the family would necessarily generate a weak, passive, and atomized self has been criti-

cized by feminist thinkers as the "patriarchal core" of Frankfurt School thought. In the article cited above, Benjamin criticizes Adorno and Horkheimer for failing to perceive that instrumental reason represents a contrast to motherly love and care, and to intersubjective principles of perception and consciousness formation (*ibid.*, p. 430). To sustain this claim, Benjamin utilizes the results of "object relations theory" in psychoanalysis (Sullivan, Fairbairn, and Kohut). In the discussion generated by C. Lasch's book *Haven in a Heartless World*, feminist writers have once more attacked the assumptions that the decline in the role of the father in the family would mean that a weak self would develop (Stephanie Engel, "Femininity as Tragedy"). It is interesting that the debate between "orthodox" and "revisionist" psychoanalysis, contrary to the assumptions outlined by Jacoby in *Social Amnesia*, does not fall into the neat dichotomies of "emancipatory" versus "reformist" social thought. An adequate analysis of this "elective affinity" between feminist psychoanalysis and "object relations" theory has yet to be undertaken; cf. also Dorothy Dinnerstein, *The Mermaid and the Minotaur: Sexual Arrangements and Human Malaise* (New York: Harper Colophon Books, 1977).

37. Adorno and Horkheimer, DA, p. 162.

38. Hegel, *Wissenschaft der Logik*, 2:17ff.; *Hegel's Science of Logic*, pp. 403ff.

39. John Locke, *An Essay Concerning Human Understanding*, A. D. Woozley, ed. (New York: Meridian Books, 1964, pp. 200ff.; and David Hume, *A Treatise of Human Nature*, A. Selby-Bigge, ed. (New York: Oxford University Press, 1978), vol. 2, book 1.

40. I. Kant, *Critique of Pure Reason*, "The Paralogisms of Pure Reason," p. 329.

41. J. G. Fichte, *Grundlage der gesammten Wissenschaftslehre*, p. 289.

42. Adorno, *Negative Dialektik*, pp. 295ff.

43. Adorno's critique of Hegel again has much in common with my rejection of the philosophy of the subject. His discussion in *Negative Dialektik* has been very instructive for me in this regard; see pp. 295–353. Only, Adorno chooses to ignore those other aspects and elements of Hegel's thought which are irreconcilable with his mystified emphasis on the *Weltgeist*.

44. G. W. F. Hegel, "Love," pp. 302–9.

45. I believe there is a deeper reason that can explain Adorno's unwillingness to locate a moment of non-identity in the realm of social and human relations. The social is, for Adorno, a category of *mediation*. The act of exchange, which is older than the commodity form, already establishes that the basis of sociality is the equivalence of the non-identical. Odysseus appeals to the gods through sacrifice; but the logic of sacrifice is already the logic of exchange. "If exchange is the secularization of the victim, the latter already appears as the magical schema of rational exchange; a display of humans to dominate the gods" (DA, p. 47). Exchange is mediation; mediation is the identity of the non-identical. The

expansion of civilization is the expansion of exchange. The continuous reduction of everything to something other than itself, which is the secret of money and later of the commodity form, is institutionalized in the course of history. The increase in social intercourse, the socialization of humanity, only means that this network of abstract acts of equivalence expands to a point where the immediate, that is, non-mediated, disappears. It could therefore be that Adorno's disregard for relations to others as a possible realm in which the compulsion of identity logic would be broken is related to the strong identification in his thought of sociality with exchange, with mediation, and with the establishment of identitary logic. See also Susan Buck-Morss, *The Origin of Negative Dialectics*, pp. 82–96.

46. Adorno, *Negative Dialektik*, pp. 277ff.

47. Adorno, *Ästhetische Theorie*, in *Gesammelte Schriften*, Rolf Tiedemann, ed. (Frankfurt: Suhrkamp, 1970), 7:111ff.

48. *Ibid.*, pp. 101–3.

49. *Ibid.*, p. 113.

50. "The naturally beautiful is the cipher [*Spur*] of the non-identical in things set upon their course of universal identity" (*ibid.*, p. 114). Susan Buck-Morss investigates the relationship of this search for "ciphers" to Walter Benjamin's method of building constellations, in *The Origin of Negative Dialectics*, pp. 96ff.

51. Baumeister and Kulenkampff, "Geschichtsphilosophie und philosophische Ästhetik," p. 87.

52. Adorno, *Negative Dialektik*, pp. 184ff.

53. *Ibid.*, pp. 184–89.

54. See J. Habermas, "Urgeschichte der Subjektivität und verwilderte Selbst-Behauptung."

55. Adorno, *Negative Dialektik*, p. 273.

56. H. Blumenberg, "Selbst-Erhaltung und Beharrung," in H. Ebeling, ed., *Subjektivität und Selbsterhaltung*, pp. 147ff.

57. Ludwig Feuerbach, "Principles of the Philosophy of the Future," pp. 175–247; Marx Wartofsky, *Feuerbach*.

58. Adorno and Horkheimer, DA, pp. 167ff.

59. In his careful and thoughtful study *The Domination of Nature*, William Leiss attempts to clarify what the term "the domination of nature" means and how this can be defended. He writes: "It is absurd to refer to man's "conquest of nature" or "man's domination of nature"; the putative subject of this enterprise does not exist. "Man" as such is an abstraction which when employed in this manner only conceals the fact that in the actual violent struggles among *men*, technological instruments have a part to play" (p. 120).

Certainly it would be absurd to suggest that Adorno and Horkheimer ignored social conflict in their reflections upon the matter; however, they used the concept of "domination" so globally that at times even the first act of name giving (which we know to be a mythological posit), the concept as the unit of abstract thought, was said to carry the germ of dominating reason. I concur with Leiss that the concept of domination is meaningless when applied to our *cognitive* relation to nature, and significant only when applied to the *technological* exploitation of nature (p. 193). As Leiss points out, the liberation of nature from such technological domination can be conceived of as a social and political task, not necessarily as a cultural and cognitive one (*ibid.*).

60. Without an extensive study of Adorno's aesthetic theory, I will venture the suggestion here that Adorno's concept of the aesthetic realm almost strikes me as being "pre-hermeneutical." What I mean is that Adorno seems to abstract aesthetic experience from that of mediated relation to a tradition and community of interpretation, which Gadamer has so decisively brought to the fore. It is almost as if Adorno believes in the possibility of an unmediated relation to the work of art, where a subject "receives" the truth of the art work. The experience of mimesis seems very much to imply such an epiphanic experience. But aesthetic experience is mediated, and it is primarily mediated by the history of the reception of the art work. See Gadamer, *Truth and Method*, pp. 91–146.

61. Habermas, "Urgeschichte der Subjektivität und verwilderte Selbst-Behauptung"; English trans., pp. 106–7.

62. *Ibid.*, p. 107. "Bilderverbot" refers to the injunction in Judaism against drawing images of God or even attempting to represent Him; this injunction was given a mystical interpretation in the Hassidic movement in particular. In using this concept, Adorno is alluding to sources of mystical and messianic experience in which he shared an interest with Walter Benjamin. On the significance of Jewish theology for the critical theorists, see Micha Brumlik, "Der revolutionäre Messianismus der Frankfurter Schule." *Merkur*, pp. 228–31.

7. The Critique of Functionalist Reason

1. All in Habermas, *Theorie und Praxis*. English translation *Theory and Practice*, John Viertel, trans.

2. For a penetrating account of this problem, see Joel Whitebook, "The Problem of Nature in Habermas." Habermas' rejection of Adorno's and Horkheimer's hopes for a mimetic reconciliation with nature has usually taken the form of the claim that in our relationship to external nature there is "only one *theoretically fruitful* attitude, namely, the objectivating attitude of the natural-scientific, experimenting observer" (Habermas, "Reply to My Critics," in Thompson and Held, eds., *Habermas: Critical Debates*, pp. 243–44). Habermas does not deny that "one can adopt a performative attitude to external nature, enter in communicative relations with it, have aesthetic experience and feelings analogous to morality with respect to it" (*ibid.*).

Although I agree that our relation to inner and outer nature cannot be made the exclusive focus of emancipatory potential, and that the concept of mimesis is best actualized in the sphere of relations to another like ourselves, I do believe that the strong objectifying cognitivism which Habermas represents here is misguided. True, when we examine chemicals in a lab or rocks under a microscope, and thus "objectify" nature, we are not "dominating" it; but when we destroy life and natural habitats through poisonous dumping, cause fish to have cancer, forests to die, and species to become extinct, there is a sense in which we are dominating nature. As long as our actions can inflict *pain* upon other sentient beings or destroy their conditions of life, we have a *prima facie* case for speaking of a moral responsibility. (Admittedly it is hard to see what it means to "pain" trees; here it seems that we have to think, not of single trees, but of a natural habitat as a totality which is in our power to preserve or destroy.) But pointing out that one can plausibly speak of a moral obligation toward nature or preserving life does not suffice to deal with Habermas' point that no other cognitive attitude toward nature other than a theoretical-objectifying one is fruitful. Here I believe that Habermas is ignoring the strong evidence from biology and from the life sciences that have shown the theoretical fruitfulness of a more holistic, expressive, performative approach to nature. A recent, striking example of this has been given by Barbara McClintock, the Nobel Prize–winning plant geneticist, who, according to her biographer Evelyn Fox Keller, literally treated her maize cells as if she were able to penetrate them and walk inside them; see Keller, *A Feeling for the Organism*.

3. See Habermas, *Theorie des kommunikativen Handelns*, 1:489; *The Theory of Communicative Action*, pp. 366ff. All future references in the next two chapters to this first volume will be to the English translation except where otherwise indicated; abbreviated in the text as ThCA. Most translations from the second volume are mine except when McCarthy has provided an English rendering in his Introduction to ThCA.

4. Cf. the following statement: "However if (as becomes even more apparent in times of recession) the bourgeois ideals have gone into retirement, there are no norms and values to which an immanent critique might appeal with the [expectation of] agreement. *On the other hand, the melodies of ethical socialism have been played through without result*" (Habermas, "Historical Materialism and the Development of Normative Structures," in *Communication and the Evolution of Society*, p. 97, emphasis added).

5. For this distinction, drawn in slightly different terms, see György Markus, "Practical-Social Rationality in Marx," part II, *Dialectical Anthropology*, p. 12.

6. These remarks, of course, do not suffice to explain the attitude of Adorno and Horkheimer during the student movement of the early six-

ties. In their Introduction, Bonss and Honneth provide an interesting account of the various phases of reaction to critical theory in light of political developments; see "Einleitung: Zur Reaktualisierung der kritischen Theorie," in *Sozialforschung als Kritik*, pp. 7ff.

7. As Manfred Riedel has shown, there is a tradition of analyzing modernity, quite distinct from the Weberian one, which runs from neo-Aristotelianism to British political economy and to Hegel ("Hegels Begriff der 'bürgerlichen Gesellschaft,'" pp. 247ff.). For this tradition, the crucial aspect of modernity is the separation of *oikos* and *polis*, or of institutional as opposed to cultural differentiation. In *Strukturwandel der Öffentlichkeit*, Habermas was more concerned with the problem of institutional differentiation than with that of cultural differentiation (see p. 13–101). For a reading of Hegel which combines both approaches, see Habermas, "Können komplexe Gesellschaften eine vernünftige Identität ausbilden?" in *Zur Rekonstruktion des historischen Materialismus*, pp. 92–129.

8. For an analysis of this phase of Habermas' thought, see Jean Cohen, "Why More Political Theory?" *Telos*, pp. 86ff.

9. Habermas, *Technik und Wissenschaft als "Ideologie,"* pp. 98ff.; English trans., "Technology and Science as 'Ideology,'" in *Toward a Rational Society*, pp. 119ff.

10. In response to this claim, Thomas McCarthy has objected that these ideals were not completely without immanent grounding even in this phase of Habermas' thought, insofar as democratic institutions seemed to correspond to them. As I will point out in the following chapter, while it is true that the ideals of a discourse free from domination and the ideal speech situation were first formulated in the context of the dilemmas of democratic societies, I still would hold that the appeal to an educated public of scientists, citizens, and politicians which is made in some of these early essays is not sufficient to show that there were tendencies in these societies which would result in leading the population to challenge the political content of technocracy and scientism (see Habermas, "The Scientization of Politics and Public Opinion," *Toward a Rational Society*, pp. 62–81).

11. See the appendix to chapter 5 on Weber, Lukács, and the Frankfurt School.

12. For a detailed account of some issues of social science methodology involved in this distinction, see Thomas McCarthy, *The Critical Theory of Jürgen Habermas*, ch. 3 and pp. 379ff. See also Habermas, *Legitimationsprobleme im Spätkapitalismus;* English trans.; *Legitimation Crisis*, pp. 3ff. All references in the text are to the English edition.

13. These terms are introduced, following George Herbert Mead, in Habermas, *Theorie des kommunikativen Handelns*, 2:27ff.

14. The central role played by the concept of "needs" in Habermas' work is often ignored, but as Thomas McCarthy empathically points out,

"For Habermas, sociology is always at the same time social psychology" (*The Critical Theory of Jürgen Habermas*, p. 334). He cites Habermas: "The system of institutions must be grasped in terms of the imposed repression of needs and of the scope for possible individualization, just as personality structures must be grasped in determinations of the institutional framework and of role qualifications" (Habermas and Luhmann, *Theorie der Gesellschaft oder Sozialtechnologie*, pp. 217–18).

15. See Habermas, *LC*, p. 95; and R. Döbert, J. Habermas, and G. Nunner-Winkler, eds., *Entwicklung des Ichs*, Editors' Introduction, pp. 18ff.

16. The early reactions to this work in English failed to grasp its significance. David Held and Larry Simon's analysis, "Habermas' Theory of Crisis in Late Capitalism," *Radical Philosophers' News Journal*, pp. 1–19 was an exception.

17. While it cannot be denied that the social-welfare state is in some measure unique in the functions it assumes, a stronger thesis could have been built around the changing role of the state if this change could also be historically documented. For it seems obvious that different countries have different state traditions, and that in some the state has played an active role in certain of these areas even in the last century; see Anthony Giddens, "Capitalism: Integration, Surveillance and Class Power" and "The Nation-State, Nationalism and Capitalist Development," both in *A Contemporary Critique of Historical Materialism*, pp. 157–203.

18. Especially significant is the replacement of the market mechanism by the state in the public sectors of transportation, health, housing, and leisure. This process generates a new orientation toward work, namely, an orientation to concrete use values. This new orientation is, in turn, significant for explaining the replacement of professional privatism by an activist professionalism among social workers, doctors, teachers, and public employees of various sorts; Habermas, *LC*, p. 66.

19. I return at the end of this section to the plausibility of Habermas' claim that these "privatisms" are eroding. As McCarthy points out, "Moreover, even if we grant that normative structures and motivational patterns are undergoing profound change, the question remains as to where these changes will lead. Might they not, for instance, issue in some altered constellation of passivity, privatism, and consumerism no less functional for the formally democratic welfare state?" (*The Critical Theory of Jürgen Habermas*, p. 374).

20. See Claus Offe, "Spätkapitalismus—Versuch einer Begriffsbestimmung" and "Tauschverhältnis und politische Steuerung. Zur Aktualität des Legitimationsproblems," both in *Strukturprobleme des kapitalistischen Staates*, pp. 7–77; "Some Contradictions of the Modern Welfare State," *Praxis International*, pp. 219–30.

21. Daniel Bell, *The Cultural Contradictions of Capitalism*.

22. In the section of *ThdkH*, vol. 2, entitled "Marx and the Thesis of Inner Colonization," Habermas undertakes a reinterpretation of the Marxian category of reification in light of his system and lifeworld distinction. The central point of this analysis is that one must preserve the Marxian thesis of the growth and accumulation tendencies of capital, but that at the social-institutional level, late capitalism generates conflicts that are not *class-specific* but encompass broader sectors of the population and are manifested in a wider variety of symptoms (pp. 489ff.).

23. For general discussions in English, see McCarthy, Introduction, in Habermas, *The Theory of Communicative Action;* David Rasmussen, "Communicative Action and Philosophy," *Philosophy and Social Criticism*, pp. 1–29; Dieter Misgeld, "Communication and Societal Rationalization"; and Anthony Giddens, "Reason Without Revolution?" *Praxis International*.

24. There are many aspects of the distinction between "system" and "lifeworld" which remain unclear in this account. I shall name only two. First, if, as Habermas suggests, we must conceive of society both as system and as lifeworld (*ThdkH*, 2:183ff.), does this imply that we can adopt the perspective of the *observer* when analyzing cultural reproduction, social integration, and socialization, or that we cannot adopt the perspective of the *participant* when examining—let us say—the everyday life of the modern factory and bureaucratic organizations? Can these perspectives be adopted at will? Or do the constraints of the object domain privilege one mode of social analysis over another? Secondly, do these categories correspond to institutional domains or do they permeate all institutions? Does the family belong to the lifeworld alone, whereas the factory belongs to the system?

Although some critics have suggested that this dualistic framework arbitrarily restricts modes of social inquiry (e.g., Johannes Berger, "Die Versprachlichung des Sakralen und die Entsprachlichung der Ökonomie" *Zeitschrift für Soziologie*, pp. 353–65), I believe it must be argued that Habermas means both methodological perspectives to be legitimate in both domains, provided that they do not become exclusive. To claim, for example, that the economy must be studied from the perspective of the modern worker is just as arbitrary as the claim that the family can only be studied functionalistically, from the perspective of its stabilizing or destabilizing consequences upon the modern economy. The real task of modern social theory is to explicate the mediation and interaction of system and lifeworld. However, an *objectivist* account alone of reproduction, system integration, and socialization is *not* possible, for communicative action can only be understood if we are capable of adopting the perspectives of alter and ego, of first and second person.

25. See Edmund Husserl, *The Crisis of European Sciences and Transcendental Phenomenology*, part II, section 33ff.; Alfred Schutz, "The

Problem of the 'Life-World,'" esp. part III, "Symbol, Reality and Society."

26. See Michael Theunissen, *The Other*, part I; David Carr, "The Fifth Mediation and Husserl's Cartesianism."

27. Hans-Georg Gadamer, "Hermeneutics and Social Science"; Paul Ricoeur, *Hermeneutics and the Human Sciences*.

28. Peter Winch, *The Idea of a Social Science and Its Relation to Philosophy* (London: Routledge & Kegan Paul, 1958).

29. McCarthy, Introduction, in Habermas, *The Theory of Communicative Action*, 1:xxiv.

30. Habermas wants to claim that the three reproduction processes (cultural reproduction, social integration, and socialization) are based on the different aspects of communicative action (understanding, coordination, sociation) which are in turn rooted in the structural components of speech acts (propositional, illocutionary, expressive). The discussion of the relationship of formal pragmatics to the sociological concept of action remains one of the most programmatic aspects of the theory of communicative action. See ThCA 1:328ff.

31. Habermas intends to define the three worlds formally and not materially. It is not so much the content or the object of these worlds that distinguishes them from one another, but the *basic attitudes* one assumes toward a given domain. The attitude toward the existing world of states of affairs is *objectivating*, that toward the intersubjective world is *norm-conformative*, and that toward the subjective is *expressive*. McCarthy shows that there are difficulties with this way of formulating matters. "If Habermas' three worlds are defined *formally*, in relation to three different basic attitudes, how is it at all possible to adopt different attitudes toward one and the same (attitudinally specified) world?" ("Reflections on Rationalization in *The Theory of Communicative Action*," *Praxis International*, p. 182.)

32. "The rationality proper to the communicative practice of everyday life points to the practice of argumentation as a court of appeal that makes it possible to continue communicative action with other means when disagreement can no longer be headed off by everyday routines and yet is not to be settled by the direct or strategic use of force" (Habermas, ThCA, 1:17–18).

33. It is important not to confuse the *semantic* and *pragmatic* aspects of this claim. Habermas is not propounding a theory of meaning. He is maintaining that understanding the meaning of the words of a sentence is not sufficient to understand what that sentence, when uttered by someone, means in the sense of understanding what is intended by the utterance in question. To give an example: suppose I say, "The moon is the goddess of light." Knowing the meaning of these words does not allow me to see what the speaker is doing or what kind of speech act he or she is performing; is she telling me that this is the nature of the universe or that I am transgressing a social rule by not falling on my knees when I see the full moon, or is she explaining to me why some

sects go out on the roof when there is a full moon? To reach an understanding with one another, we would have to know what it would mean to disagree with the statement "The moon is the goddess of light." Would this involve a theoretical dispute, a normative one, or a psychological one? Members of the same sociocultural world and milieu can usually take this kind of knowledge for granted, but we reproduce our social lifeworld over time when we can coordinate our actions, reinterpret our culture, and give meaning to the experiences of our private world.

34. Schnädelbach argues that Habermas links rationality far too narrowly with "knowledge" and with truth, and instead suggests that "we can still classify expressions and actions as rational even when the presuppositions on which they rest prove to be false." Schnädelbach, "Transformation der Kritischen Theorie", p. 167. With this claim, Schnädelbach is advocating a weak hermeneutical concept of rationality which would presumably understand what "good grounds" are for participants themselves and refrain from judging them. Habermas tries to show that understanding (*Verstehen*) and judging validity (*Geltungsansprüche zu bewerten*) are inseparable; see note 36 on this question.

35. R. Münch expresses skepticism that communicative action can accomplish all this sociologically because of its orientation to the redemption of validity claims. His contention is that Habermas has ignored the symbolic or ritualistic dimension of social action ("Von der Rationalisierung zur Verdinglichung der Lebenswelt," *Soziologische Revue* [1982], 5:390–97). I find Münch's objection far less convincing than Schnädelbach's critique. Münch almost seems to want to revive Weber's concept of "affective action" as sociologically basic (see p. 394). It is unclear what force the dimension that Münch names "the regular rituals [which] maintain a sacred character and which are anchored affectively and communally" (*ibid.*) can have in modern societies.

36. In "Reflections on Rationalization in *The Theory of Communicative Action*," McCarthy addresses the very important argument implied by this aspect of Habermas' theory. This argument suggests that meaning, intelligibility, and understanding are in the final analysis inseparable from validity, rationality, and assessment. "But if, in order to understand an expression," Habermas writes, "the interpreter must bring to mind the reasons with which a speaker would, if necessary and under suitable conditions, defend its validity, he is himself drawn into the process of assessing validity claims. For reasons are of such a nature that they cannot be described in the attitude of the third person" (ThCA 1:115–16). McCarthy rightly comments that this conclusion—that one cannot understand symbolic expressions, acts, or utterances "without taking a position on them" (ThCA 1:116)—is stronger than is warranted by the argument (p. 184). In the next chapter I try to show a similar problem arising with respect to Habermas' theory of communicative ethics, where Habermas identifies the very capacity to engage in argu-

ment with an ethical commitment. Both problems are part of the same very strong tendency in his work to "naturalize" normative and evaluative commitments by showing them to "have been always already made."

37. The concepts of "philosophy of consciousness" and "philosophy of the subject" are not equivalent. As I define it in this work, the philosophy of the subject means, first, that history can be viewed as the work of a collective singular subject that becomes through externalizing itself in the historical process, and second, that emancipation entails our reappropriating the heritage of this subject.

38. Hegel, *Hegel's Phenomenology of Spirit*, p. 111.

39. Habermas' analysis of Mead in volume 2 of *Theorie des kommunikativen Handelns* is probably one of the most successful and fascinating reconstructions in the entire work; see pp. 18ff.

40. Habermas defends the paradigmatic significance of communicative action through a consideration of alternative models of social action. Social theory provides us with three models of action: *teleological action*, according to which a responsible subject carries out a preconceived action in the world; the model of *normative action*, where it is assumed that two social actors coordinate their actions through internalizing given social norms; and *dramaturgical action* (ThCA 1:85ff.). In this latter case, social action is viewed as a mode of "self-presentation"; situation definitions are established and actions coordinated via the theatrical presentation of the self to others. Whereas the first model reduces sociality to the coordination of self-interested actors, the second model views society as a norms system alone, and the third proceeds from self-presentation to establish social contexts.

41. Habermas, ThdkH, 2:29ff.; cf. also Habermas, "Luhmanns Beitrag zu einer Theorie der gesellschaftlichen Evolution," in Habermas and Luhmann, *Theorie der Gesellschaft oder Sozialtechnologie*, pp. 27ff.

42. Max Weber, "The Social Psychology of World Religions." See note 19, chapter 5.

43. Habermas, ThCA 1:69ff., 157ff., and 186ff.

44. Habermas, 2:267ff.

45. Monetarized exchange relations abstract from affective relations among individuals and require that they be motivated by the principle of self-interest alone. Such relations initiate a real process of abstraction with respect of the identity of the persons involved, the kinds of objects they deal with, the quality of their actions, and the nature of the norms governing them. Modern exchange relations are governed by formal-legal norms that apply not to particular actions but to *action types*, not to specific individuals but to individuals qua members of a body politic.

46. This change of emphasis was most noticeable in Habermas' Introduction to *Stichworte zur "Geistigen Situation der Zeit."*

47. For an analysis of some of the ambivalences of such welfare-statist

reform processes, see Richard Cloward and Frances Fox Piven, *Regulating the Poor*.

48. See Daniel Bell's curious call in *The Cultural Contradictions of Capitalism* (pp. 146–71) for a return to the sacred and the revival of a sense of transcendence, as if such meaning contexts could be willfully and purposely made to come alive again. This kind of appeal to value contents that cannot stand cognitive tests ends up "functionalizing" them, that is to say, they are treated as belief systems that the man on the street, who is not in the business of science or reflection, gets served on a platter from intellectuals who themselves are surely beyond the sense of the sacred and the revival of transcendent values in their own cognitive practices.

49. The use of the word "pathology" instead of "crisis" is troublesome. Although not very explicit in this regard, Habermas seems to emphasize that these new phenomena are not primarily about contestations of social relations of power, but concern the preservation of the integrity of forms of life. Yet the question lingers as to whether there is not too much of an echo of Durkheimian functionalism, with its emphasis on the "health" or "sickness" of societies, in Habermas' use of this word. "We shall call 'normal' those social conditions that are most general in form, and others 'morbid' or 'pathological.' . . . [It] is clear that a phenomenon can be defined as pathological only in relation to a given type. The conditions of health and illness cannot be defined *in abstracto* and in an absolute manner. . . . [A] social fact can, then, be called normal for a given social species only in relation to an equally specific phase of its development" (Durkheim, *Rules of Sociological Method*, p. 103).

50. The one most clearly to articulate this was H. Marcuse in *Eros and Civilization*. He writes in the Preface: "This essay employs psychological categories because they have become political categories. The traditional borderlines between psychology on the one side and political and social philosophy on the other have been made obsolete by the conditions of man in the present era. . . . Psychological problems therefore turn into political problems: private disorder reflects more directly than ever before the disorder of the whole" (English ed., p. xvii).

51. See Habermas, "Dialectics of Rationalization"; ThdkH, 2:575ff.

52. As I will discuss in section 3 of the next chapter, "Communicative Autonomy and Utopia," and in my conclusion, I have doubts about the extent to which Habermas' categories can provide us with an immanent critique of the demands and potentials of these new social movements.

53. Johannes Berger, "Die Versprachlichung des Sakralen," p. 361.

54. The tendencies toward "juridification" (*Verrechtlichung*) play a special role in Habermas' theory of the colonization of the lifeworld. As he explains it:

"If it is the case that the symbolic reproduction of the lifeworld cannot be adjusted to the fundamentals of system integration without pathological side-effects, and if exactly this trend is an unavoidable side-effect of a successful organization of the social state, in the spheres of cultural reproduction, social integration and socialization, under the above conditions, an approximation [*Angleichung*] to formally organized spheres of action will take place. We name those social relations formally organized which constitute themselves first in the form of modern law. It is to be expected therefore that the adjustment of social to system integration should take the form of processes of juridification" (ThdkH 2:524ff.).

55. Claus Offe, "New Social Movements as a Meta-Political Challenge," pp. 30–31.

56. See Eli Zaretsky, *Capitalism, the Family and Personal Life* (New York: Harper & Row, 1976).

57. Christopher Lasch, *Haven in a Heartless World*, and note 37 in chapter 6.

58. Barbara Ehrenreich and D. English, *Complaints and Disorders: The Sexual Politics of Sickness* (Old Westbury, N.Y.: Feminist Press, 1973).

59. I am much indebted to Albrecht Wellmer for this formulation; see "Thesen über Vernunft, Emanzipation und Utopie," p. 3.

60. Michel Foucault, *Discipline and Punish;* for a careful analyses of Foucault's presuppositions, see Nancy Fraser, "Foucault on Modern Power," and "Is Michel Foucault a Young Conservative?" (MS, 1984).

61. Alasdair MacIntyre, *After Virtue*, pp. 35ff.

62. Marx, *Grundrisse*, p. 105.

63. For some recent accounts, see M. Berman, *All That Is Solid Melts Into Air*, and Hans Blumenberg, *The Legitimacy of the Modern Age*.

64. Talcott Parsons' translation of this passage in Max Weber, *The Protestant Ethic and the Spirit of Capitalism* (p. 13), is seriously misleading. Parsons renders "Kulturwelt" as "civilization"; where Weber mentions "der Okzident," Parsons reads "Western civilization." Above all, Parsons omits the qualifying adjectives "unvermeidlich und berechtigterweise," and misses the theoretical problem of validity by rendering "Gültigkeit" as "value." For the original German, see "Die Protestantische Ethik und der Geist des Kapitalismus," p. 1. From the standpoint of a neo-Kantian epistemology, the question of "validity" has a very specific meaning: what theoretical or moral grounds can we rationally bring forth for claiming that this is a justifiable perspective? Something may have value for us without being "gültig" in this sense. Parsons' rendering flattens the very emphatic and insistent tone of Weber's question.

65. Max Weber, "Objectivity in Social Science and Social Policy," p. 81, emphasis in the original.

66. I have dealt with Weber's methodological writings more extensively in "Rationality and Social Action."

67. On the possibility of transcendental arguments, see Peter Bieri and R. P. Horstmann, eds., *Transcendental Arguments and Science.*

68. Weber, "Science as a Vocation," p. 149.

69. *Ibid.*, pp. 152ff. Weber does allow that the scientization of values contributes to a certain axiomatic clarity and to an increase in self-reflection; yet this still does not resolve the problem of meaning. Cf. Weber, "The Meaning of Ethical Neutrality in 'Sociology' and 'Economics,'" pp. 10ff.

70. Karl Mannheim, *Ideology and Utopia,* ch. 4.

71. F. Nietzsche, *The Genealogy of Morals,* pp. 217ff., 258.

72. Cf. "After Nietzsche's devastating criticism of those 'last men' who 'invented happiness,' I may leave aside altogether the naive optimism in which science . . . has been celebrated as the way to happiness. Who believes in this?—aside from a few big children in university chairs or editorial offices" (Weber, "Science as a Vocation," p. 143).

73. In premodern systems of legitimacy, the extraordinary qualities that justify the charisma of a person can be traced back to metaphysical, cosmological, religious, and magical belief systems (Weber, *Economy and Society,* vol. 2, ch. 14, pp. 1111ff.). Subsequent to the disenchantment of worldviews, however, the belief in charismatic authority can no longer be justified in the same manner. They are irreducibly subjective. The extraordinary qualities of the leader have no metaphysical quality. Mommsen characterizes the qualities of plebiscitary leaders as follows: "The attachment of the masses to the person of the leading politican and not their objective conviction concerning the value of the aspired goal, is, according to Weber, the unique aspect of 'plebiscitary leader-democracy.' The content of the goals set do not determine the results of an election, but the personal-charismatic qualifications of the leading leader" (*Max Weber, Gesellschaft, Politik und Geschichte,* p. 137).

74. Leo Strauss, *Natural Right and History,* ch. 1.

75. Habermas, "Reply to My Critics," in Thompson and Held, eds., *Habermas: Critical Debates,* pp. 244–45.

76. "For the rationalization and conscious sublimation of men's relation to the various spheres of values, external and internal, have then pressed towards making conscious the *internal and lawful autonomy* of the individual spheres; thereby letting them drift into those tensions which remain hidden to the originally more naive relation to the external world. This results quite generally from the development of inner- and outer-worldly values towards rationality, towards conscious endeavor and sublimation by knowledge." Weber, "Religious Rejections of the World and Their Directions," in *From Max Weber,* H. H. Gerth and C. W. Mills, eds. and trans. [originally "Zwischenbetrachtung" to *Gesammelte Aufsätze zur Religionssoziologie*], p. 328

77. For the theme of the impoverishment of the lifeworld and the emergence of cultural elites, see Habermas, ThdkH, 2:479ff.; "Reply to My Critics," p. 250; and "Modernity vs. Post-Modernity." While denying

that a cognitive reintegration of separated value spheres is possible, Habermas attaches hope to the holistic logic of the everyday lifeworld to reabsorb back into itself those cultural values that are now the monopoly of elites.

78. Jean-François Lyotard, *The Post-Modern Condition;* see note 17, chapter 2.

79. Let me illustrate this problem with an example from the history of philosophy. It is *prima facie* very plausible to write a history of philosophy from Aquinas to Kant, let us say, as a learning process within a tradition responding to common problems with differing means and conceptual tools. Even Hegel, through his own lectures on the history of philosophy, showed that he stood at the pinnacle of a tradition in which he maintained there had been cumulative growth. But as Richard Rorty has also recently pointed out, Kant, no less than Hegel, had to rewrite the history of philosophy in order to make room for his own innovations (Rorty, *Philosophy and the Mirror of Nature*, pp. 131ff.). Yet, precisely after Kant and Hegel, it is no longer possible to write "the history of philosophy" in such a way as would do justice to Nietzsche as well as Kierkegaard, to Feuerbach as well as Mach and Poincaré. The self-conception of philosophy changes so radically in the aftermath of the breakdown of the Hegelian synthesis that no single history of philosophy can any longer be *the* history of philosophy. The writer's philosophical choices then lead him to have to ignore what he considers "non-philosophy" as opposed to philosophy. Bertrand Russell's *A History of Western Philosophy* (London: George Allen & Unwin, 1946) is a good example. In this account it is not clear that existentialism, Marxism, and phenomenology ever existed. I would venture the suggestion that precisely at the time when the modern culture comes of age, its relationship to its own tradition is fractured, and one can no longer speak of a *single* learning process. There are only so many strands to be followed along separate paths.

80. For a sharp treatment of this question, see McCarthy, "Reflections on Rationalization in *The Theory of Communicative Action.*"

81. "Self-reflection brings to consciousness those aspects of a process of formation which ideologically determine a present praxis of action and a worldview. . . . Rational reconstructions, by contrast, encompass anonymous rule-systems which can be followed by whatever subjects insofar as they have acquired the corresponding rule-competencies. . . . These legitimate forms of self-knowledge have remained undistinguished in the philosophical tradition under the title of reflection. However, a concrete criterion for distinguishing them is at hand. Self-reflection leads to insight through the fact that what was hitherto unconscious will be made practically conscious. A successful reconstruction also brings an 'unconscious' functioning system of rules in a certain way to consciousness: it makes explicit the intuitive knowledge which is given with rule competencies in the form of a know-how" (Habermas,

new Introduction to the 1978 edition of *Theorie und Praxis*, p. 29; my translation).

82. ThCA 1:67; see McCarthy, Introduction, ThCA 1:xvff., for a discussion of this point.

83. For a discussion of the problems in Habermas' theory of social evolution and learning, see Michael Schmid, "Habermas's Theory of Social Evolution." I find Schmid's point irrefutable. He writes: "It seems unlikely that ontogenetically possible stages of development which clearly exist, the human organism being the vehicle of such an empirically observable sequence, are really transformed into world-views of a similar sequential order, while at the same time *there is no empirically visible carrier system for these world-views*" (p. 179, emphasis in the text).

84. W. V. Quine, "Two Dogmas of Empiricism," in *From a Logical Point of View*, 2d rev. ed. (Cambridge, Mass.: Harvard University Press, 1980), pp. 20–47.

85. Robert Paul Wolff, *Kant's Theory of Mental Activity*, pp. 53ff.

86. Mary Hesse, "Science and Objectivity," pp. 111ff.

87. *Ibid.*, pp. 112–13, emphasis added.

88. Rainer Döbert gives an interesting application of this distinction to the European witch craze in the fifteenth and sixteenth centuries. He succeeds in showing that learning at one level—e.g., with regard to theological argumentation—does not automatically translate into learning at another—e.g., the use of torture in generating evidence; see "The Role of Stage-Models Within a Theory of Social Evolution."

89. See Habermas, "Historical Materialism and the Development of Normative Structures," in *Communication and the Evolution of Society*, pp. 95ff. Any such attempt will have to deal with the objection raised by M. Schmid above; see note 83.

90. See Arendt, *The Human Condition*, pp. 273–80.

91. Nietzsche, *The Genealogy of Morals*, pp. 291ff.

92. Arendt, *The Human Condition*, pp. 248ff.

93. Gadamer, *Truth and Method*, pp. 235ff.

94. Habermas, "Reply to My Critics," p. 262.

95. Wellmer, "Thesen über Vernunft, Emanzipation und Utopie," pp. 53ff.

96. Habermas, "Reply to My Critics," p. 262. Cf. also Habermas, ThCA, pp. 73ff., and note 49 on Durkheim above.

97. Hans-Georg Gadamer, "Rhetorik, Hermeneutik und Ideologiekritik," pp. 80–81; and Hans Joachim Giegel, "Reflexion und Emanzipation," pp. 249ff.

98. For this problem, see also the section in the new Introduction to Habermas, *Theorie und Praxis*, entitled "Organization der Aufklärung," pp. 33ff.

99. Of course, the possibility of massive reversals and psychological regressions cannot be precluded any more than Adorno, Horkheimer, and Marcuse could preclude the emergence of a new socialization type

that would make the categories of psychoanalysis obsolete. The structural parallelism between these claims needs to be taken seriously. In order to establish that motivational crises can occur such as to trigger legitimation crises, Habermas has to claim that according to the remnant of bourgeois ideologies, the decline of civic, professional, and familial privatisms can be reversed only at the cost of psychological regressions; but he also admits that these ideologies have become so reified that new patterns of individual and collective identity-forms such as would uncouple power from truth, authority from belief in its legitimacy, and social value from meaning may emerge. This new socialization type would mean that social systems constitute their identities independently of the individuation of their members. The consequence of societal rationalization, then, would not be socialization without repression, but socialization without individuation (LC, pp. 117ff.).

100. For an earlier formulation of this objection, cf. S. Benhabib, "Modernity and the Aporias of Critical Theory," *Telos*, p. 54.

8. Toward a Communicative Ethics and Autonomy

1. Herbert Schnädelbach, "Transformation der Kritischen Theorie," *Philosophische Rundschau*, p. 178, my translation.

2. T. McCarthy, "Rationality and Relativism," p. 59.

3. See Adorno's critique of Husserl in *Zur Metakritik der Erkenntnistheorie;* Max Horkheimer, "Zum Rationalismusstreit in der gegenwärtigen Philosophie," ZfS 1934:1–53, esp. 40ff.

4. See Richard Rorty, *Philosophy and the Mirror of Nature*, in particular part three, ch. 7, pp. 313ff., "From Epistemology to Hermeneutics."

5. See the collectively produced and authored volumes in the 1930s, *Studien über Autorität und Familie, Schriften des Instituts für Sozialforschung;* T. W. Adorno, Else Frankel-Brunswick, Daniel J. Levinson, and R. Nevitt Sanford, *The Authoritarian Personality*.

6. Habermas, "Die Philosophie als Platzhalter und Interpret," in *Moralbewusstsein und kommunikatives Handeln*, pp. 9–29.

7. See Habermas, "The University in a Democracy: Democratization of the University," "Technical Progress and the Social Life-World," and "The Scientization of Politics and Public Opinion," all in *Toward a Rational Society;* and "Dogmatism, Reason and Decision: On Theory and Practice in Our Scientific Civilization," in *Theory and Practice*, English ed., pp. 253–83.

8. "This *dialectic of potential and will* takes place today without reflection in accordance with interests for which public justification is neither demanded nor permitted. Only if we could elaborate this dialectic with political consciousness could we succeed in directing the mediation of technical progress and the conduct of social life, which until now has occurred as an extension of natural history. . . . The substance of domination is not dissolved by the power of technical control. To the

contrary, the former can simply hide behind the latter. The irrationality of domination, which today has become a collective peril to life, could be mastered only by the development of a political decision-making process tied to the principle of general discussion free from domination. Our only hope for the rationalization of the power structure lies in the conditions that favor political power for thought developing through dialogue" (Habermas, "Technical Progress and the Social Life-World," *Toward a Rational Society*, p. 61).

9. There is a strong and a weak version of this claim. The strong thesis is the one given in the text; the weak thesis claims that only the paradigmatic case of speech acts, namely, those aimed at *Verständigung*—reaching an understanding—display these four presuppositions most fully; see the exchange between McCarthy and Habermas in Willi Oelmuller, ed., *Transzendentalphilosophische Normenbegründung*, pp. 135–38.

10. Habermas, Introduction to the new edition, *Theorie und Praxis*, p. 25; the English translation renders this as the "virtualization of constraints on action," p. 18. I believe the word "suspension" better captures the Husserlian mode of phrasing this problem. Indeed, the rest of the passage quotes Husserl: "To speak as Husserl does, in discourse we bracket the general thesis" (*ibid.*). For general accounts of universal pragmatics, see further Habermas, "What Is Universal Pragmatics?" in *Communication and the Evolution of Society*, pp. 1–69.

11. Habermas points out that the establishment of the condition of truthfulness (*Wahrhaftigkeit*) as a validity claim entails placing discourses in action contexts; see Habermas, "Vorbereitende Bemerkungen zu einer Theorie der kommunikativen Kompetenz," in Habermas and Luhmann, *Theorie der Gesellschaft oder Sozialtechnologie*, pp. 138ff. In ThCA, Habermas introduces the category of an "explicative" discourse that concerns itself with the condition of comprehensibility. Such discourses include translations, interpretations, philological and textual clarifications, and the like (pp. 22ff.).

12. Habermas, "Wahrheitstheorien," p. 256, my translation; abbreviated in text as Wth.

13. That the requirement of "suspension" obscures rather than illuminates the relationship between action (*Handlung*) and discourse (*Diskurs*) has been successfully argued by Herbert Schnädelbach in *Reflexion und Diskurs*, pp. 135–71. I return to this problem in section 2.

14. R. Spaemann, "Die Utopie der Herrschaftsfreiheit"; Quentin Skinner, "Habermas's Reformation."

15. Raymond Geuss, *The Ideal of a Critical Theory*, p. 67.

16. Habermas, "Vorbereitende Bemerkungen," p. 139.

17. See McCarthy, *The Critical Theory of Jürgen Habermas*, pp. 303ff.

18. John B. Thompson discusses the lack of attention to the "evidential dimension" of truth in Habermas' theory; see John B. Thompson, "Universal Pragmatics," p. 130.

19. Although it would seem to be necessary for his ethical theory,

Habermas has never undertaken an explicit confrontation with ethical naturalism, either of the intuitionist or of the utilitarian sort. He has simply assumed that the main rival of cognitivism in ethics is decisionism, without distinguishing, however, his position from other rival cognitivist-naturalist accounts; see the reference to the ancient tradition of "natural law" as the representative of this in Wth, pp. 226–27, translated by McCarthy in *The Critical Theory of Jürgen Habermas*, p. 311.

20. *Ibid.*

21. Habermas, "Moral Development and Ego Identity," *Communication and the Evolution of Society*, p. 89.

22. Habermas, "Einige Bemerkungen zum Problem der Begründung von Werturteilen," p. 92.

23. Cf. one of the earliest formulations of this: "What raises us out of nature is the only thing whose nature we can know: *language*. Through its structure, autonomy and responsibility are posited for us" (Habermas, Appendix, "Knowledge and Human Interests: A General Perspective," in *Knowledge and Human Interests*, p. 314). Also cf.: "The ideal speech situation would be best compared with a transcendental illusion, if this illusion were not to owe its existence to an impermissible transgression (as in the use of the categories that transcend experience) but would also be the constitutive condition of rational speech. The anticipation of the ideal speech situation has the significance of a constitutive illusion for every possible communication; it is simultaneously the anticipation of a life-form" (Wth, p. 259, my translation).

24. For this formulation, see Habermas, "Vorbereitende Bemerkungen," p. 114.

25. For this formulation, see Wth, pp. 226–27.

26. Karl-Heinz Ilting, "Geltung als Konsens," *Neue Hefte für Philosophie*, pp. 22–50. Although these formulations may not appear very different, in fact they are, and their difference is significant for Habermas' attempt to ground ethical norms. If the ideal speech situation is understood as signifying the possibility of linguistic communication in general, then Habermas would want to ground ethical norms upon a very strong and incontrovertible basis. If, on the other hand, it is admitted that the ideal speech situation refers to *idealized* processes of communication, then the grounding of ethical norms is less strong and incontrovertible, for the question remains open as to how "ideal" discourses are. I hope the following discussion will clarify the strong and weak justification strategies outlined here.

27. Habermas, "Historical Materialism and the Development of Normative Structures," in *Communication and the Evolution of Society*, p. 97.

28. The following discussion is a condensed summary of the first half of my article "The Methodological Illusions of Modern Political Theory," *Neue Hefte für Philosophie*, pp. 47–74.

29. Cf. also Steven Lukes, "Of Gods and Demons," pp. 134–49; Iris

Young, "Toward a Critical Theory of Justice," *Social Theory and Practice* pp. 279–302.

30. Rawls, *A Theory of Justice*, pp. 17–22, 31ff., and 139ff.

31. Habermas, "Vorbereitende Bemerkungen," pp. 139ff.

32. These criticisms can be divided into two groups: according to the first, even the minimal interpretation of the original position, under the constraints of a "thin theory of the good"—the assumption that individuals are to be considered as moral persons whose ends are not ranked in value—is not minimal; see Thomas Nagel, "Rawls on Justice," pp. 97ff. According to the second line of criticism, not the minimal but the privileged description of the original position constitutes the problem. These critics question the so-called neutrality of Rawls' theory of primary goods (Schwartz); Rawls' criterion of intersubjective comparison in terms of average income (Wolff); the plausibility of Rawls' moral psychology, which presupposes risk aversion (Barber); and the game-theoretic and economic definition of rationality (Höffe). See A. Schwartz, "Moral Neutrality and Primary Goods," *Ethics* (July 1973), p. 83; B. Barber, "Justifying Justice: Problems of Psychology, Politics, and Measurement in Rawls," in Norman Daniel, ed., *Reading Rawls* (New York: Oxford University Press, 1975); R. P. Wolff, *Understanding Rawls;* Ottfried Höffe, *Ethik und Politik*, pp. 227–43.

33. One of the preconditions of the ideal speech situation is that "the speakers should deceive neither themselves nor others about their intentions," (Habermas, "Vorbereitende Bemerkungen," p. 138); the reciprocity and symmetry conditions require that participants should "have equal chances as *actors*" (*ibid.*) to use representatives. Cf. also Wth, p. 256.

34. Rawls, *A Theory of Justice*, p. 20.

35. Habermas, "Vorbereitende Bemerkungen," p. 138; Wth, p. 258.

36. There is a great deal of sociological evidence that all known societies regulate the relations of their members according to norms of reciprocity, but as Lévi-Strauss' discussion in *The Elementary Structures of Kinship* brilliantly shows, the question of who is to be considered the "relevant other" with whom one enters into a relation of reciprocity is not answered by establishing the presence of such a rule. The determination of the "relevant other" (in this case the males who exchange their women) presupposes what I call the "semantic" dimension of reciprocity, perhaps better referred to as the "symbolic" dimension.

37. Albrecht Wellmer, *Praktische Philosophie und Theorie der Gesellschaft*, p. 50.

38. Wth, p. 246; "Moral Development and Ego Identity," in *Communication and the Evolution of Society*, pp. 69–94; and "A Reply to My Critics," in Thompson and Held, eds., *Habermas: Critical Debates*, p. 253.

39. Habermas, "Historical Materialism and the Development of Normative Structures," in *Communication and the Evolution of Society*, pp. 116ff.

40. McCarthy, "Rationality and Relativism," p. 73.

41. *Ibid.*, p. 74.

42. Habermas, "Diskursethik," pp. 90ff.

43. Karl-Otto Apel, "Das Apriori der Kommunikationsgemeinschaft und die Grundlagen der Ethik," in *Transformation der Philosophie*, pp. 405ff.; English trans., pp. 225–301.

44. Habermas, "Diskursethik," pp. 62–63.

45. Apel, "Das Apriori der Kommunikationsgemeinschaft," pp. 394 and 397.

46. *Ibid.*, pp. 414ff.

47. *Ibid.*, pp. 432–33.

48. Apel and Habermas disagree about the "beginnings" of argument. Habermas has criticized Apel for wanting to make the conditions of normative speech binding only for those who take the "reflective turn" and who engage in argumentation; by contrast, Habermas would like to maintain that these presuppositions are always already presupposed in communicative speech (LC, p. 159*n* 16). As the next section will indicate, I do not think that Habermas himself has dispensed with what he names "the decisionistic problem" in communicative ethics. Some kind of "reflective turn" is required in order to see that the rules of discourse are normatively binding upon us in the strong sense.

49. Habermas, "Diskursethik," MukH, p. 98.

50. Habermas clarifies the meaning of "reconstruction" in moral theory in MukH, pp. 127ff.

51. This is, of course, a controversial claim. It means that neither moral sentiments nor moral virtues constitute the object domain of such a moral theory. I am not convinced, although I will not argue for this here, that ethical cognitivism need be interpreted in such a radical fashion that moral affect and disposition fall outside the realm of moral theory altogether. Actually, Habermas himself brings them back via not moral but socialization theory. See section 3 for the place of socialization theory in communicative ethics.

52. Habermas, "Moralbewusstsein und kommunikatives Handeln," MukH, p. 128.

53. Habermas, "Diskursethik," pp. 103ff. and 127.

54. It should be pointed out that this "good reasons approach" does not suffice to exclude *all* of the kinds of reasons Habermas wants to exclude. In certain cultures, theological imperatives may very well constitute good reasons, while a claim like "X is good for humans in general" may well function as an acceptable reason in certain argumentations. I want to emphasize once more that the analysis of rules of argumentation is not sufficient to deal with problems about what counts as *reasons* or as *evidence* in such arguments.

55. J. Silber, "Procedural Formalism in Kant's Ethics."

56. Kant, *Anthropologie in pragmatischer Hinsicht*, as quoted in Silber, "Procedural Formalism in Kant's Ethics," p. 202.

57. Silber, "Procedural Formalism in Kant's Ethics," p. 216.
58. As quoted *ibid.*, p. 202.
59. Alan Donagan, *The Theory of Morality*, pp. 37ff.; Alan Gewirth, *Reason and Morality*, pp. 48ff.
60. Habermas, "Labor and Interaction: Remarks on Hegel's Jena *Philosophy of Mind*," in *Theory and Practice*, pp. 155ff.
61. McCarthy, *The Critical Theory of Jürgen Habermas*, p. 326.
62. See Stephen Toulmin, *The Uses of Argument*, pp. 99ff.; Habermas, Wth, pp. 244ff.
63. Habermas, Wth, p. 245.
64. *Ibid.*
65. *Ibid.*, p. 251.
66. *Ibid.*, p. 252.
67. I thank Paul Stern for pointing out to me that the universalizability principle can be interpreted as one operating either in the context of the logic of justification or the logic of discovery. In the particular article in question, one could cogently interpret this formula as functioning as part of the logic of discovery in enabling participants to follow the line of reasoning: (1) we agree that we all have a shared need for the flexible use of scarce resources; (2) therefore we must institutionalize practices such as make this possible; (3) the practice of lending and borrowing fits this purpose; (4) hence we must respect the requirements of this practice. The universalizability principle would then function as a kind of legitimating transition from "is"—a need in this case—to an "ought" (we must act such as to fulfill this need). Although helpful, this reformulation of the principle as one of logic of moral discovery does not settle the issue, for the question is, how do we come to the agreement that we all share a need to the flexible use of scarce resources in the first place? If the differences of wealth between us are so great that I would actually stand to lose by sharing with you the flexible use of my scarce resources, then what should compel me to agree that this is a shared need? It would seem that it is exactly at this point, when a transition needs to be made from a self-regarding or egotistical point of view to one that is capable of being shared by all, that universalizability must play a role.
68. Rousseau, *The Social Contract*, pp. 30–31.
69. Habermas, MukH, p. 105. Those familiar with distinctions made in Anglo-American ethical theory will notice how confusing this formulation is in that it appears to combine a universalist-deontological with a utilitarian-teleological approach. Cf. further, "Only an actually carried out discourse offers any guarantee of the possibility of objecting to any norm that does not fulfill the following condition: that the consequences and side-effects for the satisfaction of the interests of *every* individual, which are expected to result from a *general* observance of the norm, can be accepted with good reason by *all*" ("Reply to My Critics," p. 257).

70. Karl-Otto Apel defines such pragmatic presuppositions as follows: "If I cannot challenge something without actual self-contradiction and cannot deductively ground it without formal-logical *petitio principii*, then that thing belongs precisely to those transcendental-pragmatic presuppositions of argumentation which one must always have accepted, if the language game of argumentation is expected to retain its significance. One can, therefore, call this transcendental-pragmatic way of arguing the *sense-critical [sinn-kritische] form of the fundamental grounding.*" "The Problem of Philosophical Fundamental-Grounding in Light of a Transcendental Pragmatic of Language," K. R. Pavlovic, trans., *Man and World* (1975), no. 18, p. 264; emphasis in the text.

71. See R. Alexy, "Eine Theorie des praktischen Diskurses," in W. Oelmuller, ed., *Normenbegründung, Normendurchsetzung* (Paderborn: Ferdinand Schoningh, 1978), pp. 22–59; English translation forthcoming in S. Benhabib and F. Dallmayer, eds., *The Communicative Ethics Controversy* (Cambridge, Mass.: MIT Press).

72. "βαρβαρος" (Barbaros) means someone who speaks unintelligibly; one who speaks a foreign language; strange and un-Greek; see W. Gemoll, ed., *Griechisch-deutsches Schul und Handwörterbuch*, 9th ed. (Munich: G. Freytag, 1965), p. 153. It is this distinction between those who speak Greek and who thus belong to a common culture, and those who speak a language unintelligible to the Greeks, which leads Aristotle, in my judgment, to argue in the *Politics* that the practice of slavery among the Hellenes should be abolished. *Politics*, in *The Basic Works of Aristotle*, p. 1134, 1255a29ff.

73. While commentators like H. J. Paton resist the suggestion that Kantian ethics is legalistic (see *The Categorical Imperative*, pp. 75ff.), they have a difficult time explaining why the metaphor of law and lawgovernedness plays such an important role in his ethical formulations. As Ernst Cassirer has argued, it is not at all implausible to point to the tremendous impact that Rousseau and the French Revolution had on Kant's thinking, and to search for the origins of the categorical imperative in Rousseau's concept of the general will (Cassirer, *Rousseau, Kant, Goethe*).

74. Karl-Otto Apel, "Kant, Hegel und das aktuelle Problem der normativen Grundlagen von Recht und Moral."

75. Rawls, *A Theory of Justice*, pp. 60ff.

76. The possibility of such a reconciliation is suggested by Habermas' discussion and positive evaluation of Mead's reformulation of Kant; cf. the statement "To the extent that language asserts itself as the principle of sociation [*Vergesellschaftung*], the conditions of sociality converge with conditions of communicatively asserted intersubjectivity" (ThdkH 2:143).

77. LC, p. 108; emphasis in the text. In an interesting article, "Habermas on Truth and Justice," Philip Petit distinguishes between two senses of consensus in Habermas' theory. According to the "distrib-

utive" sense of consensus, a proposition admits of consensus if and only if each person assents to it, whether or not after discussion with others and whether or not in awareness of what others think. According to the collective sense, a proposition admits of consensus if the people involved discuss it as a group and come to a unanimous decision about it. Petit comments that "it is quite gratuitous to add the requirement that the agreement must be achieved in collective discussion and it is therefore quite unnecessary for an upholder of the theory to investigate how best to guard against collective irrationality. . . . There is no reason to say that assent must be forthcoming as part of a collective consensus achieved in an ideal speech situation; it may coincide with the judgment that would appear on such a strong occasion, but that is neither here nor there" (p. 216). I agree with Petit that the collective sense of consensus has problems—epistemic as well as political ones. Yet the distributive sense of consensus Petit attributes to Habermas cannot be made compatible with a discourse theory of truth and justice, for the way he interprets this, it can very well be attained by a solitary thinker, thinking rationally for all. Habermas' valid point is that the model of the solitary thinker must be replaced by the dialogic mode of give-and-take among a community of investigators. Thus the dilemma seems to be to give the discourse theory a formulation that would not fall into the strong sense of collectivism outlined by Petit, but which would neither revert back to the model of a group of brilliant mathematicians, each solving in silence a problem set in front of him.

78. Rousseau, *The Social Contract*, p. 31.

79. See the formulation in Habermas, "Legitimation Problems in the Modern State," in *Communication and the Evolution of Society*, pp. 204ff.

80. Habermas, LC, p. 112.

81. Habermas, "Legitimation Problems in the Modern State," p. 199.

82. Raymond Geuss, *The Idea of a Critical Theory*, pp. 65ff.

83. For Habermas' critique of Rousseau, see "Legitimation Problems in the Modern State," pp. 185ff.

84. For Habermas' critique of Apel, see LC, p. 159n16.; for the critique of Lorenzen, see "Zwei Bemerkungen zum praktischen Diskurs," pp. 109ff., and LC, pp. 109ff.

85. Paul Lorenzen, *Normative Logic and Ethics*, p. 74; Otto Schwemmer, *Philosophie der Praxis*, p. 194.

86. Apel, "Das Apriori der Kommunikationsgemeinschaft," pp. 397ff.

87. Habermas, LC, p. 159, emphasis in the text.

88. Habermas, "Diskursethik," p. 110.

89. Habermas, "Reply to My Critics," p. 253.

90. Jack Mendelson, "The Habermas-Gadamer Debate," *New German Critique*, p. 73.

91. *Ibid.*; see also Habermas' own distinction between history and evolution, "Geschichte und Evolution."

92. See Andrew Arato's discussion of the problem of East European

type social formations, "Critical Sociology and Authoritarian State Socialism."

93. Rüdiger Bubner, "Habermas's Concept of Critical Theory," p. 49.

94. This neglect of the intimate sphere and the morality entailed by it is a necessary consequence of a communicative ethics that focuses on the public dimension of social life alone; see further my criticism of this bias in the following section.

95. Habermas, ThdkH 2:251ff.; "Reply to My Critics," pp. 254ff.

96. See Carol Gilligan and J. M. Murphy, "Moral Development in Late Adolescence and Adulthood," *Human Development*, pp. 77–104; Lawrence Kohlberg, "A Reply to Owen Flanagan," *Ethics*, pp. 513–28.

97. Stanley Cavell, *The Claim of Reason*, p. 265.

98. See also Richard Bernstein, *Beyond Objectivism and Relativism*, pp. 207ff., for a discussion of Arendt's concept of judgment.

99. Habermas, "Moralbewusstsein und kommunikatives Handeln," MukH, pp. 197ff.

100. Habermas, "Reply to My Critics," p. 251.

101. Habermas, "On the Actuality of Walter Benjamin: Consciousness-Raising or Rescuing Critique," in *Philosophical-Political Profiles*, p. 156. I have modified Lawrence's translation such as to render "Unterdrückung" in this context as "oppression" rather than "repression"; cf. "Zur Aktualität Walter Benjamin: Bewusstmachende oder rettende Kritik," in *Kultur und Kritik* (Frankfurt: Suhrkamp, 1973), p. 340.

102. Habermas, "On the Actuality of Walter Benjamin," p. 156.

103. Joel Whitebook, "Saving the Subject," *Telos*, pp. 81–82.

104. Habermas, "Reply to My Critics," pp. 166 and 262.

105. Habermas, "On the Actuality of Walter Benjamin," p. 158.

106. For an early formulation of the dialogic principle, see Habermas, "Labor and Interaction: Remarks on Hegel's Jena *Philosophy of Mind*," in *Theory and Practice*, pp. 142ff.

107. Habermas, "Introduction: Some Difficulties in the Attempt to Link Theory and Practice," *Theory and Practice*, p. 24; McCarthy, *The Critical Theory of Jürgen Habermas*, pp. 94ff.

108. Cf. "Moreover, evolution-theoretical statements on contemporary social formations have a direct practical relation insofar as they serve for the diagnosis of developmental problems. Thus the necessary restriction to retrospective explanation of the historical material is abandoned in favor of a *retrospective that is designed from action perspectives:* the diagnostician of our times takes the fictional standpoint of the evolution-theoretical explanation of a past lying in the future" (Habermas, "History and Evolution," p. 44).

109. Only insofar as we can assume that empirical subjects in the present can discover themselves in this presentation of the past can we say that "theories of evolution and the explanation of epoch-making developmental leaps based on them can enter those 'discourses' in which competing identity-projections are 'subject to debate'" (*ibid.*). My

question is: whose identity? Of men or of women? Of Jews or of Gentiles? Of Westerners or of Africans? While it is not incumbent upon a theoretical social scientist engaged in explaining social evolution to necessarily offer an answer to these questions, it is nonetheless necessary to specify if these theoretical constructions succeed or fail when one attempts to mediate them with the formative history of specific groups. The problem will not go away by distinguishing between history and evolution, because the suspicion remains that this evolution is really the logic of the history of one group alone.

110. Cf. the following statement of a woman historian: "Once we look to history for an understanding of women's situation, we are, of course, already assuming that women's situation is a social matter. But history, as we first come to it, did not seem to confirm this awareness. . . . The moment this is done—the moment one assumes that women are part of humanity in the fullest sense—the period or set of events with which we deal takes on a wholly different character or meaning than the accepted one. Indeed what emerges is a fairly regular pattern of relative loss of status for women precisely in those periods of so-called progressive change. . . . Our notion of so-called progressive development, such as classical Athenian civilization, the Renaissance and the French Revolution, undergo a startling reevaluation. For women 'progress' in Athens meant concubinage and confinement of citizen wives to the gynaceum. In Renaissance Europe it meant domestication of the bourgeois wife and escalation of witchcraft persecution which crossed class lines. And the Revolution expressly excluded women from its liberty, equality and 'fraternity.' Suddenly we see these ages with a new double vision—and each eye sees a different picture" (J. Kelly-Gadoll, "The Social Relations of the Sexes," pp. 810–11).

111. Habermas, Wth, p. 252.

112. Rawls, A Theory of Justice, pp. 24 and 513ff.

113. Döbert, Habermas, and Nunner-Winkler, eds., Introduction, Entwicklung des Ichs, p. 12.

114. Habermas, "Moral Development and Ego Identity," in Communication and the Evolution of Society, p. 93.

115. Habermas, ThCA, 1:41ff.

116. Kant, Critique of Practical Reason, p. 171.

117. Even Alasdair MacIntyre's definition of the virtues and the "good life" does not really reverse the Copernican Revolution, insofar as MacIntyre gives a "meta-definition" in each case that is compatible with a variety of practices and ways of life; also, there is a curious "functionalism" in MacIntyre's argument in this regard. He often does not seem to distinguish between what makes a social practice work and what individuals can choose; see MacIntyre, After Virtue, pp. 169–89 and 203–4.

118. Carol Gilligan, In a Different Voice, pp. 224–64.

119. Herbert Marcuse, One-Dimensional Man, pp. 4ff., 245.

120. Jürgen Habermas, Sylvia Bovenschen, et al., Gespräche mit Herbert Marcuse, "Theorie und Politik," pp. 30ff.

121. Hobbes, "Philosophical Rudiments Concerning Government and Society," 2:109.

122. Habermas, "A Reply to My Critics," p. 262.

123. Habermas, ThdkH 2:144–45.

124. The "suppression" of this standpoint by the tradition of modern philosophy is, without a doubt, also a consequence of the epistemic and social exclusion of women's voice and activity from the public sphere, and their denigration. Although I agree with the observation of feminist writers like Gilligan and Chodorow that the "relational" perspective of moral life, implied in taking the standpoint of the concrete other, is one that women, because of patterns of personality formation and activities confined to nurturance, love, and care, are more prone to assume and identify with, I want to restrict neither the capacity nor the willingness to assume the standpoint of the concrete other to women and the private sphere alone. See Gilligan, *In a Different Voice*, pp. 16–17; N. Chodorow, *The Reproduction of Mothering* (Berkeley and Los Angeles: University of California Press, 1978). The issues involved here point not only to a "gender gap," but to profound transformations in the nature of public and civic life in modern societies such that the standpoint of the concrete other has been banned from the light of the public to the dark recesses of the household. Aristotle, for example, crowns his discussion in the *Ethics* with a discussion of friendship, and claims that legislators most jealously guard and seek to further this sentiment among citizens (in *The Basic Works of Aristotle*, book VIII, ch. 9, pp. 1068ff.).

125. In an interesting discussion of Gilligan's moral theory, Gertrud Nunner-Winkler points out that the distinction between an ethics of principle and an ethics of care is not really a distinction between two types of ethics, but one between two types of duties—perfect and imperfect ones. She maintains that an ethics of justice formulates perfect duties which are duties of omission (do not kill, cheat, etc.), but that imperfect duties, like the wish to care for and help others, to meet obligations and responsibilities, are more properly what Gilligan names an "ethics of care." Nunner-Winkler observes that these duties necessarily require contextualization and the exercise of judgment concerning particulars. In fact, she makes the stronger claim that a universalist-ethical orientation necessarily requires situational contextualization, since no formal principle can yield a maxim of action without such additional considerations. G. Nunner-Winkler, "Two Moralities? A Critical Discussion of an Ethic of Care and Responsibility Versus an Ethic of Rights and Justice," in W. M. Kurtines and J. L. Gewirtz, eds., *Morality, Moral Behavior, and Moral Development*, pp. 348–61 (New York: Wiley, 1984).

I agree with Nunner-Winkler that to speak of two "ethics" rather than of "ethical orientations" in this case may be misleading; furthermore, the emphasis on contextualization is salutary. Yet, even when one accepts a universalist-ethical standpoint, as I do, questions remain as to what "taking the standpoint of the other" means in moral judgment. The distinction between the "generalized" and the "concrete" other does not replace universalism in ethical theory, it is only intended to suggest that there is usually an unspoken bias in defining the "generalized other" as a right-bearing, adult male whose concrete individuality appears irrelevant to us. I have tried to show how this bias has been at work in modern moral and political theory since Hobbes, and that it certainly has not been explicitly repudiated by Rawls, Kohlberg, and even Habermas. For a further discussion, see my "The Generalized and the Concrete Other: "The Kohlberg-Gilligan Debate and Feminist Theory," in *Praxis International*, Vol. 5, No. 4 (January 1986), pp. 38–60 and in the Proceedings of the Conference on "Women and Morality," E. F. Kittay and D. Meyers, eds. (New Jersey: Rowman and Allenheld, 1987).

126. Baudrillard, *The Mirror of Production;* Giddens, *A Contemporary Critique of Historical Materialism;* Gorz, *Adieu au Proletariat.*

127. "For what is characteristic of our contemporary situation is not just the playing out of powerful forces that are beyond our control, or the spread of disciplinary technics that always elude our grasp, but a paradoxical situation where power creates counter-power (resistance) and reveals the vulnerability of power, where the very forces that undermine and inhibit communal life also create new, and frequently unpredictable, forms of solidarity" (Bernstein, *Beyond Objectivism and Relativism*, p. 228).

128. Ernst Bloch, *Naturrecht und menschliche Würde*, p. 13, my translation.

BIBLIOGRAPHY

Adorno, Theodor. "Die Aktualität der Philosophie." *Philosophische Frühschriften. In Gesammelte Schriften*, Rolf Tiedemann, ed., 1:325ff. Frankfurt: Suhrkamp, 1973. Translated by B. Snow, "The Actuality of Philosophy." *Telos* (Spring 1977), no. 31, pp. 120–33.

Adorno, Theodor. *Minima Moralia*. London: New Left Books, 1974.

Adorno, Theodor. *Negative Dialektik*. Frankfurt: Suhrkamp, 1973. English translation: *Negative Dialectics*, E. B. Ashton, trans. New York: Seabury Press, 1973.

Adorno, Theodor. "Die revidierte Psychoanalyse." In Max Horkheimer and Theodor Adorno, *Sociologica II: Reden und Vorträge*. Frankfurter Beiträge zur Soziologie, 10:94ff. Frankfurt, 1962. Translated by I. Wolfrath, "Sociology and Psychology." *New Left Review* (December 1967/January 1968), nos. 46/47, pp. 67–80 and 79–90.

Adorno, Theodor. *Soziologische Schriften*. Frankfurt: Suhrkamp, 1979.

Adorno, Theodor. *Zur Metakritik der Erkenntnistheorie. In Gesammelte Schriften*, Gretel Adorno and Rolf Tiedemann, eds., 5:7–247. Frankfurt: Suhrkamp, 1975. English translation: *Against Epistemology*. W. Domingo, trans. Cambridge, Mass.: MIT Press, 1982.

Adorno, Theodor and Max Horkheimer. *Dialektik der Aufklärung*. 7th ed. Frankfurt: Fischer, 1980. English translation: *Dialectic of Enlightenment*. John Cumming, trans. New York: Herder and Herder, 1972.

Adorno, Theodor, Else Frankel-Brunswick, Daniel J. Levinson, and R. Nevitt Sanford. *The Authoritarian Personality*. New York and London: Norton, 1982. First published by the American Jewish Committee, 1950.

Althusser, Louis. *Reading Capital.* Ben Brewster, trans. London: New Left Books, 1970.

Anderson, Perry. *Considerations on Western Marxism.* Atlantic Highlands, N.J.: Humanities Press, 1976.

Apel, Karl-Otto. *Transformation der Philosophie.* Frankfurt: Suhrkamp, 1976. Selected English translation: *Toward a Transformation of Philosophy.* Glyn Adey and David Frisby, trans. London: Routledge and Kegan Paul, 1980.

Apel, Karl-Otto. "Kant, Hegel und das aktuelle Problem der normativen Grundlagen von Recht und Moral." In D. Henrich, ed., *Kant oder Hegel: Über Formen der Begründung in der Philosophie.* Stuttgart: Klett-Cotta, 1983.

Arato, Andrew. "Critical Sociology and Authoritarian State Socialism." In Thompson and Held, eds., *Habermas: Critical Debates* (q.v.), pp. 196–219.

Arato, Andrew and Paul Breines. *The Young Lukács and the Origins of Western Marxism.* New York: Pluto Press, 1979.

Arato, Andrew and Eike Gebhardt, eds. *The Essential Frankfurt School Reader.* New York: Urizen Books, 1978.

Arendt, Hannah. *The Human Condition.* 8th ed. Chicago: University of Chicago Press, 1973.

Arendt, Hannah. "Tradition and the Modern Age." In *Between Past and Future.* Cleveland: World, 1968.

Aristotle. *The Basic Works of Aristotle.* Richard McKeon, ed. New York: Random House, 1966.

Avineri, Shlomo. *The Social and Political Thought of Karl Marx.* Cambridge: Cambridge University Press, 1970.

Baier, Kurt. *The Moral Point of View.* Abridged ed. New York: Random House, 1965.

Baudrillard, Jean. *The Mirror of Production.* Mark Poster, trans. St. Louis: Telos Press, 1975.

Baumeister, Thomas and Jens Kulenkampff. "Geschichtsphilosophie und philosophische Ästhetik: Zu Adornos ästhetischer Theorie." *Neue Hefte für Philosophie* (1974), no. 6. pp. 74ff.

Bekker, K. *Marx' philosophische Entwicklung, sein Verhältnis zu Hegel.* Zurich and New York: Oprecht, 1940.

Bell, Daniel. *The Cultural Contradictions of Capitalism.* New York: Harper and Row, 1977.

Benhabib, Seyla. "The Logic of Civil Society: A Reconsideration of Hegel and Marx." *Philosophy and Social Criticism* (Summer 1982), pp. 149–67.

Benhabib, Seyla. "The Methodological Illusions of Modern Political Theory: The Case of Rawls and Habermas." *Neue Hefte für Philosophie* (Spring 1982), no. 21, pp. 47–74.

Benhabib, Seyla. "Modernity and the Aporias of Critical Theory." *Telos* (Fall 1981), no. 49, pp. 39–59.

Benhabib, Seyla. "Obligation, Contract, and Exchange: On the Significance of Hegel's Abstract Right." In Z. A. Pelczynski, ed., *The State and Civil Society*, 2:159–78. Cambridge: Cambridge University Press, 1984.

Benhabib, Seyla. "Rationality and Social Action: Critical Reflections on Max Weber's Methodological Writings." *The Philosophical Forum* (July 1981), 12(4):356–75.

Benjamin, J. "Die Antinomien des patriarchalischen Denkens." In W. Bonss and A. Honneth, eds., *Sozialforschung als Kritik* (q.v.), pp. 426–56. An earlier version of this article appeared as "The End of Internalization: Adorno's Social Psychology." *Telos* (Summer 1977), no. 32, pp. 42–64.

Berger, Johannes. "Die Versprachlichung des Sakralen und die Entsprachlichung der Ökonomie." *Zeitschrift für Soziologie* (October 1982), 11(4):353–65.

Berman, Marshall. *All That Is Solid Melts Into Air: The Experience of Modernity.* New York: Simon and Schuster, 1982.

Bernstein, Richard. *Beyond Objectivism and Relativism.* Philadelphia: University of Pennsylvania Press, 1983.

Bernstein, Richard. *Praxis and Action.* Philadelphia: University of Pennsylvania Press, 1971.

Bernstein, Richard. *The Restructuring of Social and Political Theory.* Philadelphia: University of Pennsylvania Press, 1976.

Bieri, Peter and R. P. Horstmann, eds. *Transcendental Arguments and Science: Essays in Epistemology.* Dordrecht: Reidel, 1979.

Bloch, Ernst. *Naturrecht und menschliche Würde.* Frankfurt: Suhrkamp, 1977.

Blumenberg, Hans. *The Legitimacy of the Modern Age.* R. Wallace, trans. Cambridge, Mass.: MIT Press, 1983.

Bonss, Wolfgang. *Die Einübung des Tatsachenblicks.* Frankfurt: Suhrkamp, 1982.

Bonss, Wolfgang. "Kritische Theorie und empirische Sozialforschung: Anmerkungen zu einem Fallbeispiel." Introduction to Erich Fromm, *Arbeiter und Angestellte am Vorabend des dritten Reichs: Eine sozialpsychologische Untersuchung*, W. Bonss, ed. Stuttgart: Deutsche Verlagsanstalt, 1980.

Bonss, Wolfgang. "Psychoanalyse als Wissenschaft und Kritik: Zur Freudrezeption der Frankfurter Schule." In Bonss and Honneth, eds., *Sozialforschung als Kritik* (q.v.), pp. 367ff.

Bonss, Wolfgang and A. Honneth, eds. *Sozialforschung als Kritik*. Frankfurt: Suhrkamp, 1982.

Bonss, Wolfgang and Norbert Schindler. "Kritische Theorie als interdisziplinärer Materialismus." In W. Bonss and A. Honneth, eds., *Sozialforschung als Kritik* (q.v.), pp. 33–67.

Bourdieu, P. and J. C. Passeron. "Sociology and Philosophy in France Since 1945: Death and Resurrection of a Philosophy Without Subject." *Social Research* (Spring 1983), 34(1): 162–212.

Bradley, F. H. "My Station and Its Duties." *Ethical Studies*. 2d ed. Oxford: Clarendon Press, 1927.

Brumlik, Micha. "Der revolutionäre Messianismus der Frankfurter Schule." *Merkur* (March 1983), 2(416):228–31.

Bubner, Rüdiger. "Habermas's Concept of Critical Theory." In Thompson and Held, eds., *Habermas: Critical Debates* (q.v.), pp. 42–56.

Bubner, Rüdiger. "Was ist kritische Theorie?" In *Hermeneutik und Ideologiekritik*, pp. 160–210. Frankfurt: Suhrkamp, 1971.

Buchanan, A. *Marx and Justice: The Radical Critique of Liberalism*. Totowa, N.J.: Rowman and Littlefield, 1982.

Buck-Morss, Susan. *The Origin of Negative Dialectics*. New York: Free Press, 1977.

Carlebach, J. *Karl Marx and the Radical Critique of Judaism*. London and Boston: Routledge and Kegan Paul, 1978.

Carr, David. "The Fifth Meditation and Husserl's Cartesianism." *Philosophy and Phenomenological Research* (1973), no. 34, pp. 14–35.

Cassirer, Ernst. *Rousseau, Kant, Goethe*. P. O. Kristeller and J. H. Randall, trans. New York: Harper Torchbooks, 1963.

Castoriadis, C. "From Marx to Aristotle, from Aristotle to Us." *Social Research* (Spring 1978), no. 44, pp. 3–24.

Cavell, Stanley. *The Claim of Reason*. Oxford: Oxford University Press, 1982.

Cloward, Richard and Frances Fox Piven. *Regulating the Poor: The Functions of Public Welfare*. New York: Vintage Books, 1972.

Cohen, Jean. *Class and Civil Society: The Limits of Marxian Critical Theory*. Amherst: University of Massachusetts Press, 1982.

Cohen, Jean. "Why More Political Theory?" *Telos* (Summer 1979) no. 40, pp. 86ff.

Cohen, Jean. "The Subversion of Emancipation." *Social Research* (Winter 1978), no. 45, pp. 789–844.

Derbolav, H. "Hegels Theorie der Handlung." In M. Riedel, ed., *Materialien zu Hegels Rechtsphilosophie*, pp. 201–17. Frankfurt: Suhrkamp, 1975.

Döbert, Rainer. "The Role of Stage-Models Within a Theory of Social Evolution, Illustrated by the European Witch-Craze." In R. Harré and U. J. Ensen, eds., *Studies in the Concept of Evolution*. Brighton: Harvester Press, 1981.

Döbert, R., J. Habermas, G. Nunner-Winkler. *Entwicklung des Ichs*. Köln: , 1977.

Donagan, Alan. *The Theory of Morality*. Chicago: University of Chicago Press, 1977.

Dove, K. L. "Hegel's Phenomenological Method." *Review of Metaphysics* (June 1970), 24(93):615ff.

Dubiel, Helmut. *Wissenschaftsorganisation und politische Erfahrung: Studien zur frühen kritischen Theorie*. Frankfurt: Suhrkamp, 1978. English translation by Benjamin Gregg. Cambridge, Mass.: MIT Press, 1985.

Durkheim, Emile. *Rules of Sociological Method*. In *Emile Durkheim: Selected Writings*, Anthony Giddens, ed. and trans. Cambridge: Cambridge University Press, 1972.

Durkheim, Emile. "Montesquieu's Contribution to the Rise of Social Science." In *Montesquieu and Rousseau: Forerunners of Sociology*, R. Bellah, trans. Ann Arbor: University of Michigan Press, 1960.

Ebeling, Hans, ed. *Subjektivität und Selbsterhaltung*. Frankfurt: Suhrkamp, 1976.

Engel, Stephanie. "Femininity as Tragedy: Re-examining the 'New Narcissism.'" *Socialist Review* (September-October 1980), no. 53, pp. 77–104.

Feuerbach, Ludwig. *The Essence of Christianity.* G. Eliot, trans. New York: Harper and Row, 1975.

Feuerbach, Ludwig, "Principles of the Philosophy of the Future." In *The Fiery Brook: Selected Writings of Ludwig Feuerbach.* Zawar Hanfi, trans. Garden City, N.Y.: Anchor Books, 1972.

Fichte, J. G. *The Science of Right.* A. E. Kruger, trans. New York: Harper and Row, 1970.

Fichte, J. G. *Grundlage der gesammten Wissenschaftslehre.* In *Werke in sechs Bänden,* Fritz Medicus, ed., vol. 1. Darmstadt: Wissenschaftliche Buchgesellschaft, 1962.

Foucault, Michel. *Discipline and Punish: The Birth of the Prison.* Alan Sheridan, trans. New York: Pantheon Books, 1977.

Fraser, Nancy. "Foucault on Modern Power: Empirical Insights and Normative Confusions." *Praxis International* (October 1981) 1(3):272–88.

Freedman, George. *The Political Philosophy of the Frankfurt School.* Ithaca, N.Y.: Cornell University Press, 1981.

Fulda, H.F. "These zur Dialektik als Darstellungsmethode im 'Kapital' von Marx." *Hegel Jahrbuch* (1974), pp. 204–10.

Fulda, H. F. "Zur Logik der Phänomenologie." In Fulda and Henrich, eds., *Materialien zu Hegels "Phänomenologie des Geistes"* (q.v.), pp. 391ff.

Fulda, H. F. and D. Henrich, eds. *Materialien zu Hegels "Phänomenologie des Geistes."* Frankfurt: Suhrkamp, 1973.

Gadamer, Hans-Georg. "Hermeneutics and Social Science." *Cultural Hermeneutics* (1975), no. 2, pp. 307–16.

Gadamer, Hans-Georg. "Rhetorik, Hermeneutik und Ideologiekritik." In Gadamer et al., eds., *Hermeneutik und Ideologiekritik.* Frankfurt: Suhrkamp, 1971.

Gadamer, Hans-Georg. *Truth and Method.* Garrett Barden and John Cumming, trans. New York: Seabury Press, 1975.

Geuss, Raymond. *The Idea of a Critical Theory: Habermas and the Frankfurt School.* Cambridge: Cambridge University Press, 1981.

Gewirth, Alan. *Reason and Morality.* Chicago: University of Chicago Press, 1978.

Giddens, Anthony. *A Contemporary Critique of Historical Materialism.* Berkeley and Los Angeles: University of California Press, 1981.

Giddens, Anthony. "Reason Without Revolution? Habermas's *Theorie des kommunikativen Handelns.*" *Praxis International* (October 1982), 2(3):297-318.

Giegel, Hans Joachim. "Reflexion und Emanzipation." In Gadamer et al., eds., *Hermeneutik und Ideologiekritik*, pp. 249ff. Frankfurt: Suhrkamp, 1971.

Gilligan, Carol. *In a Different Voice: Psychological Theory and Women's Development.* Cambridge, Mass.: Harvard University Press, 1982.

Gilligan, Carol and J. M. Murphy. "Moral Development in Late Adolescence and Adulthood: A Critique and Reconstruction of Kohlberg's Theory." *Human Development* (1980), 23(2): 77–104.

Godelier, Maurice. "Fetishism, Religion, and Marx's General Theories Concerning Ideology." *Perspectives in Marxist Anthropology.* New York: Cambridge University Press, 1977.

Görland, Ingtraud. *Die Kantkritik des jungen Hegel.* Frankfurt: Klostermann, 1966.

Gould, Carol. *Marx's Social Ontology.* Cambridge, Mass.: MIT Press, 1978.

Grenz, F. *Adornos Philosophie in Grundbegriffen. Auflösung einiger Deutungsprobleme.* Frankfurt: Suhrkamp, 1974.

Habermas, Jürgen. *Communication and the Evolution of Society.* Thomas McCarthy, trans. Boston: Beacon Press, 1979.

Habermas, Jürgen. "Dialectics of Rationalization: An Interview." *Telos* (Fall 1981), no. 49, pp. 5–33.

Habermas, Jürgen. "Diskursethik: Notizen zu einem Begründungsprogramm." In *Moralbewusstsein und kommunikatives Handeln* (q.v.), pp. 53–127.

Habermas, Jürgen. "Einige Bemerkungen zum Problem der Begründung von Werturteilen." In *Philosophie und Wissenschaft*, Proceedings of the 9th Deutscher Kongress für Philosophie. Meisenheim am Glan: Anton Hain, 1969.

Habermas, Jürgen. "The Entwinement of Myth and Enlightenment: Rereading *Dialectic of Enlightenment.*" *New German Critique* (Spring-Summer 1982), no. 26, pp. 13–30.

Habermas, Jürgen. "Geschichte und Evolution." In *Zur Rekonstruktion des historischen Materialismus*, pp. 200–60. Frankfurt: Suhrkamp, 1976. Abridged translation: "History and Evolution." David J. Parent, trans. *Telos* (Spring 1979), no. 39, pp. 5–44.

Habermas, Jürgen. Introduction, *Stichworte zur "Geistigen Situation der Zeit."* Frankfurt: Suhrkamp, 1979. English translation: *Observations on the "Spiritual Condition of the Age."* A. Buchwalter, trans. Cambridge, Mass: MIT Press, 1984.

Habermas, Jürgen. *Knowledge and Human Interests.* Jeremy Shapiro, trans. Boston: Beacon Press, 1971.

Habermas, Jürgen. *Legitimationsprobleme im Spätkapitalismus.* Frankfurt: Suhrkamp, 1973. English translation: *Legitimation Crisis.* Thomas McCarthy, trans. Boston: Beacon Press, 1975.

Habermas, Jürgen. "Modernity vs. Post-Modernity." Seyla Benhabib, trans. *New German Critique* (Winter 1981), pp. 3ff.

Habermas, Jürgen. *Moralbewusstsein und kommunikatives Handeln.* Frankfurt: Suhrkamp, 1983.

Habermas, Jürgen. "Die Philosophie als Platzhalter und Interpret." In *Moralbewusstsein und kommunikatives Handeln* (q.v.), pp. 9–29.

Habermas, Jürgen. *Strukturwandel der Öffentlichkeit.* Frankfurt: Suhrkamp, 1974.

Habermas, Jürgen. *Technik und Wissenschaft als "Ideologie."* Frankfurt: Suhrkamp, 1968. English translation: "Technology and Science as 'Ideology.'" Jeremy Shapiro, trans. In *Toward a Rational Society.* Boston: Beacon Press, 1970.

Habermas, Jürgen. *Theorie des kommunikativen Handelns.* 2 vols. Frankfurt: Suhrkamp, 1981. English translation: *The Theory of Communicative Action*, vol. 1. Thomas McCarthy, trans. Boston: Beacon Press, 1984.

Habermas, Jürgen. *Theorie und Praxis: Sozial-philosophische Studien.* Frankfurt: Suhrkamp, 1978. English translation: *Theory and Practice.* John Viertel, trans. Boston: Beacon Press, 1973.

Habermas, Jürgen. "Urgeschichte der Subjektivität und verwilderte Selbst-Behauptung." In *Philosophisch-politische Profile.* Bibliothek Suhrkamp. Frankfurt: Suhrkamp, 1971. English translation: "Theodor Adorno—The Primal History of Subjectivity—Self-Affirmation Gone Wild." Frederick G.

Lawrence, trans. *Philosophical-Political Profiles*, pp. 99–111. Cambridge, Mass.: MIT Press, 1983.

Habermas, Jürgen. "Wahrheitstheorien." In *Wirklichkeit und Reflexion*. H. Fahrenbach, ed. Pfüllingen: Neske, 1973.

Habermas, Jürgen. *Zur Rekonstruktion des historischen Materialismus*. Frankfurt: Suhrkamp, 1976.

Habermas, Jürgen. "Zwei Bemerkungen zum praktischen Diskurs." In *Konstruktionen versus Positionen*, Kuno Lorenz, ed. Berlin: Walter de Gruyter, 1979.

Habermas, Jürgen, Sylvia Bovenschen et al. *Gespräche mit Herbert Marcuse*. Frankfurt: Suhrkamp, 1981.

Habermas, Jürgen and Niklas Luhmann. *Theorie der Gesellschaft oder Sozialtechnologie—Was leistet die Systemforschung?* Frankfurt: Suhrkamp, 1976.

Haering, Th. *Hegel: Sein Wollen und sein Werk*. Leipzig and Berlin: B. G. Teubner, 1938.

Hegel, G. W. F. "Differenz des Fichteschen und Schellingschen Systems der Philosophie." In *Werke in zwanzig Bänden* (q.v.). English translation: *The Difference Between the Fichtean and Schellingian Systems of Philosophy*. J. P. Surber, trans. California: Ridgeview, 1978.

Hegel, G. W. F. "Glauben und Wissen." In *Werke in zwanzig Bänden* (q.v.), 2:287–434. English translation: *Faith and Knowledge*. W. Cerf and H. S. Harris, trans. Albany: State University of New York Press, 1977.

Hegel, G. W. F. *Grundlinien der Philosophie des Rechts*. In *Werke in zwanzig Bänden* (q.v.), vol. 7.

Hegel, G. W. F. *Hegel's Philosophy of Mind*. W. Wallace, trans. Part 3 of *Encyclopedia of Philosophical Sciences*. Oxford: Clarendon Press, 1971.

Hegel, G. W. F. *Hegel's Philosophy of Right*. T.M. Knox, trans. Oxford: Oxford University Press, 1973.

Hegel, G. W. F. *Jenaer Realphilosophie.*, Johannes Hoffmeister, ed. Philosophische Bibliothek, vol. 67. Hamburg: Felix Meiner, 1969.

Hegel, G. W. F. "Love." In *Early Theological Writings*. T. M. Knox, trans. Philadelphia: University of Pennsylvania Press, 1971.

Hegel, G. W. F. *Phänomenologie des Geistes*. J. Hoffmeister, ed.

Philosophische Bibliothek. Hamburg: Felix Meiner, 1952. English translation: *Hegel's Phenomenology of Spirit.* A. V. Miller, trans., with an analysis and foreword by John Findlay. Oxford: Clarendon Press, 1977.

Hegel, G. W. F. "The Spirit of Christianity and Its Fate." In *Early Theological Writings.* T. M. Knox, trans. Philadelphia: University of Pennsylvania Press, 1971.

Hegel, G. W. F. "Über die wissenschaftlichen Behandlungsarten des Naturrechts, seine Stelle in der praktischen Philosophie und sein Verhältnis zu den positiven Rechtswissenschaften." In *Werke in zwanzig Bänden* (q.v.), 2:434–533. English translation: *Natural Law.* T. M. Knox, trans.; introduction by H. B. Acton. Philadelphia: University of Pennsylvania Press, 1975.

Hegel, G. W. F. *Die Vernunft in der Geschichte.* J. Hoffmeister, ed. Hamburg: Felix Meiner, 1955.

Hegel, G. W. F. *Werke in zwanzig Bänden.* 20 vols. Eva Moldenhauer and K. Markus Michel, eds. Frankfurt: Suhrkamp, 1970.

Hegel, G. W. F. *Wissenschaft der Logik.* G. Lasson, ed. Hamburg: Felix Meiner, 1976. English translation: *Hegel's Science of Logic.* A. V. Miller, trans. New York: Humanities Press, 1969.

Heidegger, Martin. *Being and Time.* J. Macquarrie and E. Robinson, trans. New York: Harper & Row, 1962.

Heidegger, Martin. *What Is a Thing?* W. B. Barton and Vera Deutsch, trans. Chicago: Regnery, 1967.

Held, David. *Introduction to Critical Theory.* Berkeley and Los Angeles: University of California Press, 1980.

Held, David and Larry Simon. "Habermas's Theory of Crisis in Late Capitalism." *Radical Philosophers' News Journal* (1976), No. 6, pp. 1–19.

Heller, Agnes. *A Theory of Feelings.* Dordrecht: Van Gorcum, 1979.

Heller, Agnes. *The Theory of Need in Marx.* New York: St. Martin's Press, 1976.

Heller, Agnes. "Towards a Marxist Theory of Value." A. Arato, trans. *Kinesis* (Fall 1972), vol. 5, no. 1.

Henrich, D. "Karl Marx als Schüler Hegels." *Hegel im Kontext,* pp. 196ff. Frankfurt: Suhrkamp, 1975.

Hesse, Mary. "Science and Objectivity." In Thompson and Held, eds., *Habermas: Critical Debates* (q.v.), pp. 98–116.

Hindess, Barry and Paul Q. Hirst. *Pre-Capitalist Modes of Production*. London: Routledge and Kegan Paul, 1975.

Hirshman, Albert. *The Passions and the Interests: Political Arguments for Capitalism Before Its Triumph*. Princeton: Princeton University Press, 1977.

Hobbes, Thomas. *Leviathan*. C. B. Macpherson, ed. Baltimore: Penguin Books, 1971.

Hobbes, Thomas. "Philosophical Rudiments Concerning Government and Society." In *The English Works of Thomas Hobbes*. Sir William Molesworth, ed. Reprint from English ed. 1839–1854. London: John B. John (Darmstadt: 1966).

Höffe, Ottfried. *Ethik und Politik*. Frankfurt: Suhrkamp, 1979.

Honneth, Axel. "Arbeit und instrumentales Handeln." In A. Honneth and U. Jaeggi, eds., *Arbeit, Handlung, Normativität*. Frankfurt: Suhrkamp, 1980. English translation: "Work and Instrumental Action." *New German Critique* (Spring-Summer 1982), pp. 31–54.

Honneth, Axel. "Horkheimers ursprüngliche Idee: Das soziologische Defizit der kritischen Theorie." In *Kritik der Macht: Reflexionsstufen einer kritischen Gesellschoftstheorie*, pp. 12–43. Suhrkamp: Frankfurt, 1985.

Horkheimer, Max. *The Eclipse of Reason*. New York: Seabury Press, 1974. German translation: *Kritik der instrumentellen Vernunft*. A. Schmidt, trans. Frankfurt: Fischer, 1974.

Horkheimer, Max. "Egoismus und Freiheitsbewegung." In Institute for Social Research (q.v.), *ZfS*: 1936, 161–234. English translation: "Egoism and the Freedom Movement." D. Parent, trans. *Telos* (Winter 1982–83), no. 5, pp. 10–61.

Horkheimer, Max. Foreword. In Martin Jay, *The Dialectical Imagination*. Boston: Little, Brown, 1973.

Horkheimer, Max. "Die Juden und Europa." *Studies in Philosophy and Social Science*. In Institute for Social Research (q.v.), *ZfS*: 1939–40, 115–37.

Horkheimer, Max. "Materialismus und Moral." In Institute for Social Research (q.v.), *ZfS*: 1933, 161–97.

Horkheimer, Max. "Traditional and Critical Theory." In *Critical*

Theory, pp. 188–214, 244–52. M. J. O'Connell et al., trans. New York: Herder & Herder, 1972.

Horkheimer, Max. "Zum Begriff der Vernunft." *Sozialphilosophische Studien: Aufsätze, Reden und Vorträge 1930–1972.* Frankfurt: Fischer Taschenbuch, 1972.

Horkheimer, Max. "Zum Problem der Wahrheit." English translation: "On the Problem of Truth." In Arato and Gebhardt, eds., *The Essential Frankfurt School Reader* (q.v.), pp. 407–44.

Horstmann, R. P. "Über die Rolle der bürgerlichen Gesellschaft in Hegels politischer Philosophie." In M. Riedel, ed., *Materialien zu Hegels Rechtsphilosophie* (q.v.), 2:276ff.

Howard, D. "On the Transformation of Marx's Critique Into Dialectics." *Dialectical Anthropology* (1980), no. 5, pp. 75ff.

Husserl, Edmund. *The Crisis of European Sciences and Transcendental Phenomenology.* David Carr, trans. Evanston, Ill.: Northwestern University Press, 1970.

Ilting, Karl-Heinz. "Geltung als Konsens." *Neue Hefte für Philosophie* (1976), no. 10, pp. 22–50.

Ilting, Karl-Heinz. "Hegels Auseinandersetzung mit der Aristotelischen Politik." *Philosophisches Jahrbuch* (1962–63), vol. 71.

Institute for Social Research. *Studien über Autorität und Familie.* Paris: Librairie Felix Alcan, 1955.

Institute for Social Research. *Zeitschrift für Sozialforschung.* 9 vols. A. Schmidt, ed. Munich: Deutscher Taschenbuch-verlag, photomechanical reprint, 1980.

Jacoby, Russell. *Social Amnesia: A Critique of Contemporary Psychology from Adler to Laing.* Boston: Beacon Press, 1975.

Jay, Martin. *The Dialectical Imagination.* Boston: Little, Brown, 1973.

Jay, Martin. "Positive und negative Totalität: Adornos Alternativentwurf zur interdisziplinären Forschung." In Bonss and Honneth, eds., *Sozialforschung als Kritik* (q.v), pp. 67–87.

Kant, Immanuel, "Anthropologie in pragmatischer Hinsicht." In *Werke in zehn Bänden* (q.v.), vol. 10.

Kant, Immanuel. "Ideen zu einer allgemeinen Geschichte in weltbürgerlicher Absicht." In *Werke in zehn Bänden* (q.v.), vol. 9. English translation: *On History.* L. W. Beck, R. E.

Anchor, and E. L. Fackenheim, trans. New York: Bobbs-Merrill, 1963.

Kant, Immanuel. *Grundlegung der Metaphysik der Sitten*. In *Werke in zehn Bänden* (q.v.), vol. 6. English translation: *Groundwork of the Metaphysics of Morals*. H. J. Paton, trans. New York: Harper and Row, 1964.

Kant, Immanuel. *Kritik der praktischen Vernunft*. In *Werke in zehn Bänden* (q.v.), vol. 6. English translation: *Critique of Practical Reason and Other Writings in Moral Philosophy*, L. W. Beck, trans. New York: Garland, 1976.

Kant, Immanuel. *Kritik der reinen Vernunft*. In *Werke in zehn Bänden*, (q.v.), vol. 3. English translation: *Critique of Pure Reason*. Norman Kemp Smith, trans. New York: St. Martin's Press, 1965.

Kant, Immanuel. *Die Metaphysik der Sitten*. In *Werke in zehn Bänden* (q.v.), vol. 7. English translation of first part: *The Metaphysical Elements of Justice*. John Ladd, trans. New York: Bobbs-Merrill, 1965.

Kant, Immanuel, *Werke in zehn Bänden*. 20 vols. Wilhelm Weischedel, ed. Darmstadt: Wissenschaftliche Buchgesellschaft, 1968.

Keller, Evelyn Fox. *A Feeling for the Organism: The Life and Work of Barbara McClintock*. New York: W. H. Freeman, 1984.

Kellner, Douglas and Rick Roderick. "Recent Literature on Critical Theory." *New German Critique* (Spring–Summer 1981), no. 23, pp. 141–71.

Kelly, G. A. *Hegel's Retreat from Eleusis*. Princeton: Princeton University Press, 1978.

Kelly-Gadoll, J. "The Social Relations of the Sexes: Methodological Implications of Women's History." *Signs* (1976), no. 1, pp. 809–23.

Kirchheimer, Otto. *Funktionen des Staates und der Verfassung: Zehn Analysen*. Frankfurt: Suhrkamp, 1972.

Kirchheimer, Otto. *Political Justice: The Use of Legal Procedure for Political Ends*. Princeton: Princeton University Press, 1961.

Kirchheimer, Otto. *Politik und Verfassung*. Frankfurt: Suhrkamp, 1964.

Kohlberg, Lawrence. "A Reply to Owen Flanagan." *Ethics* (April 1982), no. 92, pp. 513–28.

Kolakowski, Leszek. "Karl Marx and the Classical Definition of Truth." In *Toward a Marxist Humanism*, pp. 38–67. Jane Z. Peel, trans. New York: Grove Press, 1968.

Kolakowski, Leszek. *Main Currents of Marxism—Its Origin, Growth and Dissolution.* P. S. Falla, trans. Oxford: Oxford University Press, 1978.

Korsch, Karl. "Marxism and Philosophy." In *Marxism and Philosophy*, pp. 29–89, Fred Halliday, trans., London: New Left Books, 1970.

Koselleck, R. *Kritik und Krise.* Frankfurt: Suhrkamp, 1976.

Labarrière, Jean-Pierre. *Structures et mouvement dialéctique dans la Phénoménologie de l'Esprit de Hegel.* Paris: Aubier-Montaigne, 1968.

Lacan, Jacques. "The Subversion of the Subject and the Dialectic of Desire in the Freudian Unconscious." In *Écrits: A Selection*, pp. 292–326. A. Sheridan, trans. New York: Norton, 1977.

Lange, E. M. *Das Prinzip Arbeit.* Frankfurt: Ullstein, 1980.

Lange, E. M. "Wertformanalyse, Geldkritik und die Konstruktion des Fetischismus bei Marx." *Neue Hefte für Philosophie* (1978), no. 13.

Lasch, Christopher, *Haven in a Heartless World.* New York: Basic Books, 1977.

Leiss, William. *The Domination of Nature.* Boston: Beacon Press, 1974.

Lévi-Strauss, Claude. *The Elementary Structures of Kinship.* Rev. ed. J. Bell, J. Richard, and R. Needham, trans. Boston: Beacon Press, 1969.

Lobkowitz, N. *Theory and Practice.* Notre Dame, Ind.: University of Notre Dame Press, 1967.

Locke, John. *First and Second Treatises of Civil Government.* P. Laslett, ed. Cambridge: Cambridge University Press, 1970.

Lockwood, David. "Social Integration and System Integration." In G. K. Zollochan and W. Hirsch, eds., *Explorations in Social Change*, pp. 244–57. London: Routledge and Kegan Paul, 1964.

Lohmann, Georg. "Gesellschaftskritik und normativer Mass-stab." In A. Honneth and U. Jaeggi, eds., *Arbeit, Handlung, Normativität*, pp. 270ff. Frankfurt: Suhrkamp, 1980.

Lorenzen, Paul. *Normative Logic and Ethics*. Mannheim: Bibliographisches Institut, 1969.

Lukács, Georg. *Der junge Hegel*. In *Werke*, vol. 8. Berlin: Luchterland, 1967. English translation: *The Young Hegel*. R. Livingstone, trans. London: Merlin Press, 1975.

Lukács, Georg. *History and Class Consciousness*. R. Livingstone, trans. Cambridge, Mass.: MIT Press, 1971.

Lukes, Steven. "Of Gods and Demons: Habermas and Practical Reason." In Thompson and Held, eds., *Habermas: Critical Debates* (q.v.), pp. 134–49.

Lyotard, Jean-François *The Post-Modern Condition*. G. Bennington and B. Manumi, trans. Minneapolis: University of Minnesota Press, 1984.

McCarthy, Thomas. *The Critical Theory of Jürgen Habermas*. Cambridge, Mass.: MIT Press, 1978.

McCarthy, Thomas. "Rationality and Relativism: Habermas's 'Overcoming' of Hermeneutics." In Thompson and Held, eds., *Habermas: Critical Debates* (q.v.), pp. 57–78.

McCarthy, Thomas. "Reflections on Rationalization in *The Theory of Communicative Action.*" *Praxis International* (July 1984), pp. 177–92.

MacIntyre, Alasdair. *After Virtue: A Study in Moral Theory*. Notre Dame, Ind.: University of Notre Dame Press, 1981.

Mackie, J. L. *Ethics: Inventing Right and Wrong*. New York: Penguin, 1977.

Mannheim, Karl. *Ideology and Utopia*. L. Wirth and E. Shils, trans. New York: Harcourt, Brace and World, 1946.

Marcuse, Herbert. *Eros and Civilization: A Philosophical Inquiry Into Freud*. New York: Vintage Books, 1962. German translation: *Triebstruktur und Gesellschaft: Ein philosophischer Beitrag zu Sigmund Freud*, M. von Eckhardt-Jaffe, trans. Frankfurt: Suhrkamp, 1979.

Marcuse, Herbert. *Hegels Ontologie und die Theorie der Geschichtlichkeit*. Frankfurt: V. Klostermann, 1975. English translation, by S. Benhabib. Cambridge, Mass.: MIT Press forthcoming.

Marcuse, Herbert. *One-Dimensional Man: Studies in the Ideology of Advanced Industrial Society.* Boston: Beacon Press, 1964.

Marcuse, Herbert. "Some Social Implications of Modern Technology." In Institute for Social Research (q.v.), *ZfS*, vol. 9. Reprinted from the original and from *Studies in Philosophy and Social Science* in which this article appeared in 1941, pp. 414–39.

Marcuse, Herbert. "Das Veralten der Psychoanalyse." In *Kultur und Gesellschaft*, 2:85–107. Frankfurt: Suhrkamp, 1968. English translation: "The Obsolescence of Psychoanalysis," J. Shapiro and Sherry M. Weber, trans. In *Five Lectures.* Boston: Beacon Press, 1970.

Markus, György. "Four Forms of Critical Theory—Some Theses on Marx's Development." *Thesis Eleven* (1980), no. 1, pp. 90ff.

Markus, György. "Practical-Social Rationality in Marx: A Dialectical Critique." Part I, *Dialectical Anthropology* (1979), 4(1):255–88. Part II, *Dialectical Anthropology* (1980), 5(1):1–33.

Marramao, G. "Zum Verhältnis von politischer Ökonomie und kritischer Theorie." *Ästhetik und Kommunikation: Beiträge zur politischen Erziehung* (April 1973), 4(11):79–93.

Marx, Karl. *Capital: A Critical Analysis of Capitalist Production.* Vol. 1. Frederick Engels, ed.; S. Moore and E. Aveling, trans. New York: International Publishers, 1973.

Marx, Karl. *The Civil War in France: The Paris Commune.* New York: International Publishers, 1969.

Marx, Karl. *Karl Marx: Early Writings.* Quintin Hoare, ed.; R. Livingston and G. Benton, trans. New York: Vintage Books, 1975.

Marx, Karl. *The Eighteenth Brumaire of Louis Bonaparte.* New York: International Publishers, 1967.

Marx, Karl. *Grundrisse.* Martin Nicolaus, trans. London: Penguin Books, 1973.

Marx, Karl. *Texte zur Methode und Praxis. II: Pariser Manuskripte, 1844.* Günter Hillman, ed. *Rowohlt Philosophie der Neuzeit*, vol. 9. Hamburg: Reinbeck 1966. English translation: *The Economic and Philosophic Manuscripts of 1844.* Dirk J. Struik, trans. New York: International Publishers, 1964. Also translated by R. Livingstone and G. Benton,

Economic and Philosophical Manuscripts. In *Karl Marx: Early Writings* (q.v.), pp. 279–401.

Marx, Karl. "Zur Kritik der Hegelschen Rechtsphilosophie. Einleitung." In *Werke* (q.v.), vol. 1. English translation: *Critique of Hegel's Philosophy of Right.* Joseph O'Malley, trans. and ed. Cambridge: Cambridge University Press, 1970.

Marx, Karl and Frederick Engels. *The German Ideology.* R. Pascal, ed. New York: International Publishers, 1969.

Marx, Karl and Frederick Engels. *Die Heilige Familie oder Kritik der kritischen Kritik.* In *Werke* (q.v.) 2:82ff.

Marx, Karl and Frederick Engels. *Werke.* Berlin: Dietz, 1980.

Mead, G. H. *Mind, Self, and Society.* Chicago: University of Chicago Press, 1967.

Mendelson, Jack. "The Habermas-Gadamer Debate." *New German Critique* (1979), no. 18, pp. 44–73.

Misgeld, Dieter. "Communication and Societal Rationalization." Review essay (forthcoming).

Mommsen, W. *Max Weber: Gesellschaft, Politik und Geschichte.* Frankfurt: B. Mohr, 1974.

Mouzelis, N. "Social and System Integration: Some Reflections on a Fundamental Distinction." In G. K. Zollschan and W. Hirsch, eds., *Explorations in Social Change,* pp. 395–409. London: Routledge and Kegan Paul, 1964.

Nagel, Thomas. "Rawls on Justice." In Norman Daniels, ed., *Reading Rawls.* New York: Oxford University Press, 1975.

Neumann, F. *Behemoth: Structure and Praxis of National Socialism.* London: Victor Gollancz, 1942.

Neumann, F. *Democratic and Authoritarian State.* H. Marcuse, ed. Glencoe: Free Press, 1957.

Neumann, F. *Die Herrschaft des Gesetzes.* A. Söllner, trans. and ed. Frankfurt: Suhrkamp, 1980.

Neumann, F. *Wirtschaft, Staat und Demokratie.* Frankfurt: Suhrkamp, 1977.

Nietzsche, Friedrich. *The Birth of Tragedy and the Genealogy of Morals.* Francis Golffing, trans. New York: Doubleday Anchor Books, 1956.

Oelmuller, Willi, ed. *Transzendentalphilosophische Normenbegründung.* Paderborn: Ferdinand Schöningh, 1978.

Offe, Claus. "New Social Movements as a Meta-Political Challenge." MS, 1984.

Offe, Claus. "Some Contradictions of the Modern Welfare State." *Praxis International* (October 1981), 1(3):219–30.

Offe, Claus. *Strukturprobleme des kapitalistischen Staates.* Frankfurt: Suhrkamp, 1977.

Offe, Claus. "Technik und Eindimensionalität: Eine Version der Technokratiethese." In Jürgen Habermas, ed., *Antworten auf Herbert Marcuse.* Frankfurt: Suhrkamp, 1978.

Offe, Claus. "'Unregierbarkeit': Zur Renaissance konservativer Krisentheorien." In Jürgen Habermas, ed., *Stichworte zur "Geistigen Situation der Zeit,"* 1:313. Frankfurt: Suhrkamp, 1979. English translation: *Observations on the "Spiritual Condition of the Age."* Andrew Buchwalter, trans. Cambridge, Mass.: MIT Press, 1984.

Parsons, Talcott. *The Structure of Social Action.* New York: Free Press, 1968.

Paton, H. J. *The Categorical Imperative: A Study in Kant's Moral Philosophy.* Philadelphia: University of Pennsylvania Press, 1971.

Pelczynski, Z. A., ed. *Hegel's Political Thought.* Cambridge: Cambridge University Press, 1971.

Petit, Philip. "Habermas on Truth and Justice." In G. H. R. Parkinson, ed., *Marx and Marxism.* Royal Institute of Philosophy Lecture Series, No. 14.

Plant, Raymond, *Hegel.* Bloomington: Indiana University Press, 1973.

Pöggeler, O. "Qu'est-ce-que la Phénoménologie de l'Esprit?" *Archives de philosophie* (April–June 1966).

Polanyi, Karl and C. M. Arensberg, eds. *Trade and Market in Early Empires.* Glencoe: Free Press, 1957.

Popper, K. *The Poverty of Historicism.* Boston: Beacon Press, 1957.

Postone, Moishe. "Labor, Time and Necessity." In Andrew Arato, ed., *Social Research: Marx Today* (Winter 1978), 45(44):739–89.

Postone, Moishe and Barbara Brick. "Kritische Theorie und die Grenzen des traditionellen Marxismus." In Bonss and Honneth, eds., *Sozialforschung als Kritik* (q.v.), pp. 179–240.

Rasmussen, David. "Communicative Action and Philosophy: Reflections on Habermas's *Theorie des kommunikativen Handelns*." *Philosophy and Social Criticism* (Spring 1982), 9(1):1–29.

Rawls, John. *A Theory of Justice.* Cambridge, Mass.: Harvard University Press, 1972.

Ricoeur, Paul. *Hermeneutics and the Human Sciences: Essays on Language, Action and Interpretation*, John B. Thompson, ed. and trans. Cambridge: Cambridge University Press, 1981.

Ricoeur, Paul. *Freud and Philosophy: An Essay on Interpretation.* D. Savage, trans. New Haven: Yale University Press, 1977.

Riedel, Manfred. "Hegels Begriff der 'bürgerlichen Gesellschaft' und das Problem seines geschichtlichen Ursprungs." In Riedel, ed., *Materialien zu Hegels Rechtsphilosophie* (q.v.), pp. 247ff.

Riedel, Manfred. "Hegels Kritik des Naturrechts." In Riedel, ed., *Studien zu Hegels Rechtsphilosophie*, pp. 42–75. Frankfurt: Suhrkamp, 1970.

Riedel, Manfred. "Objektiver Geist und praktische Philosophie." In Riedel, ed., *Studien zu Hegels Rechtsphilosophie*, pp. 11–42. Frankfurt: Suhrkamp, 1970.

Riedel, Manfred. Vorwort. In Riedel, ed., *Rehabilitierung der praktischen Philosophie*, vol. 1. Freiburg: Rombach, 1972.

Riedel, Manfred. *Theorie und Praxis im Denken Hegels.* Stuttgart: Ullstein, 1976.

Riedel, Manfred, ed. *Materialien zu Hegels Rechtsphilosophie.* Frankfurt: Suhrkamp, 1975.

Ritter, Joachim. *Hegel and the French Revolution.* R. D. Winfield, trans. Cambridge, Mass.: MIT Press, 1982.

Ritter, Joachim. "Moralität und Sittlichkeit: Zu Hegels Auseinandersetzung mit der Kantischen Ethik." In M. Riedel, ed., *Materialien zu Hegels Rechtsphilosophie* (q.v.).

Rorty, Richard. *Philosophy and the Mirror of Nature.* Princeton, N.J.: Princeton University Press, 1979.

Rosenzweig, F. *Hegel und der Staat.* Munich: Scientia, 1920.

Rousseau, J. J. *Discours sur l'inégalité parmi les hommes.* In *Du contrat social.* Paris: Editions Garnier, 1962. English translation: *The Social Contract and Discourse on the Origin of Inequality.* Lester Crocker, ed. New York: First Pocket Books, 1967.

Rousseau, J. J. *Emile, ou de l'éducation.* Paris: Editions Garnier, 1964.

Sahlins, Marshall. *Culture and Practical Reason.* Chicago: University of Chicago Press, 1976.

Schäfer, Wolf. "Finalization in Perspective: Toward a Revolution in the Social Paradigm of Science." *Social Science Information* (1979), 18(6):915–43.

Schäfer, Wolf. "Collective Thinking from Below: Early Working Class Thought Reconsidered." *Dialectical Anthropology* (1982), no. 6, pp. 193–214.

Schluchter, W. "Die Paradoxie der Rationalisierung." In *Rationalismus und Weltbeherrschung,* pp. 19ff. Frankfurt: Suhrkamp, 1980.

Schmid, Michael. "Habermas's Theory of Social Evolution." In Thompson and Held, eds., *Habermas: Critical Debates* (q.v.), pp. 162–80.

Schmidt, James. "Recent Hegel Literature." Part I, *Telos* (Winter 1980–81), no. 46, pp. 113–48. Part II, *Telos* (Summer 1981), no. 48, pp. 114–41.

Schmidt, James. "A Paideia for the 'Bürger als Bourgeois': The Concept of Civil Society in Hegel's Political Thought." *History of Political Thought* (November 1981), 2(3):469–93.

Schmucker, J. *Adorno-Logik des Zerfalls.* Stuttgart: Frommann—Holzboog, 1977.

Schnädelbach, Herbert. "Transformation der Kritischen Theorie." *Philosophische Rundschau* (1982), 3/4(29):151–78.

Schnädelbach, Herbert. *Reflexion und Diskurs: Fragen zu einer Logik der Philosophie.* Frankfurt: Suhrkamp, 1977.

Schnädelbach, Herbert. "Zum Verhältnis von Logik und Gesellschaftstheorie bei Hegel." In O. Negt, ed., *Aktualität und Folgen der Philosophie Hegels,* pp. 65ff. Frankfurt: Suhrkamp, 1971.

Schürmann, Rainer. "Anti-Humanism: Reflections on the Turn Toward the Post-Modern Epoch." *Man and World* (1979), vol. 12, no. 2.

Schutz, Alfred. "The Problem of the 'Life-World' as a Partial Problem Within the General Problem of Objective Science." In *The Problem of Social Reality: Collected Papers I.* Maurice Natanson, ed. Boston and London: Martinus Nijhoff, 1982.

Schwemmer, Oswald. *Philosophie der Praxis*. Frankfurt: Suhrkamp, 1971.

Silber, John. "Procedural Formalism in Kant's Ethics." *Review of Metaphysics* (December 1974), 28(2):197–236.

Skinner, Quentin. "Habermas's Reformation." *New York Review of Books* (October 1982), pp. 35–38.

Söllner, Alfons. *Geschichte und Herrschaft: Studien zur materialistischen Sozialwissenschaft*. Frankfurt: Suhrkamp, 1979.

Spaemann, R. "Bürgerliche Ethik und nichtteleologische Ontologie." In H. Ebeling, ed., *Subjektivität und Selbsterhaltung* (q.v.), pp. 76–97.

Spaemann, R. "Die Utopie der Herrschaftsfreiheit." *Merkur* (August 1972), no. 292.

Stern, Paul. *Practical Philosophy and the Concept of Freedom: Hegel's Critique of Kantian Ethics*. Ph.D. dissertation, Boston University, 1983.

Strauss, Leo. *Natural Right and History*. Chicago: University of Chicago Press, 1953.

Strauss, Leo. *The Political Philosophy of Thomas Hobbes*. Chicago: University of Chicago Press, 1973.

Tar, Zoltan. *The Frankfurt School: The Critical Theories of Max Horkheimer and Theodor Adorno*. New York: Wiley, 1977.

Taylor, Charles. "Interpretation and the Sciences of Man." *Review of Metaphysics* (1971), 25:3–51.

Taylor, Charles. *Hegel*. Cambridge: Cambridge University Press, 1977.

Theunissen, Michael. "Die verdrängte Intersubjektivität in Hegels *Philosophie des Rechts*." In D. Henrich and R. P. Horstmann, eds., *Hegels "Philosophie des Rechts": Die Theorie der Rechtsformen und ihre Logik*, p. 317–81. Stuttgart: Klett-Cotta, 1982.

Theunissen, Michael. *Sein und Schein: Die kritische Funktion der Hegelschen Logik*. Frankfurt: Suhrkamp, 1978.

Theunissen, Michael. *The Other: Studies in Social Ontology of Husserl, Heidegger, Sartre and Buber*. Christopher Macann, trans. Cambridge, Mass.: MIT Press, 1984.

Thompson, E. P. *The Poverty of Theory and Other Essays*. London: Merlin Press, 1979.

Thompson, John B. "Universal Pragmatics." In Thompson and Held, eds., *Habermas: Critical Debates* (q.v.), pp. 116–33.

Thompson, John B. and David Held, eds. *Habermas: Critical Debates*. Cambridge, Mass.: MIT Press, 1982.

Toulmin, Stephen. *The Uses of Argument*. Cambridge: Cambridge University Press, 1974.

Tugendhat, E. "Zur Entwicklung von moralischen Begründungsstrukturen im modernen Recht." In *Archiv für Rechts- und Sozialphilosophie* (1980), 34:1ff.

Walsh, W. H. *Hegelian Ethics*. New York: St. Martin's Press, 1969.

Wartofsky, Marx. *Feuerbach*. Cambridge: Cambridge University Press, 1977.

Wartofsky, Marx. "The Unhappy Consciousness." Critical review of L. Kolakowski's *Main Currents of Marxism*. *Praxis International* (October 1981), 1(3):288–307.

Weber, Max. *Economy and Society*. Guenther Roth and Claus Wittich, trans. Berkeley and Los Angeles: University of California Press, 1978.

Weber, Max. *From Max Weber: Essays in Sociology*. H. H. Gerth and C. W. Mills, eds. and trans. New York: Oxford University Press, 1974.

Weber, Max. "The Meaning of Ethical Neutrality in 'Sociology' and 'Economics.'" In *The Methodology of the Social Sciences* (q.v.).

Weber, Max. *The Methodology of the Social Sciences*. E. A. Shils and Henry A. Finch, eds. and trans. New York: Free Press, 1949.

Weber, Max. "Objectivity in Social Science and Social Policy." In *The Methodology of the Social Sciences* (q.v.).

Weber, Max. "Die Protestantische Ethik und der Geist des Kapitalismus." In *Gesammelte Aufsätze zur Religionssoziologie*. Tübingen: Mohr, 1920. English translation: *The Protestant Ethic and the Spirit of Capitalism*. Talcott Parsons, trans. New York: Scribner's, 1958.

Weber, Max. *The Religion of China*. H. H. Gerth., ed. and trans. Glencoe: Free Press, 1951.

Weber, Max. "Science as a Vocation." In *From Max Weber: Essays in Sociology* (q.v.).

Weber, Max. "The Social Psychology of World Religions." In *From Max Weber: Essays in Sociology* (q.v.). This is the 1920 Introduction to Weber's *Gesammelte Aufsätze zur Religionssoziologie*, published the same year.

Wellmer, Albrecht. *Critical Theory of Society*. John Cumming, trans. New York: Seabury Press, 1974.

Wellmer, Albrecht. *Praktische Philosophie und Theorie der Gesellschaft: Zum Problem der normativen Grundlagen einer kritischen Sozialwissenschaft*. Konstanz: University Publications, 1979.

Wellmer, Albrecht. "Thesen über Vernunft, Emanzipation und Utopie." in: *Ethik und Kommunikation*. Frankfurt: Suhrkamp, 1987.

Westphal, Merold. *History and Truth in Hegel's Phenomenology*. Atlantic Highlander, N.J.: Humanities Press, 1979.

Whitebook, Joel. "The Problem of Nature in Habermas." *Telos* (Summer 1979), no. 40, pp. 41–69.

Whitebook, Joel. "Saving the Subject: Modernity and the Problem of the Autonomous Individual." *Telos* (Winter 1981–82), no. 50, pp. 79–103.

Wildt, Andreas. *Autonomie und Anerkennung: Hegels Moralkritik im Lichte seiner Fichte-Rezeption*. Stuttgart: Kleet-Cotta, 1982.

Wimmer, R. *Universalisierung in der Ethik*. Frankfurt: Suhrkamp, 1980.

Winch, Peter. *The Idea of a Social Science and Its Relation to Philosophy*. London: Routledge and Kegan Paul, 1958.

Wolff, Robert Paul. *Kant's Theory of Mental Activity*. Cambridge, Mass.: Harvard University Press, 1969.

Wolff, Robert Paul. *Understanding Rawls*. Princeton, N.J.: Princeton University Press, 1977.

Young, Iris. "Toward a Critical Theory of Justice." *Social Theory and Practice* (Fall 1981), 7(3):279–302.

Zeitschrift für Sozialforschung. See Institute for Social Research.

INDEX

Abstract equivalence: in Lukács, 183–84

Act descriptions, 135; see also Indeterminacy, interpretive

Action: as exteriorization, 86; Hegel's inadequate account of, 87–90, 242–44; interpretive indeterminacy of, 86, 87–89, 243; narrative structure of, 348–49; as Spirit's work, 86–87; three models of in social theory, 393n40; see also Activity (all entries); Communicative action; Expressive action; Indeterminacy, interpretive; Instrumental action; Strategic action

Action, intentionalist theory of: in Hegel, 134; inadequacy of, 134–37; and interpretive indeterminacy, 136; in Marx, 134

Action theory, 13

Activity: and externalization, 68–69; as linguistically mediated, 136–37, 243; reduced through fetishism, 117–19; as self-actualization, 68–69, 123, 243; see also Activity, work model of; Self-actualization

Activity, communicative model of, 225–27; see also Communicative action

Activity, expressivist model of, 84–95, 104

Activity, interaction model of, 68–69, 242–43

Activity, objectification model of, 220

Activity, work model of: concept analyzed, 10–11; and expressive

action, 84, 87, 139–40, 367n22; Habermas' critique of, 227, 243–44; and human plurality, 140–41, 243–44; inadequacies of, 68–69, 133–40, 227, 243–44, 346–49; and morality, 70–71, 84, 200; and philosophy of the subject, 10–11, 68–69, 133–43, 346–47; and politics of class, 140

Actuality: in Hegel, 98–99; in Marx, 34–35

Actualization, 7

Adorno, Gretel, 163

Adorno, Theodor, 71, 80, 147, 160, 227, 229, 244, 254, 267, 270; and aesthetics, 11, 170; autonomy in, 188, 189, 205–12, 219–21; critique of foundationalism, 280; critique of Husserl, 19; critique of identity logic, 206–12, 220–21; critique of instrumental reason, 163–71; critique of Kantian morality, 316; critique of self-identity, 205–12; critique of historical subject, 11; defetishing critique in, 174–75; dialectic of Enlightenment in, 345; domination in, 104, 208–9, 218–19; feminist critique of, 383–84n36; and Hegel, 211–12; immanent critique in, 171–74; intersubjectivity in, 214; labor in, 167; love in, 211; nature in, 212; negative dialectics in, 171–74; the "other" in, 165, 211–13; and philosophy of consciousness, 242; and philosophy of the subject, 143, 205–12, 214–19; "priority of the objective" in, 213–14; reason in, 163–65;

—Index prepared by
Robert C. Welshon